Rationality, Bounded Rationality and Microfoundations

Rationality, Bounded Rationality and Microfoundations

Foundations of Theoretical Economics

Reza Salehnejad

palgrave
macmillan

First published 2007 by
PALGRAVE MACMILLAN
Houndmills, Basingstoke, Hampshire RG21 6XS and
175 Fifth Avenue, New York, N.Y. 10010
Companies and representatives throughout the world.

PALGRAVE MACMILLAN is the global academic imprint of the Palgrave Macmillan division of St. Martin's Press, LLC and of Palgrave Macmillan Ltd. Macmillan® is a registered trademark in the United States, United Kingdom and other countries. Palgrave is a registered trademark in the European Union and other countries.

ISBN-13: 978–0–230–00480–1
ISBN-10: 0–230–00480–6

This book is printed on paper suitable for recycling and made from fully managed and sustained forest sources.

A catalogue record for this book is available from the British Library.

A catalogue record for this book is available from the
Library of Congress.

10 9 8 7 6 5 4 3 2 1
16 15 14 13 12 11 10 09 08 07

Printed and bound in Great Britain by
Antony Rowe Ltd, Chippenham and Eastbourne

Contents

List of Figures

List of Tables

Preface

In *Principles of Political Economy*, Mill wrote 'happily, there is nothing in the laws of Value [economics] which remains for the present writer or any future writer to clear up; the theory of the subject is complete'. In his view, intuition, introspection, and pure thought were enough to tackle all the challenges of economics. Max Plank, though, dropped his involvement with economics as he thought it was too difficult. To him, physics appeared more tractable.

Whether one views economics as simple or difficult depends on how the general problem of economics is defined. An emerging literature views the economy as a society of heterogeneous, and interactive, individuals, who compete with each other over scarce resources. They learn from their past experiences, continuously modify their rules of behaviour, and thereby change the structure of the environment they face. As soon as economics is defined in this way, the incredible complexity of the issues involved in modelling the economy begins to emerge. And it immediately becomes apparent that the subject sits at the crossroads of many interesting and challenging topics including cognitive science, behavioural psychology, politics, mathematics, probability theory, statistics, and even biology.

There is currently no grand theory of the economy as an evolving system, and there may never be. Yet, any step towards establishing such a theory demands a theory of adaptive behaviour and a careful analysis of the connection between the individual and the system. This work studies some aspects of these problems. It views the economy as a society of intuitive statisticians, who follow the prescriptions of rational choice theory to make decisions. It uses this framework to study the possible contribution of rational choice theories to economic theory, and examines whether the hypothesis that 'homo economicus' behaves like an intuitive statistician helps explain the dynamics of the economy. The book then turns to the complexities that behavioural heterogeneity and interaction create for the connection between the micro- and macro-levels in the economy. The upshot is a critical understanding of the current state of theoretical macroeconomics as well as numerous insights and suggestions essential for constructing a dynamic theory of the economy.

This work has been in the making for many years, and during these years I have regularly benefited from the magnanimous help of many. I would, most notably, like to thank Colin Howson and Nancy Cartwright from whom I learnt enormously during my years at the London School of Economics. Also, my special thanks go to Cliburn Chan. Though by profession a biologist, interested in nonlinear dynamics, he was generous enough to read various parts of this work to teach me how to write and even how to restructure my arguments. I also owe a great debt to Sebastiano Bavetta, Donald Gillies, Noosheen Hashemi, Gavin Hinks, Markus Jaeger, Duncan Kelly-Lite, Jamshid Parvizian, Jochen Runde, Zhand Shakibi, and Rutang Thanawall, who in one way or another assisted me with this work. Finally I wish to thank Keith Povey, and Amanda Hamilton and Katie Button of Palgrave Macmillan, for their help in the final stages of preparing this book. I dedicate this book to my parents, and my wife Simin, and daughters Bahar and Keemia, for surrounding me with so much love, support, and aspiration.

REZA SALEHNEJAD

Introduction

> As economics pushes on beyond 'static' it becomes less like science, and more like history. (Hicks, 1979: xi)

Modern economies consist of millions of heterogeneous decision-making units interacting with each other, facing different choice situations, and acting according to a multitude of different rules and constraints. The interaction of these decision-making units at the micro-level gives rise to certain regularities at the economy level, which form the subject matter of macroeconomics. The complexity of modern economies makes it impossible to build an analytic model that represents the behaviour of all the decision-making units populating the economy. In modelling the economy, it is necessary to leave many details out, introduce aggregate variables, and focus on the relations among the aggregates. Macroeconomics is primarily the study of aggregates.

The study of the economy at the aggregate level presents a number of difficulties. For practical reasons, economists are not in a position to subject the economy to controlled experiments, and have to rely on statistical analysis of aggregate data to establish causal relations true at the aggregate level. Statistical analysis alone, however, is inadequate for causal inference, and must always be supported with substantive information regarding the structure to yield causal conclusions. Also, aggregate economic data are imprecise, rendering the outcomes of statistical analysis in macroeconomics even more uncertain. These difficulties raise the question of how it is possible in macroeconomics to acquire the non-sample information needed for modelling the economy's structure.

In response to this question, several approaches to macroeconomics have emerged. Theoretical macroeconomics, championed by new classical economists, suggests that these methodological difficulties do not arise at the individual level. We can start by establishing a theory of individual behaviour which explains how the agent interacts with the economy, defines his choice situation, and makes a decision. Once we have established a theory of behaviour, we can transform it into a theory of the economy using aggregation procedures. Since the theory is derived from the rules of individual behaviour, it correctly specifies the economy's structure. Aggregate data can then be used to transform the theory into a quantitative model of the structure.

The enterprise of deriving the theory of the economy from microeconomic theory – or the *microfoundations project* – rests on two grand assumptions. The first is that it is possible to establish an empirically adequate theory of individual behaviour. The other is that the theory can be transformed into a theory of the economy using aggregation procedures, without having to make any substantive assumption about the economy.

As regards individual behaviour, the basic idea in economics is that 'homo economicus' follows the prescriptions of decision theory, understood in terms of one or another expected utility theory, in particular the theory of subjective expected utility. The expected utility theory, in all the variants on offer, takes the agent's view of the economy as given, and says nothing about how he predicts future values of economic variables. To fill this theoretical vacuum, new classical economists have set forth the rational expectations hypothesis, which identifies the agent's beliefs about the economy with the mathematical expectations implied by the true economic model. This gives rise to a view of the economy as a society in which everyone, except the econometricians, knows the structure of the economy. The new classical paradigm, therefore, defines economics as the enterprise to derive observable economic phenomena from two assumptions: (1) people are expected utility maximizers; and (2) they maximize their expected utility with respect to the true economic model.

Theoretical problems with the rational expectations hypothesis have led to a slow paradigm shift in new classical economics that aims to remove the information asymmetry existing between the econometricians and people in a rational expectations economy by suggesting that, like econometricians, market participants also lack knowledge of the true economic model, and must learn it from available data. The new paradigm has been dubbed the bounded rationality paradigm, after Herbert Simon (1955; 1956). Though the idea of bounded rationality is relatively old, a unanimous interpretation of the paradigm is yet to emerge. One leading interpretation in new classical economics conceives of the economy as a society of 'intuitive statisticians', where everyone, like econometricians, theorizes, estimates, and adapts in attempting to learn about probability distributions that, under rational expectations, they already know (Sargent, 1993: 3). So understood, the paradigm replaces the second principle of new classical economics with the assumption that agents maximize their utility with respect to models that they, like econometricians, construct from economic data. We will refer to the proposal that homo economicus behaves like an econometrician as the *intuitive statistician* hypothesis of bounded rationality.

In light of the abundant experimental evidence on the poor statistical ability of ordinary people, the intuitive statistician hypothesis may seem as unrealistic as the assumption of full rationality (information). However, the proposal incorporates many formal models of human learning in cognitive science and psychology including connectionism, as well as most proposals on human causal inference. So, by exploring the hypothesis, we can greatly learn about the possibility of establishing an empirically precise theory of adaptive behaviour, which is essential for developing a dynamic theory of the economy. This work studies the intuitive statistician hypothesis in detail, and thoroughly investigates the complications arising in any attempt at transforming a theory of individual behaviour into a theory of the economy.

Chapter 1 begins with defining some key concepts in macroeconomics, outlines several arguments for the necessity of theory in modelling the economy, and characterizes the theoretical approach in some detail. The chapter next reconstructs the so-called atheoretical approach to macroeconomics, which offers an entirely opposing perspective on macroeconomics. The view rejects both assumptions of theoretical macroeconomics. It argues that current theories of individual behaviour lack precision and substantial difficulties face any attempt to make them precise. And, because of individual heterogeneity and interaction among decision-making units in the economy, there is no simple, and useful, relationship between the individual and economy levels. The approach confines the scope of macroeconomics to establishing models that efficiently summarize data, and are useful for short-run predictions. In one reading, the approach rejects the very existence of aggregate relations suitable for a causal account. The contrast between these views reveals that the issues regarding theories of economic behaviour and those about the link between the micro- and macro-levels are the most basic topics in macroeconomics. The conjecture that one can sensibly talk of structural relations at the economy level is of equal importance.

Chapter 2 studies the contribution of rational choice theories to economic theorizing by concentrating on Savage's theory of subjective expected utility. Using the general framework of the theory, the chapter distinguishes between several phases of human decision making which include: (i) modelling the choice situation; (ii) defining the decision problem; and (iii) solving the problem. In light of this, we distinguish between two possible types of theories of behaviour: choice-based theories of behaviour and learning-based theories of behaviour. Rational choice theories are among choice-based theories of behaviour; they take for granted how the agent models his choice situation and defines his decision problem, and explain only how he solves a well-defined decision problem. In modelling behaviour using these theories, a host of substantive assumptions therefore are needed to specify the agent's view of his choice situation and the problem he is trying to solve. These assumptions concern the agent's view of the causal structure of the economy, his values, needs and goals.

The chapter demonstrates that the resolution of economic controversies *primarily* hinges on how the agent models his choice situation and defines his decision problem, rather than on the *specific* method by which he solves it. In fact, rational choice theories are consistent with all sides of any substantive controversy in economics, and contribute very little to economic analysis. Substantial results attributed to these theories are implications of the assumptions made about how people specify their choice situation, and how they redefine it when faced with new information. As a consequence, a theory of economic behaviour cannot take as given the structure of the choice situation and how the agent defines his decision problem. Economics requires a learning-based theory of behaviour that explains how the agent models his choice situation, defines his decision problem, and redefines it as a result of experience. The rational expectations hypothesis also fails to eliminate the necessity of a learning-based theory of behaviour in economics.

Chapter 3 begins studying the intuitive statistician hypothesis. The usefulness of this hypothesis for modelling and thinking about the economy depends on whether there exists a 'tight enough' theory of statistical inference. To address this issue, we propose a preliminary conjecture about how a statistician perceives and models a choice situation: the statistician regards measurable features of the environment as realizations of some random variables, with an unknown joint probability distribution. He uses data on these variables to estimate their joint probability distribution *and* then uses the estimate of the distribution to infer the causal structure of the variables. If the model turns out to be inadequate, the initial set of variables is modified and the two phases of inference are repeated. This setting allows the separation of probabilistic inference issues from those of causal inference.

Central to learning the joint probability distribution of a set of variables is model formulation, rather than estimation or hypothesis testing. Whether there is a 'tight enough' theory of statistical learning critically depends on whether in turn there is a 'tight enough' theory of model formulation (Sargent, 1993: 23). Having said this, to study the issue of model formulation at its most general level, the chapter turns to non-parametric inference, which theoretically seeks to design algorithms that receive data on a set of variables and yield the model that, given the data, best approximates the underlying mechanism. We use the framework to explain why there cannot be such algorithms. In addition, we highlight intrinsic limitations of model-free inference, and establish the necessity of probabilistic background information for building interpretable statistical models. With the data samples normally available, one must begin with a parametric model to obtain an interpretable model of the data. As an implication, proposals to model homo economicus using tools from the neural networks literature are doomed to fail. Neural network algorithms are nothing but non-parametric estimators.

Chapter 4 studies statistical learning from the perspective of the Bayesian theory, which is said to allow the incorporation of background information into inference. We first look at some critical issues at the foundation of the Bayesian theory to explain why, contrary to the common conception in economics, it cannot be a theory of learning, and is only concerned with coherent analysis. As a result, to explain central aspects of inference such as model specification, empirical model assessment, and re-specification analysis, one has to go beyond the boundaries of the Bayesian theory. Having done this, we draw on several important themes in statistics to reconstruct a broader theory of Bayesian inference. The theory takes some steps in explaining the central aspects of inference traditionally left out in the Bayesian literature, including model formulation. Reflecting on the broader theory, we consider the possibility of establishing a 'tight enough' theory of parametric inference, and bring to the fore some important implications for the bounded rationality programme.

Chapter 5 studies the second phase of statistical learning relating to inference about causal structure. The chapter concentrates on the graph-theoretic approach to causal inference in order to investigate the possibility of a data-driven approach to causal inference. By 'data-driven' we mean any effort to draw causal conclusions from probabilistic data using only subject-matter-independent principles supposedly linking causation and probability. A claim for a data-driven approach to causal inference raises two separate issues. The first is whether there are universal principles connecting probabilistic and causal dependencies. The other is whether the principles are sufficient for inferring from the joint probability distribution of a set of variables the causal structure generating the distribution. We take up both topics and, by reflecting on the limits of data-driven causal inference, outline an alternative account of causal inference from observational data. We also explain precisely the intricate interplay between subject-matter information and observational data in causal modelling.

The analysis in these last three chapters helps us judge whether there can be a 'tight enough' theory of statistical learning that accounts for all phases of inference from data. We draw on our response to provide a partial assessment of the bounded rationality programme in new classical economics.

Chapter 6 studies the other element of the microfoundations project that has to do with the move from a theory of individual behaviour to a theory of the economy. We start with a critique of the representative agent modelling approach to the study of the economy using real examples from the literature, and explain why understanding large-scale economic phenomena, such as recession and growth, calls for thinking of the economy as a society of interactive heterogeneous individuals. Having done so, we investigate the problems that individual heterogeneity and interdependencies create for the study of the economy. In modern economies these fundamentally undercut the conception of the economy underlying the microfoundations project. In fact, they sever any simple, direct, and meaningful link between the micro- and macro-levels, casting doubt on the very existence of stable relations at the economy level which are suitable for a causal account. This, of course, makes it extremely difficult for the boundedly rational agent to learn about the economic structure from observable data.

We conclude by highlighting some of the implications of our analysis for the bounded rationality programme in particular and for the study of the economy in general. The marriage of the hypothesis that the agent behaves like a decision scientist with the one that he behaves like an intuitive statistician is not of much help in predicting the course of the economy. New advances in cognitive science, which view analogical reasoning as the core of cognition, provide a promising avenue for establishing a dynamic theory of economic behaviour. But the difficulties in moving from a theory of behaviour to a theory of the economy as a whole remain insurmountable. Atheoretical macroeconomics is perhaps closer to the truth.

1
Theoretical versus Atheoretical Macroeconomics: Concepts and Controversies

1.1 Introduction

> Human beings in society have no properties but those which are derived from, and may be resolved into, the laws of the nature of the individual man. In social phenomena the Composition of Causes is the universal law. (J.S. Mill. 1974 [1874]: 879)

The study of fluctuations in aggregate measures of economic activity and prices over relatively short periods (business cycle theory) and development of the economy over the long run (growth theory) constitutes what we call macroeconomics. The objective is to understand the causes of economic fluctuations and growth, forecast the future of the economy, and aid analysis of state policies. Following tradition, we may categorize major objectives of macroeconomics under the headings of explanation, forecasting, and policy analysis. These objectives require a quantitative model, which for most purposes must represent the causal structure of the economy. A major issue in macroeconomics is therefore the understanding of the causal structure of the economy.

An economy consists of millions of individual decision makers, firms and institutions, each solving different decision problems under diverse circumstances and subject to distinct social and economic constraints. This complexity makes it impossible to build a model which represents the behaviour of all the decision-making units of the economy. In modelling the economy, we need to leave out many details of the decision-making units, introduce aggregate variables, and focus on the relations of the aggregates. For this reason, macroeconomics is primarily the study of aggregates.

The study of the economy at the aggregate level presents a number of difficulties. To begin with, for social and practical reasons, it is impossible to subject the economy to controlled experiments in order to establish causal relations that are true at the economy level. Also, statistical analysis of aggregate data is inadequate for causal inference, and has to be supported with domain-specific information. This raises the issue of how we can acquire the subject-matter information necessary for modelling the structure.

In this chapter, we explore these difficulties in the study of the economy and review some of the responses to them. We begin by defining some central notions used throughout the work before discussing some of the limitations of statistical analysis for causal inference to explain better the need for theory in modelling the economy. We then reconstruct the current theoretical and atheoretical approaches to macroeconomics in order to define some basic issues in the study of the economy.

1.2 Macroeconomics

The variables used to describe an economy originate in the decisions made by its components – numerous individuals, firms, institutions, and the government.[1] Families make decisions about what to consume and when, how many hours to work, and what to invest in; firms make decisions about unemployment, production, pricing, marketing, borrowing, investment, and so forth. The input and output variables of these decision makers form the basic variables of the economy. Often, the eventual outcome of the decisions is not quite what was planned; poor health may disrupt work or a supply shortage may result in a lower production than expected. It is sensible to model the decision outputs of an individual or institutional decision maker as a function of its key input variables plus a stochastic residual vector. The vector of input and output variables of all participants in the economy and their linking functions form the *microstructure* of the economy. We denote the microstructure by ($\boldsymbol{m}$, $\boldsymbol{r}$), where $\boldsymbol{m}$ and $\boldsymbol{r}$ stand for the vector of micro-variables and micro-relations respectively. In place of ($\boldsymbol{m}$, $\boldsymbol{r}$), the literature often refers to the triple ($\boldsymbol{m}$, $\boldsymbol{r}$, $\boldsymbol{p}$) as the true data-generating mechanism, where $\boldsymbol{p}$ is the joint probability distribution of the micro-variables $\boldsymbol{m}$ (Granger, 1990a: 7; Hendry and Ericsson, 1991: 18; Spanos, 1986: 661–72).

The immense number of micro-variables and relations in any modern economy makes it impossible to consider the behaviours of all decision-making units in a model. Modelling an economy requires introducing aggregate variables and focusing on the patterns that emerge at the aggregate level. A fundamental assumption in economics is that the microstructure ($\boldsymbol{m}$, $\boldsymbol{r}$, $\boldsymbol{p}$) leads to a unique *macrostructure* ($\boldsymbol{M}$, $\boldsymbol{R}$, $\boldsymbol{P}$), where $\boldsymbol{M}$ stands for the set of aggregate input and output variables, $\boldsymbol{R}$ for the relations among the aggregate variables, and $\boldsymbol{P}$ for the joint probability distribution of the variables (Epstein, 1987: 65). This structure is the subject-matter of macroeconomics. Macroeconomics is the study of the aggregative relations that emerge from decisions and interactions of the basic decision-making units of the economy. By contrast, microeconomics is the study of the behaviour of the basic decision-making units of the economy in which no aggregation is involved. Aggregation is what separates these fields of study from each other (Keynes, 1936: 292–3).[2]

This view of macroeconomics is consistent with mainstream economics, which postulates the existence of stable relations at the aggregate level. There are, nevertheless, several notions of macroeconomic structure and a host of views on the connection between the micro- and macrostructures. We continue by defining the notion of structure to be found in the writings of early econometricians working in the Cowles Commission.[3] This will help us characterize some key controversies in modern macroeconomics.

1.2.1 Structure

Early econometricians usually defined 'structure' using the notion of a *structural model*. To define this, consider the simple stochastic equation:

$$Y = \alpha + \beta X + \varepsilon \tag{1.1}$$

where Y is the response variable, X is the regressor, and ε is the error term with mean zero.[4] This equation is commonly used to represent the regression of Y on X, giving the mean of the distribution of Y conditional on a particular value of X, i.e. $E(Y/X = x)$. As a regression equation, (1.1) describes the association between X and Y in the population from which the data are sampled. As opposed to this usage, the equation may be used for predicting the effects of (hypothetical) interventions in X on Y. If the equation correctly predicts how the values of Y change as we intervene to change the values of X, it is called *structural* (Hurwicz, 1962: 236–7). A difference between (1.1) as a regression equation and (1.1) as a structural equation is that in the former case the equation may cease to hold as soon as changes are made to X whereas in the latter case the equation is invariant to interventions made to the values of X. Another way to state this notion of structural equation is the following, which is borrowed with small changes from Pearl (2000: 160):

> **Definition:** An equation $Y = \alpha + \beta X + \varepsilon$ is said to be structural if in an ideal experiment where we control X to x and any other set Z of variables (not containing X or Y) to z, the value of Y would be independent of z and is given by $\alpha + \beta x + \varepsilon$.

This notion of structural equation captures the core of the manipulability account of causation (Woodward, 1999). On this view of causality, variable X causes variable Y if it is possible at least in a hypothetical experiment to change Y by manipulating X. So, the claim that equation (1.1) is structural means that it expresses a causal relation. In that case, the parameter β in (1.1) reflects the causal effect of X on Y, contrary to a regression equation in which β only represents the degree of association between X and Y in the population. The terms 'structural' and 'causal' are used interchangeably in what follows.[5]

Variables on the right-hand side of a structural equation are referred to as *exogenous*: variable X in equation (1.1) is exogenous if intervening to set $X = x$ gives the same result for Y as observing $X = x$. Similarly, the variable on the left-hand side of a structural equation is called *endogenous*. Exogeneity is also used to convey weaker meanings. Sometimes, it refers to a variable whose value is not explained within the model but is supplied to it. And, sometimes, it refers to a variable which is statistically independent of the error term in the equation. By exogeneity, we mean an independent variable in a structural equation (Engle *et al.*, 1983).

The notion of a structural equation is generalized to systems of equations. An equation system forms a *structural model* if each equation in the system is structural and remains invariant to changes that invalidate other equations in the model. This means each equation in a structural model represents an autonomous causal mechanism that can be modified without undermining the mechanisms represented by other equations in the model. As an illustration, consider a simple model of demand and price determination in economics, which has been discussed by many authors, including Goldberger (1992) and Pearl (2000: 27):

$$Q = \alpha_1 P + \beta_1 I + \varepsilon_1 \tag{1.2a}$$

$$P = \alpha_2 Q + \beta_2 W + \varepsilon_2 \tag{1.2b}$$

where Q is the quantity of household demand for product A, P is the unit price of A, I is household income, W is the wage rate for producing A, and ε_1 and ε_2 are error terms, representing unmodelled factors that affect quantity and price respectively. This model is structural if equation (1.2a) correctly forecasts the effects on Q of (hypothetical) interventions in P or I, and equation (1.2b) correctly predicts the effects on P of interventions in Q or wage W. Moreover, interventions invalidating (1.2a) must not invalidate (1.2b) and vice versa.[6] If we change the values of the parameters α_1 and β_1 by intervening in the mechanisms determining the household income I, the change must not affect α_2 and β_2. The underlying mechanisms must be unrelated. In short, what makes this model structural is that each equation characterizes an autonomous causal mechanism, one equation describing the causal process determining the demand for A, and the other the process determining the price of A.[7]

This concept of structural model captures the notion of structure implicit in the writings of the Cowles Commission econometricians. According to these researchers, a structure consists of a set of autonomous causal relations that can be utilized separately for intervening in the state of the economy. Koopmans, a leading member of the Cowles Commission, recapitulates this concept of structure:

> The study of an equation system derives its sense from the postulate that there exists one and only one representation in which each equation corresponds to a specific law of behaviour (attributed to a specific group of economic agents)... Any discussion of the effects of changes in economic structure, whether brought about by trends or policies, is best put in terms of changes in structural equations. For these are the elements that can, at least in theory, be changed one by one, independently. For this reason it is important that the system be recognisable as structural equations. (quoted in Epstein, 1987: 65)

We call this characterization – the study of autonomous causal relations emerging at the economy level – the *received view*, and use it as a benchmark against which to compare alternative views on the nature and scope of macroeconomics.

1.2.2 Objectives

A full exposition of the received view also requires an understanding of the objectives set for macroeconomics. To achieve this, it is useful to describe the framework within which economic analysis is usually carried out. In its simplest form, consider an economy whose state at time t can be described by an endogenous variable Y_t and an exogenous variable X_t.[8] The dynamics of the economy is described by a difference equation:

$$Y_{t+1} = f(Y_t, X_t, \theta, \varepsilon_t) \tag{1.3}$$

where θ is a parameter vector defining the function f, and the disturbance term (random shock) ε_t has probability distribution $P(\varepsilon_t)$. The description of the economy is completed by specifying the mechanism generating the exogenous variable X_t shown by

$$X_t = g(Z_t, \lambda, e_t) \tag{1.4}$$

where Z_t denotes the only variable affecting X_t, λ a parameter vector defining the function g, and e_t a disturbance term with probability distribution $Q(e_t)$.[9] The functions f and g are taken to be fixed but not known or at least not fully known. Data on X_t, Y_t and Z_t is used to estimate θ and λ, as well as the parameters of the distributions $P(\varepsilon_t)$ and $Q(e_t)$. The model is used for prediction, policy analysis, and explanation.

1.2.2.1 *Prediction*

Given an estimate of the model's parameters, the task in prediction is to calculate the expected value of Y_{t+1} when the values of Y_t and X_t are given. Depending on how the value of X_t is given, three types of prediction can be defined. The first is the *ex post* prediction, where the model is used to predict the future value of Y_t based on a *known* value of X_t. The second is the *ex ante* prediction, where the value of X_t is not known and instead one uses *guessed* values of X_t to forecast future values of Y_t. *Ex ante* and *ex post* predictions involve no intervention in the system. If the model closely approximates the associations in the population during the periods for which the forecasts are made, it will correctly predict future values of Y_t, regardless of whether it is structural or not. No knowledge of the structure is needed for *ex ante* and *ex post* predictions.

The third type is the *conditional* prediction, where the value of X_t is *set* through intervention. In conditional prediction, the aim is to forecast the value y_{t+1} that would arise if X_t could be set at a value different from its actual value. The model must therefore be structural or, in other words, invariant to the intervention to yield a correct prediction. A regression (non-causal) model will not be adequate.[10]

1.2.2.2 *Policy analysis*

Policy analysis aims to design changes in the economy that take it to a desired state. In its simplest form, a policy consists of a change in the value of a policy variable, say X_t, to alter the value of the target variable Y_{t+1}. Policy analysis, then, involves predicting values of Y_{t+1} that would arise if X_t were set at values differing from its actual value. If such predictions were possible, future values of Y_t could be estimated for different values of X_t to find a value that would most likely yield the desired result.

More often, a policy is defined as a change in the process that determines a policy variable. In the context of our simple economy, this amounts to a change in the mechanism:

$$X_t = g(Z_t, \lambda, e_t) \tag{1.4}$$

The idea is that each set of possible values for parameters λ defines a possible mechanism (rule) for X_t. A policy change, then, consists of a change in these parameters to influence the course of the economy (Tinbergen, 1939: vol.2, 18). For selecting a policy, the analyst considers different sets of values for λ to define alternative mechanisms for X_t. The rules are used to generate sequences of values $\{x_t\}$, which are recursively inserted in model (1.3) to simulate the future of the economy under each rule.The rule that generates the desired result is chosen as the optimal policy.

A key requirement of this exercise is that equation (1.3) be invariant to changes in the policy rule (1.4). If a change in the mechanism generating X_t

undermines the relation (1.3) that determines Y_t, then an estimated version of equation (1.3) will not correctly predict the economy under alternative policy rules.

In either sense, policy analysis involves conditional predictions and, for that reason, the model must be structural to yield correct predictions.

1.2.2.3 Explanation

Another related goal of economics is to understand why certain *particular* facts are as they are. It is of utmost importance for policy analysis to understand, for example, why the inflation rate was at 2.5 per cent in the UK last year, why the rise in the interest rate by 1 per cent did not have the expected effect on the housing market, or why there has been a stark increase in inequality within the United States over the last few decades. These queries fall under the heading of explanation, which is a major topic in the philosophy of science.

According to an early theory of scientific explanation by Hempel and Oppenheim (1965 [1948]), an explanation of a particular fact is an argument to the effect that the phenomenon to be explained was to be expected by virtue of certain explanatory facts (Hempel, 1965: 336). The premises of the argument constitute the *explanans* (that which does the explaining), and the conclusion is the *explanandum* (that which is explained). The theory requires the explanans to include at least one lawful generalization. Schematically, an explanation in this approach takes the form:

True statements of initial conditions Laws	} *Explanans*
Statement of what is to be explained	*Explanandum*

Thus, one can explain the length of the shadow cast by a flagpole from the height of the pole, the angle of the sun above the horizon, and the laws about the rectilinear propagation of light.

Universal laws are hard to find outside physical sciences. In many fields, if there are any generalizations, they are statistical. For these fields, Hempel replaces the requirement of a universal law with a statistical law. For him, then, a statistical argument forms a satisfactory explanation if its premises are true, include at least one statistical regularity, and confer a high probability on the conclusion. As an illustration, if one asks why John rapidly recovered from his streptococcus infection, an explanation is that he took a dose of penicillin, and almost all strep infections clear up quickly upon administration of penicillin. Hempel takes this to be a satisfactory explanation if the explanans are all true, and confer a high probability on John's recovery.

A problem with Hempel's theory is that it takes the explanatory relation to be symmetrical. The theory equally allows one to explain the height of a flagpole by deducing it from the length of its shadow, the angle of elevation of the sun, and the laws about the rectilinear propagation of light. Or, given a statistical association between Gaussian random variables X and Y, which have no common cause, the view suggests that X can be explained by Y and Y by X, even if X causes Y. This goes against a sound intuition that while causes explain their effects, effects do not explain their causes. Moreover, an objective in understanding a system, such as the economy or nature, is to control it. Knowledge of causes is relevant to control but knowledge of effects is not. So, the search for explanation, at least in practice, is driven by a need for information on causes.

Also, many statistical associations are spurious. A sudden drop in barometer reading is usually followed by the coming of a storm. Yet even if a drop in the barometer increases the probability of a storm, it cannot explain the occurrence of a storm. Again, the reason is that an intervention on the barometer reading, say by placing the barometer in a vacuum chamber and setting its value by some random process, can neither create nor avert the bad weather. The association between a drop in the barometer reading and the occurrence of a storm is the result of a common cause – the drop in atmospheric pressure. In general, since by controlling the effect of a cause one cannot control another effect of the same cause, effects do not explain each other.

Several theories of scientific explanation have been set forth to overcome the difficulties besetting Hempel's theory but an analysis of these theories falls outside the scope of this work. Nonetheless, reflection on the problems raised against Hempel's view shows the difficulty of developing a theory of explanation of particular facts that makes no reference to causal relations. An explanation of a particular fact must give information relating to the causal process that has generated it. As Lewis notes, to explain a particular fact is to give some information about its causal history (1986: 217). In general, whenever we try to explain a particular phenomenon, we must show that (1) the explanatory events are actually true, (2) the events are causes of the explanandum in the sense that if they were present and there were no preventive causes, the explanandum would occur too, and (3) the events are *actually* the causes of the explanandum in that if they had not been present in the situation under study the explanandum would not have occurred.[11] The reason for this last condition is that for any event there might be several sets of sufficient causes that could bring it about. In short, a satisfactory explanation of a particular fact calls for information on its causes, and a model must be structural to play a part in the explanation.

To sum up, according to the received view, there is a structure behind the aggregate data, consisting of causal relations that can be manipulated independently of each other. The prime task of macroeconomics is to model the structure. In addition, all the objectives traditionally set for macroeconomics, namely *ex ante* and *ex post* prediction, conditional prediction, policy analysis and explanation, are considered achievable.

1.3 The need for theory

A basic methodological query for the received view is how the economy's structure can be discovered. Natural and physical sciences appeal to controlled experiments to infer causal relations. Economists are not in a position to carry out controlled experiments on the economy, and should turn to statistical analysis of aggregate data to learn about its structure. Statistical analysis, however, is inadequate for causal inference, and must always be supported with subject-matter information. There are three lines of argument in the literature for this inadequacy of statistical methods, and hence the necessity of theory in macroeconomics. A brief study of these arguments sheds light on the reasons behind the emergence of competing approaches to macroeconomics.

1.3.1 Statistical control

A major argument for the necessity of theory in macroeconomics is based on the inadequacy of the regression method for causal inference (henceforth, RMCI). The regression method stands at the heart of econometrics and many controversies in macroeconomics relate to this method. It is therefore worthwhile explaining in some detail how the method is used for causal inference and why it fails in establishing causation. There are many discussions of the method as well as its limitations. We draw on Simon (1954), Clogg and Haritou (1997), Spirtes *et al.* (1998), Pearl (2000) and Spirtes (1997) to describe the method and explain why it fails.

We first focus on the simple regression equation (1.1), and then extend the analysis to cases where there are several regressors involved. Since in the following the first moment of the variables is of no interest, we assume that the variables are measured around their mean and drop the intercept from the equation. Equation (1.1) becomes:

$$Y = \beta X + \varepsilon \tag{1.5}$$

Regression analysis is primarily concerned with estimating the parameter β and the conditions under which an unbiased, efficient (minimum variance), and consistent estimate can be obtained from the data. To use this as a method of causal inference, one has to explain the conditions under which such an estimate of β can be taken as an estimate of the effect of X on Y, as well as how the conditions can be established in practice. Accordingly, there are three issues to address in order to understand the possible role of regression in causal inference. The first relates to the conditions under which an unbiased, efficient, and consistent estimate of β can be obtained from the data. The second relates to the conditions under which the estimate can be taken as an estimate of the effect of X on Y. Finally, the third relates to the possibility of establishing the conditions in practice. We review the answers given to some of these questions to explain why the regression method fails to establish causation.

To estimate β, users of the RMCI turn to the theory of ordinary least squares. This theory makes a number of assumptions about the error term ε to ensure an efficient, unbiased, and consistent estimation. First, it assumes that the expected value of ε_i conditional on observation X_i is zero; that is, $E(\varepsilon/x_i) = 0$. This implies that the unconditional mean, $E(\varepsilon)$, is zero. Likewise, the same condition implies that ε_i and X_i are uncorrelated; namely, $Cov(x_i, \varepsilon_i) = 0$. This last implication is known as the *orthogonality* condition. Given the linearity of (1.5), the orthogonality condition ensures that a least-squares estimate of β is unbiased. Secondly, the theory requires that observations on X provide no information about the variance and covariance of the error term ε. This means that the errors associated with the observations must have constant variance σ^2, and be uncorrelated with each other. Under these conditions, a least-squares estimator of β is shown to be efficient, unbiased, and consistent.

Econometricians add one or two requirements to the orthogonality condition to identify an unbiased estimate of β with the effect of X on Y. In his celebrated article (1954), Herbert Simon requires X to precede Y. By this, he intends to rule out bidirectional causation between X and Y. Others have also required that X can indeed be a causal variable to exclude nonsense inferences such as inferring that having nicotine stains on one's finger causes lung cancer. According to the RMCI, then, a least squares estimate of the coefficient of X coincides with the effect of X on Y if X is uncorrelated with ε, X precedes Y, and X can indeed be a causal variable. The validity of this answer, Simon (1954) maintains, can be shown in the context of the simple regression equation (1.5). Suppose β in (1.5) represents the effect of X on Y. If we multiply the equation through by X and take expectations of both sides, we will have

$$Cov(X, Y) = \beta V(X) + Cov(X, \varepsilon) \tag{1.6}$$

where $Cov(X, Y)$ is the covariance of X and Y, $V(X)$ is the variance of X, and $Cov(X, \varepsilon)$ the covariance of X and ε. If X and ε are uncorrelated, the least squares estimate $\hat{\beta}_{XY}$ will be equal $Cov(X, Y)/V(X)$, which is the same as β, the effect of X on Y. That is

$$\hat{\beta}_{XY} = Cov(X, Y)/V(X) = \beta$$

If the condition fails, $\hat{\beta}_{XY}$ and β will not be the same.

Simon's analysis assumes that every observed correlation arises from either a direct causal connection or latent common causes. If one rules out latent common causes by assuming the orthogonality condition, then, a correlation between X and Y reveals a direct causal connection. Evidently, if the world contained spurious correlations that were not due to common causes, the orthogonality condition would not justify inferring from a correlation between X and Y that either X causes Y or Y causes X. Such a conclusion requires excluding all possible non-causal explanations.[12]

Now, we know how the regression method is used to establish causation. Assuming the conditions, one simply regresses Y on X. If the least-squares estimate $\hat{\beta}_{XY}$ differs from zero, X causes Y, and if it is zero, X does not cause Y. The success of the method depends, on the one hand, on the adequacy of the conditions and, on the other, on the possibility of establishing them in practice. An analysis of the adequacy of the conditions falls outside the scope of this work.[13] To keep the analysis short, we confine ourselves to an examination of the orthogonality condition, as this will suffice to explain why the RMCI fails.

The RMCI comes with a method for establishing the orthogonality condition. To explain the method, note that this condition differs from other familiar statistical assumptions underlying a regression model, such as the linearity of the function linking X and Y or the normality of the distribution of Y. The validity of these assumptions can be checked by using observations on X and Y. In fact, for arbitrarily large samples, there are statistical algorithms that correctly discover the functional form of the relation between X and Y, and estimate the density function of Y. In contrast, observations on X and Y contain no information on the validity of the orthogonality condition. This follows from the fact that the true disturbances ε_i are never known. In practice, we can only estimate residuals $e_i = (y_i - \hat{y}_i)$, with $\hat{y}_i$ being the expected value of y_i. If we use the least squares method to estimate β, the residuals e_i are automatically uncorrelated with x_i. One cannot, therefore, use the residuals to establish the condition (Clogg and Haritou, 1997: 94).[14] In this sense, the condition is not a statistical assumption.

Faced with this limitation, econometricians have tried to establish the orthogonality condition by bringing in variables other than X and Y. To understand the philosophy behind this attempt, one should note that when equation (1.5) is taken as a structural relation the error term ε stands for the effects of omitted variables on Y. Any correlation between X and ε is therefore said to indicate the presence of latent common causes for X and Y. Such variables are referred to as confounders. This interpretation suggests that the correlation between X and ε can be eliminated by including all the confounders of X and Y in the regression of Y on X. In that case, the error term ε will be uncorrelated with X, and, if other conditions are in place, an estimate of β will coincide with the effect of X on Y. Thus, it is suggested that the orthogonality condition can be established by searching for all the confounders of X and Y, and including them in the regression of Y on X. To estimate the effect of X on Y, it is not enough to estimate the simple regression equation (1.5). Instead, it is necessary to regress Y on X and all the confounders of X and Y. An estimate of the regression coefficient of X in this equation corresponds with the effect of X on Y. The process of controlling for confounders is often called *conditioning* or *statistical control*.

The reasoning behind statistical control can be illustrated by considering the case where there is only one confounder Z for X and Y.[15] Suppose the process generating Y is given by model (1.7):

$$X = \alpha Z + \varepsilon_1 \tag{1.7a}$$

$$Y = \beta X + \gamma Z + \varepsilon_2 \tag{1.7b}$$

where $Cov(\varepsilon_1, \varepsilon_2) = 0$, and α, β, γ are different from zero. In this model, Z is a common cause of X and Y. If we estimate (1.5) in place of equation (1.7b), X and ε will be correlated, and a least-squares estimate of the coefficient of X will differ from β. To see this, we simply need to multiply (1.7b) through by X and take expectations of both sides to get

$$Cov(X, Y) = \beta V(X) + \alpha\gamma V(Z) \tag{1.8}$$

We then have

$$\hat{\beta}_{XY} = \frac{Cov(X, Y)}{V(X)} = \frac{\beta V(X) + \alpha\gamma V(Z)}{V(X)} \neq \beta \tag{1.9}$$

If Z is included in the regression of Y on X, the orthogonality condition is satisfied, and the least-squares estimate of β can be equated with the effect of X on Y, as shown below:

$$\begin{aligned} \hat{\beta}_{XY/z} = \frac{Cov(X, Y/Z)}{V(X/Z)} &= \frac{Cov(X, Y)V(Z) - Cov(X, Z)Cov(Y, Z)}{V(X)V(Z) - Cov(X, Z)^2} \\ &= \frac{\beta(V(X) - \alpha^2 V(Z))}{(V(X) - \alpha^2 V(Z))} = \beta \end{aligned} \tag{1.10}$$

Regression on a confounder, therefore, can change an otherwise biased estimate into an unbiased one.

A problem with this reasoning is that the set of confounders of X and Y is not known. In practice, statisticians replace the set of confounders of X and Y with a set of *potential* confounders, namely a set of measured variables that precede X and Y, and can possibly affect them. It is held that by controlling for potential confounders one is likely to control for real confounders, and eliminate possible correlation between X and ε (Black, 1982: 31). One is then advised to control for as many potential confounders as one can to achieve a reliable estimate of the effect of X on Y. The longer the list of potential confounders in the regression of Y on X, the more reliable the estimate will be:

> One must include in the equation fitted to data every 'optional' concomitant [potential confounder] that might reasonably be suspected of either affecting or merely preceding Y given X – or if the available degrees of freedom do not permit this, then in at least one of several equations fitted to the data. (Pratt and Schlaifer, 1988: 44)[16]

In this way, multivariate regression has come to dominate macroeconomics. To estimate the effect of X on Y, Y is regressed on X and a few other variables that are thought likely to affect both X and Y. The estimate of β in the equation with all the potential confounders, whose inclusion affects the estimate of β, is taken to represent the effect of X on Y. The RMCI is also generalized to multivariate regression equations. For a causal interpretation of a multivariate regression equation, all the regressors are required to precede the response variable and to be uncorrelated with the error term. Similarly, to establish the orthogonality condition, it is essential to control for all the confounders of the regressors and the response variable (Clogg and Haritou, 1997: 94).

1.3.1.1 Limitations of statistical control

A limitation of statistical control arises from the small number of variables that are measured in practice. To be precise, let $\mathbf{C}$ be the set of all potential confounders of X and Y. The plausible idea of statistical control is that if we could control for all the variables in $\mathbf{C}$, we would be able to control for all the real confounders of X and Y, and estimate the effect of X on Y. But the set $\mathbf{C}$ is never completely known. In practice, what one measures is a *proper* subset of $\mathbf{C}$, which may exclude some or even all of the actual confounders of X and Y. As a result, conditioning on measured potential confounders can never guarantee the truth of the orthogonality condition, and a non-zero estimate of β can always be due to latent common causes. The RMCI, on its own, fails to distinguish between cases of genuine causal connection and spurious correlation (Pearl, 2000: 186).

Moreover, conditioning on a measured variable, which is not a real confounder, could change a consistent estimate of the effect of X on Y into an inconsistent estimate. This occurs whenever one controls for a *barren proxy*; that is, a variable Z that is correlated with factors that influence X and Y but itself has no effect on X and Y. As an illustration, consider the following simple example discussed by Pearl (2000), Spirtes *et al.* (1998), and Spirtes (1997). Suppose that our set of measured variables consists of $\{X, Y, Z\}$, X precedes Y, and that Z precedes both X and Y. Also, suppose that the causal structure of these variables is given by the model below (Figure 1.1), where ε_X, ε_Z and

$X = U_1 + \varepsilon_x$

$Z = \alpha U_1 + U_2 + \varepsilon_z$

$Y = \beta X + \gamma U_2 + \varepsilon_y$

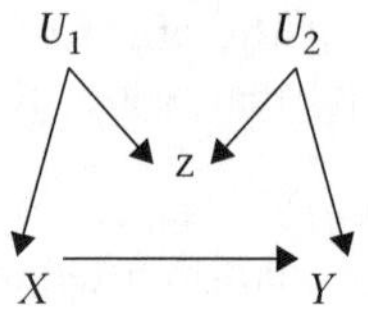

U_1= Smoking
U_2= Age
Z= Nicotine stains
X= Lung cancer
Y= Death

Figure 1.1 A barren proxy

Note: Z is a barren proxy; while Z is associated with both X and Y, X and Y are not confounded by Z.

ε_y are independent error terms, U_1 is an unmeasured common cause of X and Z, and U_2 is an unmeasured common cause of Y and Z. Further, suppose that U_1 and U_2 are uncorrelated with the error terms. In this setting, if Y is regressed on X alone, the least-squares estimate of β is consistent. However, if Y is regressed on both X and Z, the estimate of β is no longer consistent, and normally differs from the effect of X on Y. This can be seen from the least-squares estimate of β in the regression equation of Y on X and Z. To this end, first note that $Cov(X,Z) = \alpha V(U_1)$ and $Cov(Y,Z) = \beta(\alpha V(U_1)) + \gamma V(U_2)$. Also, let $Cov(X,Z) = \rho$ and $\gamma V(U_2) = \tau$. Then, we have

$$\hat{\beta}_{XY/Z} = \frac{Cov(X,Y/Z)}{V(X/Z)} = \frac{Cov(X,Y)V(Z) - Cov(X,Z)Cov(Y,Z)}{V(X)V(Z) - Cov(X,Z)^2} \tag{1.11}$$
$$= \frac{\beta V(X)V(Z) - \rho(\rho\beta + \tau)}{V(X)V(Z) - \rho^2} = \beta - \frac{\rho\tau}{V(X)V(Z) - \rho^2}$$

which generally differs from β. The estimate is consistent only if either ρ or τ is zero. Otherwise, β might be zero but the estimate $\hat{\beta}_{XY/Z}$ substantially different from zero. Therefore, 'there is no sense in which one is "playing safe" by including rather than excluding "potential confounders" in the conditioning set; conditioning on these variables could change a consistent estimate into an inconsistent estimate' (Spirtes, 1997: 7). To safely condition on a measured variable, Z, it must be ensured that Z is not a barren proxy. This, as the example illustrates, calls for some information about the causal relation between Z and unmeasured variables affecting X and Y. Clearly, such information cannot be obtained from statistical analysis of data on the measured variables.

Finally, a potential confounder must itself satisfy the orthogonality condition (Clogg and Haritou, 1997: 98). That is, to control for a potential confounder Z in estimating the effect of X on Y, Z must also be uncorrelated with the error term. Since this new requirement cannot be taken for granted *a priori*, one inevitably needs to bring in new variables to ensure that Z and ε are uncorrelated. This, of course, requires making further orthogonality assumptions. As a consequence, it is never possible to establish the condition by controlling for measured potential confounders (Freedman, 1987: 307).

To terminate the regression, one must eventually rely on substantive domain-specific information. This necessity of subject-matter information in establishing causation is viewed as a key reason for the essential role of theory in macroeconomics.

1.3.2 The identification problem

A second argument for the necessity of theory draws on the identification problem. Historically, a common belief in economics has been that the values of economic variables such as demand and supply for a good are simultaneously determined, and for that reason the economy is best represented by a simultaneous equations model. Because of feedback, the error terms across the equations in a simultaneous equation model are not uncorrelated. As a result, applying the ordinary-least-squares method to the model does not yield a consistent estimate of the parameters. For consistent estimation, the model must be transformed into a system of regression equations or, in other words, a *reduced form* model, where the errors across the equations are independent. In this context, the identification problem involves inferring the parameters of the simultaneous equations (structural) model from the parameters of the regression model (Manski, 1995). It is usually the case that a large, and often infinite, set of parameter values of the structural model is consistent with the parameters of the reduced form model, making it impossible to infer the structural parameters from those of the reduced form model.[17] Thus, the identification problem has no statistical solution.

In the context of simultaneous equations models, the identification problem can be resolved by imposing restrictions on the variables in each equation. In a linear structural model, if one can exclude from each equation one variable that enters other equations, none of the model equations can be written as a linear combination of the others, and the model becomes identifiable (Koopmans, 1971 [1949]: 169). One surely needs to rely on non-sample (domain-specific) information to decide which variable to exclude from, or include in, an equation. Similarly, in recursive models, identifiability calls for the orthogonality condition and the independence of the error terms across the equations (Boudon, 1968: 208).[18] These conditions, as we now know, are not statistical assumptions, and can be justified only by means of domain-specific information – another reason for the essential role of theory in modelling the economy.

The identification problem is not the same as the causal inference problem, as there could be more than one identifiable causal model consistent with a data set. Recursive models are always identifiable if the disturbance terms satisfy the orthogonality condition and are independent across the model equations. But there are usually many identifiable, recursive causal models consistent with a data set. This lack of uniqueness leads to a quandary regarding which is the true causal model. A solution to the identification problem is not, then, a solution to the causal inference problem.

1.3.3 The Lucas argument

The above arguments establish the need for theory by showing the limitations of statistical analysis for causal inference. The literature also offers a third argument for the necessity of theory that is based on the inadequacy of knowledge of the *existing* structure for policy analysis. Various accounts of the argument are found in the writings of Haavelmo (1944), Koopmans (1947b), and Hurwicz (1962). Yet, it was Lucas who most forcefully defended the argument in his critique of econometric policy evaluation (1976), using numerous graphic examples. The critique is aimed at the conventional theory of economic policy. Recall our simple economy, which had a single endogenous variable Y_t, whose law of motion was given by the difference equation

$$Y_{t+1} = f(Y_t, X_t, \theta, \varepsilon_t) \tag{1.12a}$$

and the rule (law) governing the policy (exogenous) variable X_t by

$$X_t = g(Z_t, \lambda, e_t) \tag{1.12b}$$

The theory interprets a policy as a sequence of values for exogenous variable X_t. So, in policy evaluation, the analyst considers different sets of values for parameters λ to define alternative mechanisms for X_t. The rules are used to generate sequences of values $\{x_t\}$ which are recursively inserted in model (1.12a) to simulate the course of the economy under each rule. The rule that generates the desired result is chosen as the optimal policy.

This practice, Lucas argues, is flawed, since it assumes that the structure $(\mathbf{f}, \theta)$ *prior* to the policy change (call it the *current* structure) and the structure *afterwards* (call it the *new* structure) are the same. But the structure emerges from the decision rules (supply and demand functions) of the agents. As the government introduces a new policy regime, it changes the environment in which they are operating, altering the constraints restricting their choice behaviour. The agents recognize the change and modify their decision rules, thereby changing the structure. This invalidates the model fitted to the data collected prior to the intervention, rendering it useless for predicting the course of the economy under the new policy rule. To predict the outcomes of a shift in a policy regime, one needs to know the structure that emerges after the intervention. By assumption, there is no data available on the new structure. For this reason, its discovery falls outside the reach of statistics.

As a simple illustration, suppose the demand for investment in the economy follows

$$Y_{t+1} = \gamma Y_t - \pi X_{t+1} + \varepsilon_{t+1}, \quad \gamma, \pi \in \theta \tag{1.13a}$$

where Y_t is the demand for investment at time t, and X_t the tax rate in period t. Also, let government's tax policy follow the rule

$$X_{t+1} = \lambda X_t \tag{1.13b}$$

A change in government's tax policy rule thus involves a change in the value of the parameter λ. Equation (1.13a) theoretically depends on the optimal decisions of investors, who take policy tax rule (1.13b) into account in making investment decisions. This means parameter π in (1.13a) depends on parameter λ, which characterizes the government's tax policy rule (1.13b). A shift in the government's tax policy, i.e. λ, then changes π. So, one cannot use an estimate of (1.13a), which is by assumption true, to analyse the effects of alternative policy tax rules on the economy. To predict the outcomes of a change in rule (1.13b), one first needs to predict the structure that would emerge after the intervention, i.e. the modified function (1.13a). Statistical analysis can at best infer (1.13a), which has been true while policy rule (1.13b) has been in place. It cannot provide any information about the new structure, for which no data are yet available. To predict the modified (1.13a), one needs a theory that explains how people respond to a policy, and how the response affects the structure.

Lucas' critique, in short, is that causal relations estimated in econometrics are not structural. The relations are so interrelated that a change in one relation could undermine others. One therefore cannot rely on the *correct* causal model fitted to the data to analyse the effects of non-trivial polices. This requires the model that would be true after the intervention. The new model, though, cannot be known by analysing existing data.

Lucas' argument has been challenged on several grounds. Notably, Sims (1982a) argued that the critique applies only to interventions involving a regime shift but such changes are rare. People are also slow in absorbing the effects of policy interventions. For these reasons, statistical models that closely describe the economy can reliably predict the policy outcomes in the short run, which is of main interest in economics. Sims' criticism contains an element of truth but does not weaken the logical force of Lucas' argument. The point is that if a policy could shift the structure, one would first have to predict the emerging structure to be able to trace the effect of the policy on the economy. Such a prediction cannot be based on the data from the current structure.

The three arguments outlined here provide a strong reason for the necessity of theory in modelling the economy. Reflection on these arguments as well as the difficulty of controlled experiments on the economy has led to rival approaches to macroeconomics. The remainder of this chapter reconstructs the theoretical and atheoretical approaches that span the spectrum of views on the scope and nature of macroeconomics.

1.4 The theoretical approach

The core idea of theoretical macroeconomics is present in the writings of early members of the Cowles Commission, including Koopmans (1947b) and Marschack (1953), as well as other early economists such as Jevons (1871) and

Hicks (1939). A rigorous and systematic defence, though, appeared in the works of new classical economists, notably Lucas and Sargent (1979), who were reflecting on the failure of Keynesian macroeconomic models during the 1970s.

A central assumption underlying the theoretical approach is that none of the difficulties hindering the study of the economy arises in the study of individual behaviour. Early on in the history of economics, economists thought that *intuition, introspection,* and *interview* were reliable means of understanding behaviour. Tjalling Koopmans, for example, held that through these means it would be possible to establish the motives of consumers, firms and investors, and understand how they make decisions. The information, he added, could be turned into a theory of economic behaviour as precise as the laws of motion of material bodies known to Kepler (Koopmans, 1947b: 166).[19] In recent years, more emphasis is placed on experimentation. It has been argued that even if current theories of behaviour are imprecise, with adequate experimental research it should be possible to establish a precise theory of economic behaviour (Lucas, 1981: 288–90). There is nothing to think that the field of human behaviour is in any intrinsic way distinct from other areas conquered by experimental research.

Another assumption underlying the approach is that the economy has no properties except those which are derived from individuals, and hence a theory of the economy can be inferred from a theory of individual behaviour. In this respect, theoretical economists follow John Stuart Mill, who wrote:

> Human beings in the society have no properties but those which are derived from, and may be resolved into the laws of the nature of the individual man. In social phenomena the Composition of Causes is the universal law. (1974 [1874]: 879)

Jevons (1965 [1871] :16) and Hicks (1939: 245) held that the general form of the laws of economics is *the same* in the case of a single decision maker and a nation, and thus the laws of the economic system can be derived from the laws of a single decision maker, be it a household or a firm. This simplistic view of the relationship between the individual and the economy, though still common, has slowly been giving way to a more elaborate view. Most economists now argue that the economy is characterized by competition over scarce resources. And to understand the laws of the economy it is vital to understand how individuals compete against each other. The laws of the economy therefore are identified with the laws of a group of competitive agents, not with the laws of a single Robinson Crusoe-type individual living on an island (Lucas, 1981: 289).

The implication of these assumptions for modelling the economy is clear. By observation and experimentation, the economist can establish a theory of individual behaviour. He can then replace the variables in the microtheory with their corresponding aggregate variables to obtain a qualitative model of the economy, and use aggregate data to estimate the model, hence transforming it into a quantitative model. Since the model is directly derived from the laws governing the basic decision-making units of the economy, it correctly represents the economy's structure. Accordingly, the main methodological objective of theoretical economics, at least as understood by the new classicals, has been to incorporate aggregative problems into the framework of microeconomics, eliminate the distinction between microeconomic and macroeconomic theory, and speak of economic theory in general. Robert Lucas lucidly states and defends this tenet in the following passage:

> The most interesting developments in macroeconomic theory seem to me describable as the reincorporation of aggregative problems such as inflation and the business cycle within the general framework of 'microeconomic' theory. If these developments succeed, the term 'macroeconomic' will simply disappear from use and the modifier 'micro' will be superfluous. We will simply speak, as did Smith, Ricardo, Marshall and Walras, of economic theory. (1987: 107–8)

The enterprise of inferring the patterns emerging at the economy level from a theory of individual or group behaviour is known as the *microfoundations* project. The project is held to enable the economist to establish a reliable theory of the economy without having to subject the economy to costly and prohibitive experiments:

> Suppose that we have some ability to predict how individual behaviour will respond to specified changes. How, if at all, can such knowledge be translated into knowledge of the way an entire *society* is likely to react to changes in its environment?...We clearly need to know something about the way a group of monkeys interacts, in addition to their individual preferences, in order to have any hope of progress on this complicated question...The ingredient omitted so far is, of course, competition...Notice that, having specified the rules by which interaction occurs in detail, and in a way that introduces no free parameters, the ability to predict individual behaviour is *nonexperimentally* transformed into the ability to predict group behaviour...This is exactly why we care about the 'microeconomic foundations' of aggregate theories. (Lucas, 1981: 289–91)[20]

The derived theory is believed to specify variables relevant for describing the economy, draw a line between endogenous and exogenous variables, determine the sign of relevant regression coefficients, and impose constraints on the algebraic form of the functions relating the aggregates. This information is adequate for modelling the structure and achieving macroeconomics' objectives.

The microfoundations project is also believed to make it possible to predict the outcomes of policies that could shift the structure. One begins by analysing how a policy might affect the way in which basic decision-making units of the economy interact with each other and make decisions. Knowing this, one will be able to infer through aggregation the impact of the policy on the entire economy, and derive the *new* structure that will prevail after the policy change. Since the same can be done for any policy, one will be able to help the state officials to select a policy that drives the economy to a desirable state. The role of statistical methods is confined to estimating and testing economic theories, and regression methods play no autonomous role in causal discovery. If a theoretical model fails to fit the data, the road to progress is to search for better theories, not to look for more sophisticated statistical methods of inference.

In the new classical school, one definition of microeconomic theory takes the basic unit of economic analysis to be a single decision maker. The consumer is modelled as an expected utility maximizer and the firm as an expected profit maximizer. When there is uncertainty, the individual is said to act according to the true model of the economy. From this viewpoint, the call for microfoundations is a call for a model of the economy in which the starting point is an expected utility or profit maximization problem. To model the relation between aggregate variables of interest, such as aggregate income and consumption, a utility maximization problem for a single consumer is set up and solved subject to his or her budget constraint. The solution defines the relation between the relevant micro-variables, say, individual income and consumption. The same relation is hypothesized to be true at the aggregate level, and the corresponding aggregate variables are inserted into the model to derive a model of the economy. Aggregate data are used to estimate the model. This method goes by the name of the 'representative agent' modelling approach.

Another definition of microeconomic theory in the new classical school takes a group of competitive individuals as the unit of analysis. In a competitive group, the outcome of an agent's decision depends on the actions of other members of the group, which means the agent must form expectations about the actions of others, and expectations about the expectations of others, and so forth. This feature of a competitive group is believed to be best captured by assuming equilibrium (Chari, 1999: 3). For this reason, new classical economists have mainly equated microeconomic theory with the Walrasian general equilibrium theory, or its successor the Arrow–Debreu competitive equilibrium theory, joined with the rational expectations hypothesis. The laws of the economy therefore are identified with the laws derived from the general equilibrium theory (Howitt, 1987: 273). In general, a model is viewed as structural if it is built on an appropriate microeconomic theory. Models that lack microeconomic foundations are viewed as non-structural (Sims, 1991: 923; 1982a: 115–16).

1.5 Atheoretical macroeconomics

Theoretical economics characterizes one extreme view on the scope and nature of macroeconomics. An alternative view that stands on the other side of the spectrum challenges all the assumptions of theoretical economics. This approach was put forward by Christopher Sims, and termed as atheoretical macroeconomics by Cooley and LeRoy (1985).[21]

Sims' atheoretical approach also emerged in response to a general discontent with the performance of macroeconomic models during the 1970s and 1980s. Most economists of the time, including Sims, blamed the failure on the identifying restrictions underpinning the models, which were supposedly derived from economic theory. Sims termed the restrictions as 'incredible' (Sims, 1980: 1). Contrary to theoretical economists, he did not think, however, that the key to improving the state of macroeconomics was to search for better theories. In his view, the problem with macroeconomics was more profound and, hence, he called for a far-reaching revision of the field and its objectives. Sims' revision is open to more than one interpretation. Two possible interpretations will be discussed here, one methodological and the other metaphysical.

Our accounts of atheoretical macroeconomics differ from a dominant interpretation criticized in a paper by Cooley and LeRoy (1985). According to these authors, Sims altogether dispenses with the role of economic theory or domain-specific information in general and seeks to achieve the goals of macroeconomics by means of statistical analysis alone.[22] A reason put forward for this reading is the use of Granger's test of causality by Sims and his followers, which is nothing but a statistical procedure for determining whether a variable helps predict another variable. Another reason is the claim by Sims that atheoretical models are useful for policy analysis. Since only a structural model can be useful for policy evaluation, any claim for the usefulness of atheoretical models for policy analysis assumes a structural interpretation of the models. Both reasons can be challenged. Sims rejects that the Granger test of causality alone can ever establish causality (1977: 29 and 42; 1986: 3). In his view, it is always necessary to rely on non-sample information to conclude that a relation that passes the test is actually structural. Moreover, according to Sims, atheoretical models, as long as they remain uninterrupted, are of no use in policy analysis (1986: 3); Sims simply challenges the claim that the interpretation derives from a well-founded theory (1982a: 138). We shall rely on Sims' writings as well as Cooley and LeRoy's paper (1985), Leamer (1985), Pagan (1987), and Swanson and Granger (1997) to give a brief review of formal aspects of Sims' modelling approach.

1.5.1 Methodological interpretation

Sims often appears to agree that the relations discernible at the economy level are suitable for a structural account but challenges the existence of a reliable method for discovering the structure. He argues that economic theories are bound to remain imprecise because of the lack of controlled experiments in economics and the nonstationarity of the economic structure. The structure, Sims says, continuously shifts through natural, social and political changes, and more critically through accumulation of experience by people. As people learn about the economy and discover the outcome of their actions, they modify their behaviour, and this shifts the structure. As a result, a theory that is approximately true of the current situation might cease to be true of a new situation, making it difficult to tell whether the failure of economic theories is due to changes in the structure or to our mistakes in theorizing about it:

> dynamic economic theories must inherently be incomplete, imprecise, and therefore subject to variation over time. One reason for this is that economic cause–effect relations involve a 'recognition delay' about which theory has little to say and may be expected to be variable... It is wrong, then, to expect economic theories to be complete, mechanical, and divorced from reference to specific historical circumstances. (Sims, 1981: 579)[23]

This inherent imprecision, Sims argues, renders economic theory necessarily subjective (2004: 282). Thus, uninterpreted statistical models of aggregate data are the only yardsticks of objectivity in macroeconomics that form a basis around which economists may come to narrow down their differences (1987: 53). These models, however, are not suitable for policy analysis. Policy analysis requires classifying the variables into exogenous and endogenous categories and deciding whether a variable can be influenced by a policy. In making such decisions, due to the lack of reliable theories, the analyst must rely on his or her personal view of the economy. Two economists with different views of the economy can arrive at conflicting interpretations of a single model of the data, and there is no objective ground to resolve the disagreement decisively.

Sims discerns three stages in modelling aggregate data. The first is to build a model that fits the data, which gives one possible account of the structure that might have generated the data. The second is to search for alternative models equally fitting the data, which provide different views of the structure. Finally, the analyst relies on his or her personal view of the economy to select a model that is most likely to approximate the structure. An appropriate modelling approach, Sims says, should distinguish between those aspects of a model that are based on the data and those that are based on subjective judgements about the structure (1982b: 317; 1987: 51). Such a distinction saves economics from the Lucas critique (1976) and that of Freedman (1981).

These critiques are solely directed at subjective features of aggregate models (Sims, 1982b: 317).

1.5.1.1 *Vector autoregression*

Sims therefore abandons the framework laid down in the Cowles Commission that requires a theory to specify relevant variables, divide them into exogenous and endogenous variables, and determine the variables in each equation in the model. As an alternative, he proposes a framework in which there is initially no division of variables into exogenous and endogenous categories, and every variable enters in the equation of every other variable (Hendry, 1993: 128).[24] The modeller relies on his view of the economy to choose relevant variables, and uses data as well as subjective and pragmatic considerations to select a model. To describe Sims' formal approach, we adopt a simple example from Swanson and Granger (1997), which models the relations between four aggregates consisting of money M_t, consumption C_t, investment I_t and gross domestic product Y_t. Let $\mathbf{Y}_t$ be the vector of current variables (M_t, C_t, I_t, Y_t) and $\mathbf{Y}_{t-i}$ the vector of lagged variables $(M_{t-i}, C_{t-i}, I_{t-i}, Y_{t-i})$. In theory, Sims' point of departure is a structural model of the following form:

$$B\mathbf{Y}_t + \sum_{i=1}^{p} \Gamma_i \mathbf{Y}_{t-i} = \varepsilon_t \tag{1.14}$$

where B and Γ_is are 4×4 matrices whose terms are polynomial in the lag operator, p is the lag length, and ε_t is a column vector of stochastic error processes with elements ε_{it}. The matrices have no zero element and all the variables are of identical lags. Moreover, the model contains only current or lagged endogenous variables. This contrasts with a structural model of theoretical economics in which the theory dictates variables to be either endogenous or exogenous, and sets some elements of the coefficient matrices to zero.

In practice, Sims works with a vector autoregression (VAR) representation of (1.14), in which each variable is regressed on its own past values and past values of other variables under study. The transformation into a VAR model leads to a model of the form:

$$\mathbf{Y}_t = \sum_{i=1}^{p} A_i \mathbf{Y}_{t-i} + u_t \quad E(u_t u_t') \equiv \sum \tag{1.15}$$

where the A_is are 4×4 matrices, u_t is a 4×1 column vector of stochastic error processes, and Σ is the contemporaneous covariance matrix, with $E(.)$ being the expectation operator. Every current variable in (1.15) is a function of two components: its best linear predictor, based on past values of all the variables considered, and its unpredictable error u_t, which is also called 'innovation' (Darnell and Evans, 1990: 120). The error terms satisfy the orthogonality condition, and the least-squares method can be used to estimate the parameters A_i.[25]

A VAR model can effectively capture patterns existing in the data and, so long as the mechanism generating the data remains the same, is useful for *ex ante* and *ex post* prediction. A VAR model, however, sweeps all the (exogenous) variables that can affect the contemporaneous variables under the blanket of the disturbance (innovation) terms and is only driven by random shocks. As a result, the model is not suitable for policy analysis in the traditional sense which involves tracing out the effects on the endogenous variables of changes in the exogenous variables. For this reason, Sims and his followers redefine a policy as a random shock to a variable in the system, and interpret policy analysis as the task of tracing out the reaction of the system to that shock. Even in this narrow sense, a VAR model cannot be used for policy analysis. In general, the contemporaneous covariance matrix $\sum$ is not diagonal. The non-zero off-diagonal elements entail that one variable, say Y_{it}, cannot be shocked through its corresponding error term, u_{it}, without having simultaneously to deliver a correlated influence on other variables (Demiralp and Hoover, 2003: 746). Without independence, it will not be possible to use the model to trace the evolution of the system caused by a shock to a single variable. Sims and other VAR modellers advocate orthogonalizing the shocks using a Choleski decomposition to diagonalize the error covariance matrix $\sum$ by pre-multiplying (1.15) with the unique triangular matrix T. This generates a Wold causal chain among the current elements of $\mathbf{Y}_t$:[26]

$$T\mathbf{Y}_t = T\sum_{i=1}^{n} A_i\mathbf{Y}_{t-i} + \eta_t \qquad E(\eta_t\eta_t') = D \tag{1.16}$$

where $\eta_t = Tu_t$ and $D = T\Sigma T'$, a diagonal matrix. The errors η_t are termed as the *orthogonalized innovations* (Sims, 1987: 52–3).

A problem with this exercise is that the causal ordering is arbitrary, since for any ordering of the variables in model (1.15) there is a unique triangular matrix which orthogonalizes the covariance matrix of the errors. In general, if we have k endogenous variables in the model, we can order them in $k!$ ways, resulting in $k!$ different causal chain models equally fitting the data. These models describe alternative causal relations among the variables, and if no way can be found to select an ordering, any policy analysis based on a model like (1.15) will be arbitrary. A crucial matter facing the VAR methodology is how to transform a VAR model into a causal chain model in a non-arbitrary way.

Sims thinks '[t]here is no unique way to do this' (1980: 21). Nevertheless, he suggests that some confidence in an ordering can be gained by checking the performance of the model against the data. In this line, if we partition the data containing a shock to a variable into two parts and fit a model to one part, and the model closely approximates the impact of the shock in the remaining data, we gain some confidence in it. If a model is fitted to all the data, and there are no other data to check the model's performance outside the sample period, the reliability of the model remains in doubt.

1.5.1.2 Selecting a causal chain model

Since Sims' paper (1980), there have been several attempts to reduce the subjectivity involved in transforming a VAR model into a causal chain model. A proposal is found in Swanson and Granger (1997), who aim to devise a *data-driven* method for causally ordering the errors.[27] These authors begin by estimating VAR model (1.15) and use it to compute the residuals associated with the observations on the variables. The residuals form the data in their study of the causal relations among the errors. An assumption behind Swanson and Granger's method is that the underlying causal ordering of the errors is recursive such that the error in the first equation in the appropriate model is exogenous and affects only the errors in the following equations (although generalization to non-recursive models is possible in principle). Having said this, a possible ordering of the errors associated with model (1.15) is the following:

$$\begin{aligned} m_t &= v_{Mt} \\ i_t &= \alpha m_t + v_{It} \\ c_t &= \gamma i_t + 0 m_t + v_{Ct} \\ y_t &= \lambda c_t + 0 i_t + 0 m_t + v_{Yt} \end{aligned} \tag{1.17}$$

where the lower-case letters stand for the error terms; m_t stands for the error term in the equation for money M_t, and so forth.[28] Swanson and Granger assume that the errors v_{it} in (1.17) have zero expectations, are contemporaneously uncorrelated, and have a non-singular definite covariance matrix. Given these conditions, they prove that a recursive model like (1.17) entails certain zero partial correlations (vanishing partials). In particular, if in the true model m_t causes c_t and c_t causes i_t, the partial correlation of m_t and i_t given c_t is zero. If partial correlation $\rho(m_t, i_t/c_t)$ is zero or close to zero in the data, variable c_t in the appropriate causal ordering lies between variables m_t and i_t. The authors exploit this and similar results to specify an ordering of the errors that is compatible with the data. The method involves using the estimates of the residuals to compute the correlation matrix of the error terms, which is used to compute all possible partial correlations among the errors. The method then searches for a model that is compatible with the vanishing partials discerned in the data.

There are twelve partial correlations among the error terms associated with the variables under study here. In the data studied by Swanson and Granger $\rho(y_t, m_t/c_t)$, $\rho(y_t, m_t/i_t)$, and $\rho(i_t, m_t/c_t)$ are lowest in absolute value, and thus the most appropriate candidates for zero partial correlations. The first vanishing partial $\rho(y_t, m_t/c_t) \approx 0$ suggests that in the appropriate causal ordering c_t lies between y_t and m_t, the second $\rho(y_t, m_t/i_t) \approx 0$ suggests that i_t lies between y_t and m_t, and the third $\rho(i_t, m_t/c_t) \approx 0$ implies that c_t lies between i_t and m_t. Altogether, these vanishing partials suggest that a causal ordering, as in the model below, is compatible with the data:

$$\begin{aligned} m_t &= v_{Mt} \\ c_t &= \alpha m_t + v_{Ct} \\ i_t &= \gamma c_t + 0 m_t + v_{It} \\ y_t &= \lambda i_t + 0 c_t + 0 m_t + v_{Yt} \end{aligned} \tag{1.18}$$

The zero partial correlations are not compatible with the causal ordering expressed by model (1.17).

Swanson and Granger's method fails to eliminate the arbitrariness involved in transforming a VAR model into a causal chain model. For one thing, partial correlation is invariant to the reversal of causal directionality in the sense that it does not matter whether m_t causes c_t and c_t causes i_t or i_t causes c_t and c_t causes m_t. In either case, partial correlation $\rho(i_t, m_t/c_t)$ is zero. Therefore, besides model (1.18), a recursive model in which the causal influences proceed from y_t through i_t and c_t to m_t is also compatible with the vanishing partials. There is usually more than one causal ordering compatible with any set of vanishing partials found in the data. This means one must draw on other considerations to select an ordering. In the present example, Swanson and Granger favour the ordering in model (1.18) on the grounds that money, consumption, or investment is a leading indicator for GDP (1997: 363).

Also, a correlation between two variables can be due to latent common causes. If the correlation of m_t and c_t given any possible combination of the rest of the variables is different from zero, it cannot still be concluded that either variable causes the other. The possibility of latent common causes widens the class of models compatible with the data, making it impossible for the present approach to distinguish between cases of causal and spurious relations. If no outside knowledge is available, the choice of a particular causal ordering of the innovation terms and hence the choice of a VAR model remains arbitrary. Empirical evidence alone is inadequate for specifying the privileged transformation that corresponds to the data-generating structure.

1.5.1.3 *Revising the objectives*

Sims emphasizes that economists are never in a position to eliminate the need for personal judgement in selecting a model as a representation of the structure. Owing to the unreliability of personal judgements, he therefore argues for revising the conventional objectives of macroeconomics (1982b: 139–40).

In particular, Sims urges economists to be sceptical of their analysis of policies that have no historical precedent. If a policy had a precedent in the data and enough data were available, it would be possible to fit a model to one part of the data, and then investigate how it performs in predicting the rest of the data. If the model performed well in mimicking the effect of the policy in the remaining data, assuming that the economic structure was still the same, it would also most likely predict the policy outcomes in the new situation (Sims, 1982a: 122). However, if a policy had no historical precedent, the choice of a model for evaluating it would be entirely subjective. In that case, there would be no guarantee that the model would correctly predict the policy outcomes. The more a policy differs from those that have precedents in the data, the less reliable the analysis will be. Sims therefore questions the objective of evaluating novel policies, the task, he claims, falls outside the domain of macroeconomics (Sims, 1982a: 119). For him, economists are observers of the economy, not engineers of reform (Lucas, 1987: 8).

Sims is equally sceptical of the reliability of explanations in macroeconomics. In his opinion, 'economists must accept that a single view of the causal structure of the record they examine will never emerge' (1977: 30). Consequently, explanations of economic phenomena are simply 'stories' that the modellers can envision about what is going on inside their models (2004: 282). The choice of a story is partly a personal matter and must be viewed with scepticism (1981: 583). Economists can be helpful in *ex ante* and *ex post* predictions over a short period of time. But, analysis of radical policies and explanation of macroeconomic events falls beyond the boundaries of their field (1987: 50).

Finally, Sims argues that the lack of controlled experiments and the inadequacy of statistical inference are not the only sources of uncertainty in economic models. Aggregate economic data are also inherently inaccurate, and this fundamentally adds to the uncertainty of the models. This uncertainty casts doubt even on the choice of a model for *ex ante* or *ex post* prediction. And so he suggests avoiding the choice of a single model, and instead urges working with a group of models best fitting the data. If the task at hand is *ex ante* or *ex post* prediction, it will be more reliable to average the models' predictions and act accordingly. It is, in general, more reasonable both in prediction and policy analysis to compare the predictions of a number of plausible models and take a decision that is close to all the models' predictions (Sims, 2004: 282). Sims' view is consistent with the Bayesian approach to model selection in which the uncertainty concerning the models is expressed in the form of a probability distribution over the models, and thus none of the models is accepted as true.

1.5.2 Metaphysical interpretation

According to the above interpretation of atheoretical macroeconomics, it makes sense to speak of the causal structure of the economy as a web of structural relationships true of economic aggregates. But Sims' early writings often suggest a more radical view that challenges the very existence of causal relations at the economy level. He argues, time and again, that economic variables can be aggregated in many different ways, and all different levels of aggregation are theoretically arbitrary and hence acceptable:

> Almost every kind of data used in economics ... is an aggregate or index number of some sort. We deal with accounting data. Household budget studies divide expenditure into a finite number of categories with somewhat arbitrary bounds. Studies of firms use the firm's own books to construct measures of input, output, and prices. This is not just a matter of aggregation of fine-grained truth in which arbitrary accounting conventions would not be necessary.... The degree of arbitrariness in classifying production into two-digit industries is not convincingly greater than that in classifying it into four-digit industries. (Sims, 1987: 50)

What is more, as the level of aggregation is varied, quite different and conflicting models of the system are achieved. And because there is no natural or non-arbitrary level of aggregation, it is wrong to attribute any causal interpretation to aggregate models. There is, Sims argues, no truth about price indices, national income accounts, or the money stock in the way there is truth about falling objects, electrical currents, or the stars:

> The contribution of econometric probability models may be to make the process of economic data cheaper, more explicit, and more easily responsible. In doing so, it might also succeed in improving decision-making. But econometricians will not find truth the way physicists do. There is no truth about price indexes, national income accounts, expenditure of household *j* on meat, or the money stock the way there is truth about falling objects, electrical currents, or the stars. (Sims, 1987: 51)

Therefore, the search for truth in macroeconomics is misguided and, as a result, structural (causal) modelling tools are irrelevant to the analysis of aggregate data. Large-scale economic models are efficient summaries of data, useful for making short-run *ex ante* and *ex post* predictions. They are not suitable for the kind of policy analysis economists have been after. The emergence of a pattern at the aggregate level may have an explanation but the explanation is not causal. The pattern is best explained by showing how it emerges from an attempt to summarize data. On this reading, Sims deprives macroeconomics of its traditional subject-matter. Macroeconomics is atheoretical because there are no truths at the economy level for a theory to represent. To Sims, economists are closer to accountants than natural scientists (Sims, 1987).

The rejection of a causal structure at the aggregate level has precedents in the history of economics. Notably, Hayek (1979) argued that the 'wholes' studied in the social sciences are merely constructs of our mind; they do not represent anything in the external world, and are not subject to scientific laws (1979: 96).[29] Also, recently, some post-Keynesian economists have emphasized the necessity of individual heterogeneity and direct interactions among market participants in explaining macroeconomic phenomena. Individual heterogeneity and direct interaction, as will be seen, enormously complicate the relation between micro- and macro-relations, making it impossible to attribute any theoretical interpretation to relations emerging at the economy level. Such considerations have led these economists to favour an atheoretical view of macroeconomics, similar to Sims' approach, and to reinterpret empirical macroeconomic models simply as efficient summaries of data (Colander, 1996: 66).

1.6 Conclusion

Theoretical economics and atheoretical macroeconomics present two squarely opposing views on the nature and scope of macroeconomics. A fundamental reason for the emergence of these views is the recognition of the intrinsic limits of statistical inference as well as the difficulty of carefully controlled experiments on the economy. Theoretical economists hold that these limits can be overcome by adopting a bottom-up approach to the study of the economy. In contrast, atheoretical macroeconomics holds that the limitations are here to stay, and there is no successful strategy to overcome them. The central question of macroeconomics is therefore whether there can be an empirically adequate theory of economic behaviour and whether the theory can be turned into a theory of the economy through aggregation. Of equal importance is the view that one can sensibly talk of structural relations at the economy level.

2 Rational Behaviour and Economic Theory

2.1 Introduction

> Unfortunately, the general hypothesis that economic agents are Bayesian decision makers has, in many applications, little empirical content: without some way of inferring what an agent's subjective view of the future is, this hypothesis is of no help in understanding his behaviour. ...To practice economics, we need *some* way ... of understanding *which* decision problem agents are solving. (Lucas, 1981: 223)

The difficulties in atheoretical study of aggregate data have led economists to propose a bottom-up approach to the study of macroeconomic phenomena. The approach involves establishing a theory of individual behaviour and transforming it into a theory of the economy using aggregation methods. As a result, even though macroeconomics is primarily concerned with aggregate phenomena such as the unemployment level or general price movements, issues of individual behaviour have come to occupy a central place in theoretical economic analysis. The chief conjecture about 'homo economicus' is that he behaves rationally. This conjecture is thought to be an 'engine of truth' that helps to discover the laws of economic behaviour. Market forces are said to eliminate irrational behaviour, and this justifies focusing on the study of rational behaviour. This chapter studies the contribution of various rationality hypotheses to theoretical economics.

While the literature provides a host of concepts of rational behaviour, the leading definition is based on the theory of subjective expected utility, developed in Savage's book, *The Foundations of Statistics* (1972 [1954]). Savage's theory identifies behavioural rationality with subjective expected utility maximization – behaviour is rational if it is the outcome of subjective expected utility maximization. Since its inception, Savage's theory has been criticized on several grounds. It has been argued that the theory's postulates are empirically wrong, its computational requirements exceed those of human beings, and people are not only after their own utility. These criticisms have initiated an exciting search for alternative theories of behaviour. Nevertheless, they have not yet shaken the central status of the theory in economic analysis.

To analyse the contributions of rationality hypotheses to economic theorizing, this chapter distinguishes two entirely different questions about the role of rational choice theories in economics. The first is whether the theories closely describe the process of human choice whereas the other is whether the theories could ever be adequate for predicting economic behaviour, regardless of whether they are true or false. While both questions are analysed in detail, the emphasis will be on the second issue.

We argue that rational choice theories give no explanation of how the agent models his choice situation, and defines his decision problem. They only state how he, given a fully specified choice situation, makes a choice that maximizes his expected utility with respect to the situation. Therefore, in using the theories to model behaviour, a host of substantive assumptions are needed to specify the agent's view of his choice situation and the problem he is trying to solve. These assumptions relate to the agent's view of the structure of the environment, values, needs and goals. It is only then that the theories become relevant and predict how the agent solves his decision problem.

A theory of behaviour, however, cannot take as given the agent's view of his choice situation and how he defines his decision problem. This is because the resolution of economic controversies more critically depends on how the agent models his choice situation and defines his decision problem than on the specific *method* by which he solves the problem. Expected utility maximization is consistent with all sides of any economic controversy, and therefore contributes very little to economic analysis. Substantial results attributed to the hypothesis are all the implications of the assumptions made about how people specify their choice situation and re-specify it in the face of new information. In practice, economists turn to the econometric analysis of aggregate data to settle economic controversies. Yet the success of the econometric method is very limited.

As an attempt to overcome some of the shortcomings of the rational choice theories, new classical economists have put forward the rational expectations hypothesis. The hypothesis identifies the agent's view of the economy with the true model of the economy, suggesting that he maximizes his expected utility with respect to the true model. Therefore, as soon as the structure of the economy is known, the agent's view of the economy is also known. The economist then only needs to discover the agent's preferences to specify the decision problem he is trying to solve, and to predict his behaviour. We will review this hypothesis to further our understanding of the current state of microeconomic theory. We end the chapter with a brief characterization of the kind of theory of behaviour that is needed for thinking about the economy.

2.2 Rational choice

A rational choice theory of behaviour consists of a characterization of rational behaviour and a claim that a rational individual chooses only acts that satisfy the description. The oldest concept of behavioural rationality defines rational behaviour in terms of pursuit of self-interest – rational behaviour is self-interested behaviour.[1] Economists flesh out the idea of pursuit of self-interest by stating that a producer prefers more profit to less profit or a consumer prefers more money to less money. Another notion identifies behavioural rationality with the requirement that choices from different subsets of the universal set of available options be maximizing solutions from the respective subsets according to some binary relation R. A person is rational if his or her choice from any subset of the set of available options is the R-maximal element of the subset (Sen, 1987: 69). These definitions do not take into account the fact that full knowledge of the states of the world is never available and one always has to make decisions whose outcomes are uncertain. A theory of rational behaviour should take this ubiquitous feature of real-life decision-making seriously, and characterize rational behaviour under uncertainty.

A theory of rational choice under uncertainty demands a formal characterization of uncertainty and a description of how the uncertainty thus characterized is taken into account in making decisions over alternative courses of actions (Sen, 1987: 72). The theory used in this context is the *expected utility* theory, which weighs the value of each of the outcomes of an action by the respective probabilities of the different outcomes of the action. On this theory, behaviour is rational if it is the outcome of expected utility maximization. Depending on one's interpretation of probability, two general classes of expected utility theories can be defined. The objective interpretation takes probability to be a measure of relative frequency. This interpretation underpins the Von Neumann–Morgenstern theory of expected utility. On the other hand, the subjective (personal) interpretation takes probability to be a measure of the degree of belief that a person has in the occurrence of an event. This interpretation underlies Savage's subjective expected utility theory, which will be the focus of analysis in what follows.

2.2.1 Savage's theory of subjective expected utility

As any axiomatic system, Savage's theory has three parts. The first concerns the definition of primitive and constructive notions, the second involves introduction of the axioms and the third involves establishing the main result of the postulates. We describe the first two parts of the theory in some detail, as they play a critical part in our understanding of the role of the rationality hypotheses in economic theorizing.

2.2.1.1 Small worlds

Savage starts with defining the primitives of his theory, including a choice set and a formal description of what the decision maker is uncertain about.[2] To this end, Savage has a colourful example. Imagine you have just broken five good eggs into a bowl to make an omelette. A sixth egg, which for some reason you must either use for the omelette or throw away, lies unbroken beside the bowl. You are about to decide what to do with this unbroken egg, which is not known whether is good or rotten. Savage calls the sixth egg, the object about which you are concerned, the *World*. A description of the world, leaving no relevant aspect undescribed, is called a *state* (of the world), herein good or rotten. Of these two states one does in fact obtain, called the *true* state. A set of states is called an *event*. The event that has every state of the world as its element is called the *universal* event, and is denoted by $\boldsymbol{S}$. There are at least three actions available to you: you may break the egg into the bowl containing the other five good eggs, you may break it into a saucer for inspection, and you may throw it away without inspection. Depending on the state of the egg, each of these acts will have some *consequences*, say, wasting five good eggs or making a clean saucer dirty. Let $\boldsymbol{Z}$ denote the set of all the consequences about which you are concerned. In deciding on an act, you must take into account possible states of the world and also the consequences that may follow from each act under each state of the world. Accordingly, an *act* is formally defined as a function that attaches a consequence to each state of the world, i.e. a mapping from $\boldsymbol{S}$ to $\boldsymbol{Z}$. Let $\boldsymbol{F}$ denote the set of available acts. The set $\boldsymbol{F}$ is the choice set. In making a decision you prefer one act to others. A binary relation $\prec$ expresses your (strict) preferences over set $\boldsymbol{F}$; thus for two acts f and g in $\boldsymbol{F}$, $f \prec g$ means g is (strictly) preferred to f. The term 'world' is also used to refer to the pair (**S**, **Z**). Table 2.1 below gives a schematic representation of a world corresponding to Savage's example (Savage, 1972 [1954]: 14).

Table 2.1 Savage's small world

	States	
Acts	**Good**	**Rotten**
Break into bowl	Six-egg omelette	No omelette and five good eggs destroyed
Break into saucer	Six-egg omelette and a saucer to wash	Five-egg omelette and a saucer to wash
Throw away	Five-egg omelette and one good egg destroyed	Five-egg omelette

Although this example illustrates the basic notions of Savage's theory, it does not describe a typical situation to which the theory is intended to apply. To be precise, Savage develops his theory around an ideal agent whose guide in life is the proverb 'Look before you leap' as opposed to 'You can cross the bridge when you come to it' (Savage, 1972 [1954]: 16). That is, in making a decision, the agent considers not only the consequences of his immediate acts but also those of the acts that he might need to take given the consequences of the immediate acts and so forth. The objects about which he contemplates are not simple acts but sequences of acts. Savage carries the maxim 'Look before you leap' to the extreme, assuming that the agent behaves as though he has only one decision to make in his entire life. 'He must ... decide how to live, and this he might in principle do once for all' (Savage, 1972 [1954]: 83). Consequently, the world $(\mathbf{S}, \mathbf{Z})$ that he constructs to represent his choice situation has an extremely large (infinite) number of states and an ultimately refined description of the consequences of the acts under each state. Savage refers to an ultimately refined pair of states and consequences $(\mathbf{S}^*, \mathbf{Z}^*)$ as the *grand world*.

In reality, no matter how refined a world $(\mathbf{S}, \mathbf{Z})$ is, it does not include every conceivable state or consequence. Even if a person is now considering a lifetime decision, she may not bother with the price of oil on 25 June 3500. Thus, the world $(\mathbf{S}, \mathbf{Z})$ she considers to represent her choice situation is, in Savage's terms, a *small world* in the sense that each element in $\boldsymbol{S}$ can still be partitioned into smaller states and $\boldsymbol{Z}$ can still be replaced with an even more refined description of the consequences.

2.2.1.2 *The postulates*

Savage's theory is based on seven postulates regarding the preference relation on $\boldsymbol{F}$. The postulates can be stated in several equivalent ways. We follow Fishburn's statement (1970: 191). Savage's first postulate is that the strict preference relation $\prec$ on $\boldsymbol{F}$ is a *weak order*. That is to say that $\prec$ is asymmetric and negatively transitive. The preference relation $\prec$ is asymmetric just in case, for every act f and g in $\boldsymbol{F}$, if f is preferred to g, g is not preferred to f. And it is negatively transitive just in case, for every act f, g and h in $\boldsymbol{F}$, if f is not preferred to g, and g is not preferred to h, then f is not preferred to h:

Postulate 1: For every f, g and $\mathrm{h} \in \mathbf{F}$
(a) if $f \prec g$ then not $g \prec f$;
(b) if not $f \prec g$ and not $g \prec h$ then not $f \prec h$.

Let '$\sim$' denote indifference, which is the absence of strict preference. That is, for every f and g in $\boldsymbol{F}$,

$$\mathrm{f} \sim \mathrm{g} \text{ if and only if neither } f \prec g \text{ nor } g \prec f.$$

It follows from the postulate that the relation $\prec$ is transitive, and $\sim$ is reflexive, symmetric and transitive. It also follows that the preference relation is complete in the sense that for every two acts f and g in $\boldsymbol{F}$ exactly one of $f \prec g$, $g \prec f$ or $f \sim g$ holds (Fishburn, 1970: 13).

The second postulate says that states with similar consequences do not affect preferences. If acts f and g have different consequences over event A but agree over the complementary event A^C, they are ranked only on the basis of their differences on A. Similarly, if act f^* agrees with f and act g^* agrees with g on A, and further f^* and g^* agree on A^C, f^* and g^* are ranked in the same way that f and g are ranked. Let $f(s)$ be the consequence that f assigns to state s in S. The postulate can be stated as follows:

Postulate 2: Suppose acts f, g, f^* and g^* are such that:
(a) $f(s) = g(s), f^*(s) = g^*(s)$ for all $s \in A^C$
(b) $f(s) = f^*(s), g(s) = g^*(s)$ for all $s \in A$
then $f \prec g$ iff $f^* \prec g^*$.[3]

The third postulate says that the relative value of consequences is invariant across the states. Two further notions are needed to make this idea precise - *null* event and *constant* act. An event E is considered as null by a person if he is indifferent among acts that only differ on E. An act is called constant if it leads to the same consequence over every state of the world. This contrasts with *concrete* acts that yield different consequences over different states. Savage identifies each consequence z in $\boldsymbol{Z}$ with a constant act, i.e. an act that leads to z over all the non-null states. The third postulate then says that if a person prefers y to x given non-null event A, he prefers y to x in general, and if he prefers y to x in general, he prefers y to x given A:

Postulate 3: If event A is not null, and

$f(s) = x,\ g(s) = y$ for all $s \in A$, and $f(s) = g(s)$ for all $s \in A^C$, then $f \prec g$ iff $x \prec y$.

So, the set $\boldsymbol{F}$ not only includes concrete acts but also, for every z in $\boldsymbol{Z}$, contains a constant act f that produces z in every state of the world. The postulate thus extends the preference relation $\prec$ from acts to consequences $\boldsymbol{Z}$.

The fourth postulate says that the consequences following from an act under a state do not affect the belief about the state. Suppose a person prefers consequence y to x and y^* to x^*. Then, if he prefers y to x when event A obtains rather than when event B obtains, he also prefers y^* to x^* when A obtains rather than when B obtains:

Postulate 4: Suppose $A, B \subseteq \mathbf{S}$; $x, y, x^*, y^* \in \mathbf{Z}$; $f, g, f^*, g^* \in \mathbf{F}$ are such that
(a) $x \prec y$ and $x^* \prec y^*$

(b) $f(s) = y$ for all $s \in A$ $\quad f(s) = x$ for all $s \in A^C$
$g(s) = y$ for all $s \in B$ $\quad g(s) = x$ for all $s \in B^C$
(c) $f^*(s) = y^*$ for all $s \in A$ $\quad f^*(s) = x^*$ for all $s \in A^C$
$g^*(s) = y^*$ for all $s \in B$ $\quad g^*(s) = x^*$ for all $s \in B^C$
then $f \prec g$ iff $f^* \prec g^*$.

This paves the way for defining a qualitative likelihood relation $\prec^*$ over ***S***. Suppose y is preferred to x. Further, suppose acts f and g are such that f is equal to y on A and equal to x on A^C, and g is equal to y on B and equal to x on B^C. If g is preferred to f, then the only explanation is that B is considered to be more probable than A:

$$A \prec^* B \text{ if and only if } f \prec g. \tag{2.1}$$

Thus, the preference ordering over ***F*** induces a likelihood ordering over ***S***. These four postulates capture all the behavioural content of Savage's theory. Savage's three remaining axioms are technical postulates to ensure the existence of a mathematical representation of preferences and likelihood judgements (Kreps, 1988: 128). We mention two of these postulates here. The first is the *non-triviality* postulate:

Postulate 5: There is at least one pair of acts f and g such that $f \prec g$.

The sixth postulate says that for every two non-indifferent acts in ***F*** and for every consequence x in ***Z***, the set ***S*** can be partitioned into arbitrarily small events so that altering either act to equal x *on just one of these events* does not reverse the ordering of the acts:

Postulate 6: For all $f, g \in$ **F** such that $g \prec f$, and for all $x \in \boldsymbol{Z}$, there is a finite partition of ***S*** such that for every event A in the partition
(a) if $f^*(s) = x$ for $s \in A$, $f^*(s) = f(s)$ for $s \in A^C$ then $g \prec f^*$
(b) if $g^*(s) = x$ for $s \in A$, $g^*(s) = g(s)$ for $s \in A^C$ then $g^* \prec f$.

The postulate, called the continuity axiom, excludes infinitely desirable consequences. It also implies that if event B is less likely than event C, there is always a partition of ***S*** such that the union of each element of the partition with B is still less likely than C. This means ***S*** can endlessly be partitioned into smaller events. The preference relation $\prec$, therefore, has a property corresponding to the Archimedean property of natural numbers.

2.2.1.3 The representation theorem

Savage shows that when preferences among acts in ***F*** satisfy the postulates, there exists a unique finitely additive probability measure P on the set of all subsets of ***S*** such that

$$A \prec^* B \text{ if and only if } P(A) < P(B) \tag{2.2}$$

and, with P as given, there exists a real valued utility function u on $\boldsymbol{Z}$ such that for a finite $\boldsymbol{Z}$

$$f \prec g \text{ if and only if } \sum P(s)u(f(s)) < \sum P(s)u(g(s)) \tag{2.3}$$

According to (2.3), act g is preferred to act f if and only if the subjective expected utility of g exceeds the subjective expected utility of f. From this perspective, individual behaviour is rational if it is the outcome of subjective expected utility maximization.

2.3 Restating the issues

Savage distinguishes between a normative and an empirical interpretation of his theory. The normative interpretation takes the postulates to be norms of rationality, providing a standard for actual people to follow. In contrast, the empirical interpretation suggests that people's actual preferences among acts by and large comply with the postulates, and hence agree with a ranking of subjective expected utility. Positive economics assumes the empirical interpretation.[4]

Reading *Foundations*, one gets the impression that, according to Savage, there are two general phases in human decision making. In the first phase, the decision maker draws on his view of the causal structure of the world to specify the acts that are available to him, the states that affect the outcomes of the acts, and the consequences that follow from each act under each state – in short, a small world. After that, he evaluates the likelihood of each state of the world, and assesses the desirability of the consequences. We refer to a small world, the likelihood ranking of the states of the world, and the preference ranking of the consequences of the world as a *choice situation*:

$$\text{Choice situation} = \begin{cases} \text{Small world} \\ \text{Likelihood judgements over the states of the} \\ \text{small world} \\ \text{Preferences over the consequences in the small} \\ \text{world} \end{cases}$$

The choice situation defines the decision problem that the agent is trying to solve. In the second phase, the decision maker solves the problem by comparing the acts in the light of the likelihood of the states of the world and the desirability of their consequences to identify an act that is most likely to yield that which is desired the most.

This general description of human decision making helps us to define two different types of theories of behaviour. The first consists of theories that explain *both* how a person models his choice situation and defines his decision problem *and* how he solves the problem. The second consists of theories that take the structure of the choice situation and the definition of the decision problem as *given*, and *exclusively* focus on how a person solves an already well-defined decision problem. We refer to the former group of theories as *learning-based* theories of behaviour and the latter group as *choice-based* theories of behaviour.[5]

Savage's theory is a choice-based theory of behaviour. The reason for this classification can be explained by examining the restrictions that the theory imposes on the various stages of decision making. According to the theory, the decision making process starts with the construction of a small world. The postulates of the theory impose two restrictions on the admissibility of a small world. Postulate 6 requires the set of the states of the world to be such that they can be partitioned indefinitely into smaller elements. On the other hand, the second, third and fourth postulates necessitate the description of the world to be such that preferences among the consequences can be stated without regard to beliefs about the states, and that likelihood judgements about the states can be expressed without regard to preferences among the consequences. These restrictions are non-trivial but leave the specific structure of the small world undetermined. Formation of a small world lies outside the theory:

> I believe ... that decision situations can be usefully structured in terms of consequences, states, and acts in such a way that the postulates of F. of S. [The Foundations of Statistics] are satisfied. Just how to do that seems to be an art for which I can give no prescription and for which it is perhaps unreasonable to expect one – as we know from other postulate systems for application. (Savage, 1971: 79)

Also, Savage's postulates make no reference to anything *outside* choice, such as information, experience, goals, needs and motivations. As should be clear by now, they only require a certain correspondence between different parts of a choice function (Sen, 1993: 495). Consequently, the theory permits any internally consistent preference and likelihood ranking, and regards the content of beliefs and values as *exogenous*. Savage's postulates can indeed be satisfied by both cognitive and moral idiots:

> [Savage's theory] can be satisfied by cognitive and moral idiots. Put another way, the consistency of computations required by the expected utility model does not guarantee the exercise of judgement and wisdom in the traditional sense. (Suppes, 1984: 207-8)

Finally, since the theory is silent about how a rational person models his small world and forms beliefs and values, it is also silent about how he defines his decision problem. All in all, then, the theory takes as *given* the first stage of decision making, i.e. the construction of a choice situation and definition of the decision problem, and only hypothesizes how a person solves an *already well-structured* choice problem. The same point applies to other rational choice theories on offer, including the Von Neumann–Morgenstern theory; they too concentrate solely on the final stage of decision making, i.e. choice, and fall into the category of choice-based theories of behaviour.[6]

In light of these preliminaries, we can distinguish two questions about Savage's theory in its capacity as a descriptive theory of behaviour: the first is whether the theory closely describes the process of human choice, i.e. the final stage of decision making. The second, but more crucial, issue is whether a choice-based theory of behaviour is ever adequate for predicting and explaining behaviour, regardless of being true or false.

2.4 A discussion of the postulates

The first question, which relates to the realism of the postulates, has mostly been investigated in experimental psychology. The second, which relates to the adequacy of choice-based theories of behaviour, has mostly been taken up in economics. Both approaches from psychology and economics are complementary. We first look at some well-known findings from experimental psychology (Kahneman, 2003). Our objective for such examination here is not to reiterate that the postulates fail. Our aim is to explain why they fail, state an alternative view of preferences emerging from the findings, highlight the implications of the view for economic analysis, and set the stage for defining the kind of behavioural theory needed in economics.

2.4.1 The constructive nature of preferences

The first postulate implies that the decision maker has a complete preference ordering among acts in $\boldsymbol{F}$. To explain what this implication means, note a distinction between 'indifference' and 'indecision'. Indifference refers to a case when the decision maker neither prefers f to g nor g to f but is ready to replace one of the options with the other in his or her preference ordering. Indecision refers to a case when the decision maker neither prefers f to g, nor g to f, and is not ready to substitute one for the other in his or her preference ordering. Thus, completeness means that there are no cases of indecision. And so the weak order postulate is most consistent with the view that people have definite and ready-made preferences, and as soon as they need to reveal them they can do so instantaneously and simultaneously (Thrall, 1954: 183).

This view of preferences is incompatible with a large body of empirical evidence. In an early study, Mosteller and Nogee (1951) observed that subjects would not always give the same answers on repeated elicitation of preferences. Similarly, Simonson and Tversky (1992) observed that varying the choice set could produce different patterns of preferences. In a set of experiments, they presented two groups of subjects with descriptions and pictures of microwave ovens taken from a catalogue. They invited one group of

60 individuals to choose between an Emerson microwave priced at $110 and a Panasonic priced at $180. The subjects were told that both items were on sale, with one third off the regular price. Of these individuals, 57 per cent chose the Emerson oven and 43 per cent the Panasonic. In contrast, they presented the second group of 60 individuals with the same items together with a $200 Panasonic at a 10 per cent discount. Only 13 per cent of the people in the second group chose the most expensive Panasonic oven, which was of the same make as the $180 oven, but its presence among the alternatives increased the percentage of the subjects who selected the less expensive oven from 43 per cent to 60 per cent. A similar pattern of preference variation has been found in a host of other experiments reported in Tversky and Shafir (1992).

If the subjects had definite and ready-made preferences or if they simply read preferences off 'some master list' (Slovic, 1995: 569), the introduction of the new expensive oven would not alter the percentage of people preferring the Emerson oven to the cheaper Panasonic one, and the subjects would exhibit a similar pattern of preferences in both experiments. The observed variation is therefore most consistent with the view that people do not have ready-made preferences. Rather, when they need to choose among options, particularly among complex alternatives, they start in a sense from a state of indecision. They identify the features of the options relevant to the decision task at hand, compare the options in accordance with the attributes and construct pro and con arguments for each option. The pro and con arguments are then used to *construct* a preference ranking of the options. From this perspective, since varying the choice set can make different attributes appear relevant or provide new information about the attributes already noted, a change in the choice set can give rise to construction of new pro and con arguments and hence a different preference ranking. In the above example, the introduction of the more expensive microwave probably brought with it new useful clues that were not available before. The subjects, when choosing among the ovens, most likely looked at the quality and the price of each brand. Since, in the first scenario, the quality difference between Emerson and Panasonic ovens appeared less dominant than the price difference, most subjects opted for Emerson. However, when the third and most expensive Panasonic was introduced, because of a maintained correlation between price and quality, the subjects were most likely led to think that the $180 Panasonic oven was of a much higher quality than previously thought. This additional clue rendered the quality difference more dominant than the price difference, driving more subjects to choose the $180 Panasonic oven, thinking that it was a bargain (McFadden, 1999: 86).

If people do not have ready-made preferences but construct them from pro and con arguments, it is natural to expect that they sometimes fail to develop necessary arguments for constructing a definite preference ranking. There may not be enough information available about the options; the options may be complex, multi-dimensional, or newly invented; or gathering information may be very costly. There is therefore every reason to expect that completeness can fail in practice.

The emphasis on the constructive nature of preferences is the hallmark of psychologists' view of preferences. There is, however, more to the claim in the psychological literature that preferences are constructed than are revealed. To further our understanding of the constructive view of preferences, let us look at another body of evidence known as preference reversals. The discovery of the phenomenon goes back to a study by Slovic and Lichtenstein (1968), in which they noticed that the selling prices of gambles were more highly correlated with pay-offs than with probabilities of winning but choices among lotteries were more highly correlated with probabilities of winning than with the pay-offs. This led the researchers to the conjecture that if subjects were offered two bets with the same expected returns, one featuring a high probability of winning a modest sum of money (called *H* for high chance of winning) and the other featuring a low probability of winning a relatively large amount of money (called *L* for low chance of winning), the subjects would most likely choose the high-probability bet *H* but price the low-probability bet *L* higher. Lichtenstein and Slovic (1971) tested this conjecture by confronting a group of subjects with pairs of bets such as the one depicted in Table 2.2.

Table 2.2 Preference reversal phenomenon

H-bet	**L-bet**
99 % of winning $4 1 % of losing $1	33 % of winning $16 67 % of losing $2

The subjects were asked to state the cash equivalent of the *H* bet (i.e. the minimum price at which they would be willing to sell the bet if they owned it), state the cash equivalent of the *L* bet and make a choice between the two bets. Most subjects, as conjectured, chose the *H* bet but assigned a higher selling price to the *L* bet. In an experiment, 127 out of 173 subjects (or 73.4 per cent) assigned a higher selling price to the *L* bet in every pair in which they chose the *H* bet, even though both bets had the same expected value.

As with any empirical finding, the preference reversal phenomenon is subject to competing explanations, arising from various assumptions that can possibly be made about preferences. There are several assumptions relevant to an explanation of preference reversals. One that has already been mentioned is that people possess well-defined and stable preferences (Stigler and Becker, 1977). A second is *description invariance* that says preferences among options do not depend on the manner in which they are represented or displayed. A third is *procedure invariance* that says strategically equivalent methods of elicitation give rise to the same preference order; it does not matter whether choice questions or evaluation enquiries are used to elicit information about preferences.[7] Let C_H and C_L denote, respectively, the cash equivalent of H and L. Procedure invariance implies that the decision maker prefers H to a cash amount X if and only if his cash equivalent for H exceeds X and that he is indifferent between H and X if and only if $C_H = X$. Finally, a fourth assumption is monetary consistency, which says people prefer more money to less. If X and Y are sure cash amounts, then $X > Y$ implies $X \succ Y$, where $>$ refers to the ordering of the cash amounts. Given these assumptions, preference reversal implies a violation of transitivity, as shown below:

$$\left.\begin{array}{l} 1.\ H \succ L \\ 2.\ C_L > C_H \end{array}\right\} \text{Preference reversal}$$

$$\left.\begin{array}{l} 3.\ C_H \sim H \\ 4.\ C_L \sim L \end{array}\right\} \text{Preference invariance}$$

$$5.\ C_L \succ C_H \ \text{Monetary consistency}$$

....

$$\therefore L \succ C_H \qquad (4 \text{ and } 5)$$

$$H \succ C_H \qquad (1, 4 \text{ and } 5)$$

which contradicts $C_H \sim H$ (hence, intransitivity). Economists initially interpreted the reversals as violations of transitivity and called for establishing an expected utility theory that could account for intransitive choices (Machina, 1987). In contrast, psychologists saw more in the phenomenon than intransitivity, and began exploring whether it could have arisen from the failure of any other assumption, particularly procedure invariance. So, they distinguished two conjectures about the causes of preference reversals – the intransitivity and non-invariance hypotheses.

To test these hypotheses, Tversky *et al.* (1990) extended Lichtenstein and Slovic's initial experimental setting by including an option of receiving a specified sure cash amount X. In this setting, they asked the subjects to state their preferences between each of the pairs in the triple $\{H, L, X\}$, and also announce their cash equivalent for bets L and H. The researchers then focused on the preference reversal cases in which X fell between the cash equivalents C_L and C_H announced by the subjects; that is, the cases in which the reversals followed the pattern

$$H \succ L \text{ and } C_L > X > C_H \qquad \text{(PR)}$$

Intransitivity and non-invariance give rise to different testable implications for preference orderings that satisfy the PR pattern. To spell out some of these implications, note that procedure invariance can fail either because of *overpricing* of L, *underpricing* of H, or both overpricing of L and underpricing of H. Overpricing of L occurs if a person offers cash equivalent C_L for L that is greater than X but in a direct choice between C_L and L he prefers C_L (i.e. $C_L \succ L$). Underpricing of H occurs if a person announces cash equivalent C_H for H that is less than X but in a direct choice between the H and C_H he prefers H to C_H (i.e. $H \succ C_H$). This distinction suggests there are at least four possible hypotheses about the causes of the preference reversals. We derive below the implications of intransitivity, overpricing of L, and underpricing of H:

Hypothesis I: intransitivity	**Hypothesis II: overpricing of L**	**Hypothesis III: underpricing of H**
1. $H \succ L$	1. $H \succ L$	1. $H \succ L$
2. $C_L > X > C_H$	2. $C_L > X > C_H$	2. $C_L > X > C_H$
3. $C_L \succ X \succ C_H$	3. $C_L \succ X \succ C_H$	3. $C_L \succ X \succ C_H$
4. $C_L \sim L$	4. $C_L \succ L$	4. $C_L \sim L$
5. $C_H \sim H$	5. $C_H \sim H$	5. $H \succ C_H$
....	....	....
$\therefore$ $L \succ X$	$\therefore$ $L \succ X$	$\therefore$ $L \succ X$
$X \succ H$	$X \succ H$	$X \succ H$

Tversky *et al.* (1990) looked at the relative frequencies of these preference rankings among the subjects' orderings. Their findings were astounding. In the study, 40 per cent to 50 per cent of the participants showed preference reversals consistent with the PR pattern. Of these subjects, only 10 per cent had preferences consistent with intransitivity while the remaining 90 per cent had preferences consistent with the non-invariance hypotheses. In particular, nearly two-thirds of the reversals were consistent with overpricing of the L bet. The researchers thus concluded that the failure of procedure invariance (overpricing of the L bet) is the major cause of the reversals.

Several theories have been proposed to explain the failure of procedure invariance, including the *scale compatibility hypothesis*, which suggests that an attribute of an object is given more weight when it is compatible with the response mode than when it is not. Since the cash equivalence of a bet is stated in, say, dollars, compatibility implies that pay-offs, which are also stated in the same units, are weighted more heavily in pricing than in choice. As a result, the L bet is overpriced relative to the H bet, leading to the observed preference reversals (Tversky, 1996: 189–90).

The conclusion that preference reversals are to a large extent due to the failure of procedure invariance fits particularly well with another significant body of evidence on framing effect which points to the systematic failure of description invariance (Tversky and Kahneman, 1986). These findings strongly support the viewpoint that there are no ready-made, well-defined, and stable preferences; preferences are constructed on demand and are *endogenous* to the decision process. The findings also indicate that preference formation is *sensitive* to the manner in which options are framed and questions are posed (Fischer *et al.*, 1999: 1074). Consequently, behaviour is likely to vary sharply across situations considered identical by the rational choice theory (Tversky and Thaler, 1990: 210).

2.4.2 The entanglement of values and beliefs

Savage's other behavioural postulates require a small world where preferences among the consequences of the world and beliefs about the states of the world are completely disentangled. Consider the third postulate that says consequence x is preferred to y given a non-null event $\boldsymbol{A}$ if and only if x is preferred to y in general. Specializing $\boldsymbol{A}$ to a single state, the postulate says that the relative value of x is invariant across the states. If beliefs about the states affected the desirability of x, the relative value of x could vary across the states. In that case, the postulate would no longer hold. Thus, for the postulate to hold, there must be a small world refined enough to permit expressing preferences among the consequences of the world without regard to beliefs about the states and expressing likelihood judgements about the states of the world without regard to preferences (Shafer, 1986: 743). Similarly, the second and fourth postulates are predicated on the existence of a refined small world where beliefs and values are entirely disentangled.

In reality, a person's preference ordering of the consequences of his actions may depend on his likelihood ordering of the states of the world, and as his beliefs about the likelihood of the states change, so does his preference ranking of the consequences. Savage was aware of this fact. Considering a person who is about to decide whether to buy a bathing suit or a tennis racket, Savage acknowledged that whether the person prefers 'possessing a bathing suit' to 'possessing a tennis racket' may depend on whether he expects to go on a picnic at a beach or in a park (1972 [1954]: 25). He took such dependence, however, as an indication of the inadequacy of the person's description of his choice situation. Possessing a bathing suit and a tennis racket, he argued, should be regarded as acts, not consequences. Appropriate consequences in this case would be things like 'having a refreshing swim with friends at a beach on a sunny day' and 'sitting on a shadeless beach twiddling a brand new tennis racket while one's friends swim'. Evaluation of these consequences does not depend on which of the two states 'picnic at the beach' or 'picnic in the park' occurs. Savage conjectured that it would generally be possible to completely disentangle values from beliefs by carrying the refinement of the consequences to '*its limits*' (Savage, 1972 [1954]: 25). In an adequately refined world there would be no link between one's values and beliefs.

The difficulty with this proposal is that an attempt at refining the consequences in $\boldsymbol{Z}$ can force a refinement of the states in $\boldsymbol{S}$. This is because the states $\boldsymbol{S}$ must be detailed enough to determine which element of $\boldsymbol{Z}$ will be achieved by each act in $\boldsymbol{F}$ (Shafer, 1986: 474). Savage's suggestion of taking 'a refreshing swim with friends' rather than 'possession of a bathing suit' as the consequence requires refining $\boldsymbol{S}$ to contain states such as whether friends come, whether the temperature is warm enough for a refreshing swim, whether the beach is clean, and so forth. These additional states can render one's ordering of the refined $\boldsymbol{Z}$ dependent on one's beliefs about which element in the refined $\boldsymbol{S}$ is true. Perhaps you would prefer twiddling a brand new tennis racket while your friends swim if you knew that your friends would bring along someone who you don't like. There is *a priori* no reason to think that, for any set of acts, there is always an ultimately refined world in which preferences among the consequences can be completely disentangled from beliefs about the states. Even if such a world existed, it would not be anything similar to a description that a typical individual would have of his choice situation. Later in his life, Savage acknowledged that an 'ultimate' analysis might not after all exist and if it existed it might be quite 'cumbersome':

> A nickel is itself a lottery ticket, and one objection to getting miserably drenched is that it seems conducive to illness. If the problem were concerned with illness or the possibility of accidentally buying poisoned food, then of course the notion of consequences would have to be further analysed. An ultimate analysis might seem desirable, *but probably it does not exist and certainly threatens to be cumbersome.* (Savage, 1971: 79; italics added)

In the small worlds we construct to represent our choice situations, our evaluation of the consequences of the world depends on our beliefs about the states of the world. This dependence defines another aspect of the constructive view of preferences.

Finally, it is important to emphasize the constructive nature of small worlds; they are also the outcome of our models of the world and evolve with the evolution of our models. Small worlds, beliefs, and preferences are not 'there like the Rocky Mountains', to use Stigler and Becker's phrase (1977: 76); they are all constructed.

These remarks, though they may seem self-evident, have a profound implication for modelling behaviour. Since different constructions of beliefs, small worlds, and preferences can systematically give rise to different choices, no theory can accurately predict or explain (dynamic) behaviour without taking into account the *factors* affecting formation of beliefs, small worlds and preferences (Bowles, 1998: 75). Therefore a satisfactory theory of behaviour should explain how beliefs, small worlds and preferences are formed; it cannot take them as *exogenous*. To illustrate the point, let us return to the preference reversal phenomenon. The phenomenon shows that pay-offs and probabilities of winning have quite different effects in pricing gambles and choosing among them. Pay-offs are weighted more heavily in pricing gambles whereas probabilities of winning are weighted more heavily in choosing among gambles. This means a theory of behaviour cannot correctly predict or explain pricing and choice behaviour in such cases without taking into consideration the dominance of pay-offs in pricing and probabilities in choice. A theory that pays no attention to the different roles of these factors is bound to yield wrong predictions. The real difficulty with Savage's theory and indeed all rational choice theories is not merely that they give a wrong description of human choice. The real difficulty is that they take things as exogenous that cannot be taken as exogenous by a theory of behaviour. In general, because of the constructive nature of beliefs, small worlds and preferences, no choice-based theory of behaviour can ever explain or accurately predict economic behaviour.

2.5 The limited role of rational choice theories

In economics, critics of the rational choice theories have until relatively recently paid less attention to the realism of the postulates, and mainly disputed the contribution that the theories can make to economic theorizing, whether they are true or not. In this section, we draw on the works of economists such as Kenneth Arrow (1986), Arthur Goldberger (1989), Robert Lucas (1976), Herbert Simon (1984; 1986) and the philosopher Patrick Suppes (1961) to argue why choice-based theories of behaviour are in principle inadequate for dealing with substantive economic controversies. The analysis complements the central lessons of behavioural psychology. We continue working within the framework of Savage's theory but the relevance of the analysis to other choice-based theories will be evident.

2.5.1 Choice-based theories and economic controversies

Savage's theory takes the structure of the small world and the content of beliefs and preferences as given, and only says how an agent solves a well-structured decision problem. This means, in using the theory for modelling behaviour, a host of *exogenous* assumptions is needed to specify the agent's choice situation and his decision problem. These assumptions are made by specifying a utility function, the variables entering the function, the physical or socio-economic laws determining the variables, their joint probability distribution, and so forth. Without such assumptions, the theory makes no *concrete* prediction about observed behaviour.[8]

Now, one way to reconstruct the economists' critique of Savage's theory is that these assumptions are not like auxiliary assumptions that are necessary for a general theory to speak about the actual world. On the contrary, they assume the solutions to the very same questions that a theory of behaviour is expected to answer. The reason is that, by varying the exogenous assumptions, every conceivable side of any substantive economic controversy can be derived as the outcome of subjective expected utility maximization. Thus, the key to settling an economic controversy lies in correctly specifying the exogenous assumptions. However, a correct specification of the assumptions necessary for making Savage's theory have any implication about a substantive controversy requires nothing less than knowing the correct side of the controversy. As a result, once the necessary exogenous assumptions in a given situation are fully specified, nothing essential remains for the theory to predict; the predictions are already in the assumptions. Savage's theory simply repackages them in terms of subjective expected utility maximization. But a satisfactory theory cannot assume the answer to the very same questions that it is expected to address. Consequently, regardless of being true or not, Savage's theory cannot function as a theory of economic behaviour.

We defend these points by examining a rational choice-based model of economic behaviour to illustrate how by varying the model's exogenous assumptions any side of an economic controversy can be rationalized. We will then explain why the analysis generally holds.

2.5.1.1 The Effect of compensatory educational programmes

We borrow our model from a paper by Arthur Goldberger (1989), who scrutinizes Gary Becker's claim about the effectiveness of public compensatory educational programmes. The effectiveness of these programmes is still a matter of controversy.[9] On the one hand, there is the view that such programmes contribute positively to the well-being of the children participating in them and improve their future earnings. On the other, there is the view that the programmes are ineffective, since parents whose children participate in them reallocate the portion of their income that they would have otherwise spent on their children. This is known as the *offsetting effect*. An adequate theory of behaviour is expected to have some implication for the truth of the offsetting effect.

Becker (1981) seems to suggest that, by extending expected utility analysis to parents' expenditure decision making, he has been able to establish the offsetting effect. Goldberger is critical of this claim. He argues that the offsetting effect implied by Becker's model is not the result of the expected utility maximization assumption but depends on the exogenous assumptions introduced to specify, in our terms, the decision problem being solved by the parent. If the parent's choice situation were defined differently, a different conclusion would be derived. The expected utility maximization hypothesis is consistent with both opposing views on the effect of compensatory educational programmes. We review Goldberger's analysis in some detail as it explains how formal economic modelling proceeds in practice.[10]

A key to resolving the controversy about the effectiveness of public education programmes is to know how parents would respond to a change in the income of their children. To address this query, Becker assumes a representative parent, suggesting that all parents whose children participate in the programmes have the same utility function, live in the same environment, and receive the same information. He speaks of 'the parent' rather than parents. Having done so, he introduces several assumptions about the representative parent. The first is that she has an *interdependent* (i.e. non-egoistic) utility function that allows a concern with the consumption patterns of others (Pollak, 2002: 10). In particular, it is assumed that the parent's utility derives from her own consumption C and her child's income Y. Becker's second assumption is that the parent has a Cobb-Douglas utility function U:

$$U = \alpha \log Y + (1 - \alpha) \log C \tag{2.4}$$

The parameter α, which lies between 0 and 1, shows relative preference for child income as against own consumption. The parent's relative preference for her child's income as against her own consumption is independent of Y and C. The parent receives income X, which is allocated between her consumption, C, and investment in her child, I:

$$X = C + I \tag{2.5}$$

Becker's third assumption relates to the mechanism generating the child's income. The child's income is taken to be an *additive* function of the parent's investment I and another general component E, called 'luck', which represents natural endowments, social status, government support, luck in the market, and so forth. The rate of return on investment I is r. Let $m = 1 + r$. The child's income Y is given by

$$Y = mI + E \tag{2.6}$$

Since the time unit is a generation, Y and X are technically wealth or permanent income. Consequently, the return factor $m = 1 + r$ can be taken to be larger than unity, say, 1.5 or even more. Finally, Becker's analysis assumes that the parent has full knowledge of her child's luck. She decides by maximizing utility function (2.4) subject to constraints (2.5) and (2.6), which yields the optimal allocation of her income as

$$I = \alpha X - (1 - \alpha)E/m \tag{2.7}$$

$$C = (1 - \alpha)X + (1 - \alpha)E/m \tag{2.8}$$

Substituting (2.7) back into (2.6) gives the income transmission rule

$$Y = bX + \alpha E \qquad b = \alpha m \tag{2.9}$$

where the parameter b is the 'propensity to invest in the child' and α is the 'fraction of family income spent on the child' (Goldberger, 1989: 506).

The income transition rule (2.9) describes how the parent responds to an increase in the child's luck. Suppose there is a dollar increase in E. According to (2.9), the child's income increases only by the fraction of α of one dollar; the parent partially offsets the increase in E by increasing her own consumption (see (2.7)). Becker takes this result to argue that 'public education and other programs to aid the young may not significantly better them because of compensating decreases in parental expenditures' (Becker, 1981: 153). This conclusion is not an inevitable implication of the utility maximization hypothesis. The offsetting result depends on the assumption that the child's income is an additive function of parental investment and child's luck. If the child's income were, for instance, a multiplicative function of parental investment and luck, the result would no longer follow. To illustrate this, Goldberger replaces (2.6) with the multiplicative function

$$Y = mIE \tag{2.10}$$

which says the rate of return to parental investment increases with luck. In this case, the parent allocates her income according to

$$I = \alpha X \tag{2.11}$$

$$C = (1 - \alpha)X \tag{2.12}$$

an allocation that is independent of E. And the income transmission rule becomes

$$Y = bXE \tag{2.13}$$

An increase in E no longer affects the parent's investment decision. If Y followed (2.10) rather than (2.6), public education programmes could have strong effects (Goldberger, 1989: 507). This means the utility maximization assumption implies neither the offsetting effect nor its negation. Becker's result is based on his hypothesis (2.6) about the structure of the environment, which says the child's income is an additive function of her luck.

Becker's offsetting result also depends on the choice of a homothetic utility function.[11] Goldberger does not consider this but a non-homothetic function undermines the result. Consider the simple non-homothetic utility function

$$U = Y + \ln C \tag{2.14}$$

while retaining the assumption that the child's income is an additive function of parental investment and child's luck. The optimizing parent will now allocate her income into

$$C = m^{-1} \tag{2.15}$$

$$I = X - m^{-1} \tag{2.16}$$

which is again independent of E. The new income transmission rule will be

$$Y = mX - 1 + E \tag{2.17}$$

As evident from (2.15) and (2.16), the parent's optimal consumption and investment are independent of the child's luck. And so, the model does not entail the offsetting effect.

The subjective expected utility maximization assumption is therefore consistent with both opposing views on the effectiveness of compensatory educational programmes. It is the exogenous assumptions about the shape of the parent's utility function, the variables entering it, and the mechanisms generating the variables that make a model entail the offsetting result or its negation (Pollak, 2002: 9). To predict the effect of the educational programmes using Savage's theory, one ought to know, among other things, whether the parent cares about the child, how she cares, whether her relative preference for her own consumption and investment in the child vary with changes in the child's income, what she thinks of the mechanism generating the child's income, how she predicts the effect of her investment on the future wealth of the child, and so forth. But if we knew the answers to these queries, we would already know how she would behave in response to a change in her child's income; the answer to the question concerning the effect of the programmes is implicit in the answers to these questions. In the end, we may need to introduce an optimization principle to infer how she actually solves her decision problem but the principle would not need to be the subjective expected utility maximization principle; satisficing would do equally (Arrow, 1986).[12] Nor is the principle an 'engine of truth', standing above all the other assumptions; it is an assumption like other substantive assumptions entering a model of parent behaviour.

2.5.2 How economic controversies are settled

The resolution of economic controversies depends on the choice of exogenous assumptions, not the expected utility maximization principle. In practice, economists turn to econometric analysis of aggregate data to select a rational choice model and thereby settle economic controversies. The analysis involves trying various combinations of exogenous assumptions to establish a rational choice model that best fits aggregate data, and using the model to answer behavioural or policy questions of interest. A crucial question is whether this approach can fill the theoretical vacuum left by the rational choice theories. This requires knowing the assumptions underlying the econometric approach. To bring some of these assumptions to the fore, we consider a typical application of the method from the history of economics and, on that basis, explain why it fails.

2.5.2.1 The effect of economic events on votes

An issue of interest in economics concerns the effect of economic events on votes. The literature contains conflicting views on the matter. Kramer (1971), for example, concluded from his analysis of US voting behaviour that economic fluctuations have a major effect on congressional elections, whereas Stigler (1973) concluded that they do not. Against this background, Fair (1978) set himself the task of presenting a model of voting behaviour that was general enough to incorporate most of the theories of voting behaviour in the literature and that allowed one to test in a systematic way one theory against the others. His goal was to use the model to analyse the effect of economic events on votes. Fair considers a two-party political system such as in the US, referred to as Democratic and Republican parties, and focuses on presidential, rather than congressional, elections. Fair's model is expectedly a rational choice model of voting behaviour.

According to the rational choice theory, a voter evaluates the past performance and current pronouncements of the competing parties, forms from this assessment an expectation of her future utility under each party, and votes for the party that offers the maximum expected utility. Let us define the following notations:

$E(U_{it}^d)$: voter i's expected utility if the Democratic candidate is elected at time t.

$E(U_{it}^r)$: voter i's expected utility if the Republican candidate is elected at time t.

These expectations are based on the information available up to time t. Also, let V_{it} be a variable that is equal to one if voter i votes for the Democratic candidate at time t and zero if she votes for the Republican candidate at time t. The theory implies that[13]

$$V_{it} = \begin{cases} 1 & if \quad E(U_{it}^d) > E(U_{it}^r) \\ 0 & if \quad E(U_{it}^d) < E(U_{it}^r) \end{cases} \tag{2.18}$$

Voter i votes for the candidate that gives the higher expected utility. Further, let us denote voter i's utility function as

$$U_{it} = f_i(\mathbf{Z}_{it}) \tag{2.19}$$

with $\mathbf{Z}_{it}$ being the variables affecting her utility. Fair interprets the differences in the literature on voting in terms of whether $\mathbf{Z}_{it}$ includes economic factors and, if so, how they affect, votes. If economic factors affect votes, the voter's expected future utility if a party were in power will depend on her forecast of the performance of the economy under the party. Fair, therefore, embarks on testing whether the voter's expected future utility under a party depends on her forecast of the performance of the economy under the party. This raises several questions about how the voter measures the state of the economy *and* how she forecasts the economy's performance.

Fair makes two assumptions about the voter's forecasting procedure:

A_1: the forecast reflects accumulated past experience;
A_2: the forecast attaches more weight to recent than to remote periods.

According to these assumptions, the voter bases her forecast of the future performance of a party on the economy's performance when the party was recently in power. If economic factors affected voting decisions, then the voter's expected future utility under a party would depend on how well the economy performed when the party was recently in power. Let

$tj1$: last election from t back that party j was in power,
$tj2$: second-to-last election from t back that party j was in power,
ξ_i^j : a vector of variables specific to voter i, assumed to be independent of the variables used to measure the performance of the economy,
M_{ih} : some measure of economic performance of the party in power during the four years prior to election h. Subscript i suggests that each voter may use different measures.

j takes two values d for the Democratic candidate and r for the Republican. When party j is in power at time t, $tj1$ is equal to t.[14] The postulates A_1 and A_2 can then be formalized as follows:

$$E(U_{it}^d) = \xi_i^d + \beta_{i1}\frac{M_{itd1}}{(1+\rho_i)^{t-td1}} + \beta_{i2}\frac{M_{itd2}}{(1+\rho_i)^{t-td2}} \tag{2.20}$$

$$E(U_{it}^r) = \xi_i^r + \beta_{i3}\frac{M_{itr1}}{(1+\rho_i)^{t-tr1}} + \beta_{i4}\frac{M_{itr2}}{(1+\rho_i)^{t-tr2}} \tag{2.21}$$

where parameters β_{i1}, β_{i2}, β_{i3}, and β_{i4} are unknown coefficients and ρ_i is an unknown discount rate. Equations (2.20) and (2.21) state that voter i's expected future utility under a party is a function of a vector of individual specific variables and the party's performance during the last two times that it was in power. The performance measure is discounted from time t back at rate ρ_i. For ρ_i greater than zero, more weight is attached to recent than to remote periods. If desired, the equations can be expanded to include more than just the last two periods each party was in power. Also, M_{ih} can be a function of several variables describing the economy.

Fair attempts to settle the theoretical disagreements about the effect of economic events on votes by fitting to aggregate voting data various possible models that arise from substituting alternative performance measures for M_{ih} in equations (2.20) and (2.21). His objective is to determine if any of the models adequately account for the data. Equations (2.20) and (2.21) are about individual behaviour, and without some justification cannot be estimated by aggregate data. To justify using aggregate data, Fair introduces four extra assumptions regarding the voters and the economy. Let

$$\psi_i = \xi_i^r - \xi_i^d \text{ and} \tag{2.22}$$

$$q_t = \beta_{i1}\frac{M_{itd1}}{(1+\rho_i)^{t-td1}} + \beta_{i2}\frac{M_{itd2}}{(1+\rho_i)^{t-td2}} - \beta_{i3}\frac{M_{itd1}}{(1+\rho_i)^{t-tr1}} - \beta_{i4}\frac{M_{itr1}}{(1+\rho_i)^{t-tr2}}. \tag{2.23}$$

It follows from equations (2.18), (2.20) and (2.21) that voter i votes for the Democratic candidate if $q_t > \psi_i$ and votes for the Republican candidate if $q_t < \psi_i$.[15] With this in mind, Fair's assumptions for linking the individual and the aggregate levels are as follows:

A_3 : all voters use the same measure of performance;
A_4 : the coefficients β_{i1}, β_{i2}, β_{i3}, β_{i4} and ρ_i in (2.20) and (2.21) are the same for all voters; index i can be deleted;
A_5 : ψ_i in (2.22) is evenly distributed across voters in each election between some numbers $a+\delta_t$ and $b+\delta_t$, where $a < 0$ and $b > 0$. a and b are constant but δ_t can vary across elections;[16]
A_6 : There are an infinite number of voters in each election.

Let V_t denote the percentage of the two-party vote that goes to the Democratic candidate in election t. It follows from equations (2.18), (2.20), and (2.21), and assumptions A_3 through A_6 that:

$$V_t = \alpha_0 + \beta_1^*\frac{M_{td1}}{(1+\rho)^{t-td1}} + \beta_2^*\frac{M_{td2}}{(1+\rho)^{t-td2}} - \beta_3^*\frac{M_{td1}}{(1+\rho)^{t-tr1}} - \beta_4^*\frac{M_{tr1}}{(1+\rho)^{t-tr2}} + v_t \tag{2.24}$$

which makes no reference to variables ξ_i^d and ξ_i^r (see Appendix 2.C). Given some restrictions on the error term v_t, equation (2.24) can be estimated from aggregate data. Fair considers several measures of performance to replace for M_h. They include the growth rate of real GNP per capita in the year of the election, in the two-year period before the election, in the three-year period before the election, and over the entire four-year period; the change in the unemployment rate for the same four periods; and the absolute value of the growth rate of the GNP deflator for the same four periods. Among the forty-eight equations considered, the equation with the growth rate of the real GNP per capita in the year of the election as the measure of performance best fitted the data. Fair therefore concludes that economic events as measured by the change in real economic activity in the year of the election have a significant effect on votes for president. Voters do not, he also concludes, look back very far. Nor do they consider the past performance of the non-incumbent party. Economic factors, after all, enter voters' utility functions.

2.5.3 Why the econometric method fails

Fair's study is a typical example of how substantive controversies – such as what variables affect votes and how – are settled in economics. In practice, substantive controversies are resolved by searching for a rational choice-based model that best fits aggregate data. A central question is therefore whether this approach can fill the theoretical vacuum left by the rational choice theories. For two reasons, the answer is negative.

First, the econometric approach requires assuming that the laws of the individual and the economy coincide; without this assumption aggregate data cannot be used to select the assumptions entering a rational choice model. Fair takes this coincidence for granted by assuming that all voters have the same utility function, use the same measure of economic performance, employ the same forecasting rules, and that individual characteristics are uniformly distributed in the population. These assumptions, which are necessary for the laws of the individual and the economy to coincide, are incredibly strong. Yet, they are not adequate to ensure the coincidence. A full justification of this point demands a proper understanding of the conditions under which the laws of the individual and the economy are the same, which is given in the final chapter. Here, it suffices to note that economic variables change status when one moves from the micro-level to the aggregate level. The individual takes, for example, prices, the rate of economic growth, inflation, and the unemployment level as given but the economy cannot take them as given. Quite the opposite, it determines them. It is therefore wrong to assume that models true of the aggregates are also true of the individuals or vice versa. Contrary to common practice in economics, the fate of rational choice models cannot be settled by analysis of aggregate data. A different type of data is needed.

Second, the exogenous assumptions in a rational choice model convey information about the agent's small world, beliefs and preferences. These are not invariants of human behaviour but are *constructed* on the basis of past experiences, goals and needs, and vary with the accumulation of experiences and information. This means even if the aggregation difficulties arising from the differences between the micro- and macro-levels did not exist, the econometric method could at best establish the model that was true of the individuals during the period from which the data were collected. It could not establish the model that would be true if they received different information, if a different policy regime were in place, or if the institutional structure of the economy were different. As a result, the econometric method is unsuitable for establishing models useful for predicting the effects of changes in the economy on individual behaviour. In a nutshell, for the very same reasons underlying the Lucas critique, econometrics fails to fill the theoretical vacuum left by the rational choice theories.

For these reasons, the marriage of rational choice theory with econometrics fails to yield models suitable for predicting the effects of change on behaviour. The key to achieve this objective is the ability to answer counterfactual queries such as those stated above. Settling such queries demands a theory of behaviour that endogenizes small worlds, beliefs and preferences. In other words, it calls for a theory that explains how a person forms beliefs about the causal structure of the economy, updates his beliefs in light of new information, adapts preferences on the basis of past experiences, and accordingly defines his decision problem. If such a theory is established there remains no *essential* role for the subjective expected utility theory to play in predicting and explaining behaviour. The theory, in one sense, becomes otiose:

> The psychologist resists accepting them [subjective probability and utility] as basic or primitive concepts of behaviour. Ideally, what he desires is a dynamic theory of the inherent or environmental factors determining the acquisition of a particular set of beliefs or values. If these factors can be identified and their theory developed, the concepts of probability and utility become otiose in one sense. (Suppes, 1961: 614)

Two general implications of our analysis of Savage's theory are worth noting. First, the inadequacy of Savage's theory arises from the fact that it provides no explanation of how the agent models his choice situation and defines his decision problem. In this respect, other rational choice theories on offer are the same. They are also solely concerned with the final stage of decision – choice, and cannot serve as a satisfactory theory of economic behaviour. Secondly, but equally importantly, economists have long argued for the necessity of economic theory to specify explanatory variables in econometric models, the functional form of the model, the sign of the model parameters, and even the joint probability distribution of the variables under study (Fair, 1987: 270). And by economic theory, they mean a theory of rational choice or a model based on it (Becker, 1976: 5). Our analysis reveals that rational choice theories do not provide any information useful for specification of econometric models; they just take them for granted. The so-called theoretical information in economics is simply disparate assumptions that are not derived from any theory, certainly not from rational choice theories (Peltzman, 1991: 206). They are accepted because they intuitively sound plausible (Sims, 2004: 282) or are part of a model that fits aggregate data.

2.6 Expectations

To understand the dynamics of behaviour, it is essential to model both the process of preference and expectations (beliefs) formation. Notwithstanding this, economists have treated expectations and preferences differently. Stigler and Becker (1977) famously suggested that economics should take preferences not only as exogenous but also as homogeneous across individuals, arguing that differences in actions are best explained in terms of differences in perceived opportunities (Vriend, 1996: 279). While there have been some attempts to study preference formation, Stigler and Becker's view still strongly dominates economics. In sharp contrast, a central position in economics has always been that economic theory cannot take expectations as exogenous (Harsanyi, 1965: 450), and a variety of proposals have been put forward to model expectations. An influential proposal is the rational expectations hypothesis. We study some aspects of this hypothesis to further our understanding of the current state of economic theory.

2.6.1 Adaptive expectations

The rational expectations (RE) hypothesis emerged as a result of reflection on the shortcomings of the so-called adaptive expectations (AE) hypothesis. According to this hypothesis, the agent considers only the recent values of a variable to form expectations of its future values and, when the truth of his forecasts transpires, he uses his forecasting error to revise his future forecasts of the variable (Cagan, 1956). The AE hypothesis restricts relevant information on a variable to its recent history. As a consequence, it implies that people do not take note of changes in the economy until the effects of the changes are fed into their forecasting errors and therefore make systematic mistakes in perceiving the course of the economy (Bicchieri, 1987: 506). Moreover, according to the hypothesis, the effect of interventions on behaviour begins to bear only after previous expectations badly go wrong. Because of this strictly backward-looking feature, the hypothesis rules out any immediate effect of policies on expectations and hence behaviour. These implications go against a common conviction in economics that people optimally use all available information in making decisions. It is claimed that they realize the interrelations among economic variables and utilize the information on their movements to form expectations. The AE hypothesis has therefore been viewed as an inadequate conjecture about people.

2.6.2 Rational expectations

The RE hypothesis is an extreme response to the backward-looking feature of the AE hypothesis. In its strong form, it posits that economic agents know the true model of the economy and their subjective expectations of the variables representing the economy are the same as the objective expectations entailed by the true model (Pesaran, 1987: 165):

> Expectations, since they are informed predictions of future events, are essentially the same as the predictions of relevant economic theory. At the risk of confusing this purely descriptive theory...with a pronouncement as to what firms ought to do, we call such expectations 'rational'. (Muth, 1961: 316)

The RE hypothesis stands on several assumptions. An assumption is that the vector of exogenous and endogenous variables of the economy follows a *jointly* stationary stochastic process. Another assumption is that the variables have an objective joint probability distribution in the sense understood in the frequency interpretation of probability. In characterizing this assumption, following Knight (1964 [1921]), new classical economists divide uncertainty into 'reducible' and 'irreducible' components. Reducible uncertainty is defined as risk, which is the uncertainty that is analysable according to the laws of mathematical probability. Irreducible uncertainty is taken to be the 'true' uncertainty, which falls outside the bounds of numerical probability. The RE hypothesis is, by definition, restricted to risky situations (McCann, 1994: 63). However, nothing is said about how it can be known whether a given situation is risky or truly uncertain, and so in practice the hypothesis is applied generally. A further assumption is that the agents correctly know the objective probability distribution of the variables describing the economy.[17] Finally, the agents are also assumed to know the true values of all the exogenous and endogenous variables through to the end of the present period.

These assumptions have strong implications for modelling the economy. Since the agents know the true economic model, their forecasts are always confirmed by the course of events and their views are always consistent with each other. They therefore never have an incentive to revise their view of the economic structure. Moreover, since they maximize their expected utility with respect to the true model, they also never have an incentive to revise their actions. Their actions are always optimal with respect to the environment and with respect to the actions of fellow agents in the economy. The economy is therefore permanently in equilibrium. Disequilibrium, by definition, becomes a vacuous notion, and all supposed disequilibrium phenomena are *a priori* defined out of existence. This last point plays a critical role in solving rational expectations models. These models are solved by requiring the collective outcomes of individual decisions to be an equilibrium state.

To understand the hypothesis better, it is useful to look at the way a rational expectations model is built and solved. To this end, we use a perfect foresight version of the *quantity theory* about the relation between money supply and prices.[18] Versions of this model are found in Blanchard and Watson (1982), Sargent (1993) and MacCallum (1983). The account here is based on

Sargent (1993), who uses it to discuss a theoretical difficulty with rational expectations models. This is done in three steps.

First, the economy runs in discrete time, and each individual lives for two periods. The same number of individuals, normalized to one, is born every period. An individual born at time t is young at time t and old at time $t+1$. Each individual receives an endowment of $2e_1$ when young and $2e_2$ when old. The endowment is non-storable, and can only be saved by holding money. Let p_t be the price level at time t, and $E(p_{t+1})$ the value of p_{t+1} expected as of period t. The individual decides on his or her level of nominal balances m_t to carry from time t to time $t+1$ by maximizing the utility function:

$$\ln(2e_1 - m_t/p_t) + \ln(2e_2 + m_t/E(p_{t+1})) \tag{2.25}$$

The function describes how the agent is ready to forfeit m_t/p_t units of goods in this period against $m_t/E(p_{t+1})$ units that he expects his real money balances will offer next period. The agent chooses m_t, taking as given the current price level p_t and what he expects the price level will be next period, $E(p_{t+1})$. The maximizing choice of m_t yields the money demand function

$$m_t/p_t = e_1 - e_2 E(p_{t+1})/p_t \tag{2.26}$$

Second, the laws of the variables entering the model are specified – here the money supply and the price level. Suppose the government supplies money according to the rule:

$$M_{t+1} = \alpha M_t \tag{2.27}$$

Because expectations about future price levels affect current prices, $E(p_{t+1})$ enters the price function. The RE hypothesis requires the price function to be a function that ensures equilibrium. A method for finding the function is to conjecture a price function, and check if it leads to equilibrium, which here means if it makes the demand for money m_t equal to its supply M_t.[19] A possible conjecture is the following:

$$p_t = \beta M_t \tag{2.28}$$

Since the agent, by assumption, knows the economic structure, he knows (2.27) and (2.28) as well as their parameters. He uses these laws to estimate $E(p_{t+1})$. It follows that

$$E(p_{t+1}) = \alpha\beta M_t \tag{2.29}$$

Finally, (2.28) and (2.29) are substituted into (2.26) and the demand for money m_t is set equal to the money supply M_t. This yields the equilibrium price as

$$p_t = (e_1 - \alpha e_2)^{-1} M_t \tag{2.30}$$

The agent holds money if $m_t/E(p_{t+1})$ is greater than m_t/p_t and stops giving up his endowment $2e_1$ if the two ratios are equal.

The RE hypothesis significantly reduces the complexity of predicting behaviour. A person's maximization behaviour is considered to be solely a function of his environment, preferences and budget constraint. That is, given his preferences and budget constraint, he behaves exactly in the way that is optimal with respect to the environment. For predicting behaviour, there is then no need to study the person's beliefs about the economy or how he has arrived at those beliefs. We only need to know the person's preferences, budget constraint and the economy (Simon, 1990: 6). Issues of human learning and adaptation can be left entirely to psychologists (Sargent, 1993: 21). Furthermore, since individual preferences are taken to be homogeneous, the RE hypothesis leads to the representative agent modelling approach that enormously simplifies the study of economic phenomena.

2.6.3 Problems with the RE hypothesis

The RE hypothesis has been one of the most influential proposals in economics, and has influenced the views of economists on many aspects of policy analysis and inference from aggregate data. At the same time, like any bold conjecture, it has been the subject of bitter controversies. A full analysis of these controversies is beyond the scope of this chapter. Here, we only look at some of the theoretical debates that are directly related to the role of the hypothesis as a means for specifying people's view of the economy, a role Lucas assigned to the hypothesis (1981: 223).

2.6.3.1 The true model

A problem with the RE hypothesis relates to the notion of the 'true model'. There are certain situations where it makes sense to speak of a true model. In computer simulations designed to investigate an estimation procedure, the modeller writes down a model, uses it to generate data and studies whether the procedure can uncover the model from the data if the sample size is let to grow arbitrarily large. Outside such situations, it is not clear what a true model means, particularly in macroeconomics where model construction heavily involves aggregation, idealization, and simplification. Aggregation over interactive heterogeneous units generates relations that are absent at the individual level. Also, as one varies the aggregation level one encounters quite different models. What guides a modeller to choose a specific aggregation level are pragmatic considerations, not correspondence to reality, and this casts doubt on the notion of a true model. Moreover, even if the notion of a 'true model' were unproblematic, the true model would be so complex in macroeconomics that it would be of no use for prediction or explanation of economic phenomena. These quandaries in making sense of a 'true' model and the difficulties in establishing it reduce the RE hypothesis to the idea that the agent's model of the economy coincides with whatever model the economist uses to describe the economy (Bullard, 1994). The question then arises as to whose model really reflects the people's view of the economy. A possible response is to search for a model that best fits aggregate data. This, however, takes us back to where we started the search for microfoundations. Many models can fit the data equally well, and the greatest challenge is to determine which model best approximates the economy.

2.6.3.2 *Multiple equilibria*

A step in building a rational expectations model is to conjecture the mechanisms or laws determining the variables describing the economy, such as money supply in the above example. To explain a difficulty with this, it is crucial to distinguish between two types of variables entering an economic model. First, there are variables whose values do not depend on their own expected values. One such variable is weather that often enters agricultural models. The state of weather over the next few years does not depend on people's expectations about future weather. Second, there are variables whose current values depend on people's expectations of their future values. Current prices, for example, depend on people's expectations of future prices. This means the way people form expectations about future prices is part of the process determining prices. In such cases, the RE hypothesis requires people's expectations to be *consistent* with each other so that the economy is in equilibrium. In the present example, this means that people's expectations of future prices are such that they make the demand for and supply of money equal (i.e. the market clears). However, this consistency requirement is not enough to ensure a unique solution for rational expectations models with expected endogenous variables. Many expectations formation rules yield consistent expectations, raising the question of which rule is true of the economy. An alternative mechanism for the price level in the above economy is (Sargent, 1993: 11):

$$p_t = \beta M_t + \lambda^t c \tag{2.31}$$

Like the forecasting rule (2.27), this rule also clears the market. In fact, for every $c > 0$, there is an equilibrium price.[20] Due to this multiplicity, a complete description of the fundamentals of the economy (i.e. tastes, technology, and initial resources endowments) and the requirement of belief consistency across individuals are not sufficient for predicting the equilibrium price. It is also essential to know how people converge on a particular expectation formation rule. The RE hypothesis falls short of specifying people's beliefs about the future of the economy.[21]

2.6.3.3 *A paradox*

In addition to the multiple equilibria problem, there are other less known issues with the RE hypothesis. Recall the hypothesis implies that the vector of exogenous and endogenous variables of the economy follow a jointly *stationary* stochastic process. It also implies that people's subjective expectations of the variables coincide with the mathematical expectations implied by the variables' objective probability distribution. Taken together, these implications exclude the possibility of discretionary policy interventions. For if there were some free parameters that could be controlled by public officials there would be, according to the hypothesis, an objective probability distribution for the parameters that were known to the people. In that case, people would already know the likelihood of any variation in the parameters, and would have taken the information into account when making their decisions. And so, the likelihood of any change by a policy maker would already have been known to the people and would already have been fed into their behaviour. This means there can be no discretionary policy intervention under the RE hypothesis (Bicchieri, 1987: 510; Vercelli, 1991: 150). To allow for policy interventions, the assumption that the economy is permanently stationary must be relinquished, which requires abandoning the RE hypothesis.[22]

2.6.3.4 The peril of redundancy

There is another paradoxical implication of the RE hypothesis that is worth noting. The hypothesis, as just said, excludes the possibility of policy interventions by assuming the stationarity of the economic environment. As a consequence, it excludes all the practical objectives of macroeconomics except *ex ante* and *ex post* predictions. Such predictions do not require a structural model built on the optimal rules of behaviour. A regression model that closely represents the relations among relevant aggregate variables is enough. Therefore, with the impossibility of policy interventions, there is no practical necessity to model expectations and, for that reason, there remains no direct role for the hypothesis in economic modelling. The RE hypothesis implies its own practical redundancy. Sims notes this quandary at the heart of Lucas' programme (1982a: 115–16). He seems to argue that, having assumed stationarity, Muth should have excluded expected variables from the realm of large-scale economic modelling altogether rather than requiring macroeconomic models to be explicitly built on an expectation formation mechanism. In a stationary environment, a vector autoregression model tracking the past movements of relevant aggregate variables suffices for the purpose of economic analysis (Sims, 1982a: 115–16). In an interesting comparison of Lucas and Sims' approaches to macroeconomic modelling, Sargent also acknowledges that the RE hypothesis, taken seriously, can be used equally 'to support Sims' style of more or less uninterpreted vector autoregressive empirical work' (Sargent, 1984: 408).

2.6.3.5 The no-trade theorems

The RE hypothesis has also contributed to the emergence of a class of no-trade theorems that are in sharp conflict with observed data (Milgrom and Stokey, 1982). In economics, preferences are taken to be homogeneous across individuals. This assumption, joined with the RE hypothesis, implies a view of the economy as a society of identical individuals. Such an economy provides no place at all for security markets. Security markets exist because people have diverse information, think of the economy differently, have heterogeneous preferences, and differ in their attitudes towards risk (Arrow, 1986: 212). Even though rejecting homogeneous preferences is enough for eliminating the theorems, it is equally plausible to reject the RE hypothesis to account for the emergence of security markets.

The RE hypothesis is a bold attempt to specify people's view of their choice situation by studying the economy. It assumes that people have already learnt the structure of the economy, adapted their optimal rules of behaviour, and that the economy is in equilibrium. While these suppositions are incredibly strong, they are inadequate for predicting economic outcomes, due to the ubiquitous existence of multiple equilibria. The inadequacy remains even when the fundamentals of the economy are fully known. Therefore, the marriage of rational choice theory with the RE hypothesis fails to provide a predictive theory of the economy. Predicting whether the economy converges to equilibrium after an intervention, and the equilibrium to which it converges, requires a theory of how people model their choice situation, remodel it as a result of a policy change, and adapt their behaviour as a result of subsequent experiences. Until an adequate theory of how people learn about the economy and adapt is established, macroeconomic theory cannot hope to produce the policy predictions that are its ultimate goal (Bicchieri, 1987: 512).

2.7 Conclusion

We distinguished two different questions regarding the possible contribution of rational choice theories to the development of a theory of economic behaviour. The first was whether the theories closely described the process of human choice. The second was whether the theories were *in principle* adequate for explaining and predicting behaviour, i.e. regardless of whether they were true or false. We analysed both queries using the general framework of Savage's theory.

As regards the first issue, we argued that Savage's postulates were predicated on two further basic assumptions that preferences are fixed and ready-made, and that there always exists a description of the world that allows complete disentanglement of values from beliefs. Drawing on the lessons of experimental psychology, we argued that preferences, beliefs and small worlds are constructed. Since different constructions of preferences, beliefs and small worlds lead to different choices, prediction and explanation of behaviour in a dynamic situation demand a theory that explains the *process* of preference, belief and small world formation. We also noted that a description of the world, allowing complete disentanglement of beliefs and values, was hard to find and even if it existed, it would be too cumbersome to be of any use in guiding decisions.

As regards the second issue, our central point was that rational choice theories take small worlds, likelihood judgements and preferences as given, and only state how an ideal agent solves an already well-structured decision problem. Therefore, in predicting behaviour, a very large list of substantive assumptions is needed to specify the agent's view of his choice situation and the decision problem he is trying to solve. These assumptions implicitly assume the answer to the very same question that a theory of behaviour is expected to answer. In fact, by varying the exogenous assumptions in a rational choice model all sides of any economic controversy can be rationalized. Rational choice models answer no substantive economic question; they only repackage what has already been stated in the assumptions. In practice, economists try to select a rational choice model based on econometric analysis of aggregate data. But the econometric approach is unsuitable for settling queries regarding individual behaviour.

Moreover, evaluating policy interventions requires predicting how the agents would react to the intervention. This requires predicting how, in response to the intervention, they modify their view of their choice situation and redefine their decision problem. These queries fall entirely outside the scope of rational choice theories, which take the structure of the choice situation and definition of the decision problem as given. Contrary to common belief, the critical difficulty with rational choice theories is not that they are false. It is that they in principle have very little to contribute to economic theorizing.

The RE hypothesis also fails to overcome the shortcomings of rational choice theories. Economic decisions involve expectations of endogenous variables such as prices. In these cases, the hypothesis is reduced to the requirement of belief consistency across individuals. Yet, there are always many ways in which beliefs can be consistent across people. And so, the hypothesis falls short of specifying people's view of the economy.

These remarks demonstrate that understanding economic behaviour requires a different type of theory of behaviour. It requires a theory that explains how people form preferences, learn about the economy, model their choice situation, define their decision problem, and redefine it as new information arrives. In a nutshell, economics needs a *learning-based* (adaptive) theory of behaviour, not a choice-based theory.

3
'Homo Economicus' as an Intuitive Statistician (1): Model-Free Learning

3.1 Introduction

> This is our key bounded rationality assumption: we back away from the rational expectations assumption, replacing it with the assumption that, in forecasting prices, firms act like econometricians. (Evans and Honkapohja, 2001: 28)

The subjective expected utility theory is a method for solving an already well-defined decision problem. But prediction of behaviour in dynamic situations requires a theory that explains how the agent models his choice situation and defines his decision problem. The subjective expected utility theory, even if true, is inadequate as a theory of economic behaviour. New classical economics have proposed the rational expectations (RE) hypothesis as a way of specifying the agent's view of the economy. The hypothesis identifies the agent's subjective expectations with the mathematical expectations implied by the true economic model, suggesting that he maximizes his expected utility with respect to the true model. So, the new classical paradigm defines economics as the enterprise to derive economic phenomena from two hypotheses: (1) people are expected utility maximizers; and (2) they maximize their expected utility with respect to the true economic model.

Attempts to overcome the theoretical shortcomings of the RE hypothesis have resulted in the re-emergence of the bounded rationality project, originally proposed by Herbert Simon (1955; 1956). While there has been a burst of interest in the topic over the last two decades or more, there is no consensus yet on the definition of bounded rationality or what the critical questions of the project are (Rubinstein, 1998). The general goal of the project is to replace the behavioural assumptions of economics with more realistic assumptions and investigate the implications of the changes for our understanding of the economy (Conslik, 1996). Depending on what behavioural assumptions of economics are withdrawn and what assumptions are retained, various notions of bounded rationality can be defined. Most studies of bounded rationality in new classical economics retain the subjective expected utility maximization principle but replace the RE hypothesis with the assumption that the agent constructs a model from the available economic data, which may not coincide with the true model. Thus, in new classical economics, the project of bounded rationality is a programme to derive observable economic phenomena from the general principles that: (1) the agents are subjective expected utility maximizers; and (2) they maximize their expected utility with respect to models constructed from the available economic data.

Thus understood, the primary issue of the bounded rationality programme is to theorize how the agent learns about the economy and models his choice situation. Several proposals are on offer. The conjecture that has received most attention is that the 'homo economicus' is an *intuitive* statistician; i.e. he intuitively models the economy like a statistician (Arthur *et al.*, 1997: 4). Thomas Sargent, a leading economist from the new classical camp, nicely summarizes this view of the programme as follows:

> I interpret a proposal to build models with 'boundedly rational' agents as a call to retreat from the second piece of rational expectations (mutual consistency of perceptions) by expelling rational agents from our model environments and replacing them with 'artificially intelligent' agents who behave like econometricians. These 'econometricians' theorise, estimate, and adapt in attempting to learn about probability distributions which, under rational expectations, they already know. (Sargent, 1993: 3)

This conjecture will be called the *intuitive statistician* (IS) hypothesis of bounded rationality. A pioneering work on this view of bounded rationality is Bray (1982), who considers an economy in which the agents know the correct model up to a small number of parameters and use the least-squares method to estimate the unknown parameters. Letting the agents live indefinitely, she investigates whether they ever learn the true parameters, which is essential for forming rational expectations. The significance of this question lies in the fact that the learning problem facing the agents in Bray's model economy is not identical with ordinary parameter estimation. As the agents learn about the economy, they modify their expectations and behaviour, which in turn alter the relations being learnt. It is not then possible to use textbook convergence theorems on the long-run behaviour of the least-squares estimator to argue that the agents will asymptotically learn the truth. The question addressed by Bray is different. Her objective is to examine the conditions under which her model economy converges to rational expectations equilibrium, even though feedback from learning can change the relations being learnt. Since Bray's publication, a sizeable number of similar studies have emerged. Bray (1983), Honkapohja (1995), Marrimon (1997), Williamson (1997), Kirman and Salmon (1995), Evans and Honkapohja (2001), Sargent (1993), and Sobel (2000) contain original contributions as well as surveys of the literature on learning in economics.[1]

The relevance of these theoretical studies is unclear for several reasons. These studies usually assume that the agents already know the correct unestimated model of the economy, without any explanation of how the model was learnt in the first place (Sargent, 1993: 166; Sobel, 2000: 256).[2] The assumption that the agents know the correct model is crucial, since starting with a wrong model can make the learning of rational expectations impossible (Nyarko, 1991). Therefore, the convergence results established are contingent on the model economies being studied; they do not generally hold. Furthermore, the results are invariably of an asymptotic nature. But what is needed for evaluating policies are short-run predictions of how agents would revise their view of the economy in response to a policy change, redefine their choice situation, and modify their behaviour. As Keynes put it, in the long run we are all dead. Finally, the dynamics of the economy in these studies come exclusively from people's adjustments of their behaviour. However, the economic structure can change for reasons other than feedback from learning, entirely altering the inference problem facing the agent.

The possibility of convergence to rational expectations equilibrium is not an immediate concern here. The goal is to investigate if the IS hypothesis helps us predict how the agent models his choice situation and defines his decision problem. A positive response to this query presumes that there is a 'tight enough' theory of statistical (scientific) inference, describing how statisticians learn about the world, turn economic data into a model of the economy, and revise the model in the face of new information (Sargent, 1993: 23).[3] Otherwise, the IS hypothesis would not be of much help in predicting how the statistician and thus the agent models their choice situation. And *a fortiori*, no general conclusion could be derived from the hypothesis about the conditions under which an economy converges to equilibrium.

Therefore, a major aim here is to investigate whether there is a 'tight enough' theory of statistical inference. To clarify this query, it is useful to begin with a conjecture about how a statistician models a choice situation. In statistics, the environment is perceived through a collection of measurable features (quantities), which are conceived as realizations of some random variables with a joint probability distribution. The statistician first uses the data on these quantities to estimate their joint probability distribution. He next uses the estimate of the joint distribution to uncover the causal relations among the variables. If the resulting model is inadequate, the initial set of variables is modified, and the two phases of inference repeated.

This description, though imprecise, helps in separating issues relating to inference about probabilities from issues relating to inference about causes, and provides a framework for defining certain important questions about the possibility of establishing a precise theory of statistical learning. This chapter and the one following examine some basic issues relating to learning about the joint probability distribution of a set of variables describing a choice situation. The fifth chapter investigates if there can be a theory that tells us how to move from the joint probability distribution of a set of variables to the causal structure linking the variables.

Several approaches to statistical inference are on offer. The diversity partly arises from disagreements about the nature of probability and partly from alternative methodologies that, given an interpretation of probability, can be adopted to solve inference issues. The debates about the nature of probability are not crucially related to whether there exists a 'tight enough' theory of statistical inference, and will not be taken up here. Instead, two general methodological approaches to statistical modelling are studied, based on the frequency and subjective interpretations of probability. An analysis of these approaches provides an adequate ground for understanding the possibility of a 'tight enough' theory of statistical inference, which is essential for assessing the bounded rationality programme.

The current chapter investigates the possibility of a 'tight enough' theory of statistical learning by looking at non-parametric statistics – a branch of statistics that avoids restrictive non-sample, probabilistic assumptions, and seeks to leave model discovery to data. We use this framework to investigate two queries. The first is whether it is possible with a reasonably sized sample to obtain a good approximation of the joint probability distribution of several variables using non-parametric estimators, or whether substantial non-sample information is required to achieve this. The second is whether there exist inferential procedures that receive observations on a set of variables and yield the 'best' estimate of their joint probability distribution, which is possible given the data. If not, statistical model discovery cannot be left to data, raising the question of where statistical models come from. Both issues are clearly important for the bounded rationality programme.

3.2 Statistical model specification

In statistics, the environment is perceived in terms of a collection of measurable quantities, some of which are known and some of which are not known. The quantities are considered as realizations of random variables with some unknown joint probability distribution. The goal of statistical inference is to infer the values of the unknown quantities from the known quantities, which in theory requires modelling the joint distribution of the random variables. So, an appropriate point of departure for our study is to disentangle problems that arise in modelling the joint distribution of a set of variables, give a precise definition of a statistical model, and highlight the basic issues that a theory of statistical learning has to explain.[4]

A problem in model building, which in a sense precedes any statistical inference, concerns the choice of variables that characterize the environment. Two forms of variable selection should be separated. Sometimes the objective in building a model is to generate accurate *ex ante* and *ex post* predictions of a response variable Y. In that case, variable selection requires specifying some variables that are systematically related to Y, and there is no need for them to be the causes of Y. Alternatively, if the goal is to use the model to analyse the effect of changes in the environment on Y, variable selection requires finding the causes of Y. In either case, variable selection poses difficult questions that must, at least tentatively, be solved before one is able to construct a useful model. The problems in mind concern the appropriate form of the variables, the right method of measurement, the correct level of aggregation, and so forth. The emphasis here is on variable selection in the second sense. A solution to this problem calls for a theory of causal inference, which is taken up in the fifth chapter. For now, we assume that the relevant variables are known, and concentrate on issues relating to learning probabilities. We continue with a description of various issues arising in modelling the joint distribution of a set of variables.[5]

Let us proceed with the simplest case where there is only one variable of interest. Specifically, let Z_t denote the variable and $\mathbf{D} = \{z_1, z_2, ..., z_{T-1}\}$ the past values of Z_t. The task is to predict the future values of Z_t from the known values in $\boldsymbol{D}$. This requires estimating the joint distribution of $\mathbf{Z} = \{Z_1, Z_2, ..., Z_T\}$, which we denote by $p(Z_1, Z_2, ..., Z_T, \Theta)$ or simply $p(\mathbf{Z}, \Theta)$, where Θ is the parameter space defining the distribution. However, the problem of inferring $p(\mathbf{Z}, \Theta)$ from the sample, $\boldsymbol{D}$, alone is ill-posed, since it has no unique solution regardless of the size of the sample. To show this, note that using sequential conditioning the joint distribution $p(\mathbf{Z}, \Theta)$ can be decomposed into a product of univariate marginal and conditional distributions:

$$p(\mathbf{Z}, \Theta) = p(Z_1/\Theta_1) \prod_{t=2}^{T} p(Z_t/z_{t-1}, \ldots, z_1, \Theta_t) \quad \text{for all } \mathbf{z} \in R_{\mathbf{Z}}^{T} \tag{3.1}$$

For each sample size T, the conditional distribution $p(Z_T/z_{T-1}, \ldots, z_1, \Theta_T)$ involves $T-1$ conditioning variables. This means, with each increase in the sample size, the conditional distribution for Z_T changes, making it impossible to infer $p(\mathbf{Z}, \Theta)$ from the data. Spanos terms this phenomenon the *increasing conditioning set* problem (1999: 266).

Furthermore, the notion of conditional density is defined only for specific values of the conditioning variables. Thus, for each $\mathbf{z} \in R_{\mathbf{Z}}^{T}$, estimating $p(\mathbf{Z}, \Theta)$ involves estimating one marginal and $T-1$ different conditional distributions. This is impossible since the number of parameters to be estimated always exceeds the sample size. Spanos calls this phenomenon the *stochastic conditioning* or *heterogeneity* problem (1999: 267).[6] It is therefore necessary to introduce certain simplifying assumptions to make any inference about the target distribution $p(\mathbf{Z}, \Theta)$.

To explain the kind of assumptions necessary for inference from data, note that the increasing conditioning set problem arises because Z_t is allowed to depend on the whole past history of the stochastic process. The problem can be circumvented by restricting the dependence of Z_t on its past. To illustrate, one possibility is to assume that Z_t is *completely* independent of its past. Complete independence reduces the joint distribution $p(\mathbf{Z}, \Theta)$ into a product of univariate distributions:

$$p(\mathbf{Z}, \Theta) = \prod_{t=1}^{T} p(Z_t/\Theta_t) \quad \text{for all } \mathbf{z} \in R_{\mathbf{Z}}^{T} \tag{3.2}$$

Another possibility is to assume that Z_t conditional on its immediate past Z_{t-1} is independent of the rest of the history of the process. This assumption, called the first-order Markov condition, simplifies (3.1) into

$$p(\mathbf{Z}/\Theta) = p(Z_1/\Theta_1) \prod_{t=2}^{T} p(Z_t/z_{t-1}, \Theta_t) \quad \text{for all } \mathbf{z} \in R_{\mathbf{Z}}^{T} \tag{3.3}$$

In any case, inference about $p(\mathbf{Z}, \Theta)$ necessarily requires some independence restriction to cut the link between conditional distribution $p(Z_T/z_{T-1}, \ldots, z_1, \Theta_T)$ and the sample size.

The stochastic conditioning problem arises because conditional densities $p(Z_t/z_{t-1}, \ldots, z_1, \Theta_t)$ are allowed to vary for each possible $\{z_{t-1}, \ldots, z_1\} \in R^{T-1}$. The only way to deal with the problem is to impose some homogeneity restriction across the conditional densities $p(Z_t/z_{t-1}, \ldots, z_1, \Theta_t)$ defined over all possible values $\mathbf{z} \in R_{\mathbf{Z}}^{T}$. The strongest form of homogeneity is *complete* homogeneity, which takes the conditional densities $p(Z_t/z_{t-1}, \ldots, z_1, \Theta_t)$ defined over all $\mathbf{z} \in R_{\mathbf{Z}}^{T}$ to be the same. Complete homogeneity renders the indices in Θ_t, which distinguish different densities $p(Z_t/z_{t-1}, \ldots, z_1, \Theta_t)$, redundant, simplifying (3.2) to

$$p(\mathbf{Z}, \Theta) = \prod_{t=1}^{T} p(Z_t/\Theta) \quad \text{for all } \mathbf{z} \in R_{\mathbf{Z}}^{T} \tag{3.4}$$

A set of completely independent and homogeneous random variables $\{Z_1, Z_2, \ldots, Z_T\}$ forms a random, or an independently and identically distributed (IID), sample. An alternative concept of homogeneity, which will be used later, is *strict stationarity*. The stochastic process $\{Z_t, t \in T\}$ is strictly stationary if

$$p(Z_{t_1}, Z_{t_2}, \ldots, Z_{t_n}; \theta) = p(Z_{t_1+\tau}, Z_{t_2+\tau}, \ldots, Z_{t_n+\tau}; \theta) \quad \text{for any } \tau (t_i + \tau) \in T \tag{3.5}$$

i.e. the joint distribution remains unchanged when each point $1, 2, \ldots, T$ is shifted by a constant τ. When n is equal to 1, strict stationarity is reduced to complete homogeneity.

These two types of assumptions, though necessary, are not sufficient to transform the problem of inferring $p(\mathbf{Z}, \Theta)$ from data into a well-posed problem. With a finite sample, it is also necessary to restrict *a priori* the class of density functions to which $p(Z_t, \Theta)$ may belong to a class F that is smaller than the class of all possible density functions.[7] The proposed distribution family must be small enough to warrant a unique solution. The distributional hypothesis allows restating (3.4) as

$$p(\mathbf{Z}, \Theta) = \prod_{t=1}^{T} f(Z_t/\theta) \quad \text{for all } \mathbf{z} \in R_{\mathbf{Z}}^{T} \tag{3.6}$$

The independence, homogeneity and distributional assumptions reduce the inference problem to the task of finding a distribution $f(Z_t/\theta)$ from the distribution family F that best fits the data. If the non-sample assumptions are appropriate, and if the sample size is adequately large, then $f(Z_t/\theta)$ can be reliably estimated from the data.

In light of this analysis, we may define a statistical model as a set of assumptions drawn from the three categories of independence (I), homogeneity (H), and distribution (D) hypotheses (Spanos, 2000: 239). To make this definition more precise, several further remarks about the basic assumptions are in order.

First, these assumptions are *basic*. That is, once we choose the assumptions for a vector of observables $\boldsymbol{Z}$, no other assumption is needed to specify the marginal and conditional distributions of the variables in $\boldsymbol{Z}$, the regression function of any of the variables on the others, or the distribution of the error terms. All these are determined by the three assumptions made about $\boldsymbol{Z}$. As an example, consider a bivariate random variable $\mathbf{Z}_t = (X_t, Y_t)$, with data being $\mathbf{D} = \{(x_t, y_t)\}_{t=1}^{N}$. Suppose $\mathbf{Z}_t$ is randomly distributed and has a bivariate normal distribution. Then we have the following model:

Bivariate normal model

A_1: Data distribution: $\begin{pmatrix} Y \\ X \end{pmatrix} \sim N\left(\begin{pmatrix} \mu_Y \\ \mu_X \end{pmatrix}\begin{pmatrix} \sigma_Y^2 & \sigma_{XY} \\ \sigma_{XY} & \sigma_X^2 \end{pmatrix}\right)$

A_2: Independence: $(\mathbf{Z}_1, \mathbf{Z}_2, \ldots, \mathbf{Z}_N)$is C-Independent

A_3: Homogeneity: $(\mathbf{Z}_1, \mathbf{Z}_2, \ldots, \mathbf{Z}_N)$ is C-Homogeneous

The model completely defines the marginal distribution of X, the conditional distribution of X given Y, the marginal distribution of Y, and the conditional distribution of Y given X. It also determines the algebraic form of the regression function of Y on X, and X on Y. If Y is the response variable, the model implies (Spanos, 1986, ch.22):

$$X \sim N(\mu_x, \sigma_x^2)$$
$$(Y/X = x) \sim N(\mu^*, \sigma^2)$$
$$\mu^* = E(Y/X = x) = \beta_0 + \beta_1 x$$
$$\beta_0 = \mu_y - \beta_1 \mu_x; \beta_1 = \sigma_{xy}/\sigma_x^2; \sigma^2 = \sigma_y^2 - \sigma_{xy}^2/\sigma_x^2$$

Second, these assumptions cannot be combined arbitrarily. An assumption from one of these categories can restrict possible choices from the other two categories. For example, the choice of a first-order Markov condition for $\mathbf{Z} = (X_t, Y_t)$ and a bivariate normal distribution are not compatible. The independence assumption necessitates a multivariate distribution. Finally, all these assumptions are of a probabilistic nature; all have to do with the distribution of the observables.

We can now more precisely redefine a statistical model as a set of *internally consistent* probabilistic assumptions drawn from the three categories of independence, homogeneity and distribution hypotheses (Spanos and McGuirk, 2001). From this perspective, statistical model specification involves positing *a priori* appropriate independence, homogeneity and distribution assumptions to make inference from data possible.

To sum up, any inference from data demands three types of assumptions – a model. In theory, once these assumptions are introduced, the inference problem is reduced to parameter estimation, for which there are usually routine procedures. So, the most challenging aspect of inference (learning) from data consists in model specification. And, as a consequence, the most immediate task facing a theory of statistical inference (learning) is to explain where the models come from, and how to go about selecting the three basic assumptions in any inference problem.

3.3 Non-parametric statistical inference

We find two responses to these queries in theoretical statistics. This chapter analyses a response found in *non-parametric* statistics. The concern in this branch of statistics has mostly been with estimating a density (regression) function from a random sample, and less attention has been paid to inference from non-random samples. We begin by assuming a random sample to spell out the core idea of non-parametric inference, and then explain how it can be extended to inference from non-random samples. Having done so, we define the IS hypothesis within the framework of non-parametric statistics, linking the definition to the economic literature on learning.

3.3.1 The basic idea

Suppose $\mathbf{D} = \{x_i\}_{i=1}^N$ is a random sample from an unknown distribution with density function $f(x)$ and that the concern is to use the data to estimate $f(x)$. This requires restricting *a priori* the class of density functions to which $f(x)$ belongs to a class smaller than the class of all possible density functions. In ordinary (parametric) statistics, inference begins by assuming that $f(x)$ belongs to a particular distribution family defined by a small number of parameters, e.g. the exponential family. Non-parametric inference avoids starting with such a restrictive distribution assumption. Instead, it assumes only that $f(x)$ belongs to the general class of *smooth* functions. Intuitively, smoothness means that, for each x in a 'small' neighbourhood of point x_0, $f(x)$ is almost the same as $f(x_0)$ and therefore a small shift away from x_0 to x does not greatly alter $f(x_0)$.[8] The smoothness restriction allows estimating $f(.)$ at each point x_0 by averaging over the observations falling in a 'small' neighbourhood around it. The degree (strength) of smoothing is determined by the size of the neighbourhood over which averaging takes place. A larger neighbourhood size implies a greater degree of smoothing, and hence a smaller class of functions to which $f(x)$ is *a priori* thought to belong.

Non-parametric inference ties the strength of smoothing, or equivalently the neighbourhood size over which something takes place, to the size N of the sample. As the sample size grows, the size of the neighbourhood is reduced so as to enable the data to reveal the details of $f(x)$. In the limit, when the sample size approaches infinity, the neighbourhood size is forced to zero so that the shape of the density function is determined by the data alone. In this way, non-parametric inference aims to do away with the need for specifying the functional form of the density function, and to base that decision on the data alone. If successful, non-parametric inference turns model building (here, finding the right distribution assumption) into an integral part of inference from data, and evades mis-specification.[9]

The reason for naming this approach 'non-parametric' should be clear now. It is called non-parametric because it avoids beginning with the assumption that $f(x)$ belongs to a distribution family defined by a finite number of parameters. Since the approach leaves the determination of the functional form of $f(x)$ to the data, non-parametric procedures are also called 'model-free' or 'distribution-free' procedures.

3.3.2 The naïve estimator

Non-parametric statistics has flourished over the last three decades, producing a remarkable list of procedures for model-free inference. Here, to set the stage for our discussion and to give a brief glimpse of the field, we review a well-known group of procedures for local averaging that has evolved from attempts to improve on an estimation method called the *simple* or *naïve* estimator (Silverman, 1986: 12).[10]

It follows from the definition of a probability density that if variable X has density $f(x)$, then

$$f(x_0) = \lim_{h \to 0} \left[\frac{P(x_0 - h < X < x_0 + h)}{2h} \right] \tag{3.7}$$

For any given h, the naïve estimator estimates $f(.)$ at point x_0 by replacing the probability $P(x_0 - h < X < x_0 + h)$ with the proportion of the observations falling in the interval $(x_0 - h, x_0 + h)$.[10] That is

$$\hat{f}(x_0) = \frac{\sum_{i=1}^{N} I[X_i \in (x_0 - h, x_0 + h)]}{2Nh} \tag{3.8}$$

where $I(.)$ is the indicator function and parameter h controls the neighbourhood size for averaging. When the support of $f(x)$ is densely populated with data and h is sufficiently small, estimator (3.8) is likely to generate a reliable estimate of the density function.

The naïve estimator has several drawbacks. To begin with, it assigns equal weights to all observations in the interval $(x_0 - h, x_0 + h)$, thus allowing them to contribute *equally* to the estimate $\hat{f}(x_0)$. But it is plausible to assume that $f(x)$ is more similar to $f(x_0)$ for points which are closer to x_0 than those further away. A more accurate estimate of $f(x)$ at point x_0 can be obtained by giving greater weights to data points closer to x_0. The estimator also takes the width of the interval $(x_0 - h, x_0 + h)$ as fixed across the entire sample space. Consequently, it has the tendency to miss the details of the density function in the main part of the distribution where the data are plentiful and create noise in the tail area where the data are sparse. This suggests that the estimator can be improved by a procedure that adjusts the width of the smoothing interval to match the local density of the data.

3.3.3 Kernel-based estimators

These considerations have led to the development of numerous estimators that outperform the naïve estimator. Let us restate the naïve estimator employing a weight function w:

$$\hat{f}(x_0) = \frac{1}{Nh} \sum_{i=1}^{N} w\left(\frac{x_0 - X_i}{h}\right) \tag{3.9}$$

$$w(z) = \tfrac{1}{2} \text{ if } |z| < 1 \text{ and } 0 \text{ otherwise.}$$

It is clear that the naïve estimator assigns equal weight to every point in $(x_0 - h, x_0 + h)$. One way to improve on (3.9), as hinted, is to replace $w(z)$ with a function that assigns weights to points in $(x_0 - h, x_0 + h)$ so that points closer to x_0 receive higher weights while those further from it receive lower weights. A convenient class of such functions, termed *kernel* functions, is the family of unimodal functions centred at zero that decline in either direction at a rate controlled by a scale parameter. A common kernel function is the normal density function $K(z) = (2\pi)^{-1/2}\exp(2^{-1}z)$, where $z \in [-1/2, 1/2]$. In general, let K be a bounded function that integrates to one and is symmetric around zero. Substituting $K(z)$ for $w(z)$ in (3.9) yields the general class of kernel estimators, defined by

$$\hat{f}(x_0) = \frac{1}{Nh}\sum_{i=1}^{N} K\left(\frac{x_0 - X_i}{h}\right) \tag{3.10}$$

where the scale parameter h is called the *bandwidth, smoothing* parameter, or *window width*. A large h places a greater weight on observations far apart from x_0 whereas a small h allows only observations very close to x_0 to influence the estimate. If kernel function K is a probability density function, the estimate $\hat{f}(x)$ is also a probability density function. Estimator (3.10) improves on (3.9) but still takes the bandwidth as fixed across the x-region. The so-called adaptive kernel estimator improves on (3.10) by varying h in accordance with the local density of the data. To decide on the window width at each data point, 'an initial (fixed bandwidth) density estimate is computed to get an idea of the density at the data points'. This pilot estimate is then used to adjust 'the size of the bandwidth over the data points when computing a new kernel estimate' (Silverman, 1986: 100–10).[11]

The kernel density estimator (3.10) is generalized to multivariate cases. Let $\boldsymbol{Z}$ be a vector of variables with p elements. The p-variate kernel estimator with kernel K and bandwidth h is defined by

$$\hat{f}(\mathbf{z}) = \frac{1}{Nh^p}\sum_{i=1}^{N} K\left(\frac{(\mathbf{z}_0 - \mathbf{Z}_i)}{h}\right) \tag{3.11}$$

K can be any radially symmetric unimodal p-variate probability density function such as the standard p-variate normal density function. A common method for multivariate non-parametric density estimation is the product kernel method that replaces p-dimensional kernel K in (3.11) with a product of p one-dimensional kernels. In the bivariate case, where $\mathbf{Z} = (X, Y)$, the bivariate product kernel estimator is given by

$$\hat{f}(x, y) = \frac{1}{Nh^2}\sum_{i=1}^{N} K\left(\frac{x - x_i}{h}\right) K\left(\frac{y - y_i}{h}\right)^{12} \tag{3.12}$$

An important aspect of a multivariate probability distribution is the regression function of each of the variables under study on the remaining variables. This describes how the mean value of the variable in question, conditioned on the values of the rest of the variables, varies. The theoretical regression function of Y on X is given by

$$r(x) = E(Y|X = x) = \int yf(y|x)dy = \frac{\int yf(x,y)dy}{\int f(x,y)dy} \tag{3.13}$$

Substituting the density estimate (3.12) into (3.13) yields the kernel regression estimator:

$$\hat{f}(x_0) = \frac{\frac{1}{Nh}\sum_{i=1}^{N} K(\frac{x_0 - x_i}{h})}{\frac{1}{Nh}\sum_{i=1}^{N} K(\frac{x_0 - x_i}{h})} y_i \tag{3.14}$$

Since (3.14) is *linear in the observations* $\{y_i\}$, it can simply be written as (Scott, 1992: 220):

$$\hat{f}(x_i) = \mathbf{W}(h)\mathbf{y} \tag{3.15}$$

where $\mathbf{W}(h)$ is known as the smoother matrix, and $\mathbf{y}$ is the vector of observed response values. $\mathbf{W}(h)$ is an $n \times n$ matrix whose elements w_{ij} denote the weight assigned to point x_j in estimating the target function at point x_i. As is evident from (3.13), estimating a density function or a regression function is theoretically the same.

Non-parametric estimator (3.11) (or, 3.14) is consistent. Consistency means that the estimator approximates the target density function arbitrarily closely as the sample size approaches infinity, regardless of the form of the function. A proof for the consistency of (3.14) is found in Yatchew (1998). Therefore, non-parametric statistics theoretically provides a way of learning a density (regression) function from random data, without having to posit *a priori* a parametric distribution family.

In practice, data is not usually known to be random, making the choice of independence and homogeneity assumptions as crucial as the choice of a distribution family. An issue for non-parametric inference is how to generalize model-free inference to non-random samples. There is no non-parametric algorithm for selecting independence and homogeneity assumptions. The only way to use non-parametric inference for selecting these assumptions is to follow a hypothetic-deductive method. That is, one has to conjecture an independence or homogeneity condition, and non-parametrically test it against the data. Consider the first-order Markov condition which implies that $p(Z_t/z_{t-1}, z_{t-2}) = p(Z_t/z_{t-1})$. One can proceed by hypothetically assuming that the vectors (Z_t, Z_{t-1}, Z_{t-2}) and (Z_t, Z_{t-1}) are randomly distributed to non-parametrically estimate the probabilities $p(Z_t/z_{t-1}, z_{t-2})$ and $p(Z_t/z_{t-1})$. The estimates can be used to check if the equality holds. In theory, this proposal extends model-free inference to non-sample data. But the manoeuvre, as will be seen, encounters intractable practical problems.

3.4 The homo economicus as a non-parametric statistician

While the flourishing of non-parametric statistics is relatively recent compared to ordinary statistics, there have been a good number of attempts by economists to model the 'homo economicus' as a non-parametric statistician. Historically, Bray's work (1982) can be viewed as an early proposal to view the agent as a non-parametric statistician. She studies an economy in which the agents know the supply curve $p_t = a + bE(p_{t+1}) + u_t$ but must form expectations $E(p_{t+1})$ to plug into it. She conjectures that they form expectations $E(p_{t+1})$ by taking the average of past prices, which is equivalent to learning with the naïve estimator. Commenting on Bray's work, Lucas suggests that 'learning by averaging' seems to be a plausible conjecture about human learning (1986: 236). Sargent also considers using histogram and kernel estimators for modelling learning behaviour (1993: 106–7).

Chen and White (1998) criticize early works on learning in economics such as Bray and Savin (1986), which assume that the agents already know the correct unestimated model of the economy without any explanation as to how the model was learnt in the first place. To eliminate this shortcoming, Chen and White model the agents as non-parametric statisticians who utilize an *online* kernel regression estimator to learn about the economy. To explain what this means, note that the above estimators, including (3.14), are all defined from the whole data, meaning that the estimate must be recomputed from the whole sample for every newly arriving observation. In learning situations of interest in economics, data arrives as an ongoing sequence $\{(x_1, y_1), (x_2, y_2), \ldots\}$. It is thus more plausible that the agent works with an estimator that at any time t can be represented as a function of the estimator at time $t-1$ and the new pair of observations (x_t, y_t). Interestingly, estimator (3.14) can be reformulated to achieve this (Härdle, 1990: 66):

$$\hat{f}_{N+1}(x_0) = \hat{f}_N(x_0) + (hN)^{-1} K_{N+1h}(x - x_{N+1})(y_{N+1} - \hat{f}_N(x_0)) \qquad (3.16)$$

which dispenses with the need for re-computing the estimate from the whole sample each time. With this proposal, the person uses the data available at time t to obtain $\hat{f}_N(x)$ and uses the estimate to make predictions necessary for his future decisions. As new data comes in, he uses rule (3.16) to update the estimate.[13] Chen and White establish the necessary and sufficient conditions under which regression estimator (3.16) asymptotically converges to the true regression function in spite of the fact that feedback from learning may alter the relation being learnt.[14]

This chapter follows these economists in viewing the economy as a society of non-parametric statisticians, and investigates whether the conjecture helps shed light on some critical issues in theoretical economics. Specifically, we investigate whether agents in such a society can learn the probabilistic features of their environment from ordinarily available data samples, whether it is possible to predict what the agents think given the data generated by the economy, and finally whether the conjecture helps us understand how the agents revise their view of the economy in the face of a new policy.

3.5 Intrinsic limitations of model-free inference

Non-parametric estimators are asymptotically consistent, in that they uncover the target function as the number of observations approaches infinity. The asymptotic results teach us how learning is possible, in principle, and provide some general insights into the working of non-parametric estimators and what must be done, as the sample size increases, to obtain an accurate estimate (White, 1992: 121). In reality, we only have access to a finite and usually small number of observations, and since the economy changes over time, remote past data are uninformative. Thus, the relevant question for economics is not whether there are model-free estimators that can asymptotically discover the truth or whether the opinions in a society of statisticians asymptotically converge to truth. The relevant question is whether it is possible with a 'reasonably sized' sample to learn a 'good' approximation of a relatively complex target function using non-parametric methods. This section argues that accurate approximation of 'complex' functions using non-parametric techniques is practically impossible. Even a 'crude' model-free approximation of a function relating several variables requires a gigantically large sample that is rarely available in practice. The argument is inspired by a critique of the claims surrounding the theory of neural networks given in Geman *et al.* (1992).

3.5.1 The bias–variance decomposition

Essential for investigating the limitations of non-parametric methods with 'reasonably sized' samples is a precise definition of what is meant by a 'good' or 'accurate' estimate. This can be achieved by considering non-parametric estimation of a simple regression function. Suppose we are given a random data set $\{(x_i, y_i)\}_{i=1}^{N}$, and interested in estimating the regression function $f(x)$ in

$$y = f(x) + \varepsilon \tag{3.17}$$

where ε has mean zero and is independent of X. An objective in searching for an estimate of $f(x)$ is to predict the value of Y when only x is known. A possible way to define the accuracy of an estimate is in terms of the accuracy of its predictions. A measure of predictive accuracy is the mean-squared prediction error (*MPE*):

$$MPE = E[y - \hat{f}(x)]^2 \tag{3.18}$$

which provides a measure of the accuracy of the estimate $\hat{f}(x)$ when X takes value x and Y takes value y. The expectation $E(.)$ is taken with respect to the joint probability distribution of Y and X. The error (3.18) can be decomposed into two distinct elements (White, 1992: 97–8):

$$MPE = E[(y - f(x)]^2 + E[\hat{f}(x) - f(x)]^2 \qquad (3.19)$$

The first term on the right-hand side is the variance of Y at point x. It is independent of the estimate and hence plays no role in evaluating accuracy. The second term gives the mean-squared distance between the estimate and the regression function at point x, providing a natural measure of approximation accuracy. The term is known as the *mean-squared estimation* (MSE) error:

$$MSE = E[\hat{f}(x) - f(x)]^2 \qquad (3.20)$$

where the expectation is taken with respect to $p(x)$. From this viewpoint, a 'good' approximation refers to an estimate that yields a 'negligible' MSE error. Since the estimate $\hat{f}(x)$ depends on the data, it can be viewed as a realization of a random variable defined over all samples D of fixed size N that can possibly be drawn from the system. This means we can define the mean and variance of the estimate. Letting $E[\hat{f}(x)]$ be the mean of $\hat{f}(x)$ taken over all hypothetical samples D of fixed size N, the MSE error can be decomposed into two distinct components (Geman *et al.*, 1992: 10):

$$\begin{aligned}
E[(\hat{f}(x) - f(x))^2] \\
&= E\{[(\hat{f}(x) - E[\hat{f}(x)]) + (E[\hat{f}(x)] - f(x))]^2\} \\
&= E[(\hat{f}(x) - E[f(x)])^2] + E[(E[\hat{f}(x)] - f(x))^2] \\
&\quad + 2E[(\hat{f}(x) - E[\hat{f}(x)]) \times (E[\hat{f}(x)] - f(x))] \\
&= E[(\hat{f}(x) - E[\hat{f}(x)])^2] + (E[\hat{f}(x)] - f(x))^2 \\
&\quad + 2[E[\hat{f}(x)] - E[\hat{f}(x)])] \times [E[\hat{f}(x)] - f(x)] \\
&= E[(\hat{f}(x) - E[\hat{f}(x)])^2] + (E[\hat{f}(x)] - f(x))^2 \qquad (3.21)
\end{aligned}$$

The first term is the *variance* of the estimate at point x, measuring the dispersion of $\hat{f}(x)$ around its mean. The second is the *squared bias* of the estimate at point x, giving the squared distance between the mean estimate value $E[\hat{f}(x)]$ and the regression function at point x. Since both the variance and bias components contribute to the MSE error, they must approach to zero for a good approximation or accurate learning to occur. Therefore, the question posed earlier is in fact whether it is possible in interesting inference problems to make both the squared bias and variance 'small' with 'reasonably' sized samples, using non-parametric procedures such as kernel regression estimators (Geman *et al.*, 1992: 44).

3.5.2 The bias–variance trade-off

The estimate (estimator) $\hat{f}(x)$ depends on three factors: the estimator family (say, the kernel family); the smoothing parameter (or parameters); and the data. By altering any of these elements it is possible to vary the estimate, and hence control the MSE error. To answer our question, it is enough to consider the effect of varying the smoothing level and the data. We begin by examining the effect of varying the smoothing level on the squared bias and variance components of the MSE error.

Increasing smoothing reduces the variance part of the MSE error. In the extreme case, if each neighbourhood (bandwidth) is so chosen to cover the whole x-region, the kernel estimate becomes equivalent to the average of the response values everywhere. In that case, the variance part of the MSE error is at its lowest possible value, namely zero. However, when each bandwidth is so chosen to cover the whole x-region, the estimator always yields a straight line, which is most likely quite different from the target function. In that case, the response value y corresponding to each x will be significantly different from the estimate, leading to a substantial bias (Hastie and Tibshirani, 1990: 17). An attempt at eliminating variance by increasing smoothing can cause an increase in the bias component that may be greater than the reduction in MSE error obtained by reducing the variance. Decreasing variance by increasing smoothing does not necessarily reduce the overall error; it may in fact increase it.

Conversely, decreasing smoothing reduces the squared bias part of the MSE error. In the extreme case, if each neighbourhood is so chosen to contain only one observation the kernel estimator interpolates the data. In that case, the squared bias term achieves its lowest possible value at the data points and, if the target function is smooth, is also small in the close neighbourhoods of the points. The reduction in the bias term, however, can sharply increase the variance of the estimator, since the estimate at each point x would most likely be different from its average value (Bishop, 1995: 336; Hastie and Tibshirani, 1990: 17). As a general rule, then, for a fixed sample, an attempt at reducing the squared bias part by decreasing smoothing could increase the variance part of the error, thus increasing the overall value of the error.

These considerations about the effect of varying the smoothing level, which can be made formally precise, point to a trade-off between the squared bias and variance components of the MSE error. For a fixed sample, the squared bias component can be reduced at the expense of increasing the variance factor and the variance factor can be reduced at the expense of increasing the bias component (Silverman, 1986: 35). Geman *et al.* (1992) term this trade-off the bias–variance dilemma.

Given that this dilemma plays a central role in the analysis to follow, it is worth illustrating it with a simple example, which we adopt from Wahba and Wold (1975). Suppose $x \in [0, 3]$ and that y is related to x by

$$y = f(x) + \varepsilon \tag{3.22}$$

where $f(x) = 4.26(e^{-x} - 4e^{-2x} + 3e^{-3x})$ and ε is distributed as $N(0,0.2)$. We generate 100 data points from the model to investigate the effect of varying the smoothing level on the performance of a kernel regressor. If the bandwidth is so chosen to cover the whole x-region (e.g. if it is set at 6) as in Figure 3.1, the estimate is a straight line, significantly different from the true function. Alternatively, if the bandwidth is reduced to 0.01 as in Figure 3.2, the estimator interpolates the data, and again the estimate drastically differs from the true function. When the bandwidth is set to an intermediate value of 0.7 as in Figure 3.3, the variance and bias of the estimate are reduced, and the estimator closely approximates the function.

An immediate consequence of the bias and variance dilemma is that, given a data set, smoothing cannot be reduced arbitrarily. Quite the opposite, for a fixed sample, there is a unique (set of) smoothing parameter value (values) that ensures an optimal trade-off between the squared bias and variance in the sense of minimizing MSE error (Friedman, 1994: 32). The optimal value fixes the class of functions that the estimator can approximate given the data, and hence fixes the minimum bias possible. If the optimal neighbourhood size relative to the data is, for instance, the whole x-region, the estimator will only be able to approximate straight lines. In that case, if the true function is considerably different from a straight line, the estimator will produce a highly biased estimate. With a finite sample, there is essentially no difference between parametric and non-parametric estimators; they both search through a proper subset of the class of all possible functions (White, 1992: 117).

The bias–variance dilemma can be resolved only by increasing the sample size. As the sample size increases, and the input variable space (x-region) is increasingly densely populated with data everywhere, smoothing can be reduced without increasing variance. And, as smoothing is reduced, the estimator becomes able to search over an increasingly larger class of functions, thus reducing the chance of bias. To illustrate the point, let us return to the above example. This time, we hold the level of smoothing fixed but vary the sample size. If we simulate a sample of 100 observations from the model, and fit a model using a kernel regressor with bandwidth 0.03, the result is a highly variable curve significantly different from the target function (Figure 3.4). If the sample size is increased to 1,000 data points, the same smoothing level yields a much smoother curve, with lower bias and variance (Figure 3.5). When the sample size is increased to 10,000 observations, we get an estimate that closely matches the regression function (Figure 3.6). By increasing the sample size, it is possible to reduce both bias and variance simultaneously.

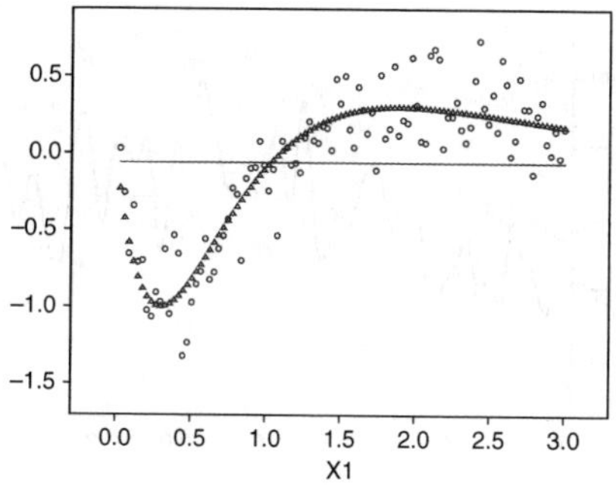

Figure 3.1 Kernal smoothing (bandwidth = 6.0)

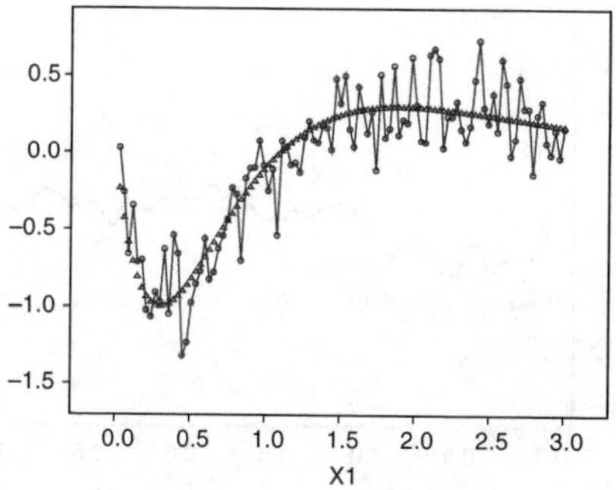

Figure 3.2 Kernal smoothing (bandwidth = 0.01)

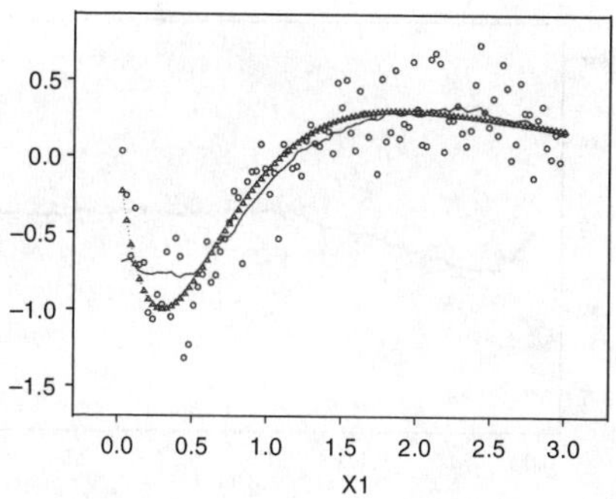

Figure 3.3 Kernal smoothing (bandwidth = 0.7)

Note: The thick curve shows the true regression function whereas the thin line in Figure 3.1, the wiggly curve in Figure 3.2, and the thin curve in Figure 3.3 show the estimates.

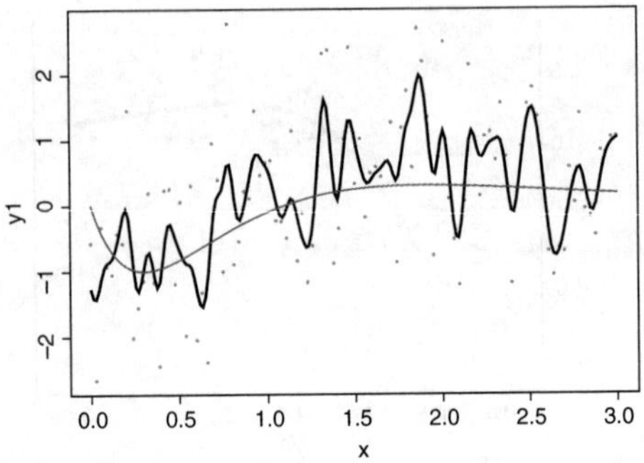

Figure 3.4 Kernal regression estimate, h=0.03, N=101

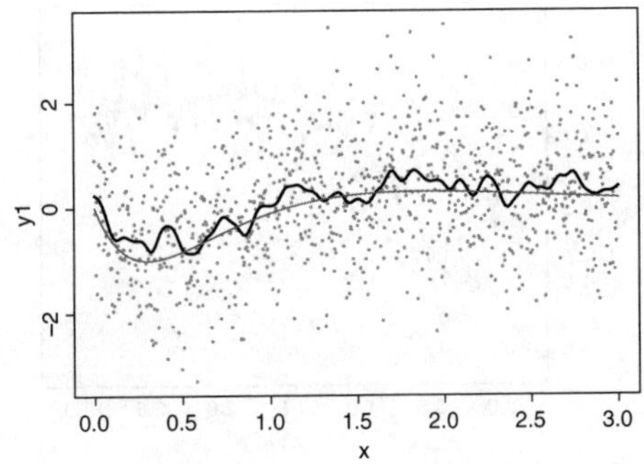

Figure 3.5 Kernal regression estimate, h=0.03, N=1001

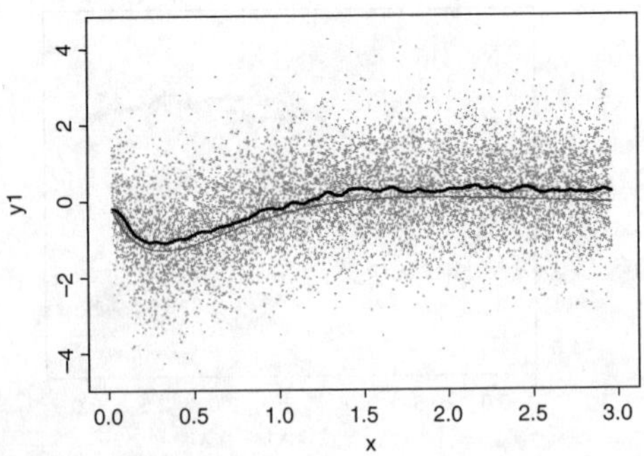

Figure 3.6 Kernal regression estimate, h=0.03, N=10001

Note: The smooth curve shows the true regression function whereas the wiggly curves show the estimates.

The key to driving both the bias and variance components of the MSE error of local averaging (fitting) estimators towards zero is to populate the input variable space (x-region) densely with data. If this turns out to be impossible, because of the bias–variance trade-off, non-parametric estimators can only search through a proper and most likely small subset of the class of all possible functions. In that case, they may not be able to produce an accurate approximation of the target function.

3.5.3 The curse of dimensionality

Although it may be possible to densely populate low-dimensional input variable spaces (i.e. one or two predictors) with ordinarily available samples, this is impossible in high-dimensional spaces due to the *curse of dimensionality* problem (Bellman, 1961). Recall that the basic idea of local averaging (or fitting) is to divide the input variable space ($\mathbf{x}$-region) into a number of cells and take the average of the responses in each cell as the estimate of the regression (or density) function in that cell. The curse of dimensionality refers to the fact that the number of cells increases exponentially with the dimension of the input variable space (i.e. the number of regressors). In general, if d indicates the dimension of $\mathbf{X}$, ($\mathbf{x} \in R^d$), and each regressor coordinate is divided into M divisions, the total number of cells will be M^d. Since each cell must contain some data points to make any inference, the number of data points required for local averaging also grows exponentially with the dimension of the input variable space. For example, if M is taken to be 10, and ten observations are required for densely populating each cell, a sample of 10×10^2 observations will be needed to populate densely a two dimensional input variable space (two regressors). On the same ground, a sample of 10×10^{10} observations will be required to equally populate a ten-dimensional input variable space (ten regressors). Therefore, the curse of dimensionality makes it impossible to adequately densely populate high-dimensional input variable spaces with ordinarily available samples.

To provide more insight into the problem, suppose we have 10,000 data points uniformly distributed over the ten-dimensional unit cube $[0, 1]^{10}$. A bandwidth of diameter 0.2 in each regressor coordinate results in a volume of $0.2^{10} \approx 1.02 \times 10^{-7}$ for each cell, and the expected number of observations in each cell is approximately 1×10^{-3}. Obviously, no local averaging is possible with this number of data points. Alternatively, if we increase the neighbourhood size to include at least ten observations, the bandwidth must cover at least 0.5 of each coordinate. In that case, averaging is carried out over at least half of the range along each coordinate and is no longer local. The lesson is that in high-dimensional spaces, if the neighbourhood is 'local' (i.e. small), it is almost surely empty, and if the neighbourhood is not empty, it is not 'local'.[15]

Moreover, to drive both elements of the MSE error of a local averaging estimator towards zero, which is necessary for it to arbitrarily closely approximate the target function, it is necessary to increasingly divide the input variable space into smaller and smaller cells, and, in parallel, the number of data points in each cell must increasingly grow larger and larger. In the limit, the number of cells M and the number of data points in each cell must approach infinity to ensure a good approximation. This means that densely populating an even low-dimensional input variable space (say with four or five regressors) demands an astronomically large sample, which is impossible to achieve in practice or at least in situations of interest in economics.

Taken together, the curse of dimensionality and the bias–variance trade-off imply that an astronomically large sample is required to arbitrarily closely approximate a target function even for moderate numbers of regressors (say four or five). Ordinarily available samples in situations of economic interest do not even allow for a crude approximation of a high-dimensional function using local averaging techniques. This intrinsic limitation of model-free inference reveals that even with an unusually large sample the agent is not able to learn accurately the probabilistic relations characterizing his choice situation from data alone. Learning the probabilistic relations of a choice situation calls for substantive probabilistic non-sample information.

3.5.4 Defeating the curse of dimensionality

The impossibility of local averaging (or fitting) in high-dimensional input spaces has prompted an intensive search for non-parametric inference methods that build an approximation of a high-dimensional function that takes the form of expansions in low-dimensional (univariate) functions. If a complex high-dimensional function could be approximated with a sum or product of low-dimensional (univariate) functions, non-parametric inference would only involve estimation of low-dimensional functions. In that case, the curse of dimensionality would raise no intrinsic issue, and the argument for the impossibility of model-free learning of high-dimensional functions would break down at a closer scrutiny. To explain that this is not really the case, and to draw some further important methodological conclusions about the boundaries of model-free learning, it is useful to look briefly at the project pursuit regression method developed by Friedman and Stuelzle (1981). The method is directly aimed at extending the idea of non-parametric inference to high-dimensional data.[16]

In multivariate regression analysis the objective is to model the conditional expectation of response variable Y given predictor variables $\mathbf{X} = \{X_1, \ldots X_p\}$ using a sample $\{y_i, x_{1i}, ..., x_{pi}\}_1^N$. The data are assumed to have come from a system described by

$$y = f(x_1, \ldots, x_p) + \varepsilon \tag{3.23}$$

The projection pursuit regression (PPR) estimator models the conditional expectation of Y given $\mathbf{X}$, $f(\mathbf{x})$, as a sum of functions of linear combinations of the predictors, i.e.

$$\hat{f}(\mathbf{x}) = \alpha_0 + \sum_{m=1}^{M} g_m(z_m) \qquad z_m = \sum_{i=1}^{p} \alpha_{mi} x_i \tag{3.24}$$

where the univariate variable z_m denotes a projection of the vector $\boldsymbol{X}$ onto a one-dimensional space, and g_m is a univariate smooth function, called basis function. The PPR estimator constructs an approximation $\hat{f}(\mathbf{x})$ in an iterative manner. It begins by setting α_0 equal to $\bar{y}$, the average of the observed responses, and computes the residuals $r_{1i} = y_i - \bar{y}$. Next, it assigns some initial values to projection parameters α_{1i} to define a univariate variable $z_1 = \sum_{i=1}^{p} \alpha_{1i} x_i$ and regresses r_{1i} on z_{1i} using some univariate non-parametric estimator. It updates the parameters α_{1i} by minimizing the squared residuals sum $\Delta = \sum_{(r_{1i} - \hat{g}(z_{1i}))^2}$ over all possible choices of α_{1i}, inserts the optimal values of α_{1i} into $z_1 = \sum_{i=1}^{p} \alpha_{1i} x_i$, and re-estimates $\hat{g}_1(z_1)$. Again, it uses the new estimate to update α_{1i} and repeats the process until no further reduction of the sum of residuals can be achieved. It then adds the final estimate $\hat{g}_1(z_1)$ to $\bar{y}$ and computes the new residuals $r_{2i} = [y_i - (\bar{y} + \hat{g}_1(z_1)]$. These steps are repeated to obtain a second basis function $\hat{g}_2(z_2)$, and the process of constructing new basis functions is continued until no further reduction can be achieved in the residuals. Diaconis and Shahshahani (1984) show that if the number of basis functions M in equation (3.24) is let to grow to infinity, the function can arbitrarily closely approximate any continuous function. That is, with an arbitrarily large number of basis functions M, the PPR estimator can approximate any continuous target function arbitrarily closely.[17]

This consistency result is reassuring but is of not much help in practice. The number of basis functions M in a projection pursuit regression estimator plays the same role as the smoothing parameter in the kernel estimators. If M is taken to be small, the estimator can only search through a small subset of continuous functions, which may neither include the target function nor a good approximation thereof, and will therefore be biased. If M is taken to be large, the estimate interpolates the data and will be highly variable. Again, the bias–variance trade-off restricts the number of basis functions that can be included in a projection pursuit estimate given a data set, thus limiting the class of functions that the estimator can approximate in practice. As a result, the sample size must be adequately large to include an adequately large number of basis functions so as to ensure a good approximation.

Moreover, as Huber (1985) points out, there are simple functions that cannot be approximated by a sum of a finite number of additive basis functions. An example is $f(x_1, x_2) = e^{x_1 x_2}$. Any use of projection pursuit regression in practice assumes that a good estimation of the target function can be obtained with a small number of basis functions. There is, however, no *a priori* reason to take this for granted. To justify the assumption, some substantive knowledge about the target function is essential.

3.5.5 The loss of interpretability

There is another important aspect of non-parametric inference in high-dimensional data that is worth noting. In practice, as explained, any extension of non-parametric inference to high-dimensional input spaces takes the form of expansions in low-dimensional functions (Barron and Xiangyu 1991: 80). And, a good estimate may require a large number of basis functions. In that case, the estimate is a model like (3.24) with a large number of basis functions g_m. Such a model gives no clear description of how each regressor X_i *separately* relates to the response variable Y; each regressor X_i relates to Y in a very complex way (Hastie and Tibshirani 1994: 67). As a result, even if it were known that $X_1, \ldots, X_p$ are causes of Y and have no latent common causes with Y, it would still be impossible to use the model to trace the distinct effect of each X_i on Y. The model is useful only for *ex ante* and *ex post* predictions; it is not suitable for analysis of actions and policies or understanding of the system. A similar remark is true of the outcome of other non-parametric multivariate approximation methods, including the neural network approach (Warner and Manavendra, 1996). The price to pay for extending non-parametric inference to high-dimensional data is the loss of interpretability (Friedman, 1994: 9).

A general lesson learnt from this consideration is that establishing an interpretable model suitable for evaluating actions and policies requires substantive probabilistic information. To be precise, one has to begin with a parametric model to ensure interpretability. If no substantive probabilistic assumption is made at the outset, the outcome is a black box model that lacks interpretability, and is useful only for *ex ante* and *ex post* predictions. There is, therefore, a trade-off between a model's interpretability and the amount of *probabilistic* information used to obtain it.

We have so far explained some of the limitations of non-parametric inference from *random* data. It is appropriate to close this section by looking again at the possibility of extending non-parametric inference to any sample, random or not. Any such attempt, as stated earlier, requires tentatively assuming that the data are random, and non-parametrically estimating the joint distributions of various subsets of the variables to assess alternative independence and homogeneity assumptions. Since accurate estimation of the joint distribution of several variables with ordinary samples is not possible, successful non-parametric evaluation of these assumptions is not practically possible either. Alternative methods are needed for selecting independence and homogeneity assumptions.

3.6 Model selection

The analysis of the bias–variance trade-off demonstrates that, for any data set, there is an optimal smoothing parameter value that minimizes the MSE error. The optimal value fixes the class of functions over which the estimator can search, determining the best possible approximation of the target function given the data. A crucial issue in non-parametric inference therefore concerns the choice of the smoothing parameter value that is optimal given the data. We refer to this issue as the smoothing parameter or model selection problem. The assumption in non-parametric statistics is that nothing is known about the target function apart from smoothness. This implies that one has to look at the data or, more precisely, assess the predictive accuracy (error) of possible models to select a model. This is indeed the approach pursued in non-parametric statistics. Broadly speaking, a number of models with different smoothing parameters are fitted to the data, the predictive error of each model is estimated, and the model with minimum prediction error is chosen (Moody, 1994: 149). A question is whether this approach provides a unique, and entirely data-driven, method for finding the optimal model.

3.6.1 Alternative model selectors

A model selector is consisted of a discrepancy (distance) function and an estimation strategy. The discrepancy function is to measure the distance between the predicted value of the response variable and its actual value, i.e. the prediction error. The estimation strategy is to estimate the accuracy of the model with respect to the population. To explain the basic approaches to prediction error estimation, we continue working with the squared Euclidean distance $[y_i^* - \hat{f}_h(x_i)]^2$, where $\hat{f}_h(x_i)$ is the response value predicted by the model for a new observation at x_i, and y_i^* is the actual response value. For the purpose of this section, we propose to measure the prediction error rate of a model using the *average mean-squared prediction error* (APE):

$$\text{APE}(h) = N^{-1} \sum_{i=1}^{n} E(y_i^* - \hat{f}_h(x_i))^2 \tag{3.25}$$

The error depends on the smoothing parameter h. A problem is that future data are not known, and except for the strategy of 'wait and see' any attempt at estimating error (3.25) involves exploiting exiting data. However, the same data cannot be used for both obtaining a model and estimating its predictive accuracy. An attempt to do so amounts to estimating APE using the average squared residuals (ASR):

$$\text{ASR}(h) = N^{-1} \sum_{i=1}^{n} \{y_i - \hat{f}_h(x_i)\}^2 \tag{3.26}$$

Following a technique explained in Eubank (1988), the expected value of ASR can be decomposed into (see Appendix 3.B):

$$E(\text{ASR}(h)) = \delta^2 + f(x)'(I - \mathbf{W}(h))^2 f(x) + N^{-1}\delta^2 tr[\mathbf{W}(h)^2] - 2N^{-1}\delta^2 tr[\mathbf{W}(h)] \tag{3.27}$$

$\mathbf{W}(h)$ is the smoother matrix with bandwidth h, $f(x)$ is the regression function, δ^2 is the variance of Y (given x), and $tr[\mathbf{W}(h)]$ is the trace of the smoother matrix.[18] Applying the same technique to the average mean-squared prediction error yields:

$$\text{APE}(h) = \delta^2 + f(x)'(I - \mathbf{W}(h))^2 f(x) + N^{-1}\delta^2 tr[\mathbf{W}(h)^2] \tag{3.28}$$

A comparison of (3.27) and (3.28) shows that ASR on average underestimates the mean prediction error APE by factor $2N^{-1}\sigma^2 tr[\mathbf{W}(h)]$. As a result, this estimate of prediction error is usually called the *apparent rate* of error or the *substitution* error (Efron, 1983). In fact, substitution error (3.26) can be reduced arbitrarily by selecting a sufficiently small smoothing parameter value so that the model interpolates the data. This would not necessarily lead to a model that minimizes the MSE error, which is essential for minimizing prediction error. The literature provides three avenues for obtaining an unbiased estimation of prediction error.

A strategy is to split the data into two sets, a *training* set and a *test* set. The training set is used to obtain a model and the test set is used to evaluate its performance. By using different data for model construction and evaluation, the data-splitting strategy evades the problem with the apparent rate of error. Nevertheless, it has several drawbacks. First, by leaving part of the data aside as a test set, the strategy fails to make optimal use of the data in estimating a model. In a non-parametric setting, a smaller sample necessitates a greater degree of smoothing, which reduces the class of functions over which an estimator can search. Consequently, the procedure is likely to lead to the choice of a biased model. To be precise, the strategy estimates the predicting error of a model built from (say) half of the data but the primary concern is to estimate the predictive accuracy of a model that can be constructed from the whole data (Zucchini, 2000: 19). Secondly, when the sample size is small, as is usual in practice, splitting the data leads to a small test set, which may also be inadequate for a reliable estimate of the model's prediction error (Faraway, 1998: 335). Finally, the strategy involves an arbitrary decision in dividing the data into a training set and a test set, which could affect estimation of the prediction error and hence model selection (Glymour *et al.*, 1996: 37).

Another strategy attempts to overcome the inefficiency of the simple data-splitting method by utilizing resampling techniques to create a test set. Cross-validation is the oldest resampling technique used for estimating prediction error, attributed to Stone (1974). The method, in its most common form, involves leaving a data point (x_i, y_i) aside at a time as a test set, fitting a model to the remaining $N - 1$ data points, and using the model to predict the omitted observation. The process is repeated for all the N observations, and the average of the errors is taken as the estimate of the model's prediction error. Let $\hat{f}_h^{-i}(.)$ be the model estimated from sample $\boldsymbol{D}$ excluding data point (x_i, y_i), and $\hat{f}_h^{-i}(x_i)$ the response value predicted by $\hat{f}_h^{-i}(.)$ at point x_i. The cross-validation estimate of prediction error is given by

$$CV(h) = \frac{1}{N} \sum_{i=1}^{N} [y_i - \hat{f}_h^{-i}(x_i)]^2 \tag{3.29}$$

This technique is called 'leave-one-out' cross-validation, as each time only one observation is left out. Alternative cross-validation error estimators can be defined by holding out a different number of observations (say, five) each time. A cross-validation-based model selector chooses a smoothing parameter h that minimizes error estimate (3.29) or a similar one.

This resampling strategy yields an unbiased estimate of the mean prediction error. The unbiasedness of an estimator such as (3.29) can intuitively be understood by noting that

$$E[y_i - \hat{f}_h^{-i}(x_i)]^2 = \sigma^2 + E[f(x_i) - \hat{f}_h^{-i}(x_i)]^2 \tag{3.30}$$

and

$$E[y_i^* - \hat{f}_h(x_i)]^2 = \sigma^2 + E[f(x_i) - \hat{f}_h(x_i)]^2 \tag{3.31}$$

As the sample size grows, the estimate $\hat{f}_h^{-i}(x_i)$ becomes closer to the estimate $\hat{f}_h(x_i)$, which is based on the full data, i.e. $\hat{f}_h(x_i) \approx \hat{f}_h^{-i}(x_i)$. As a result, the mean value of $CV(h)$ becomes increasingly close to the mean prediction error, i.e. $E(CV(h)) \approx APE(h)$. This means that $CV(h)$ is an approximately unbiased estimator of the mean prediction error (Hastie and Tibshirani, 1990: 43). Hall (1983) establishes that a sequence of smoothing parameters produced by the cross-validation procedure (3.29) leads to consistent density estimation. A sequence of smoothing parameters minimizing $CV(h)$ is therefore expected to minimize the mean prediction error.

Although cross-validation techniques give a glimpse of the resampling approach, we also need to mention bootstrap estimators that exploit a different resampling strategy for constructing a test set. Basically, the bootstrap method takes the original data set in place of the *unknown* distribution, considers each observation in the set as equally probable, and draws N new observations from the set with *replacement*. The new sample is called the *bootstrap* sample. It fits the model to the sample and estimates its prediction error by applying it to the original data set. The technique generates B bootstrap samples, estimates the model on each, and applies each fitted model to the *original* data to obtain B estimates of the model's prediction error. The average of these estimates is taken as the model's prediction error. A bootstrap model selector chooses the smoothing parameter that minimizes the average prediction error (Efron and Tibshirani, 1993). Appendix 3.C defines some bootstrap error estimators which will be mentioned in the text.

There is also a third avenue for obtaining an unbiased estimate of mean prediction error. The mean average-squared residuals E(ASR), as said, differs from the mean prediction error APE by factor $2n^{-1}\delta^2 tr[\mathbf{W}(h)]$. If this term could be estimated, it would be possible to transform ASR into an unbiased estimate of APE by adding an estimate of the term to ASR. In that case, the expected value of the augmented ASR would be the same as APE, and there would remain no need for computationally intensive resampling procedures. One would be able to estimate APE by correcting ASR with a term that cancels the bias term out. This possibility is the drive behind an ongoing search for estimates of prediction error that take the form:

$$E(\text{ASR}(h)) + 2N^{-1}\delta^2 tr[\mathbf{W}(h)] \tag{3.32}$$

To further illustrate the variety of ways of estimating prediction error, it is worth looking at one of the model selectors that proceed by minimizing an estimate of (3.32). Note that the cross-validation criterion can also be written as

$$CV(h) = \frac{1}{N}\sum_{i=1}^{N}\{y_i - \hat{f}_h^{-i}(x_i)\}^2 = \frac{1}{N}\sum_{i=1}^{N}\left\{\frac{y_i - \hat{f}_h(x_i)}{1 - w_{ii}}\right\}^2 \tag{3.33}$$

where w_{ii} are the diagonal elements of the smoother matrix $\boldsymbol{W}$ (Eubank, 1988: 30). Thus, the leave-one-out cross-validation estimator corrects the bias of ASR by multiplying it with function $(1-w_{ii})^{-2}$. Craven and Wahba (1979) suggests an approximation to (3.33) by replacing the diagonal elements w_{ii} with their average, namely $tr(\mathbf{W})/N$, calling it *generalized cross-validation* (GCV). That is, they replace (3.33) with

$$\text{GCV}(h) = \frac{1}{N}\sum_{i=1}^{n}\left\{\frac{y_i - \hat{f}_h(x_i)}{1 - tr(\mathbf{W}(h))/N}\right\}^2 \tag{3.34}$$

as an estimate of the mean prediction error. While CV corrects the bias of ASR by multiplying it with function $(1-w_{ii})^2$, GCV corrects ASR by multiplying it with $\{1 - tr(\mathbf{W}(h))/N\}^{-2}$. If we take a first-order Taylor expansion of this function and ignore its reminder, we obtain $1 + 2N^{-1}tr(\mathbf{W}(h))$. Using this approximation, GCV can be restated as

$$\text{GCV}(h) \approx \text{ASR}(h) + 2N^{-1}tr[\mathbf{W}(h)]\text{ASR}(h) \tag{3.35}$$

As shown in Härdle (1990: 155), the expected value of the second term in (3.35) is approximately the same as the second term in (3.32) and asymptotically cancels out the bias term in ASR. Eubank (1988: 35-6) also sketches an alternative proof for the consistency of GCV as an estimator of APE. Now, an important point is that there is nothing unique about the correcting function $\{(N - tr(\mathbf{W}))/N\}^{-2}$. Any function with the same first-order Taylor expansion as $1 + 2N^{-1}tr(\mathbf{W}(h)$ can equally correct the bias term in ASR. This possibility opens the way for producing alternative unbiased model selectors and is behind most known selectors such as Akaike's information criterion (Akaike, 1974), finite prediction error (Akaike, 1974), Shibata's model selector (1981) and Rice's bandwidth selector (1984). All these selectors are based on an estimate of prediction error that corrects ASR by a function whose first-order Taylor expansion is $1 + 2N^{-1}tr(\mathbf{W}(h)$ (Härdle, 1990: 167).[19]

These are some of the strategies for estimating prediction error, each leading to different model selectors. It is also important to bear in mind that the estimation strategies can be combined with other discrepancy functions than the squared Euclidean function to generate alternative model selectors. One can use, for instance, the Kullback-Leibler discrepancy. In general, alternative model selectors can be invented by varying the discrepancy function or the estimation strategy (Amemiya, 1980: 325).

3.6.2 Which model selector should be used?

The existence of alternative model selectors raises the question of which selector to choose in practice. If these methods picked up the same model, one could arbitrarily select any of the methods. But, since the methods use different estimation strategies, when applied to ordinarily available samples, they often suggest different models. Consider the data set plotted in the figures below, which consists of 100 observations simulated from the model used earlier to illustrate the bias–variance trade-off. Two selection criteria have been applied to find the optimal bandwidth in kernel regression of Y on X – the leave-one-out cross-validation and generalized cross-validation method. The former suggests the optimal bandwidth to be 0.25, producing the model in Figure 3.7 while the latter suggests it to be 0.07, producing the model in Figure 3.8. These models are different.

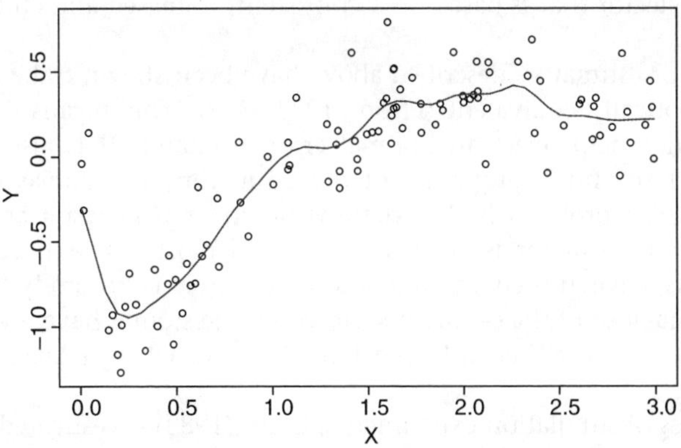

Figure 3.7 Kernel regression with leave-one-out cross-validation

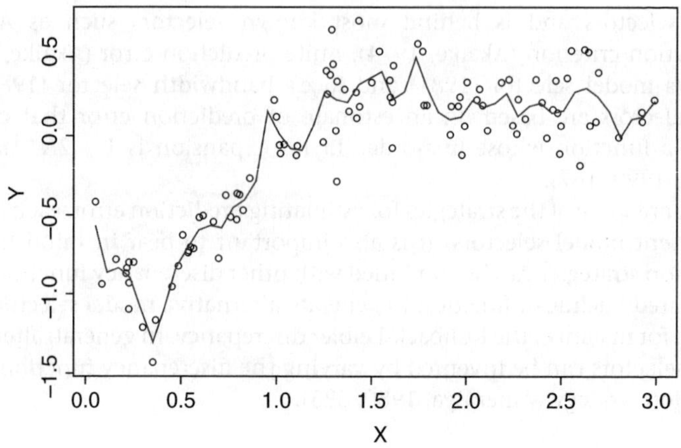

Figure 3.8 Kernel regression with generalized cross-validation

Similar findings have been observed in numerous extensive studies of the behaviour of the selectors in small samples.[20] So, in small samples the selectors can lead to different models, raising the question of which selector to choose in practice. A selector, as seen, consists of a discrepancy function and an error estimator. The latter influences the selector's performance more critically. An error estimator should be consistent, unbiased and efficient. Consistency is to ensure that the estimator is asymptotically able to estimate the error correctly; unbiasedness is to ensure that the estimates, on average, coincide with the object of inference; and efficiency (i.e. minimum variance) is to ensure that there is no other unbiased consistent estimator yielding a more precise estimate. This means one has to choose a selector that is based on a consistent, unbiased and efficient error estimator.

Most error estimators described above have been shown to be consistent or asymptotically equivalent (Efron, 1983: 328). This means consistency alone cannot help select an optimal error estimator. It is also necessary to consider the finite properties of the estimators, i.e. unbiasedness and efficiency. The problem is that there is no theoretical result as to which type of error estimator is both unbiased and most efficient. As a result, statisticians have turned to simulation experiments to study the finite-sample behaviour of the estimators. However, the studies have revealed that the estimators are either unbiased but highly variable or biased and less variable.

In a series of simulation experiments, Efron (1983) investigated the finite sample behaviour of the leave-one-out cross-validation method, several variants of the bootstrap method, and some other error rate estimators not mentioned here. The studies revealed that the leave-one-out cross-validation estimator was of low bias but suffered from a high degree of variability across different samples of fixed size. Other estimators in the study showed either high bias and less variability or high variability and low bias. Comparing the bias and variance of the estimators, Efron observed that a bootstrap estimator, called the 0.632 estimator, though biased, was comparatively less variable.[21] He recommended it for model selection. Likewise, Breiman and Spector (1992) compared the finite sample properties of leave-one-out cross-validation, *k*-fold cross-validation, and a variant of the bootstrap method in a number of subset (variable) selection experiments. The simulations showed that the leave-one-out cross-validation had low bias but suffered from high variability while five-fold cross-validation method suffered from a large bias and less variability. Comparing the results, the authors suggested using the ten-fold cross-validation method. Finally, Efron and Tibshirani (1997) report a number of simulation studies that seem to support a bootstrap estimator different from the 0.632 estimator. If a lesson can be learnt from these studies, it is that no error estimator outperforms others in all respects. Either they are unbiased but highly variable or they are biased and less variable. A judgement is needed about the relative importance of unbiasedness and efficiency to pick out an estimator.

Beside this, the real problem with the use of simulation studies is that their results cannot be generalized automatically. The fact that an estimator outperforms others in a series of simulations does not imply that it always outperforms others. In experiment with different models a different estimator may outperform the rivals. To give a historically interesting example, as mentioned above, in a series of studies Efron (1983) found that the 0.632 bootstrap estimator outperformed several other methods, and so recommended it for estimating prediction error. Not long after, Breiman *et al.* (1984) noted that the estimator badly fails in predicting the error rate of highly overfit models, such as a one-nearest-neighbour classifier (estimator), where the apparent rate of error is zero.[22] For example, if Y takes either 0 or 1 with probability 1/2, independently of (useless) predictor vector $\boldsymbol{X}$, then, the true error rate for any classifier equals 0.50. Yet, the 0.632 estimator predicts the expected error rate of a one-nearest-neighbour classifier to be $0.632 \times 0.5 = 0.316$. In this case, both the leave-one-out cross-validation estimator and the simple bootstrap estimator correctly predict the error rate of 1/2. Similar counter-examples have been found for hold-out error rate estimators. For example, in a no-information dataset, where the assignment of cases to each class is completely random (e.g. Fisher's iris dataset), the best an estimator can predict is to predict majority.[23] But if the number of cases for each class in the data set happened to be equal, the leave-one-out cross-validation method would wrongly predict 0 per cent predictive accuracy for a majority prediction rule (Kohavi, 1995). The hold-out methods including the cross-validation techniques work only if leaving part of the data aside as a test set does not destroy the structure of the data. The validity of simulation results is confined to the type of models (and data) considered and cannot be generalized automatically (White, 1992: 110). All in all, the question of which selector to choose in practice has no theoretical answer. In the end, the choice of a selector is to some extent left to the modeller's judgement (Leamer, 1983: 217):

> In this paper I have compared several simple criteria on the basis of which we can select one regression equation among many other candidates. ... the general picture that has emerged from this paper is that all of the criteria considered are based on a somewhat arbitrary assumption which cannot be fully justified, and that by slightly varying the loss function and the decision strategy one can indefinitely go on inventing new criteria. This is what one would expect, for there is no simple solution to a complex problem. (Amemiya, 1980: 352)

The predictive model selectors do not provide an entirely *objective* (data-driven) solution to the model selection problem. They only provide an *automatic* solution in the sense that, given the choice of a discrepancy function and an error estimator, the method fixes the model that minimizes the error, as measured by the estimator (Green and Silverman, 1994: 24). The idea of designing an inference procedure that receives data and yields the model that, given the data, best approximates the true model has no foundation. Any non-parametric inference is founded at a deep level on a decision about the optimal level of smoothing that cannot be fully justified by the data:

> The absence of theoretical guidance on setting the bandwidth, and more generally on defining nearness, leaves the empirical researchers with enormous discretion. This discretion gives applied nonparametric regression analysis a subjective flavor. (Manski, 1991: 44)

3.6.3 Extrapolation error

The difficulty in choosing an optimal selector is not the only factor that limits the power of the model selection strategy available in non-parametric statistics. Even if an optimal selector could be located, there would still be no satisfactory, and entirely data-driven, solution to non-parametric model selection. An explanation of this point requires distinguishing *in-sample* and *extra-sample* prediction error. In-sample prediction error (accuracy) refers to the predictive performance of a model at the locations in the input variable space from which the data have been drawn. We refer to these locations in the input variable space as the *sample region*. On the other hand, extra-sample prediction error refers to the predictive performance of a model over the locations in the input variable space for which no data are available. Given this distinction, an important point to note is that in-sample predictive accuracy is not necessarily the evidence for extra-sample predictive accuracy. The reason is that two models can be exactly alike over the sample region but

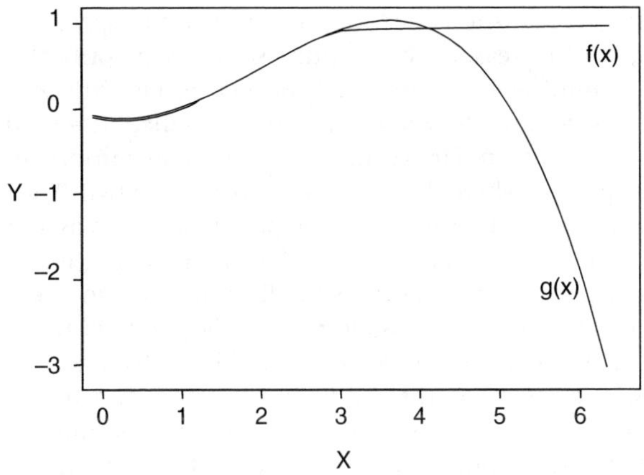

Figure 3.9 Extrapolation

Note: Functions $f(x)$ and $g(x)$ are alike over interval [0,4].

behave considerably differently outside the region. In that case, if the data produced by one of the models belonged to the points in the input variable space where the models are alike, the other model would equally predict the data despite the fact that it yields quite wrong predictions elsewhere.[24] Consider the following two models:

$$\text{(I) } y = f(x) + e_1 \qquad f(x) = 1/2 + 1/2\tanh(x - 2) \qquad e_1 \sim N(0, 0.2)$$
$$\text{(II) } y = g(x) + e_2, g(x) = 0.05 - 0.2x + 0.3x^2 - 0.002x^4 \qquad e_2 \sim N(0, 0.2)$$

where X takes values in interval [0,6.5].[25] As shown in Figure 3.9, while these models are alike over interval [0,4], they fall apart over interval [4,6.5]. Suppose model (I) was true. If the data were drawn from the first interval, model (II) would also accurately predict the data. But the model's accurate performance over this interval gives a wrong indication of its performance over the second interval. This means an estimate of in-sample prediction error cannot be taken as an estimate of extra-sample prediction error. On the same ground, the fact that a model minimizes in-sample prediction error is not a guarantee that it also performs well outside the sample region. Extrapolation demands an estimate of extra-sample accuracy. An estimate of in-sample accuracy is neither necessary nor sufficient.

Now, any error estimator is an estimator of in-sample prediction error. Consider cross-validation or bootstrap estimators. These estimators work by correcting the optimism of the apparent rate of error (Efron and Tibshirani, 1993: 249), which is a measure of how a model predicts the same data used to obtain it.[26] The correction is to remove the effect of noise in the data so as to enable the estimator to estimate correctly the prediction error of future observations drawn at the same locations in the input space where the data were drawn. For this reason, the resulting selectors are only able to locate a model that minimizes in-sample prediction error. Put differently, they can only tell what sort of model will yield accurate prediction if we draw a 'similar' sample, where by 'similar' we mean a sample drawn from the same points in the input space as where the original sample was drawn. The selectors are silent about the model that is true of the population, and as a result give no guidance as to how to generalize beyond the sample region (Browne, 2000: 8).

This conclusion has an important implication for non-parametric inference. In general, if it were possible to densely populate the input region everywhere with data, every prediction would involve only in-sample prediction and, as a result, a cross-validation estimate of a model's error, for instance, would provide an estimate of the predictive accuracy of the model with respect to the population. In that case, the distinction between in-sample and extra-sample prediction error would be irrelevant. However, the discussion of the curse of dimensionality makes it clear that in 'interesting' inference situations, the input space is almost everywhere empty, which means non-parametric prediction in 'interesting' inference situations almost always involves extrapolation (extra-sample prediction). Since the model selection criteria are silent about the predictive performance of a model outside the sample region, non-parametric extrapolation is almost always arbitrary (Geman *et al.*, 1992: 44). As a consequence, in interesting inference situations, such as modelling a choice situation, that involve a relatively large number of variables, reliable prediction with ordinary sample sizes necessarily calls for substantive prior background information. That is to say, one needs to posit *a priori* a parametric model and be sure that the model is correctly specified:

> One can usually be confident that the regression of interest is continuous. Hence one can usually trust nonparametric estimates to be consistent. On the other hand, these estimates are often imprecise in practice. Moreover, they cannot be extrapolated off the support of x. Parametric modelling permits more precise estimation and makes extrapolation possible. The problem, of course, is that an assumed parametric model may be misspecified. (Manski, 1991: 44)

The difficulty in locating the 'best' error rate estimator is not the only trouble with the predictive approach to model selection in non-parametric inference. The more serious problem is that in interesting non-parametric inference settings, such as modelling a complex choice situation, prediction almost always involves extrapolation about which data are silent. Non-parametric extrapolation is inevitably arbitrary in interesting cases. Non-parametric models are only reliable for in-sample prediction.

3.7 Conclusion

Economics needs a theory that explains how the agent learns about the economy, defines his choice situation, and redefines it in response to policy interventions. In this regard, a basic unifying hypothesis is that he behaves like an econometrician. Theoretical economists hope this conjecture helps them predict the model that the agent builds of his choice situation based on available data. The aim is to combine the information with information about the agent's preferences and budget constraint to specify the decision problem he is trying to solve, which is essential for predicting his behaviour. The success of this hypothesis critically depends on the existence of a 'tight enough' theory of statistical learning that describes how, given a data set, the statistician constructs a model of the mechanism generating the data.

Any statistical inference necessitates three types of assumptions that define a model. The central concern of a theory of statistical inference should therefore be model specification. To study model specification, we looked at non-parametric statistics that suggests starting with a very general and highly flexible model and leaving the data to determine the precise form of the model. If the goal of non-parametric inference could be accomplished, we would have inference methods that receive data and yield the best approximation of the underlying distribution given the data. And there would then be a 'tight enough' theory of learning.

As seen, in order for a non-parametric estimator to deliver a good approximation of a function, both the variance and squared bias component of the MSE error of the estimator must approach zero. Because of the bias–variance dilemma, this is only possible through densely populating the input variable space. But, due to the curse of dimensionality problem, it is practically impossible to densely populate input variable spaces in interesting inference situations, where the number of input variables considered exceeds three or four. In such situations, local averaging inference demands an astronomically large sample that is usually impossible to achieve in practice. With a reasonably sized sample, a good approximation of the relations among several variables using local averaging-based techniques is impossible.

This impossibility also rules out the possibility of extending non-parametric inference to non-random data. The extension requires estimating the joint distributions of various subsets of the variables under study in order to assess the appropriateness of alternative independence and homogeneity assumptions. Since non-parametric density estimation of high-dimensional data is practically impossible, the choice of appropriate independence and homogeneity assumptions cannot be left to non-parametric methods either. Modelling probabilistic relations among a set of variables characterizing a choice situation requires substantive probabilistic assumptions. This means one has to work within the framework of parametric inference. In that case, learning will only be possible if the model is correctly specified.

The bias – variance trade-off implies that, given a data set, there is an optimal value for the smoothing parameter of a non-parametric estimator that fixes the class of functions that it can approximate. The only avenue available to non-parametric statistics for specifying the optimal smoothing parameter value is to consider the predictive performance of various models arising from alternative smoothing parameters. There are competing procedures for non-parametric model selection. While asymptotically equivalent, the methods pick up different smoothing parameters in practice, leading to different models. There is no general theoretical consideration that can help to choose a model selector. The performance of the methods depends on the target function. For some functions, cross-validation techniques may work better and, for some others, other methods may work better. As a consequence, in a purely non-parametric inference situation, there is an element of arbitrariness in the choice of a model selector and hence a model.

Even after choosing a model selector, the smoothing parameter selection problem is not entirely resolved, as these selectors often have local minima. More importantly, the estimators underlying the selectors only measure in-sample prediction error. What they tell us at best is how to simplify the model to avoid overfitting. They do not tell us how to extrapolate beyond the sample. These considerations rule out the possibility of inventing procedures that receive data and yield the best possible approximation of the underlying model given the data. Data only speak in the light of background information and, as the information differs, they speak differently.

There are also numerous non-parametric estimators. Besides kernel estimators, one may mention nearest-neighbours estimators, spline regression methods, neural network methods, local polynomials, and many others. With an arbitrarily large sample, this multiplicity may pose no problem, since all these methods are consistent. However, when the sample is small, they often produce different estimates, raising the question of which method to choose in practice (Breiman and Spector, 1992). Modelling learning demands some decision about the agent's choice of an estimator.

Finally, due to the curse of dimensionality, in high-dimensional input variable spaces, non-parametric models take the form of expansions in low-dimensional functions. In such models, the relation between the dependent and independent variables are entirely blurred. This seriously limits the models' usefulness in analysing how the dependent variable would vary if the independent variables were changed by intervention. Consequently, the models are not suitable for analysis of actions and policies. Analysis of actions and policies requires an interpretable model, which necessitates working with a parametric model from the start.

These limitations of non-parametric inference define the boundaries of any theory of learning that fails to take the role of non-sample information seriously. It is a combination of background information and sample data that enables a person to come up with an intelligible model of a choice situation. A theory of learning ought to explain how non-sample information is obtained, how the information interacts with sample data, and how the interaction leads to a specific model. Some of these issues will be discussed in the next chapter that concentrates on the theory of Bayesian inference.

4
'Homo Economicus' as an Intuitive Statistician (2): Bayesian Diagnostic Learning

4.1 Introduction

> Learning takes place through Bayesian updating of the individual prior beliefs... However, since the use of Bayesian updating is a consequence of expected utility maximisation, assumption (2) [Bayesian updating] is already a consequence of assumption (1) [subjective expected utility maximisation]. (Kalai and Lehrer, 1993: 102)

> ... hypothesis and model generation is far more important to problem solving than is hypothesis testing and that it is very much the statistician's business to be involved with model generation and regeneration. (Box, 1994: 218)

The bounded rationality programme views the economy as a society of intuitive statisticians. The key for the success of this programme is the existence of a 'tight enough' theory of statistical inference. We have so far shown that there is no entirely data-driven algorithm that receives a finite sample of data and yields the model that best approximates the process generating the data. Learning an interpretable model of a choice situation requires starting with a parametric probability model. To analyse the programme further, we now examine the possibility of a 'tight enough' theory of learning within the general framework of the Bayesian theory, which is primarily a theory of parametric inference.

A sizeable literature on learning has emerged in economics that models the agent as a Bayesian statistician. These studies consider economies of Bayesian statisticians, who know the true economic model except for a small number of parameters, and use Bayes' theorem to learn the parameters from data generated by the economy. The papers investigate the conditions under which the opinions of these intuitive statisticians converge on the true parameter values. As noted earlier, since feedback from learning can shift the structure, the issue in question is not ordinary parameter estimation but involves estimation of shifting parameters. Various convergence theorems of probability theory have been employed to demonstrate that if the agents do not entertain extreme priors excluding the true parameter values, they eventually learn the parameters with probability one. This result is often claimed to justify the use of the solution concepts of rational expectations equilibria in solving economic models and Nash equilibria in game theory. Good reviews of, and original contributions to, Bayesian learning are found in Blume and Easley (1995), Bray and Kreps (1987), Cyert and DeGroot (1974), Kiefer and Nyarko (1995), Nyarko (1997) and Nyarko (1998).

The relevance of these studies to the study of the economy is unclear. The studies assume that the agents know the true model except for a finite number of parameters, providing no explanation of how the model has been learnt in the first place. This is a critical issue because starting with a mis-specified model can make learning of rational expectations impossible (Nyarko, 1991). Moreover, the results are of an asymptotic nature, and do not bear on real inference situations where the samples are usually small. In fact, the economic structure can shift for reasons other than learning, rendering past data irrelevant. A theory of human learning should first and foremost explain how a person builds a model of his or her choice situation from ordinarily available samples. This chapter departs from the dominant trend in the studies of Bayesian learning by focusing on the issue of parametric model formulation and problems arising in learning from small samples.

The chapter begins by arguing that the Bayesian theory is solely concerned with coherent (consistent) analysis of uncertainty regarding a closed set of specified possibilities (events, hypotheses, models) which are assumed to be adequate as a description of the (inference) situation at hand. Coherent analysis constitutes only one phase out of several in the whole process of statistical learning. A vital activity preceding coherent analysis is the initial generation of models. Another critical activity following coherent analysis is appraising the empirical adequacy of the models (Smith, 1986: 250). In practice, these phases of learning are iterated in a cyclical manner. New data cast doubt on the adequacy of the current models, calling for generation of new models. Construction of the new models necessitates forming a new coherent system of beliefs, which raises the question whether the new models include one that captures the salient features of the data. A satisfactory account of statistical learning should explain how models are built, how they are assessed and how they are modified. This chapter therefore generalizes the framework of Bayesian inference by introducing some additional proposals to shed light on those aspects of inference such as model formulation that are usually left unexplained in Bayesian statistics. Having done so, it spells out the implications of the broader theory of Bayesian inference for the bounded rationality project.

4.2 Foundational issues

In economics, a choice situation (the environment) is viewed through the perspective of a collection of measurable quantities. These quantities are of two kinds: those whose numerical values are known and those whose are not. The general problem facing the modeller is to infer the unknown quantities from the known ones. Knowledge of the known quantities usually fails to determine uniquely that of the unknown quantities, and, given the known quantities, there remains uncertainty about the values of the unknowns. The hallmark of the Bayesian position is that our uncertainty attitudes towards these unknowns should accord with the laws of probability. A foundational question is whether the Bayesian theory prescribes how these uncertainties should be updated as some of the unknowns become known. To address this query, it is first essential to understand the reasons why subjective uncertainties ought to accord with the laws of probability.

Chapter 2 studied some aspects of the decision theoretic approach to probability theory that took personal probability to be part of a theory of coherent preferences in the face of uncertainty. Since the concern in this chapter is not directly with decision making but with learning from data, it is more convenient to consider another approach to establishing the probability axioms that makes no formal reference to preference considerations. We consider the so-called Dutch book (DB) theorem, which aims to justify the probability axioms as coherence (rationality) constraints by establishing that partial beliefs are 'coherent' if and only if they conform to the axioms. We study the assumptions underlying the DB theorem to explore if they impose any restriction on how learning from experience should take place. Our exposition is mainly built on Skyrms (1986) and Howson's various writings.[1] The DB theorem stands on three assumptions.

The first assumption consists of two related components: one is that you (the agent) have a degree of belief in any hypothesis H you may ever consider. The other is that the strength of your belief in H is reflected in the price that you are ready to pay in a bet on or against it.[2] It is therefore considered possible to measure your degree of belief in H in terms of the price you are ready to pay in some appropriate bet on or against it. Several definitions are required to elaborate on this point. A bet on a statement H is an arrangement between you (the bettor) and the bookie whereby you pay the bookie amount $\$d$ to receive amount $\$c$ if H is true, and receive nothing if H is false.[3] The total amount involved $(d + c)$, is called the *stake*, the ratio d/c the *odds*, and the ratio $d/d + c$ the *betting quotient*.[4] Finally, the price that you are ready to pay for a bet in which both the stake and whether you bet on or against H is decided by your opponent is considered to be *fair* in your eyes. Given these preliminaries, the first assumption identifies your degree of belief in H with the betting quotient in a bet on or against H whose price you consider as fair (Howson, 2000: 126). Following de Finetti (1980), a bet is sometimes defined

Table 4.1 Equivalent bets (1)

P	*Q*	**Bet 1 on *P***	**Bet II on *Q***	**Sum of Bet I and II**	**Bet III on PVQ**
T	F	(1 – p)s	−qr	(1 – p)s – qr	(1 – p*)s*
F	T	−ps	(1 – q)r	(1 – q)r – ps	(1 – p*)s*
F	F	−ps	−qr	−(ps + qr)	−p*s*

differently. Let *s* stand for the stake in the above bet and *p* for the betting quotient. The bet can be restated as an arrangement in which you agree to pay *ps* in order to receive *(1–p)s* if *H* turns out true and nothing otherwise. Your fair betting quotient *p* then represents your degree of belief in *H*.

A corollary of the definition of a bet, which plays a vital role in the DB theorem, is that the sum of a collection of bets on some propositions, under certain conditions, determines a bet on another proposition. Note that a bet on a statement *H* admits only two possibilities – *H* is true or *H* is false – and specifies a unique pay-off in each case. The sum of a collection of bets then equals a new bet if it admits only two possibilities and specifies a unique pay-off in each case. As a simple illustration, consider the case involving two mutually exclusive propositions *P* and *Q*. Let B_1 be a bet on *P* with stake *s* and betting quotient *p*, and B_2 be a bet on *Q* with stake *r* and betting quotient *q*. If the stakes *s* and *r* are equal, then, the sum of these bets is equivalent to a bet on *PvQ* with stake $s^* = s = r$ and betting quotient $p^* = p + q$ (Skyrms, 1986: 176). Table 4.1 shows this.

The second assumption underlying the DB theorem is that the value of the sum of a set of bets is the total value of the bets and therefore, if a set of bets is regarded as individually fair, they are also considered as collectively fair. Thus, if in the above situation the betting quotients *p* and *q* are viewed as fair, the betting quotient p^* for the third bet is also viewed as fair. Schick (1986) was the first to note the significance and independence of this assumption in establishing the DB theorem, calling it the value additivity assumption. The principle, he argues, presumes that the value that people assign to a bet is independent of whether other bets are in effect. But people are usually risk averse. If they have already committed themselves to a bet, the highest price that they would pay for a new bet is less than it otherwise would be (1986: 114). In such cases, people are hedging against the possibility of losing both bets, and there is nothing irrational about this behaviour. The value additivity principle cannot, therefore, be taken for granted.

The literature provides several considerations in support of the value additivity assumption. Skyrms (1986: 179) defines a fair bet as a bet with expected utility zero, and seeks to derive the assumption from this definition. This move assumes that your belief distribution obeys the probability calculus, which undermines the appeal of the DB theorem as an independent approach to establishing the probability axioms.[5] Howson (2000) defends a view of the probability calculus as an extension of deductive logic to partial beliefs. In this setting, he envisages a parallel between the value additivity assumption and the closure principle applied in deductive logic. Just as the closure principle is taken for granted in deductive logic to define the truth-value of a compound sentence in terms of the truth-value of its components, it is equally 'natural', Howson suggests, to take value additivity for granted to determine the value of a compound bet from the value of its components (2000: 129).[6] This suggestion is plausible but applies only when the concern, as in deductive logic, is solely with bets that are *simultaneously* made. The proposal does not counter Schick's worries in sequential betting scenarios. The validity of the principle, if valid at all, is confined to static betting scenarios.

An implication of the value additivity principle plays a crucial role in establishing the DB theorem. Note that a fair bet can informally be interpreted as a bet that confers zero advantage to either side. Since any sum of zeros is zero, the net advantage of a collection of fair bets is also zero. Given the value additivity assumption, if you consider a collection of bets as individually fair but the net advantage of the bets is non-zero, then the *only* explanation is that you are evaluating a bet (or equivalent bets) at two different rates, regarding both as fair.[7] In that case, it is possible for a cunning bookie to invite you to accept a set of bets that all are individually fair in your eyes but, taken together, lead you to a sure loss. The trick for the bookie is simply to sell you the bet at your higher fair price and buy back an equivalent bet or an equivalent set of bets at your lower fair price. A collection of bets that guarantees a loss no matter what the outcome of the events upon which the wagers are made is called a Dutch book (Skyrms, 1986: 185).

The third assumption is a coherence (rationality) condition. Some statements of the DB theorem identify the condition with a simple behavioural criterion – essentially that a rational agent ought to avoid a combination of decisions that leads to a sure loss (Dawid, 2002: 3). For several reasons, discussed in Christensen (1991), this criterion fails to support the laws of probability as rationality constraints on partial beliefs. In a nutshell, there are situations where a person accepts a combination of bets which leads to a sure loss but he or she does not *actually* hold any beliefs violating the probability axioms. The person might, for example, recognize that a collection of bets offered to him or her by a friend leads to a sure loss but accepts them to avoid harming the friend's confidence. Such a decision is not usually considered as *irrational*. On the other hand, a person may have beliefs that breach the laws of probability or even logic but consciously refuses to participate in any decision which entails a sure loss. In such cases, even though he or she actually escapes a sure loss, there still seems to be something amiss about his or her beliefs. If the concern is to establish the probability axioms as rationality constraints on partial beliefs, the coherence condition must do more than point to some dire practical consequences; it must be directly concerned with relations among beliefs (Christensen, 1991: 238).

Another notion of coherence appears in Ramsey's brief allusion to the DB theorem in his seminal work 'Truth and Probability' (1926 [1980]). There, he regards the theory of probability as 'an extension to partial beliefs of formal logic, the logic of consistency' (1980: 41).[8] From this perspective, the underlying notion of coherence is logical consistency. This deals directly with the internal structure of a belief system and can well support a justification of the probability axioms as rationality constraints on partial beliefs. In what follows, we therefore build our analysis around this notion of coherence, which has also increasingly been adopted in the recent philosophical literature on the Bayesian theory.

These assumptions state all that is needed for proving the DB theorem. The proof starts by establishing that if your fair betting quotients for a collection of bets violate the probability axioms, a Dutch book can be made against you; that is, there will exist a finite series of bets that you consider as individually fair but collectively lead to a sure loss. The converse of this result is also shown to be true. If your fair betting quotients conform to the probability axioms, no Dutch book can ever be made against you. Given the value additivity assumption, the susceptibility to a Dutch book is the evidence that you are rating two equivalent bets at two different prices, considering both as fair. This means you believe in a pair of contradictory propositions that a bet is simultaneously fair and unfair. Since conformity with the probability calculus is both necessary and sufficient to avoid a Dutch book, the only way to avoid such a contradiction is to arrange your fair betting quotients or, in other words, your partial beliefs, in accordance with the probability axioms. And finally, since logical consistency is a rational desideratum, the laws of probability become rationality constraints on partial beliefs.[9]

The notion of conditional probability plays a key role in understanding whether the Bayesian theory furnishes a model of learning from experience. To pave the way for the discussion, it is useful to review the DB argument for the quotient rule:

$$P(H/E) = P(H\&E)/P(E) \tag{4.1}$$

which relates conditional probability to non-conditional probabilities. A central element in the argument is a definition of conditional bet, rooted in de Finetti's writings. He defines a bet on H conditional on E as a bet on H that proceeds if E turns out to be true and is called off if E is false (1980: 69). Thus, the conditional probability $P(H/E)$ is taken to stand for the price at which you will buy or sell a bet that pays \$1 if H is true, with the understanding that the purchase is called off if E turns out to be false. Another element is the fact that the sum of a bet on $H\&E$ and a bet against E, when

Table 4.2 Equivalent bets (2)

E	*H*	Bet I on *H*&*E*	¬*E*	Bet II against *E*	Sum of bets I and II	Bet III on *H* given *E*
T	T	(1 − q)r	F	−(1 − r)q	r − q	(1 − q/r)r
T	F	−qr	F	−(1 − r)q	−q	−(q/r)r
F	T	−qr	T	qr	0	0
F	F	−qr	T	qr	0	0

the loss of the first bet is the winning of the second bet, is equivalent to a bet on *H* conditional on *E* (Skyrms, 1986: 189). To be precise, let q be your fair betting quotient for a bet on *H*&*E* with stake r, and r be your fair betting quotient for a bet against *E* with stake q. The sum of these bets is equivalent to a bet on *H* conditional on *E* with fair betting quotient q/r and stake r, as shown in Table 4.2.

The ratio q/r corresponds to the ratio of the fair betting quotients for bet *H*&*E* over bet *E*. This suggests that if your fair betting quotient p for the conditional bet differed from q/r, there could be a Dutch book made against you. Since the conditional bet is called off if *E* turns out false, the trick to construct such a collection of bets is to introduce an additional bet on *E* with a suitable stake. Specifically, consider a bet on *H*&*E* and a bet against *E* with betting quotients and stakes as given above. Further consider a bet against *H* conditional on *E* with betting quotient p and stake r, as well as a bet on *E* with stake $q–pr$. Taken together, these bets lead to a net loss (gain) of $r(pr–q)$ regardless of whether *H* is true or false. Assuming that r is greater than zero, the net loss (gain) will be zero only if p equals the ratio q/r. This happens only if the fair betting quotient for the conditional bet is equal to the ratio of the fair betting quotients of *H*&*E* over *E*. Like the basic probability axioms, the quotient rule also becomes a theorem of the probability calculus.[10]

The quotient rule has a number of implications, including Bayes' theorem:

$$P(H/E) \propto P(E/H)\,P(H) \tag{4.2}$$

This theorem is usually thought to express a fundamental model of learning from experience. Savage remarks that by entailing Bayes' theorem the theory of coherent preferences gives a natural interpretation, or at least one important sense, of the phrase 'learning from experience'. The theorem, he says, 'prescribes, presumably compellingly, exactly how a set of beliefs should change in the light of what is observed' (1967: 602). A similar view is also held in economics. Kiefer and Nyarko (1995: 40) argue that economics needs no assumption beyond the subjective expected utility maximization assumption to model learning behaviour, since by implying Bayes' theorem the assumption yields a rational model of learning. Any additional assumption about how people learn about the economy is claimed to be ad hoc.

This interpretation of the role of the theorem is unwarranted, as Ian Hacking argued long ago (1967: 315). The theorem is a consequence of the quotient rule, which only says how conditional probabilities ought to be related to non-conditional probabilities where all the probabilities involved refer to the time before the conditioning event is learnt. So, like the quotient rule, the theorem is just a coherence constraint. In more detail, given $P(E/H)$, the theorem constrains the compatible pairs of $P(H)$ and $P(H/E)$; given $P(H)$, it defines the mapping from $P(E/H)$ to $P(H/E)$; given $P(H/E)$ and $P(E/H)$, it fixes $P(H)$; and given $P(./H)$ and $P(H)$, it defines the mapping from E to $P(H/E)$ (Smith, 1986: 98). The theorem is silent about where one has to begin. It is common to begin with $P(H)$ and $P(E/H)$ and use the theorem to infer $P(H/E)$, but one can begin by fixing $P(H/E)$ and use the theorem to determine a pair of $P(H)$ and $P(E/H)$ that is compatible with it. As far as the theorem's justification is concerned, both routes are equally permissible (Lindley, 1983: 7). The theorem is therefore silent about how a set of beliefs should be changed in light of what is observed.

Savage's interpretation of Bayes' theorem supposes an extra assumption that the probability of H after having learnt E is the same as the probability of H on the supposition that E were true (Hacking, 1967: 317). This assumption is known as the Bayesian conditionalization rule (BCR). The rule states that if your degree of belief in H conditional on E is $P(H/E)$, and you learn E for sure and nothing else, your new degree of belief in H, denoted by $Q(H)$, ought to be the same as $P(H/E)$:

$$Q(H) = P(H/E) \tag{4.3}$$

Thus, the question becomes whether the rationality considerations behind the probability axioms lend any support to the BCR. A response is found in Teller (1973), who argues that if you violate the rule there will be a finite series of bets that you consider as individually fair but collectively result in a loss no matter the outcomes. This has been taken to support the BCR just as the DB arguments support the probability axioms. We analyse Teller's argument to show why it fails and to hint at why there can be no justification for the rule anyway. We draw on a simple statement of the argument given in Howson (1997).

Suppose your updating strategy differs from the BCR. This means, upon learning E, you assign to H either a probability less than $P(H/E)$ or a probability greater than $P(H/E)$. Consider the first case where $Q(H) < P(H/E)$. Further, suppose in your opinion $P(H/E) = x$, $P(E) = y$ and $Q(H) = z$. In this case, a bookie can ensure a net gain by adopting the following betting strategy. He first sells you a conditional bet on H given E:

B_1: [\$1 if H, \$0 otherwise]

and a bet on E:

B_2: [\$(x–z) if E, \$0 otherwise]

at your fair prices. Later the truth of E becomes known. If E is false, the conditional bet is called off and you end up losing $(x - z)y$. If E is true, he buys from you a third bet on H:

B_3: [\$1 if H, \$0 otherwise]

at your fair price. But, then, regardless of whether H is true or false, you will end up losing $(x - z)y$. If your updating strategy were to assign a new probability to H greater than $P(H/E)$, i.e. $Q(H) > P(H/E)$, the trick for the bookie would be to buy from you a bet on H given E at your lower fair price and later sell you back a bet on H at your higher fair price. In either scenario, your net loss would be zero if your new probability for H were equal to its old probability conditional on E. It is concluded that a rational person must update his or her probability function in accordance with the BCR. Since the bookie needs to be aware of your updating strategy at the outset in order to be able to devise a collection of bets that guarantees a sure loss, Teller's argument is referred to as the *Dutch strategy* (DS) argument.

Although Teller's argument *prima facie* appears similar to the DB argument for the quotient rule, there are fundamental differences between them that are detrimental to the justificatory power of the DS argument. First, in the argument for the quotient rule, assuming that you violate it, the bookie only has to know your current partial beliefs to make a Dutch book against you. The susceptibility to a Dutch book originates solely from the internal structure of your beliefs and, as a consequence, points to an undesirable feature of your belief system. In contrast, in devising a DS argument, the bookie needs to know not only your fair betting quotients (partial beliefs) but also the direction in which you intend to depart from the BCR. If you do not reveal your updating strategy in advance, he cannot make a Dutch strategy against you. Thus, the susceptibility to a Dutch strategy arises from a conjunction of your partial beliefs with a decision to pre-announce your updating strategy. The susceptibility to the sure loss does not automatically indicate a defect in your belief system. You can avoid it simply by refusing to pre-announce your updating strategy. And there is nothing irrational about it.

Secondly, the success of the DB argument for the quotient rule depends on the validity of the value additivity principle. If the principle is not granted, susceptibility to a Dutch book will have other explanations including the failure of value additivity and cannot be taken as an indication of belief inconsistency. The postulate, as we saw, is not a logical principle. The only support for it is that whenever a number of bets are made *simultaneously*, it seems plausible to require that the value of a bet equivalent to the sum of the bets be the sum of the values of the individual bets. Like the DB argument, the DS argument also requires the assumption of value additivity to interpret susceptibility to a sure loss as an indication of belief inconsistency. However, the concern in the DS argument is with decisions made over time. In a dynamic decision-making scenario, there is no reason why an individual should not take note of his or her earlier commitments, and for this reason value additivity cannot be taken for granted. As a result, vulnerability to a Dutch strategy cannot be taken as an indication of belief inconsistency. The susceptibility can in fact arise from the failure of value additivity.

Thirdly, the bets involved in the DB argument are made simultaneously; all the underlying beliefs belong to a single point in time and the coherence requirement is deemed to be a rational ideal. In contrast, the possibility of devising a DS argument hinges on the bookie being given the opportunity to sell to or buy from you bets that are fair in your eyes at different times. This means that the beliefs underpinning a Dutch strategy belong to different times. So, even if the value additivity assumption is not challenged, the most that the possibility of a Dutch strategy can reveal is temporal inconsistency. But temporal consistency is not a rationality requirement. Otherwise, the very idea of rational belief updating would be self-contradictory. Therefore, the DS argument has no implication for how to shift from one belief system to another in light of new evidence (Christensen, 1991: 264).

These criticisms show why there can be no argument for the BCR similar to the DB argument. But, they do not establish that there can be no justification for the rule whatsoever. The Bayesian literature in fact offers several alternative attempts to justify the rule, as well as a generalization of it by Richard Jeffrey (1968).[11] An analysis of these endeavours is beyond the scope of this chapter. Some general considerations nevertheless indicate why they are also bound to fail. Note that the rule applies only when the probability of the conditioning event E shifts to unity.[12] The law of total probability then implies that $Q(H) = Q(H/E)$,[13] which means the rule holds if and only if

$$Q(H/E) = P(H/E) \tag{4.4}$$

This equality, called the *invariance* condition, implies that in order for the rule to hold, the new information must have no effect on the conditional probabilities in the domain of one's probability function. That is, having learnt E, the old and new conditional probabilities must agree with each other (Diaconis and Zabell, 1985: 36). Any attempt at establishing the BCR as a general updating rule requires showing that the invariance condition must hold under any circumstances. There are certain cases where new information not only shifts the probability of the conditioning event but also justifiably demands reassessing some of the conditional probabilities in the domain of one's probability function. Howson (1997) provides a case in which by learning E one is logically forced to change some of the conditional probabilities in the domain of one's probability function. Another case, closer to statistical practice, occurs when new observations cast doubt on the adequacy of the models considered, calling for constructing new models. When a new model is added or the existing models are modified, one should inevitably revise the probability of each model given the conditioning event (proposition) E. Since such legitimate belief shifts, which arise from introduction of new models, cannot be ruled out *a priori*, there can be no prospect for establishing the invariance condition as a general rationality requirement. And so, there can never be an argument establishing the BCR as a general rationality constraint.

Justificatory issues aside, the BCR is subject to some severe limitations. The rule applies only to situations where the new information shifts the probability of the conditioning event to unity. In reality, new information is usually vague, imprecise and fraught with errors, and rarely shifts the probability of an event to unity (Jeffrey, 1968: 171). In most real cases, the rule does not then apply anyway. The rule also requires both $p(E)$ and $p(H\&E)$ to be specified prior to learning E and hence does not apply to unanticipated information (Diaconis and Zabell, 1985). Finally, the rule does not apply to situations where a zero probability event occurs. All in all, the circumstances in which the rule applies are extremely limited.[14]

With these remarks, we end our study of some of the issues regarding the Bayesian theory that directly bear on the possibility of establishing a statistical learning theory. The main issue is whether the rationality considerations behind the probability axioms impose any constraint on how to shift from a coherent system of beliefs to a new coherent belief system in the light of new information. The answer, as seen, is in the negative. The only claim of the Bayesian theory left standing is that, for the sake of consistency, one's likelihood judgements at each moment of time ought to accord with the laws of probability. This requirement, though substantive, does not prescribe how to shift from a coherent system of beliefs to a new coherent belief system. The Bayesian theory, in itself, is not a theory of learning from experience. And, contrary to some economists, the expected utility maximization assumption does not entail a theory of learning from experience.

4.3 The orthodox view of Bayesian inference

Coherent analysis has a place in a theory of statistical inference but there is much more to a theory of statistical inference than coherent analysis. As a step towards explaining the key issues that a theory of parametric inference must address, and to define some necessary notions, we first give a brief account of the orthodox theory of Bayesian statistical inference, which views inference from data *solely* in terms of prior to posterior analysis. Suppose we want to model the relation of random variable Y with X. According to the orthodox Bayesian theory, the modeller somehow knows the set of models W that can be true of the relation of Y with X:

W = {All possible models that could possibly be true of the observables X and Y}

The assumption that W is known reduces the problem of inference from data to that of inferring the member of W that is most likely given the data. The Bayesian approach requires the modeller to express his uncertainty about the models in terms of a probability distribution that captures the confidence he has in each model prior to seeing the data. Let $D = \{x_t, y_t\}_{t=1}^{N}$ denote the data on X and Y, and let W contain only two models:

$$M_1: \quad Y \sim N(\beta_1 X, \delta_1^2) \qquad \beta_1, \delta_1^2 \in \theta_1$$

$$M_2: \quad Y \sim N(\alpha_1 + \beta_2 X, \delta_2^2) \qquad \alpha_1, \beta_2, \delta_2^2 \in \theta_2$$

Inferring the model, which is most likely given the data, requires estimating the parameters in each model. The hallmark of the Bayesian approach is to regard the parameters as random quantities, requiring the modeller to express his uncertainty towards them in the form of a (joint) probability distribution. Thus, a Bayesian model consists of at least two components, a data model $f(./\theta)$ and a (joint) prior density $\pi(\theta)$:

$$M_1: \quad Y \sim N(\beta_1 X, \delta_1^2) \qquad \pi(\theta_1) \qquad \beta_1, \delta_1^2 \in \theta_1$$

$$M_2: \quad Y \sim N(\alpha_1 + \beta_2 X, \delta_2^2) \quad \pi(\theta_2) \quad \alpha_1, \beta_2, \delta_2^2 \in \theta_2$$

$\pi(\theta_i)$ is the prior probability distribution for the parameters in M_i, representing the analyst's belief regarding the parameters prior to seeing the data.[15] The parameters in the prior density $\pi(\theta_i)$ are called hyperparameters as opposed to those in the data model $f(./\theta_i)$. Bayes' theorem combines the information in the prior density with the data to derive the distribution of the parameters θ_i of each model, namely

$$p(\theta_i/D, M_i) = p(D/\theta_i, M_i)\pi(\theta_i/M_i) \Big/ \int p(D/\theta_i, M_i)\pi(\theta_i/M_i)d\theta_i \tag{4.5}$$

$p(\theta_i/D, M_i)$ stands for the posterior distribution of θ_i and $p(D/\theta_i, M_i)$ for the likelihood function under model M_i.

Assuming M_i is true, the posterior distribution $p(\theta_i/D, M_i)$ expresses all the information required for making inference about θ_i. A point estimate of θ_i is obtained by computing the posterior mean:

$$\bar{\theta}_i = E(\theta_i/D, M_i) = \int \theta_i p(\theta_i/D, M_i) d\theta_i \tag{4.6}$$

Prediction is also obtained using posterior distribution $p(\theta_i/D, M_i)$. Suppose y_{t+1} is a future observation, independently drawn from the same distribution that has generated the data. The predictive distribution of y_{t+1} is given by

$$p(y_{t+1}/x, D, M_i) = \int p(y_{t+1}/\theta_i, M_i) p(\theta_i/D, M_i) d\theta_i \tag{4.7}$$

This distribution, termed the *posterior predictive* distribution, summarizes the information concerning the likely value of a new observation given the information in the data model, the prior and the data. If the posterior distribution $p(\theta_i/D, M_i)$ is replaced with the prior density $p(\theta_i/M_i)$, one obtains the *prior predictive* distribution:

$$p(y_{t+1}/x, M_i) = \int p(y_{t+1}/\theta_i, M_i) p(\theta_i/M_i) d\theta_i \tag{4.8}$$

which summarizes one's information about an observation y_{t+1} before having seen any data.

As in parameter estimation, the orthodox theory treats the model selection problem within the framework of prior to posterior analysis. It uses Bayes' theorem to derive the probability of each model given the data:

$$p(M_i/D) = \frac{p(D/M_i)p(M_i)}{p(D/M_1)p(M_1) + p(D/M_2)p(M_2)} \tag{4.9}$$

where $p(D/M_i)$ is the marginal probability distribution of the data under model M_i, obtained by integrating over the model parameter space:

$$p(D/M_i) = \int p(D/\theta_i, M_i) p(\theta_i/M_i) d\theta_i \tag{4.10}$$

with $p(D/\theta_i, M_i)$ being the likelihood of θ_i under model M_i. The theory suggests choosing the model that scores the highest posterior probability. Also, the degree to which the data confirm M_1 over M_2 is measured by the posterior odds for M_1 against M_2, i.e. the ratio of their posterior probabilities. By equation (4.9), this is

$$\frac{p(M_1/D)}{p(M_2/D)} = \frac{p(M_1)}{p(M_2)} \times \frac{p(D/M_1)}{p(D/M_2)} \tag{4.11}$$

The first ratio on the right-hand side of (4.11) is the prior odds ratio and the second is the Bayes factor. The numerator and the denominator of the Bayes factor are respectively the marginal likelihood of models M_1 and M_2. When the posterior odds ratio is above one, the data is said to support M_1 over M_2, and vice versa; when the posterior odds ratio equals unity, the data is said to equally support the models; and when the models are *a priori* equally likely, the posterior odds ratio is reduced to the Bayes factor.[16]

From the perspective of the orthodox theory, the agent knows the models that are possibly true of his choice situation or the economy. He uses data to estimate the models and selects the model with the highest posterior probability. When new data come in, he re-estimates the models, computes their probabilities conditional on the data, and again searches for the model with the highest posterior probability.

4.4 Bayesian statistical inference: a wider view

The orthodox Bayesian theory gives an incomplete description of the process of inference. The theory begins with the assumption that the candidate models are known in advance, and therefore the central inference problem is to find the model that is most likely given the data. This assumption is theoretically and empirically indefensible. Candidate models are never known in advance, and the most important aspect of inference from data consists of model specification (formulation).

A number of activities precede model formulation, including initial examination of the data, choosing appropriate transformations of the data, producing descriptive statistics, and finding possible outliers (Cox and Snell, 1981; Chatfield, 1995; and Leamer, 1978). This means there are at least two important phases of inference before the orthodox Bayesian theory, which interprets inference in terms of prior to posterior analysis, becomes relevant. The first is initial examination of data and the other is formulation of an initial model.

The objective in initial model formulation is to specify a model that can serve as an informed basis for searching for a model that can accurately account for the data. A Bayesian model is made of at least two components: a data model and a (joint) prior probability density for the model parameters. A data model, as explained in the last chapter, consists of a set of internally consistent hypotheses of independence, homogeneity, and distribution. The initial specification of a Bayesian model involves postulating appropriate assumptions of independence, homogeneity, and data distribution, *as well as* specifying a joint prior density for the data model parameters. Since *initial* specification of the basic assumptions concerns creating the objects (models) to which uncertainty applies, it is by definition a non-Bayesian matter. Any attempt at explaining initial model formulation necessitates stepping out of the framework of prior to posterior analysis (Hill, 1990: 57). Once a model has been formulated, the next phase of inference is estimation (model fitting), where coherent analysis begins to become relevant.

Initial model formulation is a complex activity involving many decisions. There is no guarantee a model generated in the early stages of research can adequately account for the data and yield accurate predictions. Before making any use of the model, an important question is whether it is empirically adequate. As seen, in assessing the merits of candidate models $M_1, M_2, \ldots, M_K$, the orthodox Bayesian theory requires specifying a prior probability distribution over the models, and computing the posterior probability of each model using Bayes' theorem:

$$P(M_i/D) = \frac{P(D/M_i)P(M_i)}{\sum P(D/M_i)P(M_i)} \tag{4.12}$$

This approach only allows the comparison of relative probabilities (Lindley, 1982: 81), which is not indicative of empirical adequacy. The high probability of a model can be the result of the choice of a particular prior for the parameters. As in Lindley's paradox, it is possible by adopting flat priors to arbitrarily increase the posterior probability of a model, and this can happen even if the sample size is very large (Gelfand *et al.*, 1992: 151; see Appendix 4.A for a statement of the paradox). Moreover, the posterior probability of a model is always *conditional* on the set of candidate models considered (Box, 1980: 427). When the set of candidate models contains only a single model, by Bayes' theorem the model automatically receives posterior probability one, and as the number of models in the set grows, the probability of the initial model can decrease and in fact approach zero (Box, 1983: 73). Thus, the high probability of a model may be due to the analyst's failure to include among the candidates the true model or a close approximate thereof, rather than the adequacy of the model. Only if the set of candidate models is known to be wide enough to contain an adequate model, can a connection be made between the high posterior probability of a model and its empirical adequacy. Any attempt at ensuring this, though, calls for investigating the compatibility of each model with the data (Anscombe, 1963: 34), which cannot be done using Bayes' theorem. Model assessment also necessitates an analysis different from prior to posterior analysis. To be precise, it requires a method that directly deals with the relation between a model and the data, not with apportioning of uncertainty across models (Barnard, 1962: 42-3; Mallow, 1970: 77).

The process of empirical adequacy assessment may reveal the failure of the initial model, calling for model re-specification. This involves varying the model assumptions one at a time, monitoring the effect of the variation, and continuing the process until an adequate model is obtained. Since in *re-specification analysis* the concern is with the adequacy of a single model, the analysis cannot be cast in terms of prior to posterior analysis. Re-specification analysis is also a non-Bayesian issue.

The process of initial model formulation, empirical model assessment, and re-specification analysis may produce several models fitting the data. For practical purposes, it may be necessary to choose a model from among the candidates. It is here that coherent analysis can become relevant again.

Finally, the steps from the initial examination of data to model selection are not a one-off process. In real life, statistical inference is an iterative process. The statistician formulates a set of models, estimates them, assesses their adequacy, modifies them if necessary, chooses a model and derives the predictions required for decisions. As new data arrive, she reassesses the adequacy of the models, expands or modifies the set of candidate models, derives new predictions, and waits for future data to disclose the models' adequacy. Accordingly, it is plausible to think of parametric statistical inference as a process with the following key phases:

(a) Data description
(b) Initial model formulation (or specification)
(c) Model fitting (or estimation)
(d) Model assessment (or criticism)
(e) Model re-specification
(f) Model selection
(g) Iteration

The Bayesian theory is only relevant to model estimation and model selection. It leaves out other central aspects of inference, namely initial model formulation, empirical model assessment, and re-specification analysis. If the theory is to be a satisfactory account of statistical inference, it must be broadened to cover these critical aspects of inference. The rest of this chapter joins together various pieces from the literature to define a broader view of Bayesian inference that goes some way towards explaining the inferential issues left out by the orthodox Bayesian theory.

4.5 Initial Bayesian model formulation

Is there a theory of (initial) model specification? Fisher is said to be the first to raise the issue of model specification in his seminal paper (1922) 'On the mathematical foundations of theoretical statistics'. In this paper, he divides the problems of statistics into three types; (i) problems of *specification*; (ii) problems of *estimation*; and (iii) problems of *distribution*. Fisher's discussion of specification problems is confined to a single paragraph, dominated by the first sentence: 'As regards problems of specification, these are entirely a matter for the practical statistician...' (1922: 314). This suggests 'that in his view there can be no theory of modelling, no general modelling strategy, but that instead each problem must be considered entirely on its own merits' (Lehmann, 1990: 160). Fisher's view of model specification has continued to dominate the statistics community, and has been endorsed by most statisticians, including Savage (1971), Mallow (1970), Dawid (1982), and Poirier (1988). However, a look at the modern statistical literature suggests that the view of model specification as an art with no general strategies is unduly pessimistic. Modern statistics provides a great deal of teachings that are highly relevant to establishing an exploratory theory of statistical model formulation. This chapter pieces together various elements of an exploratory theory of Bayesian modelling that takes us some way towards understanding how a statistician proceeds to build a model. The theory addresses three aspects of the model-building process: 'initial model formulation', 'empirical model assessment' and 're-specification analysis'. The current section outlines a framework for initial model formulation by drawing on proposals found in D'Agostino (1986), Lehmann (1990), Rubin (1984), Spanos (1986; 1999) and Spanos and McGuirk (2001).

4.5.1 Initial data model specification

A theory of initial model formulation requires a clear definition of the problem and a method to solve it. To provide a definition, we can divide the whole issue of Bayesian model formulation into specification of a data model and a prior distribution. We first consider the initial specification of a data model. As argued in the last chapter, when the concern is to establish an interpretable model of several variables it is necessary to start with a parametric model, which raises the question of where the models come from. An interesting response to this question is found in Lehmann (1990): a line of research in mathematical statistics has been to define alternative notions of independence, homogeneity and probability distribution families. The research has resulted in a rich variety of independence and homogeneity hypotheses, as well as a large list of univariate, bivariate, and multivariate probability distribution families. Consistent combination of these independence and homogeneity hypotheses with the distribution families produces a large collection of primitive data models, which can be used as building blocks to create numerous and, in a sense, countless mixture models. In this way, theoretical statistics provides a rich *reservoir* of models, to use Lehmann's apt term (1990: 161). Figure 4.1 schematically shows the structure of the model reservoir.[17]

So, in response to the question of where the models come from, Lehmann suggests that they come from the model reservoir of statistics. In light of this proposal, the issue of initial data model specification can be defined as the problem of selecting a set of internally consistent hypotheses from the three categories of known independence, homogeneity, and distributional assumptions to form a model that can account for the data (Spanos, 1999: 756). To provide a theory of initial model formulation, it remains to explain how the initial selection of these hypotheses can take place.

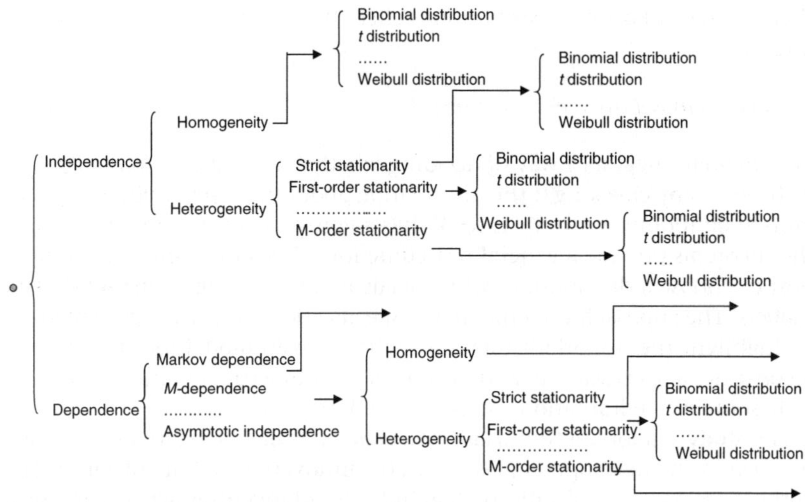

Figure 4.1 The structure of the model reservoir

Note: The model reservoir grows with advances in theoretical statistics.

4.5.1.1 The theoretical approach to data model specification

Theoretical statistics provides the ingredients for two complementary methods for initial selection of the basic hypotheses, one drawing on subject-matter information and the other on data. The first procedure, also cited in Lehmann (1990), emerges from a class of theorems known as characterization theorems. A characterization theorem, roughly speaking, defines a set of sufficient conditions that if they were true of a variable (or a set of variables), the probability distribution of the variable (or variables) would belong to a certain distribution family (Galambos, 1982). A well-known characterization theorem is the Poisson process theorem that describes the conditions under which a univariate distribution has a Poisson distribution. In one form, the theorem goes as follows:

Consider variable Y_t and let t stand for time. For each $t > 0$, if

A_1: Y_t is an integer-valued random variable
A_2: $Y_0 = 0$
A_3: Y_t and $Y_{t+s} - Y_t$ are independently distributed, $s > 0$
A_4: Y_t and $Y_{t+s} - Y_t$ are identically distributed
A_5: limit $t \to 0 \frac{p(Y_t=1)}{t} = \lambda$
A_6: limit $t \to 0 \frac{p(Y_t>1)}{t} = 0$

then, Y_t has a Poisson distribution (Feller, 1971). That is, for any positive integer n:

$$p(Y_t = n) = f(n) = e^{-\lambda_t}(\lambda_t)^n(n!)^{-1} \tag{4.13}$$

The theorem suggests a way of deciding whether a variable Y_t has a Poisson distribution by checking if the information about the distribution of Y_t warrants assumptions A_1 to A_6. If so, Y_t has a Poisson distribution. In this way, the theorems provide a general procedure for using subject-matter information to choose a distribution, which leads to a narrowing of the set of data models. The approach underlies many specification studies in econometrics. To highlight the important role of the theorems in model formulation, we reconstruct a specification study from the econometric literature, and then state some of the limitations of the method in practice.

The study is adopted from Hausman *et al.* (1984), who examine the effect of research and development (R&D) on the innovation activity of a firm. The authors use patent applications as an indicator of inventive activity and seek to model its relationship with R&D. Let Y_t represent the number of patents applied for or received during period $(0, t)$ and X_t the expenditure on research and development during the period. To model the relation of Y_t with X_t, the authors list a number of conceptual and simplifying assumptions that seem plausible about Y_t. Specifically, they propose that

A_1: Y_t is a discrete random variable taking a finite number of positive values;
A_2: The value of Y_t at time zero $t = 0$ is zero (innovation takes time);
A_3: The numbers of patents received during *non-overlapping* time intervals are *independent* of each other (independence assumption);
A_4: If Y_t is the number of patents received during $[0, t]$ and Z_t the number of patents received during $[t_1, t_{1+t}]$, Y_t and Z_t have the same distribution (homogeneity assumption);
A_5: The probability of receiving two or more patents in a sufficiently small interval is negligible; and
A_6: The probability of receiving n patents during $[t, t+s]$ is proportional to the length of $[t, t+s]$, barring extremely large intervals.

These hypotheses match with the conditions of the Poisson process theorem. Accordingly, the authors conclude, as a first conjecture, that Y_t has a Poisson distribution and model the dependence of Y_t on X_t using a Poisson regression model (Hausman *et al.*, 1984: 911):

$$\begin{aligned} p(Y_t = n/x_t) &= e^{-\lambda_t}(\lambda_t)^n(n!)^{-1} \\ \ln(\lambda_t) &= \alpha + \beta x_t \end{aligned} \tag{4.14}$$

for any integer n. The authors next consider the effect of weakening the independence assumption, and investigate the possibility of adopting a more robust model, such as the negative binomial regression model. A vast number of phenomena are similar to patent data, including the number of spells of sickness in a year, the number of records purchased per month, the number of cars owned, the number of jobs held during a year, and so forth. At one stroke, the Poisson theorem provides a unified approach to creating an initial data model for a large number of economic phenomena. Many other specification studies in econometrics can easily be interpreted as an application of a characterization theorem.[18]

This study illustrates how the theoretical approach, which emerges from the characterization theorems, enables one to use subject-matter information to narrow down the class of data models that could possibly be true of a set of variables. The method is nonetheless subject to some limitations in practice. A trouble relates to the probabilistic conditions that enter the theorems. As is explicit in the example, the theorems assume that the data are identically and independently distributed. In the natural sciences, there may be reliable subject-matter information to justify these assumptions *a priori*. In the social sciences, theories are imprecise, lack adequate empirical support, and the mechanisms generating the data undergo changes. The fate of these assumptions can rarely be decided on subject-matter information alone. If there is any way of deciding on the appropriateness of the independence or homogeneity assumptions, which go into the theorems, it must be by looking at the data.

Also, the information available about the distribution of a variable is usually imprecise and, as a result, consistent with more than one distribution family. In general, if the information is consistent with the assumptions defining a distribution family (say, exponential), it is also consistent with any distribution family that is robust with respect to it (say, Weibull). So, the approach does not usually lead to the choice of a single distribution hypothesis. These reservations aside, the theorems can effectively narrow down the class of appropriate models in the model reservoir. Even the information that the variable is continuous, finite, positive, or falls within the unit interval substantially reduces the space of appropriate data models within which an exploratory search must take place.

4.5.1.2 The empirical approach to data model specification

The second method, which emerges from theoretical statistics, uses data for initial selection of the basic probabilistic assumptions. To explain the method, let us return to the definition of a data model as a set of internally consistent hypotheses drawn from the three categories of independence, homogeneity, and distribution assumptions. Each combination of these hypotheses, which forms a data model, implies a series of consequences that are true of the model *under all its possible parameterizations*. We term such consequences *ex ante* or *pre-estimation* implications, as they can be derived before estimating the model. Theoretical statistics has a rich literature on the *ex ante* consequences of alternative combinations of the basic assumptions defining the model reservoir. With this in mind, a plausible methodological principle is that a model worthy of further consideration must not have *ex ante* consequences grossly incompatible with the data. Granting this, the class of candidate data models, warranted by subject-matter information, can be substantially narrowed down by investigating the *pre-estimation* consequences of the models. If the *ex ante* consequences of a model are compatible with the data, it is kept as a candidate model. Otherwise, it is excluded. Moreover, each *ex ante* implication of a data model can be traced to one of its assumptions. If an *ex ante* consequence of a model fails to appear in the data, then the failure can be traced to a particular assumption, and this information can be used to search systematically for a model capable of accounting for the data. The search for a first model need not be entirely blind.

Essential to using data for initial model formulation is a judgement of whether the *ex ante* consequences of the model are consistent with the data. In the frequentist setting, this judgement of consistency is usually made by computing p-values. An exploratory theory of Bayesian model formulation can also follow a similar route. But, since most *ex ante* consequences of a model are of a graphical nature or can be rephrased graphically, and since at this stage the objective is simply to make educated guesses about the nature of the statistical model that might be appropriate for the data, it is sufficient to work with an informal concept of incompatibility. Later, it will be explained how the frequentist idea of p-value can justifiably be assimilated within a broader view of Bayesian inference.

The following three subsections describe in some detail the process of data-driven initial model specification using a simple data set on the quarterly US unemployment rate over twenty-five years from 1948 to 1972, given in Fuller (1976), which we use later to illustrate Bayesian diagnostic learning. An objective is to emphasize the relevance of classical methods for an exploratory theory of Bayesian model formulation. Another is to bring to the fore the kind of heuristic principles that are necessary for using data in initial model specification. The exposition will also illustrate modes of inference that cannot be understood in terms of prior to posterior analysis but occupy a central place in a wider view of statistical inference.

4.5.1.2.1 *The independence assumption.* The choice of an independence and homogeneity assumption restricts the choice of a distribution family. This means the empirical search for an initial data model should begin by looking for an appropriate independence and homogeneity assumption. The starting-point in this search is whether the assumptions of complete independence (C-independence) and complete homogeneity (C-homogeneity) are appropriate or, in short, whether the data are random. To focus on one assumption at a time, we first take *C*-homogeneity for granted. Let *Y* denote the unemployment rate, and *N* the sample size. Given *C*-homogeneity, the task of *ex ante* assessment of *C*-independence involves assessing the implications of the following model:

Unrestricted data model
A_1 Distribution: Unrestricted
A_1 Independence: $(Y_1, Y_2, ..., Y_N)$ is *C*-Independent
A_1 Homogeneity: $(Y_1, Y_2, ..., Y_N)$ is *C*-Homogeneous

This model has several consequences that underlie a number of classical tests of independence, usually named distribution-free tests of randomness. Some of these tests are discussed in Bradley (1968) and Lehmann and D'Abrera (1975). Here, we follow Bradley (1968: 271–8). Let us arrange the *N* observations in the order they were obtained. Suppose, for simplicity, none of the observations are identical so that they constitute *N* distinct numbers.[19] The *N* numbers can be arranged in *N*! distinguishable ways, creating a sample space *S* with *N*! elements. If the hypothesized model were true of *Y*, each element in *S* would *a priori* be as likely as the actual sequence. In other words, if one believed that the observations on *Y* were random, one would *a priori* have to consider each element in *S* as equally likely. An assumption to the contrary entails the failure of either *C*-independence or *C*-homogeneity (Bradley, 1968: 277). The same conclusion is also true of any sample space formed from a sub-sequence of the *N* observations. This consequence leads to several procedures for *ex ante* assessment of *C*-independence. To explain one possible method, consider the *t*-plot of the unemployment data given below:

If an increase in the ordered sequence of observations is designated by '1' and a decrease by '0', the first quarter of the sequence of the unemployment data plotted in Figure 4.2 can be shown as:

0 1 1 1 1 1 1 0 0 0 0 0 0 1 1 0 1 1 1 0 0 1 0 1

An unbroken sequence of increasing observations (ones) or decreasing observations (zeros) is called a *run*. There are a total of ten runs in the above sub-sequence. Let *R* be the total number of runs of any size in the entire sequence, $A_{R,N}$ the total number of arrangements of the *N* observations that contains *R* runs, and $R_{(\geq m)}$ the number of runs of size *m* or greater. Given the equal probability of each element in *S*, Levene (1952) establishes that

$$P(R/N) = \frac{A_{R,N}}{N!}$$

$$E(R) = (2N-1)/3 \quad Var(R) = (16N-29)/90 \tag{4.15}$$

$$E(R_{(\geq m)}) = \frac{2 + 2(N-m)(m+1)}{(m+2)!} \quad m \leq (N-2)$$

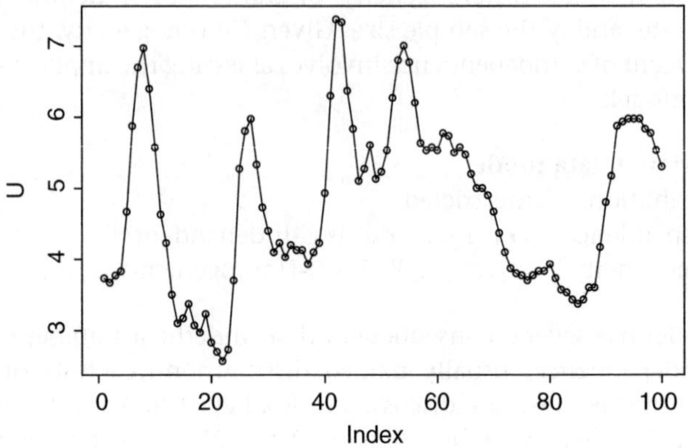

Figure 4.2 Unemployment data

and that R is asymptotically normally distributed. These consequences are in the form of expected and probability values, and as such say nothing about a particular sample. Nonetheless, it is plausible to assume that if the assumptions of the unrestricted model are appropriate, in an 'adequately' large sample, the sample values of these quantities come close to their theoretical values. In general, to bridge between theoretical (expected) quantities and their sample analogues, the following heuristic principle, present in many areas of statistics, commands plausibility:

> **Heuristic principle I**: If the hypothesized model is appropriate, in an adequately large sample, the theoretical values implied by the model for variables defined from the sample and the sample values of the variables are 'close' to each other.

In light of this, the appropriateness of C-independence can be assessed by comparing, say, the actual values of R and $R_{(\geq m)}$ with their expected values $E(R)$ and $E(R_{\geq m})$. A sharp difference casts doubt on the assumption. The sample in Figure 4.2 contains 100 observations, with $E(R)$ and $E(R_{\geq 3})$ being 66.33 and 6.48 respectively. The actual values of R and $R_{(\geq 3)}$ are 32 and 14 respectively, which are considerably different from the theoretical values. The large difference strongly points to dependence in the data, suggesting the inappropriateness of C-independence.

There is a wealth of techniques that can be used for pre-estimation assessment of alternative independence hypotheses. Notably, one may examine the sample partial autocorrelation function (SPACF) of various orders to select an independence assumption tentatively. In general, if a p-order Markov independence assumption were true of Y, the sample partial autocorrelation

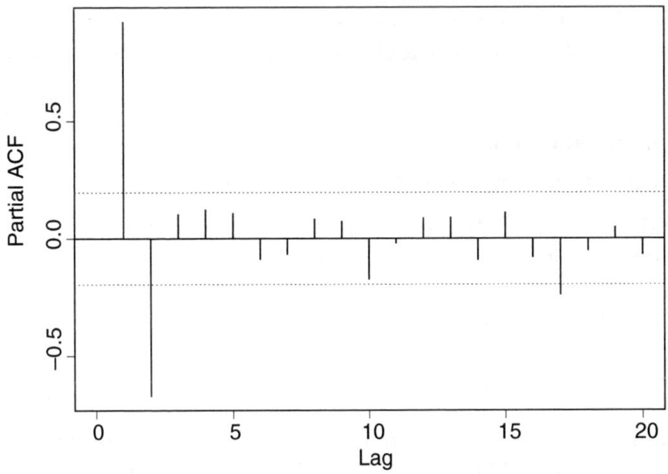

Figure 4.3 Unemployment data: sample PACF

function would be expected to 'cut off' (i.e. be equal to zero) after p lag (Box and Jenkins, 1976). Figure 4.3 plots the SPACF of the unemployment data. The plot suggests a second-order Markov independence condition. However, for illustration purposes, we will work with a first-order Markov condition, which leads to a simpler data model.

4.5.1.2.2 *The homogeneity assumption.* The starting-point in the search for a homogeneity assumption is an assessment of C-homogeneity, which is the simplest of the homogeneity assumptions. Classical statistics provides a host of distribution-free tests useful for investigating the pre-estimation implications of C-homogeneity. A class of such procedures is developed in Cox and Stuart (1955). For illustration, we look at these authors' test of trend in location, described in Bradley (1968: 175). Suppose the sample consists of N different observations, with N being an even number. If N is an odd number, the middle observation dividing the sequence into two parts is removed. Arrange the observations as an ordered sequence $Y_1, Y_2, \ldots Y_i, \ldots, Y_n, Y_{n+1}, \ldots, Y_{n+i}, \ldots, Y_{2n}$ with the subscripts indicating the order in which they were obtained. Now, for every $i \leq n$ form the difference-score $Z_i = (Y_i - Y_{n+i})$, and let S be the number of positive difference-scores. Considering the signs of Z_i, the difference-scores can be viewed as the outcomes of n Bernoulli trials. If the unrestricted model is true, Z_i is as likely to be positive as it is to be negative, i.e. $p(Y_i < Y_{n+i}) = p(Y_i > Y_{n+i}) = 0.5$. In that case, S can be regarded as the number of successes in n Bernoulli trials, with probability $p = 0.5$ of success on each trial. This results in the binomial data model:

Binomial data model

A_1 Distribution: binomial, $S \sim Bin(n, \pi)$; $P(S = s) = \binom{n}{s} \pi^s (1 - \pi)^{n-s}$

A_2 Independence: $(Z_1, Z_2, \ldots, Z_n)$ is C-Independent

A_3 Homogeneity: $(Z_1, Z_2, \ldots, Z_n)$ is C-Homogeneous

with first and second moments

$$E(S) = n/2 \qquad Var(S) = n/4$$

Cox and Stuart's test of trend in location is based on computing p-value of the observed value of S. As a less formal check, one may assess the appropriateness of C-homogeneity by comparing the expected values $E(S)$ and $Var(S)$ with their sample analogues. In an adequately large sample, a significant departure points to the failure of C-homogeneity. In particular, when S is considerably greater than $E(S)$, the data points to a negative trend in location, and when it is considerably less than $E(S)$, it points to a positive trend in location. Cox and Stuart (1955) also establish analogous procedures for testing trend in dispersion or cyclical trend.[20]

As for the unemployment data, the expected values $E(S)$ and $Var(S)$ are 25 and 12.5 respectively, which are close to the sample values of 24 and 11.06. Similar results are obtained when the data are examined for trend in dispersion or cyclical trend. Thus, the data cast no doubt on C-homogeneity. The choice of the first-order Markov condition, however, necessitates replacing C-homogeneity with strict stationarity, which is an extension of C-homogeneity to an independently distributed vector of random variables (Chapter 3). With this choice, we obtain the following model:

Unrestricted data model

A_1 Distribution: Unrestricted

A_2 Independence: $(Y_1, Y_2, \ldots, Y_T)$ is first-order Markov independent

A_3 Homogeneity: $(Y_1, Y_2, \ldots, Y_T)$ is strictly stationary

4.5.1.2.3 *The distribution assumption.* The outcome of a pre-estimation search among the independence and homogeneity hypotheses is a data model of the form stated above. Given such a model, the pre-estimation search for a distribution family involves inserting alternative distributions, suggested by subject-matter information, into the model, and assessing the *ex ante* implications of the model relating to the distribution assumption. In the current case, since Y_t is continuous, the first-order Markov assumption restricts the class of plausible distribution families for Y_t to bivariate continuous families. To illustrate, we consider the bivariate normal family. This gives rise to:

Bivariate normal data model

A_1 Distribution:	$\mathbf{X} \sim N(\mu, \Sigma)$, bivariate normal, $\mathbf{X} = (Y_t, Y_{t-1})$
A_2 Independence:	$(Y_1, Y_2, \ldots, Y_T)$ is first-order Markov independent
A_3 Homogeneity:	$(Y_1, Y_2, \ldots, Y_T)$ is strictly stationary

The *ex ante* consequences of a distribution family are mainly defined by the invariant features of the density curve, or the cumulative distribution function (cdf) of the family. These include symmetry and skewness. So, with a reasonably large sample, the appropriateness of a distribution family can be assessed by comparing the density curve or the *cdf* of the family with their sample analogues. The justification for this practice arises from another typical exploratory principle, which can be stated as follows:

Heuristic principle II: If the data come from a distribution family, when the sample is adequately large, an appropriate plot of the data should show, within sampling error, the invariant features of the density curve or *cdf* of the family such as symmetry, positive or negative skewness, kurtosis, and so forth.

This methodology works well for assessing univariate and bivariate distribution families. However, since graphical features are difficult to investigate in high-dimensional data, it cannot directly be extended to multivariate families. Nevertheless, the multivariate families have other types of *ex ante* implications that pave the way for their assessment. We briefly refer to three categories of such implications.

A general feature of the exiting multivariate (bivariate) families is that if they are true of a set of variables, the marginal distributions of the variables also belong to the same distribution family. This means an initial assessment of a multivariate family can be achieved by checking the marginal distribution families of the variables. The converse of this result is not true though. If the univariate distributions of a set of variables belong to a distribution family, it does not follow that the joint distribution of the variables also belongs to the same family (Seber, 1984: 141).

In the current case, if the bivariate normal family is true of $\mathbf{X} = (Y_t, Y_{t-1})$, the marginal distribution of Y_t is also normal. The density curve of a normal distribution is symmetric. This means that, with a large sample, a judgement about normality can be achieved by checking the symmetry of a histogram or stem and leaf plot of the data. A more informative graph for assessing symmetry is obtained by plotting the upper half of the ordered observations

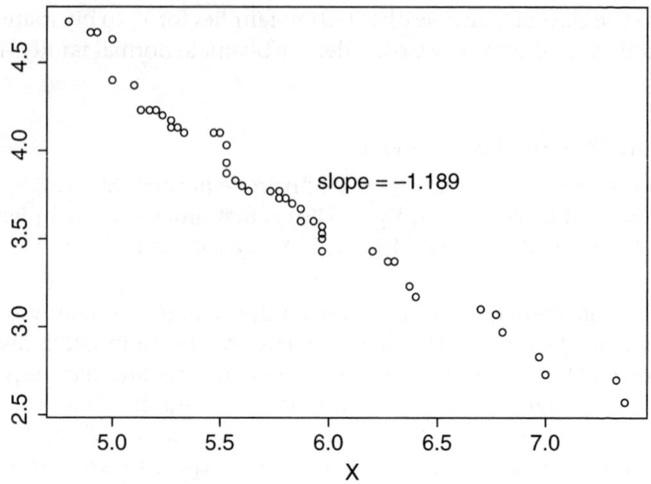

Figure 4.4 Symmetry plot unemployment data

Note: Y stands for $Y_{(N+1-i)}$ and X stands for $Y_{(i)}$.

against the lower half. Let $Y_{(1)}, Y_{(2)}, \ldots, Y_{(N)}$ represent the ordered observations. If the data arise from a symmetric distribution, a plot of $Y_{(N)}$ versus $Y_{(1)}$, $Y_{(N-1)}$ versus $Y_{(2)}$, and in general $Y_{(N+1-i)}$ versus $Y_{(i)}$ for $i \leq N/2$ should create a straight line with a negative unit slope (D'Agostino, 1986: 13). Figure 4.4 plots $Y_{(N+1-i)}$ versus $Y_{(i)}$ for the US unemployment data.

The data points are mostly scattered around a straight line with a negative slope close to one, suggesting that they could have come from a symmetric distribution family such as the normal family. To narrow down the class of symmetric families to the normal family, further assessment of the *ex ante* consequences of the family is needed, which can be done, say, by checking the normal probability plot of the data.

A second type of *ex ante* consequences of a multivariate distribution consists in restrictions on the form of the regression function of each of the variables on the rest of the variables. The distribution family determines whether the functions are linear, non-linear, or how they look. In the present case, if the bivariate normal distribution is true of $\boldsymbol{X}$, the regression function of Y_t on Y_{t-1} is given by the linear function:

$$E(Y_t/Y_{t-1} = y_{t-1}) = \alpha + \beta y_{t-1} \tag{4.16}$$

Alternatively, if the variables (Y_t, Y_{t-1}) have, for instance, a bivariate exponential distribution, the regression of Y_t on Y_{t-1} is given by the non-linear

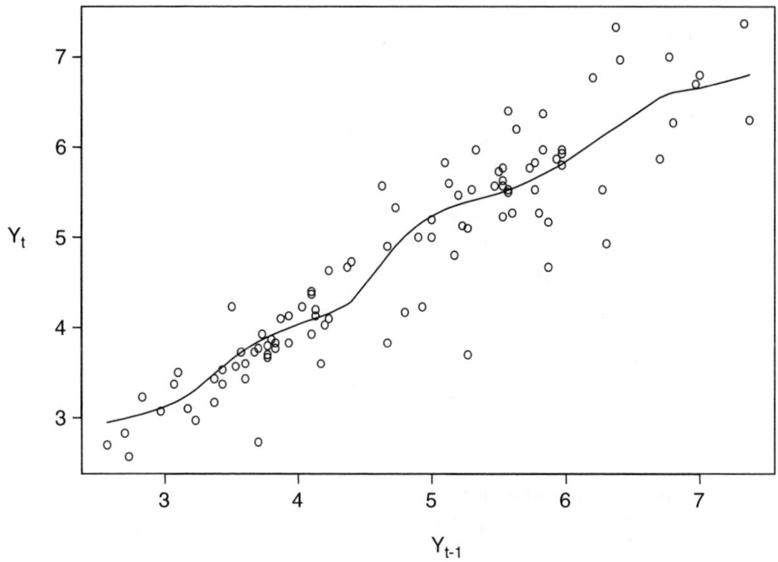

Figure 4.5 Linearity assessment unemployment data

Note: Kernel regression of Y_t on Y_{t-1}: the optimal level of smoothing was selected using leave-one-out cross-validation.

function (Mardia, 1970):

$$E(Y_t/Y_{t-1} = y_{t-1}) = \frac{(1 + \theta + \theta y_{t-1})}{(1 + \theta y_{t-1})^2} \tag{4.17}$$

The linearity of the regression of Y_t on Y_{t-1} can be assessed by using a non-parametric regressor to obtain a curve of the dependence of Y_t on Y_{t-1}, and checking if it can be approximated by a linear function. Figure 4.5 shows the kernel regression curve of Y_t on Y_{t-1}.

The curve comes close to a linear function, further confirming the consistency of the data with the normal family. In addition to non-parametric tools, a Bayesian statistician may also use the numerous classical means developed for checking linearity and curvature (Cox and Small, 1978; Abrevaya and Jiang, 2005).

Finally, a third type of *ex ante* consequences of a multivariate distribution family consists of the implications for new variables defined from the variables under study. To give an example, let $\mathbf{X}_i$ be the ith point in a sample of data on $\boldsymbol{X}$, $\overline{\mathbf{X}}$ the vector of sample means, and $\boldsymbol{S}$ the sample covariance

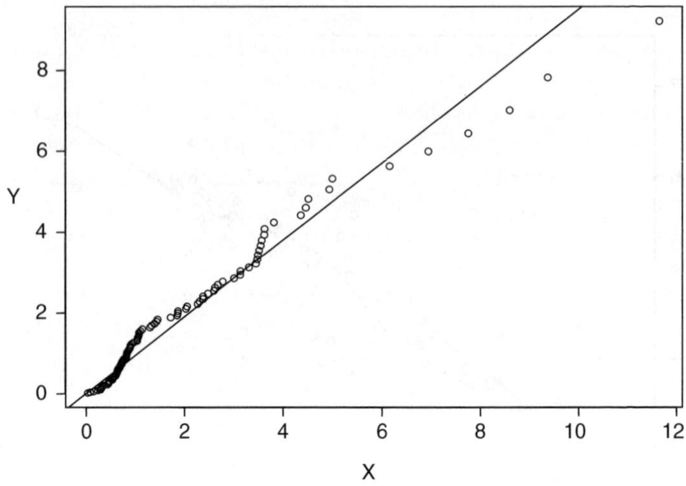

Figure 4.6 Bivariate normality test
Note: X stands for d_i^2-values and Y for $\chi^2(2)$ percentiles.

matrix. Further, define a new random variable:

$$d_i^2 = (\mathbf{X}_i - \overline{\mathbf{X}})^T \mathbf{S}^{-1} (\mathbf{X}_i - \overline{\mathbf{X}}) \tag{4.18}$$

It has been shown that when $\boldsymbol{X}$ has a multivariate normal distribution, for large samples, d_i^2-values are approximately distributed as $\chi^2(p)$, where p stands for the dimension of $\boldsymbol{X}$. In that case, a probability plot of the $\chi^2(p)$ percentiles against the ordered d_i^2-values will generate a straight line from the origin (Gnanadesikan, 1977: 172–4), allowing direct assessment of joint normality. Figure 4.6 plots the $\chi^2(2)$ percentiles against the ordered d_i^2-values for the unemployment data.

Though the data points are fairly closely scattered around a straight line, the fit is not perfect. The departure could be because the data have come from another symmetric family, the first-order Markov condition is inappropriate, or there is noise in the data. All these possibilities can be investigated. Since the concern here is illustrative, we will not further the analysis, and will take the bivariate normal model as our initial model. In general, if the *ex ante* implications of a distribution family depart from the data, a similar approach can be pursued to assess the appropriateness of alternative distributions.

The unemployment data is very simple, and so is the above analysis. The analysis, nevertheless, gives a reasonable description of how a statistician formulates an initial model. Similar methods also give guidance for dealing with complex data sets. An issue in dealing with complex data sets, for instance, is to decide whether to fit a mixture model and, if so, how complex the mixture model should be. Significant insight on this matter can be achieved by using probability plots. When the data come from different members of a distribution family, an appropriate probability plot generates several straight lines, each representing a specific distribution (D'Agostino, 1986: 42–6). The complexity of the model can be based on the number of inferred distributions. Initial data model specification is no longer without principles and procedures.

4.5.2 Prior specification

A Bayesian model also requires a (joint) probability distribution of the model parameters. While the Bayesian literature provides very little on data model specification, it offers a substantial body of literature on prior modelling. O'Hagan (1994), to give an example, devotes a full, long chapter to prior modelling but says nothing at all about selecting data model assumptions. This exclusive emphasis on prior modelling is without doubt unbalanced. The prior assumption is like any other assumption entering a model, if not the least critical one. If the data model is mis-specified, it is hard to make sense of a good prior. And, if it is correctly specified, when the sample is adequately large, the choice of a particular prior is not often critical. In any case, the central issue in prior modelling is whether there is a method to find a prior density for the parameters of the data model that enables it to best account for the data. Our response to this question will come in a later section. Here, to pave the way, we briefly look at various conventional approaches to prior modelling, explain the merits and shortcomings of each approach, and show why the focus of attention in these approaches is mistaken.[21]

4.5.2.1 The summary-based method

The aim of prior modelling is traditionally defined as specifying a joint density function that best represents the modeller's opinion about the parameters before seeing the data. A prior density that represents substantive information is called an *informative* prior. In the literature we find two general methodologies for quantifying a person's qualitative information in terms of a density function. The *summary-based* method builds on the idea that a distribution can be characterized in terms of a number of summaries. A univariate distribution, for instance, can be summarized using location measures (mean, median, and mode), dispersion measures (variance, standard deviation, and range), skewness, and fractiles. The method requires expressing certain summaries about the distribution of the parameters and searching for a probability distribution that best fits the summaries (O'Hagan, 1994: 143). This strategy underlies several apparently differing prior modelling techniques, whose only difference consists of the type of summaries they require and the way in which the summaries are used to select a density function.

As a simple illustration, following Berger (1980: 66), consider the case of a univariate parameter θ, say, the mean of a normal distribution with a known variance. Suppose it is thought the median of the distribution $\pi(\theta)$ is close to zero and the first quartile (1/4 fractile) and the second quartile (3/4 fractile) of the distribution are respectively -1 and 1.[22] These summaries suggest that $\pi(\theta)$ is symmetric around its median. It may then be concluded that $\pi(\theta)$ belongs to the family of normal distributions, which are symmetric about their median. Since the mean and median of a normal distribution is the same, it follows that $\pi(\theta)$ is a normal distribution with mean zero, i.e. $N(0, \delta^2)$. At this point, the normal distribution table can be used to conclude from the information on the quartiles that the variance $\delta^2 = 2.16$.[23]

The summary-based method is fraught with difficulties. The approach requires thinking directly about parameters, which is difficult. To appreciate this point, recall the parameter in the simple exponential regression model mentioned earlier. The parameter enters the model in various ways, making it difficult to think directly about its role and distribution. The difficulty is compounded as more complex non-linear models are considered (Kadane, 1980: 90). Also, the distribution summaries obtainable in practice are usually consistent with more than one distribution family. The above summaries about θ are equally consistent with the Cauchy distribution $C(0, 1)$.[24] Distinguishing these two distributions requires accurate summaries that cannot be easily obtained. What is more, according to a dominant reading of the Bayesian position rooted in de Finetti's representation theorem, parameters have no independent role but to simplify the relations among the observables (Lindley, 1982: 77; Poirier, 1988: 131).[25] Consequently, there is no guide for formulating a prior density other than the instrumental role of the parameters in generating an empirically adequate model. Finally, there is no guarantee that the priors resulting from a person's distribution summaries lead to an empirically adequate model. It may be that the data model is correctly specified but, because of the choice of inappropriate priors, the overall model is inadequate.

4.5.2.2 *The hypothetical prediction-based method*

The difficulties in thinking directly about parameters have given rise to an alternative approach to prior modelling that only demands distribution summaries of observables. Suppose the interest is to model the distribution of X, with data density $f(x/\theta)$. Let $\pi(\theta)$ stand for the (joint) prior density function of the parameters θ. Further, let Y denote some statistic defined from (hypothetical) observations $\{x_1, \ldots, x_N\}$. The distribution of Y before seeing the data is given by the prior predictive distribution:

$$m(y) = \int_{\Theta} f(y/\theta)\pi(\theta)d\theta \qquad \theta \in \Theta \tag{4.19}$$

which does not depend on the parameters θ, since they are integrated out. Equation (4.19) contains one known term, which is the data density of the statistic $f(y/\theta)$, and two unknown terms, which are the predictive distribution of the statistic $m(y)$ and the prior distribution $\pi(\theta)$. Suppose it was possible to estimate the predictive distribution $m(y)$ for some values of Y, or to state some summaries of $m(y)$, such as mean, median, and fractiles, which were enough to infer the distribution. This would reduce the number of unknowns in equation (4.19) to one unknown, the prior density $\pi(\theta)$. The prior specification problem could then be solved by searching for a density function that renders the two sides of (4.19) equal. There would remain no need to think directly about parameters to formulate a prior.

A problem with this strategy is that if the search for a prior density is carried out among the class of all possible densities, it will be difficult to solve the inference problem analytically. It is not clear where to start the search, and there can be many different densities equalizing the two sides of (4.19). Any attempt at solving the inference problem requires restricting *a priori* the class of densities to which $\pi(\theta)$ belongs to a class smaller than the class of all possible densities.

A common restriction is to assume that $\pi(\theta)$ is a member of the distribution family that is conjugate with respect to the data density $f(y/\theta)$.[26] This assumption reduces the search for a prior into the search for a set of hyperparameters of the conjugate family that renders the two sides of (4.19) equal (Winkler, 1980: 99). Thus, an alternative approach to prior modelling is to begin by restricting the class of distribution functions to which the priors belong to a class smaller than the class of all possible functions, and providing certain relevant summaries of the prior predictive distribution of the observable of interest. One can use the predictive assessments to infer values of the hyperparameters that equalize the two sides of (4.19). There is then no need to directly think about parameters.

A simple example, adapted from Winkler (1980: 99), illustrates the method. Suppose the data come from a Bernoulli process so that each observation can be considered as either a success ($x = 1$) or a failure ($x = 0$). Let Y stand for the number of successes in N trials. And, suppose the observations are random. We can describe the process generating Y using a binomial data model, with a parameter θ representing the probability of success on any given trial. The conjugate family for a binomial parameter is the beta family, leading to beta-binomial model:

The beta-binomial model

A_1 Data distribution: binomial, $p(y/\theta) = \binom{N}{y}\theta^y(1-\theta)^{n-y}$, $Y = \sum_{i=1}^{N} X_i$

A_2 Independence: $(X_1, X_2, \ldots, X_N)$ is C-Independent

A_3 Homogeneity: $(X_1, X_2, \ldots, X_N)$ is C-Homogeneous

A_4 Prior distribution: beta, $\pi(\theta) = B(\alpha, \beta)^{-1}\theta^{\alpha-1}(1-\theta)^{\beta-1}$

where $B(.)$ is the beta function, $0 \leq \theta \leq 1$, $\alpha > 0$, and $\beta > 0$. The prior predictive distribution of Y is given by the 'beta-binomial' distribution (N, α, β):

$$p(y) = \binom{N}{y} \frac{\Gamma(\alpha+\beta)}{\Gamma(\alpha)\Gamma(\beta)} \frac{\Gamma(\alpha+y)\Gamma(N+\beta-y)}{\Gamma(\alpha+\beta+N)} \tag{4.20}$$

for $y = 0, 1, \ldots, N$, where Γ is the gamma function. Let y_i be the number of successes in i trials. Thus, $y_2 = 1$ represents one success in two trials. Given the properties of the gamma function, equation (4.20) entails the following simple equalities:

$$\frac{p(y_1 = 1)}{1 - p(y_1 = 1)} = \frac{\alpha}{\beta} \quad \frac{p(y_2 = 0)}{p(y_2 = 2)} = \frac{\beta(\beta+1)}{\alpha(\alpha+1)} \quad \text{and} \quad \frac{p(y_2 = 1)}{p(y_2 = 2)} = \frac{2\alpha\beta}{\alpha(\alpha+1)} \tag{4.21}$$

These equalities can be used to infer α and β from some estimates of $p(y_i)$. For instance, the estimates $p(y_1 = 1) = 0.5$, $p(y_2 = 0) = 0.25$ and $p(y_2 = 2) = 0.25$ imply that α and β are equal to one.

Over the last two decades or so, the predictive method has been extended to some common models such as the normal linear regression model (Kadane *et al.*, 1980; Kadane and Wolfson, 1998). For these models, we know what prior predictive assessments to obtain, and how to use them to infer a prior fitting the assessments.

The predictive approach conquers one serious problem with the summary-based method by relinquishing the need for directly thinking about parameters. But it has its own limitations. For one thing, the form of the prior predictive distribution is not known for most interesting models encountered. This limits the usefulness of the method in practice (Winkler, 1980: 99). Also, as the complexity of the data model grows, a larger number of predictive estimates are needed for finding necessary priors, making the method impractical (Kadane, 1980: 91). Above all, the method requires specifying a distribution family to which the priors belong. This raises the possibility that none of the members of the family leads to an adequate model. On this score, the predictive approach offers no improvement on the summary-based method. Like the older approach, this method is concerned with eliciting beliefs about parameters rather than with building an empirically adequate model.

4.5.2.3 Default priors

The analysis of these two major approaches to prior modelling demonstrates the difficulties in specifying an informative prior. In addition to these methods, a line of research in Bayesian statistics has been to establish formal rules for specifying priors that contain no information and let the data rapidly dominate the posterior distribution. Historically, the origin of these rules is traced to the theory of objective Bayesianism, according to which, given any information set, there is only one probability distribution in relation to the information set (Jeffreys, 1973 [1931]: 10). And, when there is no information about a parameter, there exists a unique prior density representing the state of initial knowledge (ignorance). Such priors go by the name of non-informative, default, reference or invariant priors.

The earliest formal rule for prior specification is the principle of insufficient reason that assigns equal probabilities to all possible outcomes when there is no information to the contrary. The rule is subject to a re-parameterization (partitioning) paradox; applying it simultaneously to all the equivalent representations (coarsenings and refinings) of the parameter space yields inconsistent probability assignments (Kass and Wasserman, 1996: 1347). Consider a single parameter θ and a one-to-one transformation of it such as $\phi = \theta(1-\theta)^{-1}$. If ignorance is claimed about θ, the rule requires choosing a uniform distribution. The change of variable formula then entails the prior density for ϕ to be $\pi^*(\phi) = (1+\phi)^{-2}$, which is not uniform. If one is ignorant about θ, however, one is also ignorant about ϕ, and in either case, according to the insufficient reason principle, one should select a uniform density. Since there is no such thing as the 'correct' representation of the parameter space, the principle falls short of identifying a unique representation of the initial state of knowledge (Leamer, 1978: 61).

What is required is a rule that chooses a prior that is parameterization invariant. In the context of the above example, this means it should not matter whether the rule is first applied to θ to obtain $\pi(\theta)$ and $\pi^*(\phi)$ is derived by means of the change of variable formula or it is first applied to ϕ to obtain $\pi^*(\phi)$ and $\pi(\theta)$ is derived by means of the change of variable formula. In either case the priors should assign equal probabilities to the corresponding regions under both parameterizations.[27] Recognizing this minimal requirement, Harold Jeffreys (1946) pioneered an approach to non-informative prior modelling, known as the invariance approach.

This approach links the choice of a prior to the model chosen for the data. To be precise, it considers one-to-one differentiable transformations of the random variables or the model parameters that do not change the model, and accordingly defines certain invariance requirements. It next searches for a prior that satisfies the requirements (Seidenfeld, 1979: 419). To elaborate on this, following Dawid (1983), denote a data model by the triple $M = (X, \Theta, P)$, where X is a variable, Θ the parameter space, and $P = \{f(x, \theta), \theta \in \Theta\}$ the distribution family to which $p(x)$ belongs. Let $Y = g(X)$ be a one-to-one differentiable transformation of X (e.g. $Y = X + c$) and $\Phi = h(\Theta)$ the parameter space induced by the transformation of X (i.e. $\Phi = \Theta + c$). Although the change transforms $M = (X, \Theta, P)$ into a new model $M^* = (Y, \Phi, P)$, the distribution families in both cases are still the same; if $p(x)$ belongs to distribution family P (say, the normal family), so does $p(y)$. This means if M is true of a situation, M^* is also true of the situation, and the models are in this sense equivalent. Moreover, in the state of ignorance it is as likely that $\theta \in A \subset R$ as $\phi \in A \subset R$. The prior should then satisfy the invariance condition $\pi(\theta \in A) = \pi^*(\phi \in A)$, known as the *context invariance* condition.

Jeffreys (1961: 181) proposes a rule that fulfils the context invariance condition and a few others. The rule is to take the prior density to be proportional to the square root of the expected Fisher information measure. In the univariate case, it is given by

$$\pi(\theta) = [I(\theta)]^{1/2} \tag{4.22}$$

where $I(\theta) = E[-\partial^2 \log f(x/\theta)/\partial\theta^2]$ is the expected Fisher information for the parameter θ, with the expectation being taken with respect to the distribution function $f(x/\theta)$. In the multi-parameter case, $I(\theta)$ is replaced with the determinant of the expected Fisher information matrix. This prior is invariant with respect to one-to-one transformations of the model's random variables or parameters. That is

$$\pi^*(\phi) = [I(\theta)]^{1/2} \left| \frac{d\theta}{d\phi} \right| \tag{4.23}$$

Directly computing Jeffreys' prior for ϕ produces the same prior as computing the prior for θ and subsequently using the change of variable formula to obtain $\pi^*(\phi)$.

There has been a great deal of debate concerning the use and status of invariant priors. The debates mainly arise from the fact that invariant priors are inevitably improper; i.e. they do not integrate to one. As a result, the context invariance condition is not strictly valid (Dawid, 1983). The most that can be assumed is that if in the state of initial knowledge it is as likely that $\theta \in A \subset R$ as $\phi \in A \subset R$, the priors $\pi(\theta)$ and $\pi^*(\phi)$ must be proportionally related to one another, i.e. $\pi(\theta) = h(c)\pi^*(\phi)$. This weaker condition is satisfied by many priors other than Jeffreys' prior, making invariant priors non-unique. On noting this multiplicity, Jeffreys proposed to select a prior on the basis of an international agreement (1955: 277).[28]

This proposal overlooks the possibility that a prior, chosen on the basis of international agreement, may not give rise to an empirically adequate model. A more reasonable proposal for selecting from among invariant priors is to tie the acceptability of the priors to the overall adequacy of the model. There is no difference between the prior assumption and other assumptions entering a model, and just as the plausibility of other assumptions are to be judged by looking at the overall adequacy of the model, the appropriateness of a prior must also be judged in light of the adequacy of the model. From this perspective, the insufficient reason principle, Jeffreys' rule and other possible formal rules for formulating priors constitute valuable modelling tools. Since formulating informative priors is difficult, it is sensible to pick out first a prior using these rules and assess if it gives rise to an adequate model. If the model is adequate, the posterior distribution can be used as a prior in future inferences. If the model turns out to be inadequate, it is necessary to search for alternative priors. Thus, we regard invariant priors as default priors. This is not, however, to deny that invariant priors must be used with care, especially because they can lead to improper posteriors (O'Hagan, 1994: 79).

4.5.3 Some limitations

Mathematical statistics provides a rich reservoir of models, characterizes the conditions under which a model can be true, and offers valuable information on the *ex ante* consequences of the models. These contributions constitute essential building blocks for a theory of initial model formulation. According to the theory, initial model formulation begins by investigating qualitative assumptions about the distribution of the variables under study to narrow down the class of appropriate data models. It then involves examining the *ex ante* consequences of the models to find a model that can account for the data. Essential for the theory is certain heuristic principles for linking theoretical concepts with their sample counterparts.

The possibility of a theory of model formulation hinges on the existence of a model reservoir, and the scope of the theory grows with advances in theoretical statistics. As the list of the independence and homogeneity assumptions grows, new distributions are characterized and new *ex ante* consequences are derived, the scope of the theory expands. While there is a relatively large list of univariate and bivariate distribution families, to date only a few multivariate distribution families have emerged in statistics. Of the four volumes of the reference work by Johnson *et al.* (1994), only the last deals with multivariate distributions and this is dominated by the multivariate normal distribution. In addition, all the known multivariate families are based on the restrictive assumption that the marginal and conditional distributions of the variables also belong to the same distribution family. This scarcity of multivariate families defines the boundary of parametric inference. It also constrains the scope of the specification approach outlined above, which starts with modelling the joint distribution of the observables, and uses it to derive the marginal and conditional distributions, as well as the regression functions of interest. The scarcity also further renders prior formulation difficult, as none of the few multivariate families may actually fit one's prior information.

Due to the scarcity of multivariate distribution families, it has become common to consider the values of independent variables as constant, and to concentrate on the univariate distribution of the dependant variable conditional on the fixed values of the independent variables. The above exploratory approach assists in selecting the univariate distribution but is not of much help in specifying the regression function beyond indicating whether it is linear, convex, or concave. Precise specification of the algebraic form of the function becomes a matter for trial and error.

In addition, initial model formulation requires subjective judgements as to whether the sample size is large enough to permit comparison of theoretical and sample values, whether the discrepancies between the theoretical and actual values are large enough to call for searching for an alternative model, and whether an incompatibility between the model's *ex ante* consequences and the data is due to chance or inappropriateness of the model. Because of the necessity of such judgements, an assessment of *ex ante* consequences should be used solely for finding a model capable of accounting for the data, not for rejecting a model as false.

A final word may be needed on the compatibility of the Bayesian theory with the exploratory methods outlined here. Bayesian theory is applicable only after having formulated a model or a set of models, and is silent about the steps preceding specification of a model. Since the theory and the exploratory methods operate at two different levels, there is no incompatibility between them. Savage's last papers also reveal a high regard for 'puttering about with the data' (Savage, 1977: 5), which can be construed as learning by means other than Bayes' theorem (Draper *et al.*, 1993: 25).

4.6 Bayesian empirical model assessment

Our analysis exposes the complexity of initial model formulation, the uncertain decisions involved in selecting basic hypotheses, the difficulties in prior formulation, and the inconclusiveness of data and subject-matter information in locating a single model. There is every reason to expect that the initial model may fail to account for important features of the data, and yield poor predictions. An important aspect of data modelling, therefore, is to assess the empirical adequacy of the initial model or models. The concern in empirical model assessment is with assessing the relation between a single model and the data, which falls outside the scope of the orthodox Bayesian theory. In this section, we reconstruct and defend a trend in the literature that seeks to broaden the Bayesian framework by enriching it with a Fisherian notion of empirical adequacy and a method for assessing adequacy. The trend began with proposals by Barnard (1962), Anscombe (1963), and Dempster (1971), and culminated in the works of Box (1980; 1983), Rubin (1984), and Gelman *et al.* (1996). Drawing on the works and ideas of these statisticians, we first define the notion of empirical adequacy of a Bayesian model and describe various complementary ways to investigate a model's adequacy. We then show how the ideas lead to a general procedure for Bayesian specification searches.

4.6.1 A general framework for model assessment

The key to a theory of Bayesian empirical adequacy is the notion of *ex post* consequences and a method for judging their conformity with the data. Let a Bayesian model be denoted by $M(Z, \Phi, \pi)$, with Z being the variable (or variables) under study, Φ the parameter space, and π the (joint) prior density. Further, let $D^o = \{z_1^o, \ldots, z_N^o\}$ be the actual sample, which, in statistics, is perceived as a realization of a vector of random variables $\mathbf{Z} = \{Z_1, \ldots, Z_N\}$. The set of all possible realizations of variables $Z_1, \ldots, Z_N$ is called a sample space, denoted by S. The actual data $\{z_1^o, \ldots, z_N^o\}$ is thus a point in the N-dimensional sample space S. Next, let $T_i(.)$ be a function that maps each point of S into the real line, and let $T = \{T_1(.), \ldots, T_k(.)\}$ be the set of all such functions of interest. We refer to $T_i(.)$ as a diagnostic or checking function. Each $T_i(.)$ takes the points in S into a new sample space S_i, leading to a collection of sample spaces $S^* = \{S_i, \ldots, S_k\}$, defined by the checking functions in T. Any fully specified model for Z implies a probability distribution for the points in S, and through $T_i(.)$ a distribution $p(S_i)$ over S_i. By *ex post* consequences of a model, we mean the set of probability distributions $C = \{p(S_i), \ldots, p(S_k)\}$ that the model implies for the sample spaces in S^*.

In this setting, the issue of consistency of a model's *ex post* consequences with the data boils down to the consistency of the induced probability distribution $p(S_i)$ with the actual value $T_i(D^o)$, for every checking function $T_i(.)$ of interest. Now the core of the Fisherian theory of goodness-of-fit test is that the consistency in question has to do with the location of $T_i(D^o)$ in the distribution $p(S_i)$, which is termed the *reference* distribution, following Box (1980). If $T_i(D^o)$ falls in the central part of $p(S_i)$, the distribution is consistent with the data. If it falls in the (extreme) tail area of the distribution, it is inconsistent with the data, since in that case the actual value $T_i(D^o)$ receives a lower probability as compared to the most points in the sample space S_i (Anscombe, 1963). Having said this, a model $M(Z, \Phi, \pi)$ may be defined as empirically adequate if, for each relevant diagnostic function $T_i(.)$ in T, the reference distribution $p(S_i)$ confers a 'high' probability on the realized value $T_i(D^o)$ as compared with other possible points $T_i(D)$ in the sample space S_i.

The distribution of the observables under a Bayesian model is given by the predictive distribution or, in other words, the marginal distribution of the data. In view of this, Guttman (1967), Dempster (1971), Box (1980), and Rubin (1984) have suggested taking the predictive distribution as the basis from which to derive the distributions of the statistics $T_i(.)$. From this perspective, a Bayesian model is empirically adequate if the predictive distribution $p(S_i)$ for each diagnostic function $T_i(.)$ of interest confers a high probability on the realized value $T_i(D^o)$ as compared with other points $T_i(D)$ in S_i. The adequacy of a Bayesian model, thus, goes hand in hand with the predictive accuracy of the model; they are in fact the same thing.

In light of this, the adequacy of a Bayesian model can be assessed by (i) selecting appropriate diagnostic functions $T_i(.)$ to capture relevant features of the data; (ii) deriving the predictive (reference) distributions of the functions $p(T_i(.))$ under the model; (iii) computing the realized values of the functions, i.e. $T_i(D^o)$; and (iv) determining the location of $T_i(D^o)$ in the distribution $p(T_i(.))$. This may be done in more than one way. It may be done by computing the probability $\Pr\{p(T_i(D)) \geq p(T_i(D^o))\}$ or $p(T_i(D) \geq T_i(D^o))$. If these probabilities are not extreme, the model is consistent with the data in respect of the statistic in question (Anscombe, 1963: 84).

The justification of this approach lies in two uncontroversial facts. The first is that any assessment of the empirical adequacy of a single model necessarily involves looking at the compatibility of the model's consequences with data. The other is that statistical models have no deductive consequences; a statistical model is logically consistent with any observed data (Dawid, 2002). Therefore, either we abandon the idea of assessing the empirical adequacy of a single model, in which case the process of model formulation remains a mystery, or we admit it. In the latter case, we are naturally led to the Fisherian idea of goodness-of-fit test. The only way to decide on the compatibility of a statistical model with data is by looking at the location of the data in the distribution of the observables under the model.

4.6.1.1 *The variety of predictive distributions*

Two types of predictive distributions were defined earlier, prior and posterior predictive distributions. The prior predictive distribution describes the distribution of the observable given the information in the data model and prior density; it takes no account of the data. In contrast, the posterior predictive distribution describes the distribution of future data given the information in the data model, prior density, and the data. These distributions give rise to different approaches to model assessment.

4.6.1.2 *Prior predictive checks*

Suppose our assumptions A regarding the process-generating data D lead us to a density function $p(D/\theta, A)$ and prior $p(\theta/A)$. The joint distribution of D and θ is given by

$$p(D, \theta/A) = p(D/\theta, A)p(\theta/A) \tag{4.24}$$

and the prior predictive distribution of D by

$$p(D/A) = \int p(D/\theta, A)p(\theta/A)d\theta \tag{4.25}$$

which gives the distribution of the totality of all possible samples D that could occur if the assumptions A were true. The belief in the appropriateness of $p(D, \theta/A)$ implies that the outcome of a contemplated data acquisition experiment would be calibrated with adequate approximation by a simulation involving appropriate random sampling from distributions $p(D/\theta, A)$ and $p(\theta/A)$. This means if the model were correct, actual data D^o would fall well within the support of the predictive distribution $p(D/A)$ (Box, 1983: 59). One can therefore assess the model's adequacy by investigating the location of D^o in the prior predictive distribution $p(D/A)$ or by checking the location of some relevant diagnostic function $T(D^o)$ in prior predictive distribution $p(T(D)/A)$. The following examples, adapted from Box (1983) and (1980), illustrate the approach.

The first example concerns modelling the number of successes in a sequence of random Bernoulli trials $X_1, X_2, \ldots, X_N$, with X_i being either 0 (failure) or 1 (success). The distribution of the number of successes Y in a sequence of random Bernoulli trials is given by the binomial distribution, with parameter θ standing for the probability of success on each trial. Suppose a member of the beta distribution family with $E(\theta) = 0.2$, and $Var(\theta) = 0.01$ represents our belief about θ. As seen earlier, with a beta prior, the prior predictive distribution of Y in N Bernoulli trials is given by the 'beta-binomial' distribution (n, α, β):

$$p(y/A) = \begin{pmatrix} N \\ y \end{pmatrix} \frac{\Gamma(\alpha+\beta)}{\Gamma(\alpha)\Gamma(\beta)} \frac{\Gamma(\alpha+y)\Gamma(N+\beta-y)}{\Gamma(\alpha+\beta+N)} \tag{4.26}$$

where A represents the model assumptions.[29] It can be shown, using the formula for the mean and variance of a beta distribution, that our belief about the distribution of θ implies that $\alpha = 3$ and $\beta = 12$. The prior predictive approach involves assessing the adequacy of the model by locating the probability of the observed data $p(y^o/A)$ in the distribution (4.26) by computing the probability:

$$\Pr(p(y/A) \le p(y^o/A)). \tag{4.27}$$

Consider two scenarios. In the first scenario, the experiment is carried out ten times and three successes are observed. The prior predictive probability $p(3/A)$ is 0.16, which is not unusually small. In fact

$$\Pr(p(y/A) \le p(3/A)) = 0.33$$

The data provides no reason to doubt the model. In the second scenario, suppose there are eight successes. The prior predictive probability $p(8/A)$ is 0.0018, and

$$\Pr(p(y/A) \le p(8/A)) = 0.0021$$

which is quite small. The data casts doubt on the model, calling for a revision of the underlying assumptions.

As a different illustration, consider modelling the distribution of a continuous random variable X for which we have data set $D^o = (34, 32, 38, 35, 39)$. Suppose we think a normal distribution with unknown θ and variance $\sigma^2 = 1$ fits the data. Also, suppose a normal prior with mean $\theta_0 = 30$ and variance

$\tau^2 = 3$ captures our belief about the location parameter θ. These assumptions suggest the following model:

Simple Bayesian normal model

A_1 Distribution: normal, $X \sim N(\theta, \sigma^2)$, $\sigma^2 = 1$
A_2 Independence: $(X_1, X_2, \ldots, X_n)$ is C-independent
A_3 Homogeneity: $(X_1, X_2, \ldots, X_n)$ is C-homogenous
A_4 Prior distribution: normal, $\theta \sim N(\theta_0, \tau^2)$, $\theta_0 = 30$, $\tau^2 = 3$.

The posterior distribution of θ is given by

$$\theta \sim N(\varphi, \phi),\ \phi = (\tau^{-2} + n\delta^{-2})^{-1},\ \varphi = \phi(\theta_0\tau^{-2} + \delta^{-2}\sum x_i)$$

$$\theta \sim N(36, 0.19)$$

Let $s^2 = \sum_{i=1}^{n}(x_i - \bar{x})^2$. The prior predictive distribution of X is given by (Berger, 1980: 93–4):

$$p(x/A) = (2\pi)^{-n/2}\sigma^{-n}(\sigma^2\tau^2/\sigma^2 + n\tau^2)^{-1/2} \exp\left\{\frac{-1}{2}\left[\frac{s^2}{\sigma^2} + \frac{(\bar{x} - \theta_0)^2}{n^{-1}\sigma^2 + \tau^2}\right]\right\} \tag{4.28}$$

A possible checking function for the model is the quantity in the bracket, namely

$$T(X) = \left[\frac{s^2}{\sigma^2} + \frac{(\bar{x} - \theta_0)^2}{n^{-1}\sigma^2 + \tau^2}\right] \tag{4.29}$$

The adequacy of the model may be assessed by computing the prior predictive probability:

$$\Pr(p(T(X)/A) \leq p(T(x^o)/A)) \tag{4.30}$$

Given the assumptions about X, the quantity $T(X)$ has a χ_n^2 distribution.[30] Since $T(X)$ is inversely related to $p(x/A)$, for computing (4.30) it is sufficient to calculate:

$$p = P(\chi_n^2 \geq T(x^o)). \tag{4.31}$$

The diagnostic function:

$$T(x^o) = \frac{5 \times 6.64}{1} + \frac{(35.6 - 30)^2}{3.2} = 43$$

and

$$p(\chi_5^2 > 43) < 0.001$$

This low predictive probability reveals that the occurrence of the data is quite unlikely under model $N(36, 0.19)$.

These simple examples illustrate how prior predictive checks can be used to assess the empirical adequacy of a model. The success of the approach rests on the ability to derive necessary predictive distributions. In most useful models, obtaining the full predictive distribution is intractable, and approximation must be made via sampling. Modern sampling-based methods allow for obtaining accurate approximations to the predictive distribution of almost any Bayesian model. This opens the way to extend the predictive method beyond simple models studied in textbooks.

A limitation of the prior predictive approach is that it applies only to models with proper priors. When the prior is improper, the prior predictive distribution is also improper and, as a result, prior predictive *p*-values are not defined (Bayarri and Berger, 1999). More importantly, prior predictive checks are sensitive to the choice of priors. A choice of inappropriate priors can lead to wrongly questioning a well-specified data model. The approach is primarily suitable for exploring the effect of alternative priors within a model, and should not be used to question a data model unless the appropriateness of the priors has already been ascertained (Hodges, 1987: 264).[31]

4.6.1.3 Posterior predictive checks

Another possible approach to Bayesian model assessment is to use posterior predictive distributions (Rubin, 1984; Gelman *et al.*, 1996). Let D^o be the observed data on random variable Y, and A the assumptions forming a candidate model, with parameter vector $\boldsymbol{\theta}$. The posterior predictive distribution of Y is given by

$$P(y^f/A, D^o) = \int P(y^f/A, \theta)\pi(\theta/D^o)d\theta \tag{4.32}$$

with y^f standing for a future observation. If the model assumptions are appropriate, we could think of actual data D^o as a random sample from predictive distribution (4.32). In that case, if we could simulate random samples of size N (the size of D^o) from the distribution, we would expect the samples to be on average 'similar' in 'relevant ways' to the actual sample (Rubin, 1984: 116). This means useful information on the adequacy of the model can be obtained by randomly simulating samples of size N from (4.32), and examining their similarity with the realized sample D^o.

To elaborate on the process, consider checking if a normal model fits data $D^o = \{x_1, \ldots, x_n)$. Suppose a pair of conjugate priors well capture our beliefs about the location and scale parameters of the data distribution. Assuming the data are random, the task involves assessing the adequacy of the following model (Lee, 1997):

Bayesian normal/chi-squared model
A_1 Distribution: normal, $X \sim N(\theta, \phi)$
A_2 Independence: $(X_1, X_2, \ldots, X_N)$ is C-Independent
A_3 Homogeneity: $(X_1, X_2, \ldots, X_N)$ is C-Homogeneous
A_4 Prior distribution: normal/chi-squared distribution

The posterior distribution for ϕ is given by inverse chi-squared distribution $\phi \sim S_1 \chi_{v_1}^{-2}$ and for θ given ϕ by normal distribution $\theta \mid \phi \sim N(\theta_1, \phi/N)$, where S_1, θ_1, and v_1 are defined in Appendix 4.B. The posterior predictive distribution of X is given by

$$P(x/A, D) = \int\int N(x/A, \theta, \phi) N(\theta_1, \phi/n) S_1 \chi_{v_1}^{-2}(\phi) d\theta d\phi. \tag{4.33}$$

To simulate samples from (4.33), a value ϕ^* is drawn from the posterior distribution $S_1 \chi_{v_1}^{-2}$, say by means of Markov chain Monto Carlo simulation, and then, given ϕ^*, a value θ^* is drawn from $N(\theta_1, \phi^*/N)$. Next, using the simulated parameter values, a sample $D^{repi} = \{x_1, \ldots, x_N\}$ is drawn from $X \sim N(\theta^*, \phi^*)$. These steps are repeated k times (say, 10,000) to obtain k random samples.[32]

Assessing the model's adequacy, as said, involves checking the similarity of these samples with the actual sample, D^o. This requires some statistics $T_i(.)$ to define salient features of the data. Given some relevant diagnostic functions, we can decide on the similarity of the hypothetical samples with the actual sample by computing the percentage of cases where hypothetical values $T_i(D^{repi})$ exceed (or are less than) the realized value $T_i(D^o)$. This is known as *posterior predictive p-value* (Gelman *et al.*, 1996):

$$\textit{Posterior predictive p-value} = \alpha = \frac{1}{k}\sum_{i=1}^{k} I_{T(D_i^{rep}, \theta_i) > T(D_i^o, \theta_i)} \tag{4.34}$$

where I is the indicator function. If α for the diagnostic functions of interest are close to 0 or 1, the model is suspect. The posterior predictive approach is consistent with the main thrust of Bayesian reasoning, which is conditioning on the whole data (Rubin, 1984: 1166).

The posterior predictive approach evades the difficulties of prior predictive diagnostics. Since posterior distributions are usually proper regardless of whether the priors are proper or not, the use of posterior predictive diagnostics is not limited to models with proper priors. Also, when the sample is adequately large, posterior predictive distributions are not sensitive to the choice of priors. This makes posterior predictive diagnostics suitable for assessing data model assumptions. These successes come at a price, however. Posterior predictive checks use the data twice, once to derive the posterior predictive distribution of the observables under the model and once to assess the model. This makes the checks prone to overestimating the model's adequacy (O'Hagan, 2003: 7). Even so, it is true that if a model fails to generate data similar to the data used to obtain it, there is something amiss about it. So, posterior predictive checks of the type proposed by Rubin and others provide valuable exploratory tools for specification searches.

4.6.1.4 *Cross-validated posterior predictive checks*

Box's prior predictive approach leaves the whole data out as a test set whereas Rubin's posterior predictive approach takes the whole data as a training set. There are many alternatives between these extremes, arising from various ways in which the data can be split into a training and a test set. Of these alternatives, as noted in the last chapter, resampling methods are more promising. Gelfand *et al.* (1992) and Bernardo and Smith (1994) suggest using cross-validation for model selection. But the technique can equally be utilized for adequacy assessment. In its simplest form, cross-validation holds the *i*th observation y_i out, and fits the model to the remaining data D^{-i} to derive the posterior predictive distribution of the deleted observation y_i:

$$p(y_i/D^{-i}) = \int f(y_i/\theta)\pi(\theta/D^{-i})d\theta \qquad \text{for all } i = 1, \ldots, N \qquad (4.35)$$

This gives the probability distribution of y_i conditional on $f(y_i/\theta)$, $\pi(\theta)$, and data D^{-i}. So, when $f(y_i/\theta)$ and $\pi(\theta)$ are appropriate, hypothetical samples randomly drawn from $p(y_i/D^{-i})$ should on average be 'similar' to actual sample D^o. As in the previous approach, we can judge the adequacy of the model by sampling k observations from distribution (4.35) for each observation y_i to form k hypothetical samples, and using the samples to derive the posterior predictive distributions of diagnostic functions $T_i(.)$ of interest. The model is empirically adequate if these distributions confer a high probability on the actual value of the functions.

Distributions (4.35) can also be used to define other important types of *ex post* consequences of a Bayesian model. A number of these implications are listed in Gelfand *et al.* (1992), of which the following two are the simplest:

(i) Let $e_{1i} = y_i - \hat{y}_i$ measure the difference between the realized value y_i and its predicted value $\hat{y}_i$ (i.e. $E(Y_i/D^{-i})$), and σ_i^2 be $Var(Y_i/D^{-i})$. Standardizing e_{1i} yields $d_{1i} = e_{1i}/\sigma_i$. If the errors e_{1i} are approximately normally distributed, d_{1i} approximately has a standard normal distribution.[33] In that case, 95 per cent of the standardized errors d_{1i} must fall within the interval -2 to $+2$. If this is not the case, the model fails to capture systematic information fully in the data. Also, the squared sum of the standardized errors $D_{2i} = \sum d_{1i}^2$ can be taken as an overall index of adequacy.

(ii) Let $e_{2i} = 1$ if $\hat{y}_i \leq y_i$, otherwise 0. The expected value $d_{2i} = E(e_{2i})$ is equal to $P(Y_i \leq y_i/D^{-i})$. Viewing y_i as a random draw from the predictive distribution $p(Y_i/D^{-i})$ implies that d_{2i} is uniformly distributed over the unit interval, i.e. $d_{2i} \sim U(0, 1)$. If the model is correctly specified, the average $A(e_{2i}) = \sum e_{2i}/N$ is expected to be close to 0.5. Extreme values for $A(e_{2i})$, i.e. values close to 0 or 1, point to inadequacy.

In addition, the predictive errors e_{1i} can be used for graphical residual analysis to investigate different aspects of the model. The variance homogeneity of the errors e_{1i} can be checked by plotting them against the predictive values $\hat{y}_i$; the independence of the errors can be assessed by plotting them against time; and the normality of the errors can be checked by plotting them as a histogram (Gilchrist, 1984: 138–44).

Resampling techniques such as cross-validation overcome double use of the data. Yet, as explained in the last chapter, they are not free of limitation. Holding part of the data out as a test set can destroy important features of the data such as dependence, which can lead to a wrong estimate of the model's accuracy. Resampling techniques are suited only for unstructured data. The remarks about the strengths and weaknesses of the predictive approaches to adequacy assessment reveal that none of the methods outperforms others in all respects. Their applicability depends on the kind of data under study and the aspect of the model being considered.

4.6.2 Bayesian specification searches

The notion of *ex post* consequences of a Bayesian model combined with the Fisherian approach to assessing the compatibility of a model's consequences with data leads to a powerful procedure for searching the space of data models. The method involves choosing a data model, adopting a (joint) prior distribution for the model parameters, and assessing the compatibility of the model's *ex post* consequences with the data. If the model is inadequate, its assumptions are varied one at a time, the effect of the variation on the model's adequacy is assessed, and the process is repeated until a model that accounts for the data is found. In practice, when a data model assumption is varied, it is also often essential to modify other model assumptions to preserve consistency among the basic hypotheses. This learning procedure, which captures the way in which a serious (Bayesian) statistician builds a model, might be named Bayesian diagnostic model searching. This section illustrates the procedure by further analysing the example discussed in Section 4.5.

4.6.2.1 Exploring prior distributions

The traditional approaches to informative prior modelling require arbitrary choices about the distribution families to which the priors belong. They also require distributional summaries or predictions that are hard to obtain. There is then the possibility that the priors may not enable the *data* model to account for the data, even if it is correctly specified. Consequently, when the data model is the outcome of a careful initial exploratory analysis, the first step in *ex post* assessment of the model should be to find priors that enable the model to best account for the data. Only after this, is it possible to judge the adequacy of the data model. The objective of modelling is to specify a model capable of accounting for the data. For this reason, the choice of priors should be linked directly to the adequacy of the model. As an alternative to the traditional methods, we therefore propose to choose a prior by looking at the compatibility of the *ex post* consequences of the model with the data. Specifically, following Box (1980), Hill (1990), and Geweke (1999), we propose a two-stage method for prior specification. Subject-matter considerations are first brought in to limit the class of candidate priors *tentatively*. Next, the effect of the candidate priors on the model's adequacy is investigated, while holding the data model fixed. A set of priors that enables the model to best account for the data is selected.

To illustrate the process, let us return to the US unemployment data. Initial examination of the data suggested a bivariate normal data model. This implies that Y_t follows a first-order normal autoregression model (Spanos, 1986: ch. 22 app.):

Normal AR (1) data model

$$Y_t \mid y_{t-1} \sim N(\pi, \sigma^2)$$
$$\pi = \alpha + \beta y_{t-1}$$

with parameters α, β and σ^2. The search for priors needs a *tentative* decision about the distribution families to which they might belong. Suppose we start with the following conjugate prior densities:

Bayesian normal AR (1) model I

$$Y_t \mid y_{t-1} \sim N(\pi, \sigma^2)$$
$$\pi = \alpha + \beta y_{t-1}$$
$$\alpha \sim N(0, 0.001),\ \beta \sim N(0, 0.001), \tau \sim Gamma(1, 30), \tau \sim 1/\sigma^2$$

Assessing empirical adequacy also requires choosing some statistics to characterize salient features of the data. In general, any summary statistics may be chosen, such as minimum sample value, maximum sample value, standard deviation, skewness, and so forth. However, when the concern is to check a specific assumption, it is vital to adopt statistics that capture those aspects of the data that relate to the assumption. The unemployment data shows strong positive dependence. A critical modelling concern is thus to select an appropriate independence hypothesis. This demands using statistics that

Table 4.3 Definition of vector of interest

Preliminary statistics:

$$\bar{y}_T = \sum_{t=1}^{T} y_t/T \quad s_T = \sum_{t=1}^{T} (y_t - \bar{y}_T)^2/T$$

$$\bar{y}_T^{(2)} = \sum_{t=1}^{T} y_t^2/T$$

$T_1(.)$	Minimum sample value	$y_{\min}$
$T_2(.)$	Maximum sample value	$y_{\max}$
$T_3(.)$	Standard deviation	$(s_T)^{1/2}$
$T_4(.)$	Skewness	$\sum_{t=1}^{T}(y_i - \bar{y})^3/T(S_T)^{3/2}$
$T_5(.)$	Excess kurtosis	$\left(\sum_{t=1}^{T}(y_i - \bar{y})^4/T(S_T)^2\right) - 3$
$T_6(.)$	1st order autocorrelation	$\sum_{t=1}^{T-1}(y_t - \bar{y}_T)(y_{t+1} - \bar{y}_T)/\sum_{t=1}^{T}(y_t - \bar{y}_T)^2$
$T_7(.)$	2nd order autocorrelation	$\sum_{t=1}^{T-2}(y_t - \bar{y}_T)(y_{t+2} - \bar{y}_T)/\sum_{t=1}^{T}(y_t - \bar{y}_T)^2$
$T_8(.)$	3rd order autocorrelation	$\sum_{t=1}^{T-3}(y_t - \bar{y}_T)(y_{t+3} - \bar{y}_T)/\sum_{t=1}^{T}(y_t - \bar{y}_T)^2$

capture the dependence feature of the data.[34] To this end, we may include among our diagnostic statistics autocorrelation functions of different order. Table 4.3 defines the statistics used here.

In principle, any of the predictive approaches can be used to search for priors. However, since in the current case the data shows strong dependence, cross-validation techniques are not appropriate; they destroy the dependence feature of the data. For simplicity, we adopt Rubin's approach both for prior modelling and data model assessment. To derive the posterior predictive distributions of the statistics, 10,000 samples are simulated from the posterior predictive distribution of the observable under the model (with 5,000 burnt in), and the values of the statistics for each sample is calculated. The values are used to calculate the quantiles of the predictive distributions of the statistics. Table 4.4 gives the quantiles as well as the predictive p-values for the observed values of the statistics.[35]

The observed value of the skewness and maximum value statistics are within the support of their distributions. But the observed values of the rest of the statistics either fall outside the support of their distributions or lie in their extreme tail areas. Notably, none of the realized values of the autocorrelation functions falls within the interval (2.5%, 97.5%) of the predictive distributions; the simulated values of the functions are invariably smaller than their observed values. The model strikingly fails to account for most aspects of the data, and is empirically inadequate.

Table 4.4 Posterior predictive distribution of vector of interest

		Data	Median	(2.5%, 97.5%)	*p-value*
	Normal AR (1) model I				
$T_1(.)$	Minimum value	2.57	1.557	(032, 2.37)	0.9937
$T_2(.)$	Maximum value	7.37	8.189	(7.306, 9.449)	0.0365
$T_3(.)$	Standard deviation	1.172	1.412	(1.197, 1.648)	0.0152
$T_4(.)$	Skewness	0.2068	0.077	(−0.292, 0.441)	0.757
$T_5(.)$	Excess kurtosis	−0.9009	−0.386	(−0.876, 0.46)	0.0185
$T_6(.)$	1st order autocorrelation	0.919	0.541	(0.358, 0.680)	1
$T_7(.)$	2nd order autocorrelation	0.743	0.4402	(0.2608, 0.5746)	1
$T_8(.)$	3rd order autocorrelation	0.534	0.3192	(0.151, 0.460)	0.9997

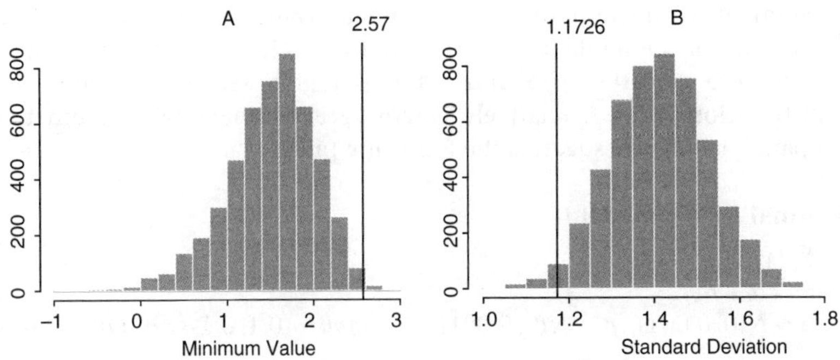

Figure 4.7 Model AR(1) I

Note: Posterior predictive distributions and the observed values for the sample minimum value and sample standard deviation statistics.

Another way of assessing the compatibility of the model with the data, suggested in Gelman *et al.* (1996), is to plot the simulated values of each statistic in the form of a histogram to obtain a non-parametric estimate of the distribution of the statistic. The consistency of the distribution with the data is determined by locating the observed value of the statistic in the histogram. The following histograms show the distributions of the minimum value and standard deviation statistics under the model.

The lines indicate the position of the actual values of the statistics in their distributions, showing that the simulated samples D^{rep} almost invariably

Table 4.5 Posterior predictive distribution of vector of interest

		Normal AR (1) model II			
		Data	**Median**	**(2.5%, 97.5%)**	***p-value***
$T_1(.)$	Minimum value	2.57	2.343	(1.672, 2.824)	0.799
$T_2(.)$	Maximum value	7.37	7.524	(6.973, 8.245)	0.302
$T_3(.)$	Standard deviation	1.172	1.176	(1.056, 1.303)	0.4741
$T_4(.)$	Skewness	0.2068	0.149	(−0.083, 0.377)	0.687
$T_5(.)$	Excess kurtosis	−0.9009	−0.685	(−1.02, −0.201)	0.122
$T_6(.)$	1st order autocorrelation	0.919	0.785	(0.707, 0.840)	1
$T_7(.)$	2nd order autocorrelation	0.743	0.6391	(0.5572, 0.701)	0.9993
$T_8(.)$	3rd order autocorrelation	0.534	0.4638	(0.3709, 0.520)	0.9581

differ from the actual sample D. The failure of the model demands searching for alternative priors.

Experiments with alternative hyperparameter values reveal that the empirical adequacy of the model is not sensitive to the choice of hyperparameter values for the densities of α and β but is highly sensitive to those for the distribution of τ. A relatively extensive experiment with alternative hyperparameter values suggests the following priors:

Normal AR (1) model II

$$Y_t \mid y_{t-1} \sim N(\pi, \sigma^2)$$
$$\pi = \alpha + \beta y_{t-1}$$
$$\alpha \sim N(0, 0.001),\ \beta \sim N(0, 0.001), \tau \sim Gamma(0.1, 0.1), \tau \sim 1/\sigma^2$$

The posterior predictive distributions implied by these new priors are given in Table 4.5 above.

As the quantiles in the table show, the new priors enable the model to better account for the features of the data captured by the statistics. Unlike the previous model, the actual values of the statistics minimum sample value, standard deviation, excess kurtosis, and the third-order autocorrelation fall within the support of the distributions, i.e. the (2.5%, 97.5%) predictive interval. The model still fails to account for the first-order and second-order autocorrelation functions. Experiments with alternative priors for τ do not improve on the adequacy of the model, and the performance of the model is not sensitive to the choice of priors for α and β. There is therefore every reason to think that the data model is not correctly specified.

In general, if experiment with a wide range of hyperparameters fails to produce good priors, other distribution families consistent with the subject-matter information should be considered. If, after an adequate search among alternative distribution families, a model still fails to account for the data, a revision of the data model assumptions becomes necessary (Geweke and McCausland, 2001: 7). As the analysis shows, the diagnostic approach to adequacy assessment presents a powerful alternative to the traditional prior modelling methods. The approach forgoes the need for qualitative distribution summaries or hypothetical predictions. More importantly, it overcomes the risk of rejecting a correctly specified data model because of the choice of inappropriate priors. The approach ties the choice of priors to the model adequacy.

4.6.2.2 Exploring data model assumptions

When a model fails to account for the data regardless of the choice of priors, the focus of investigation must be turned towards alternative data models. The exploration involves varying the data model assumptions one at a time, searching for a set of priors that best enables the model to account for the data, and checking the model's adequacy. While the failure of the above model may be due to any of the basic assumptions, because of its specific failure in accounting for the dependence feature of the data, it is more plausible to explore first the effect of varying the first-order Markov condition. We proceed by replacing it with the second-order Markov condition. Modifying the distribution assumption appropriately, this hypothesis leads to a second-order normal autoregression model:

Normal AR (2) model

$$Y_t \mid y_{t-1}, y_{t-2} \sim N(\pi, \sigma^2)$$
$$\pi = \alpha + \beta y_{t-1} + \gamma y_{t-2}$$

Experiments with alternative priors suggest that the following set of priors enables the model to best account for the data:

$$\alpha \sim N(0, 0.01),\ \beta \sim N(0, 0.01),\ \gamma \sim N(0, 0.01),\ \tau \sim Gamma(1, 3),\ \tau \sim 1/\sigma^2$$

Table 4.6 gives the (2.5%, 97.5%) predictive intervals of the posterior predictive distributions of the statistics, which result from these priors. The predictive intervals are computed from 10,000 samples simulated from the posterior predictive distribution of the observable under the model (with 5,000 burnt in).

These quantiles are not improved by considering alternative hyperparameter values or prior distribution families. The parameterization seems to enable the model to best fit the data. The model does not, then, improve on the second AR(1) model. Contrary to the latter, it neither accounts for the excess kurtosis nor for the third autocorrelation statistic.

Replacing the first-order Markov condition with higher-order Markov conditions does not create a more adequate model. Nor do the data show

Table 4.6 Predictive distribution of vector of interest

		Normal AR (2) model			
		Data	**Median**	**(2.5%, 97.5%)**	***p-value***
$T_1(.)$	Minimum value	2.57	2.21	(1.265, 2.771)	0.876
$T_2(.)$	Maximum value	7.37	7.668	(7.081, 8.442)	0.1836
$T_3(.)$	Standard deviation	1.172	1.172	(1.055, 1.296)	0.5
$T_4(.)$	Skewness	0.2068	0.1872	(−0.088, 0.448)	0.558
$T_5(.)$	Excess kurtosis	−0.9009	−0.46	(−0.854, 0.158)	0.0127
$T_6(.)$	1st order autocorrelation	0.919	0.688	(0.573, 0.768)	1
$T_7(.)$	2nd order autocorrelation	0.743	0.576	(0.482, 0.6503)	1
$T_8(.)$	3rd order autocorrelation	0.534	0.376	(0.272, 0.4666)	0.9999

any heterogeneity to consider alternative homogeneity assumptions. Experiments with alternative distributions such as student *t*-distribution also fail to yield a better model. In all these cases, the residual autocorrelation function has some large spikes at low lags, indicating that the errors are correlated. This suggests using an autoregressive moving average (ARMA) model.[36] To continue, consider an ARMA (1,1) model:

Normal ARMA(1,1) model

$$Y_t \mid y_{t-1}, y_{t-2} \sim N(\pi, \sigma^2)$$

$$\pi = \alpha + \beta y_{t-1} + \gamma \varepsilon_{t-1}$$

Experiments with alternative priors soon lead to the following densities,

$$\alpha \sim N(0, 0.3),\ \beta \sim N(0.1, 0.1),\ \gamma \sim N(0.1, 0.1),$$

$$\tau \sim Gamma(0.01, 0.01),\ \tau \sim 1/\sigma^2$$

Table 4.7 gives the (2.5%, 97.5%) posterior predictive intervals for the statistics under the model. The intervals are computed from 10,000 samples simulated from Y_t's posterior predictive distribution (with 5,000 burnt in).

The normal ARMA (1,1) model accounts for all the aspects of the data captured by the diagnostic functions. In particular, it accounts for the dependence features of the data. Moreover, the performance of the model is not sensitive to particular hyperparameter values, as a very wide range of values preserves the ability of the model to account for the data. We at last have a candidate model fitting the data.

Table 4.7 Predictive distribution of vector of interest

		Normal ARMA (1,1) model			
		Data	**Median**	**(2.5%, 97.5%)**	***p-value***
$T_1(.)$	Minimum value	2.57	2.538	(2.315, 2.538)	0.624
$T_2(.)$	Maximum value	7.37	7.399	(7.189, 7.629)	0.398
$T_3(.)$	Standard deviation	1.172	1.177	(1.149, 1.204)	0.39
$T_4(.)$	Skewness	0.2068	0.1576	(0.085, 0.229)	0.413
$T_5(.)$	Excess kurtosis	−0.9009	−0.886	(−1, −0.755)	0.91
$T_6(.)$	1st order autocorrelation	0.919	0.914	(0.906, 0.921)	0.909
$T_7(.)$	2nd order autocorrelation	0.743	0.741	(0.724, 0.757)	0.598
$T_8(.)$	3rd order autocorrelation	0.534	0.5395	(0.514, 0.564)	0.355

The analysis of the unemployment data illustrates the essence of the Bayesian diagnostic approach to model specification. The approach offers a very powerful tool for searching the space of candidate models to find a model that adequately fits the data. Joined with the procedures introduced for initial model formulation, it furnishes the key elements of a theory of exploratory Bayesian model formulation.

4.7 Model selection

Exploratory searches may generate several models equally fitting the data, raising the issue of how a model should be chosen from among the candidates. We earlier described the Bayesian solution to this problem, and now return to it to discuss some controversies surrounding it and highlight some complexities in establishing a theory of statistical learning. Following Bernardo and Smith (1994), it is important to distinguish between two possible views that can be held with respect to a set of candidate models:

Closed view: the set of candidate models $\{M_1, \ldots, M_k\}$ is complete in the sense that it includes the true model.
Open view: the set of candidate models $\{M_1, \ldots, M_k\}$ is incomplete in the sense that it excludes the true model, either because the model is not among the candidates or because there is no true model anyway.

The closed view stands on two assumptions: a metaphysical assumption that there exists a *true* model and an epistemological assumption that the true model is *actually* among the candidate models. The model selection problem is therefore defined as that of finding the true model from among the candidates. The open view emerges from the rejection of at least one of these assumptions, and can be interpreted in two ways. One interpretation takes the existence of a true model for granted but acknowledges that it may not be among the candidates. In this case, the model selection issue involves selecting the model that best approximates the true model. The other interpretation rejects the reality of a true model outright, considering the candidate models simply as a set of models contending to account for the data. In this case, the model selection issue is basically to find a simple model that best fits the data and yields accurate predictions.

The Bayesian theory of model selection takes the closed view for granted. The theory interprets the probability of a model as the probability that it is true (Hill, 1990: 61), and requires the probabilities over the candidate models to add up to one, meaning that the true model is among the candidates (Wasserman, 2000: 103). Accordingly, it recommends selecting the model that scores the highest probability in light of the data. Both assumptions underpinning the closed view are flawed.

The assumption of a true model encounters problems of interpretation. From the Bayesian perspective, probability is the product of thinking consistently about the universe, with no external counterpart (Dawid, 2002: 8), and there is no true probability model involving parameters that attain an objective existence (Poirier, 1988: 122; Leamer, 1990: 188). As a result, the truth of a model can be defined only in terms of the observables. To elaborate on this, suppose it was possible to observe endlessly a socio-economic or physical process generating data sets of size N. Suppose it was possible also to simulate endlessly samples of the same size from a candidate model purporting to describe the system. The model could be said to be true if the stylized features of the simulated samples (such as sample mean, median, minimum value, maximum value, covariance, and so forth) *arbitrarily closely* resembled those of the actual samples. This seems to be the only way to define a true model in the subjectivist framework. If so, the question arises about the rationale for supposing a unique model generating samples most closely resembling the actual samples. To define 'arbitrarily closely', it is necessary to introduce some distance function. There are, however, many possible distance functions, and depending on the choice of metric, different models may turn out to be true. There is no natural choice of a distance function. All in all, even in the abstract it is not clear how to defend the existence of a true Bayesian model.

The epistemological assumption that the true model is among the candidate models is also indefensible for several reasons. The number of models that can be considered in practice is restricted by the finiteness of the reservoir of known models. None of the models may approximate the 'true' model. More importantly, in empirical modelling, due to the possibility of overfitting, the complexity of the models considered must always be tied to the sample size. With small samples, only simple models can be considered, since highly parameterized models are prone to overfitting. This restriction arising from the smallness of actual samples constrains the set of models that can be considered in practice, giving rise to the possibility that the allowed set may include neither the true model nor even a good approximation thereof (Spiegelhalter, 1995: 72). Also, constructing models is costly, time-consuming, and severely constrained by computational capabilities of the day. The cost of developing a complex model with a better chance of approximating the reality may outweigh the practical benefit that may ensue. Such real pragmatic considerations compel the analyst to consider only a handful of models that may be very different from the true model. Thus, even if the metaphysical quandaries surrounding the existence of a true model are ignored, there are still serious reasons to doubt that the model is among the candidates considered.

Some supporters of the Bayesian position have argued that these objections do not undermine the heuristic role played by the closed view in the advancement of science. Scientists usually proceed by assuming that one of their models is true in order to analyse the merits of the models and conduct further research. This tentative assumption allows viewing the models as a closed set and assigning to them probabilities that add up to one (Wasserman, 2000: 103). But, to consider the merits of alternative models, there is no need to think of them as an exhaustive set containing the true model. Models can be compared in respect of their predictive accuracy, simplicity, broadness, computability, and so forth. For comparing the performance of two models, there is no need to think one model is true and the other false.

Another attempt to retain the closed view involves adding to the candidate models $\{M_1, \ldots, M_k\}$ a 'catchall' model M^C to represent 'all unspecified models'. This formally transforms the candidate models into an exhaustive set but raises two difficult questions. First, it is not clear how to assess the probability of the catchall model, $p(M^C)$. What is the probability that the 'true' model is not among the candidate models (Winkler, 1994: 109)? Equally important, Bayesian model selection requires specifying the probability of the data given the model, i.e. $P(D/M^c)$. How can the probability of the data conditional on a totally unknown model or set of models be estimated (Anscombe, 1963)? The proposal to use a catchall model makes no headway in addressing the problems facing the closed view.

A satisfactory account of model selection should take into account the fact that the candidate models might exclude the 'true' model. A departure from the closed view requires reinterpreting the probability of a model, redefining the goal of inference, specifying the features a model must have to be conducive to the goal, and describing methods for selecting a model with the requisite features. Interestingly, the Bayesian literature provides the elements of an alternative account of model selection that takes some steps in these directions. The account, defended by Geisser and Eddy (1979), Lane (1986), and Bernardo and Smith (1994) has its roots in de Finetti's representation theorem. On this theorem, as said earlier, statistical inference is primarily concerned with observables, and parameters enter the model just to simplify the relations among the observables, and have no independent meaning (Lindley, 1982: 77). Since the distribution of the observables under a Bayesian model is given by the predictive distribution, the probability assigned to a model is best understood as the confidence that one has in the model's ability to yield accurate predictions. This permits comparing the relative probability of any set of models, regardless of whether the set is exhaustive or not (Lane, 1986: 256). From this perspective, the primary objective of inference is to generate an accurate predictive distribution (Lane, 1986: 254; Poirier, 1988: 132), and a highly desirable feature of a Bayesian model is its ability to generate accurate predictions.

What is more, constructing accurate models and hence accurate predictive distributions is always costly, time-consuming, and subject to computational and tractability constraints. A satisfactory account of model selection should also take these features of the real-life inference situations into account. All in all, these considerations demand redefining the Bayesian model selection issue as the problem of selecting a model that is likely to produce the most accurate predictions, subject to computational, time, cost, and other pragmatic constraints faced by the analyst.

Turning these remarks into a formal theory of model selection may require introducing a preference function weighting the competing goals of predictive accuracy, tractability, and affordability, and treating the whole model selection problem within the framework of the expected utility theory. The call for establishing such a theory of model selection is by now old (Anscombe, 1963: 89; Lindley, 1968) and still being insisted on (Draper, 1996: 763; Hodges, 1987: 262). Yet, no serious contender has yet emerged. This is partly because pragmatic considerations are very difficult to quantify (Poirier, 1988: 137). In the end, a fully formal theory of model selection may be as elusive as a 'true model' (Pesaran and Smith, 1985).

4.8 Objections revisited

The theory of diagnostic searches characterized here is founded on the core idea of the Fisherian concept of the goodness-of-fit test, which has been criticized by both Bayesian and non-Bayesian statisticians. To complete the discussion, we review some of the criticisms levelled against the use of *p*-values and data-driven model-building in general.

A central objection to the use of *p*-values is that they imply an abrogation of the likelihood principle (LP), which follows from two basic principles: the conditionality principle (CP) and the sufficiency principle (SP). Consider a parameter θ standing for the proportion of successes in a sequence of independent Bernoulli trials, say, the proportion of non-defective items produced by a machine. Further, consider two scenarios for collecting data to estimate θ. In the first scenario, E_1, N items are collected and the number of non-defectives

k is counted, with N being predetermined. In the second scenario, E_2, sampling from the machine continues until k non-defective items are obtained, where $k > 0$ is a predetermined integer, and the sample size happens to be N. The first experiment leads to the choice of a binomial distribution and the second to a negative binomial.

The CP states that if we decide which of the experiments E_1 and E_2 to do by the flip of a coin, the final inference must be the same as if the experiment had been chosen without flipping the coin (Cox, 1958). The SP, on the other hand, says when there exists a sufficient statistic for θ, two samples that yield the same value for the statistic provide the same evidence for θ.[37] These principles, as shown by Brinbaum (1962), necessitate the LP, which for the current purpose, can be stated as:

> **The likelihood principle**: Consider two experiments $E_1 = \{Y_1, \theta, f_1(y_1|\theta)\}$ and $E_2 = \{Y_2, \theta, f_2(y_2|\theta)\}$ involving the same parameter θ. Suppose that for particular realizations y_1 and y_2 of the data, $L_1(\theta, y_1) = cL_2(\theta, y_2)$ for some constant c not depending on θ. Then, $Ev[E_1, y_1] = Ev[E_2, y_2]$, where $Ev[E_j, y_j]$ denotes the *evidence* about θ arising from experiment E_j and realized data y_j.

The principle 'states that two experiments providing evidence about the same parameter θ which give rise to data realisations yielding likelihoods which are proportional, must provide the same evidence regarding θ' (Poirier, 1988: 125). Since both CP and SP seem plausible, the LP has become for many statisticians the yardstick against which to gauge the acceptability of a statistical procedure. Agreement with the LP is argued to be a minimal requirement that no statistical procedure can fail to fulfil.

Some simple examples reveal that frequentist-based hypothesis-testing procedures, which are based on assessments of p-values, abrogate the LP. A simple example, due to Lindley and Phillips (1976), is concerned with estimating θ in experiments similar to those described above. Suppose in the first experiment twelve items are collected and nine non-defective items are found while in the second it has taken sampling twelve items to collect nine non-defectives. The likelihoods are given respectively by

$$L_1(\theta, k) = \frac{12!}{9!3!}\left[\theta^9(1-\theta)^3\right] = 220\left[\theta^9(1-\theta)^3\right] \tag{4.36}$$

and

$$L_2(\theta, k) = \frac{11!}{2!9!}\left[\theta^9(1-\theta)^3\right] = 55\left[\theta^9(1-\theta)^3\right] \tag{4.37}$$

These likelihoods are proportional to each other, i.e. $L_1(\theta, k) = 4L_2(\theta, k)$. According to the LP, both experiments provide the same information about

θ and must lead to the same inferences about it. However, consider testing the null hypothesis:

$$H_0 \equiv \theta = 1/2$$

The p-value $p_{\theta=0.5}(Y \geq 9)$ is 0.075 under E_1 and 0.0325 under E_2. If the significance level is set at 0.05, the first experiment suggests accepting the null hypothesis but the second suggests rejecting it. Thus, the frequentist-based hypothesis-testing procedures, which require calculating p-values, violate the LP. To see the cause of the conflict, note that even though the observed data are the same in E_1 and E_2, the sample spaces are different. In E_1 the sample space is given by $\{0, 1, \ldots, N\}$ and in E_2 by $\{m, m+1, \ldots\}$, with m being the number of defectives. Since in computing p-values the whole sample space is considered, not the realized data alone, the difference leads to conflicting inferences (Poirier, 1988: 126).

Accordingly, Lindley and Phillips (1976) and others have criticized the frequentist-testing methods, arguing that inferences about statistical hypotheses must be conditioned only on the observed data, which requires abandoning p-values.[38] And when Box (1980) proposed prior predictive p-values for adequacy assessment, Lindley repeated the criticism that they would lead to an abrogation of the LP (Lindley, 1980: 423). This critique is misplaced. The LP conditions upon the choice of a model, and is only relevant to the estimation phase of inference, where the truth of the model is taken for granted. When the concern is to construct a model that fits the data and no decision has yet been made about whether the model is true or not, the principle has no regulative force at all (Box, 1983: 74). The conflict between the LP and p-values can be resolved by recognizing that the former belongs to the estimation phase of inference while the latter to the model formulation phase (McCullagh, 1995: 178). There is, then, no inconsistency between the LP and the use of p-values. As a final point, the LP also loses its regulative force if one takes the role of parameters to be solely instrumental (Lane, 1986: 257).

A second critique of p-values is that in large samples they lead to the rejection of any model by locating minor deficiencies that are otherwise unimportant (Pratt, 1965). This is not really a deficiency at all. In practice, all models are imperfect, and it is highly desirable to have exploratory methods that can reveal deficiencies in currently held models as the sample grows (Hodges, 1990: 87–8). The deficiencies with a model might be ignored for various practical reasons but it is still useful to discover them with an eye to ultimately improving it (Gelman *et al.*, 1996: 800).

Thirdly, it has been objected that there is no guidance to decide when a p-value is extreme enough to warrant rejecting a model. This criticism fails to appreciate that Bayesian p-values are not for testing or rejecting models. They are just to show whether a model fits the data and, if not, help searching for a model with a better goodness of fit (Dempster, 1983: 124). The right question to ask is when a *p*-value is extreme enough to justify the search for an alternative model. There is no purely epistemic response to such a question. The decision whether to take a discrepancy between a model and the data seriously and search for an alternative model is to a large extent driven by pragmatic considerations, which are by no means unique to the use of *p*-values (Anscombe, 1963: 89); they are needed at every stage of modelling.

Finally, a serious matter about any exploratory procedure concerns the borderline between model-searching and data-mining. It is always possible to find a model with a better goodness of fit by exploring increasingly more complex models but such a model may not necessarily perform better over future data. Why should one then search for a model that best fits the data? Several things can be done to meet this concern. First of all, predictive searches must be carried out within the class of models warranted by the existing subject-matter information. Secondly, having found a model fitting the data, an essential aspect of modelling is to assess the sensitivity of the model to the underlying assumptions that are in doubt. In the end, the only way to gain serious confidence in a model is to try it over new and diverse data. There is never a substitute for new data. Model-building is a complex problem and there is rarely a simple solution to a complex problem.

4.9 Conclusion

According to the Bayesian learning theory presented here, model specification starts with examining the *ex ante* consequences of known basic hypotheses to construct a set of initial candidate models that are capable of accounting for the data. The process next involves assessing the *ex post* consequences of the models to locate a model that accurately accounts for the data. There is also a pragmatic side to statistical inference. Model construction is costly, time-consuming, constrained by computational capabilities, and influenced by the intended use of the model. If the objective is to explain how a statistician models a choice situation or constructs a model for a data set, the entire modelling process should be thought of as a constrained optimization problem. This account of the model-formulation process has significant implications for establishing a theory of statistical learning, and hence the bounded rationality project, some of which are stated below.

First, in the above theory of model-formulation background information enters inference in many forms: most notably, in the form of a reservoir of models (Arthur, 2000), knowledge of the conditions under which the models are appropriate, and knowledge of the *ex ante* implications of the models. An extremely significant point is that a theory of parametric learning takes such information as *given*, which means there can be no general theory of parametric inference that can also explain where the models or, more precisely, basic probabilistic hypotheses come from in the first place. Only after a reservoir of models is given is it possible to speak of a theory of parametric learning. The necessity of a model reservoir, whose generation cannot be explained by a theory of parametric learning, might have been the principal reason for Fisher and other statisticians' negative feeling concerning the possibility of a theory of model specification (Lehmann, 1990: 161). The search for a theory of statistical learning therefore encounters a dilemma. If a non-parametric approach to learning is pursued, it would be impossible to build an interpretable model of several variables with ordinarily available samples. If, on the other hand, a parametric approach is taken, the question arises as to where the models come from in the first place.

Second, the scope of a theory of parametric learning is defined by the scope of the model reservoir. So far, only a few multivariate distribution families have emerged and, because of this scarcity, any set of models in practice is likely to exclude the 'true' model or a good approximation thereof. It therefore seems fair to question the relevance of the convergence results established in the learning literature; all these results are based on the presumption that the true model is among the candidate models.[39] The relevance of the results becomes even more suspect when we realize the necessity of subjective and pragmatic considerations in modelling data.

Third, since pragmatic considerations influence decisions about the adequacy of a model, the hypothesis that the agent behaves like a Bayesian statistician, even if true, would not be adequate for predicting his model of the economy. To this end, it is also necessary to know his goals, preferences, and constraints. This makes it even more difficult to establish a precise and informative theory of how he actually models the economy.

All in all, the claim that by modelling people as intuitive statisticians one can predict the models that they construct of the economy should be treated with scepticism. The most that can be predicted on the basis of this hypothesis, the history of the observables, and the expected utility maximization principle, is that the agent takes an action that is optimal with respect to his utility function and view of the environment. The serious issue with the IS hypothesis is not that people are not perfect statisticians but that, even if they were, the hypothesis would still fall short of producing informative predictions. More will be said on this in the next chapter.

5

'Homo Economicus' as an Intuitive Statistician (3): Data-Driven Causal Inference

5.1 Introduction

'I would rather discover a single causal relationship than be king of Persia.' (Democritus)[1]

The bounded rationality programme, as understood in new classical economics, views the economy as a society of intuitive statisticians – the intuitive statistician hypothesis. This hypothesis raises the question of whether there is a 'tight enough' theory of statistical inference. Without a tight enough theory of statistical inference we will not learn much about the economy by studying the dynamics of an economy of intuitive statisticians. As a general framework for studying this question, we conjectured that the agent (statistician) first seeks to learn the probability distribution of the variables representing his or her choice situation and next uses the probabilistic information to learn about the causal structure of the situation. The last two chapters studied some of the issues relating to learning the probability distribution of a set of variables. This chapter studies in detail the second general stage of inference that is concerned with inferring the causal structure of a set of variables from their joint distribution.

We earlier studied the regression method of causal inference. According to this method, to infer whether X causes Y, one has to include in the regression equation of Y on X various combinations of potential confounders of X and Y. If the coefficient of X differs from zero regardless of the potential confounders included in the equation, X is said to cause Y. This method fails to establish whether an association between X and Y is due to a direct causal link or latent common causes. Conditioning on potential confounders can also turn an otherwise consistent estimate of the effect of X on Y into an inconsistent estimate. And, controlling for the effects of the response variable Y can lead to wrong causal conclusions. A common belief is that these problems can only be overcome by relying on subject-matter information about the underlying system.

An approach pioneered by Spirtes *et al.* (1993) and Judea Pearl is claimed to evade the difficulties facing the traditional methods of causal inference. These authors hold that the reason for the failure of the traditional methods lies in their lack of an efficient language for representing causal structures *and* in their lack of a precise characterization of the connection between probability and causation. Once an adequate language for representing causal structures is developed and the principles connecting causation and probability are precisely defined, reliable causal conclusions can be derived from data alone. The claim for the necessity of subject-matter information in casual inference is exaggerated:

> In the social sciences there is a great deal of talk about the importance of 'theory' in constructing causal explanations ...In many of these cases the necessity of theory is badly exaggerated. (Spirtes *et al.*, 1993: 133)
>
> In the absence of very strong prior causal knowledge, multiple regression should not be used to select the variables that influence an outcome or criterion variable in data from uncontrolled studies. So far as we can tell, the popular automatic regression search procedures [like stepwise regression] should not be used at all in contexts where causal inferences are at stake. Such contexts require improved versions of algorithms like those described here to select those variables whose influence on an outcome can be reliably estimated by regression. (Spirtes *et al.*, 1993: 257)[2]

The approach proposed by these authors, termed as the graph theoretical (GT) or Bayes net approach, has been the source of many significant advances. The approach has led to the development of an efficient language for representing causal structures, a precise formulation of the principles underpinning the causal inference methods, and to a variety of algorithms for causal inference. The approach has also advanced our understanding of the key issue of statistical indistinguishability of causal models. We use the approach to study the intrinsic limits of data-driven causal inference. By data-driven causal inference, we mean any effort to draw causal conclusions from probabilistic data using only general subject-matter-independent principles supposedly linking causation and probability. A claim for a data-driven method of causal inference raises two queries. The first is whether there are any *universal* principles linking probabilistic and causal dependencies. The second is whether the principles are sufficient for inferring the causal structure of a set of variables from their joint probability distribution.

We investigate both topics by focusing on the principles underlying the GT approach, which are the most general principles that can be true of the connection between probability and causation. After defining some basic concepts and a brief description of the approach, we take up the issue of model equivalence. We argue that for every causal model consistent with the data there are simple rules that allow generating a class of statistically equivalent causal models with very little or nothing in common. Even if the GT principles were valid, very little could be learnt from data alone. We next examine the validity of the principles. We argue that none of the defences put forward for the principles justifies their universal validity. In addition, we show how the possibility of selection bias undermines the claim that the GT approach outperforms other methods by being able to establish whether a correlation is *definitely* due to latent common causes. Moreover, we show why, because of the possibility of mistaking the concomitant of a cause for the cause, the GT approach cannot establish the existence or absence of a direct causal link either. In the end, by reflecting on the limitations of the GT approach, we sketch out an alternative account of causal inference from observational data, explain the role that the GT techniques play in the account and spell out some implications of the analysis for the bounded rationality project.

5.2 Preliminaries and principles

This section begins by defining the notions of causation, causal structure, and causal model used here. Next, it briefly describes the path analysis method which will later be used to introduce some graph theoretic concepts. The section also characterizes the class of candidate causal models for every set of variables, the data used for causal inference in the GT approach, and the principles proposed to link the data with the models.

5.2.1 Causal structure

Central to an analysis of actions and polices is a manipulative account of causation defended in the writings of philosophers such as Collingwood (1948), Gasking (1955) and von Wright (1971). On this account, a causal relationship primarily obtains between single events. An event x is a cause of an event y if it is *in principle* possible to alter y by wiggling x. Or in Collingwood's terms, 'that which is "caused" is an event in nature, and its "cause" is an event or state of things by producing or preventing which we can produce or prevent that whose cause it is said to be' ([1940], 1948: 285). If it were not even hypothetically possible to alter y by wiggling x, x would not be a cause of y.

The relation 'event x causes event y' is transitive, irreflexive and antisymmetric. Particular events can be grouped into types of events and event types can be coupled with their complementary event types to form variables. Consider the rise in the Dow-Jones Industrial Average last Monday. We may classify this event into event type of 'rises in the Dow-Jones Industrial Average'; call it D. And, we may further put together this event type with its complementary event type 'declines in the Dow-Jones Industrial Average' to define the random variable 'the Dow-Jones Industrial Average'; call it $X \equiv (D, D^c)$.[3] Similarly, we may join together the event types 'rises in the FTSE 100' and 'declines in the FTSE 100' to define the random variable 'the FTSE 100; call it $Y \equiv (C, C^c)$. We say that variable X causes variable Y if and only if at least one member of types (D, D^c) causes at least one member of types (C, C^c)(Sobel, 1995: 8). Having said this, we will not make further mention of particular events in the rest of this work.

Let $\mathbf{V} = \{X_1, \ldots, X_n\}$ be the set of variables necessary for describing a choice situation or a certain aspect of the economy. A proper subset of $\boldsymbol{V}$, $\boldsymbol{X}$, is a *full* cause of $X_m \quad (X_m \notin \mathrm{X})$with respect to $\boldsymbol{V}$ if (i), there is a set of values $\boldsymbol{x}$ for $\boldsymbol{X}$ and a value x_m for X_m such that were it possible to set $\boldsymbol{X}$ at value $\boldsymbol{x}$, X_m would take on value x_m regardless of the value of other variables in $\boldsymbol{V}$ and (ii), no proper subset of $\boldsymbol{X}$ satisfies condition (i). In line with Spirtes *et al.* (1993: 44), variable X_i is a *direct cause* of X_m relative to $\boldsymbol{V}$ if X_i is a member of a full cause $\boldsymbol{X}$ of X_m in $\boldsymbol{V}$. Similarly, X_i is an *indirect cause* of X_m relative to $\boldsymbol{V}$ if there is an ordered sequence of variables in $\boldsymbol{V}$ starting with X_i and ending at X_m such that each variable in the sequence is a direct cause of the next variable in the sequence, provided that m is greater than two. Also, X_i is a *common cause* of X_m and X_n in $\boldsymbol{V}$ if X_i is a direct or indirect cause of both X_m and X_n.

We define a *causal structure* over variables $\boldsymbol{V}$ as an ordered pair $\langle \mathbf{V}, \mathbf{E} \rangle$, where $\boldsymbol{E}$ is a set of ordered pairs of $\boldsymbol{V}$ such that $\langle X, Y \rangle$ is in $\boldsymbol{E}$ if and only if X is a direct cause of Y with respect to $\boldsymbol{V}$. The variables in $\boldsymbol{V}$ that have no direct cause in $\boldsymbol{V}$ are called *exogenous*, and the rest *endogenous*. A structure $\langle \mathbf{V}, \mathbf{E} \rangle$ is *deterministic* if the value of each endogenous variable in $\boldsymbol{V}$ is uniquely determined by its direct causes in $\boldsymbol{V}$. A structure that is not deterministic but forms part of a deterministic structure is called *pseudo-indeterministic*. Each variable X_i in a pseudo-deterministic structure $\langle \mathbf{V}, \mathbf{E} \rangle$ is a deterministic function of its direct causes in $\boldsymbol{V}$ and a disturbance term ε_i, which represents the net effects of variables outside $\boldsymbol{V}$ on X_i. A particular causal structure, called a *causally sufficient* structure, plays a special role in the GT literature:

> **Causal sufficiency**: A set of variables $\boldsymbol{V}$ is called causally sufficient for a population if and only if in the population every common cause of any of two or more variables in $\boldsymbol{V}$ is in $\boldsymbol{V}$, or has the same value for all units in the population.[4]

An extra assumption in the GT literature is that the disturbance terms associated with the variables in a causally sufficient structure are independently distributed. For the time being, when we refer to a causally sufficient structure, we also assume the independence of the errors. Finally, in a pseudo-deterministic structure, once the functions linking the endogenous variables to the exogenous variables are defined, a specification of a joint probability distribution for the disturbance terms generates a unique probability distribution for $\mathbf{V}$. With this remark, a causal model can be defined as:

> **Causal model**: Let S be a causal structure defined over variables $\mathbf{V}$, F a distribution family over $\mathbf{V}$ and Θ a parameter space compatible with S. The triple $M = \langle S, F, \Theta \rangle$ forms a *causal model*. Each particular parameterization of M defines a causal hypothesis.

5.2.2 Path models

The causal structure is unknown but the presumption is that if enough data become available, the joint probability distribution of the variables under study can be estimated. The issue of data-driven causal inference involves using the estimate of the distribution to learn about the structure. To explain how this problem is solved by the GT approach, it is useful to begin with a description of the more familiar field of path analysis, which also addresses a similar inference issue. In a nutshell, path analysis starts with a conjecture about the causal structure of the variables under study, translates the structure into a system of equations, introduces certain causal principles to derive the implications of the model, and tests them against the data.[5] Consider variables $\mathbf{V} = \{X_1, \ldots, X_5\}$. Model I describes a possible structure that can be true of these variables:

$$
\begin{aligned}
&X_1 \\
&X_2 = \alpha X_1 + \varepsilon_2 \\
&X_3 = \beta X_1 + \varepsilon_3 \\
&X_4 = \gamma X_2 + \phi X_3 + \varepsilon_4 \\
&X_5 = \varphi X_4 + \varepsilon_5
\end{aligned}
\qquad \text{Model I}
$$

where the term ε_i in each equation represents the effect of unrecorded variables on X_i. According to this model, X_1 is a direct cause of X_2 and X_3 but an indirect cause of X_4 and X_5. X_2 and X_3 are direct causes of X_4, and X_4 is a direct cause of X_5. Since there is no reciprocal causal influence among the variables, the model is called a *recursive model*.

For estimation, path analysis assumes that: (i) the disturbance term ε_i is uncorrelated with the exogenous variables in the equation for X_i; (ii) the disturbance terms across the equations are uncorrelated; (iii) the errors are normally distributed with mean zero; and (iv) the endogenous variable in each equation *linearly* depends on the exogenous variables in the equation. A recursive model satisfying these conditions is called a path model. In addition, path analysis assumes that (v), the existence of a direct causal connection between two variables appears as a non-zero coefficient and (vi) the absence of a direct causal connection always appears as a zero coefficient (Goldberger, 1971: 35). These assumptions lead to two principles that allow deriving the implications of a path model for the data (see Appendix 5.A for a proof):

(i) The screening-off principle: If in a path model X causes Z only through the mediate of a set of variables $\mathbf{Y}$, X and Z are statistically independent conditional on $\mathbf{Y}$. In short, direct causes screen off their remote causes. Given the linearity assumption, this means that partial correlation $\rho_{XZ.\mathbf{Y}}$ is zero.
(ii) The common cause principle: If in a path model Z is a common cause of X and Y and neither X is a cause of Y nor Y is a cause of X, then $\rho_{XY.Z} = 0$.

Assuming that Model I satisfies the path-analytic conditions, the model entails the following zero partial correlations:

$$\rho_{X_2X_3.X_1} = 0;\ \rho_{x_4x_1 \cdot x_2x_3} = 0;\ \rho_{X_5X_2.X_4} = 0;\ \rho_{X_5X_3.X_4} = 0;\ \rho_{X_5X_1.X_4} = 0$$

The practice in path analysis is to derive the zero partial correlations of the model and test them against the data. If the vanishing partials are approximately zero in the data, the data is said to confirm the model. If they are significantly different from zero, the model is considered as incompatible with the data. Path analysis solves the causal inference problem by finding a model whose vanishing partials are consistent with the data. A limitation of this approach is that conflicting models can imply the same vanishing partials, making it impossible to infer the true model by testing its zero restrictions. Path analysis can at best eliminate models whose zero restrictions are inconsistent with the data. It cannot establish the model that has actually generated the data.

5.2.3 Graphical representation

The GT approach seeks to improve on path analysis. To this end, it replaces the language of equations with the language of graphs to represent causal structures. A graph consists of two parts - a set of variables (*vertices* or *nodes*) $\mathbf{V}$ and a set of *edges* (or *links*) $\mathbf{E}$. Each edge in $\mathbf{E}$ is between two distinct variables in $\mathbf{V}$. There are two kinds of edges in $\mathbf{E}$, directed edges $X \to Y$ and bidirected edges $X \leftrightarrow Y$. In either case, X and Y are called *endpoints* and when there is an edge between X and Y, X and Y are said to be *adjacent*. If there is an edge between X and Y and towards Y, X is called a *parent* of Y and Y a *child* of X. A directed edge between X and Y (i.e. $X \to Y$) in graph G stands for the claim that X is a direct cause of Y relative to G. The absence of an edge means that neither X causes Y nor Y causes X. The error terms are not represented in a graph. So, Model I can be expressed as Figure 5.1.

This graph depicts a *directed acyclic graph* (DAG). It is *directed* because the arrows lead from one variable into another and *acyclic* because one cannot return to any of the variables by following the arrows leading away from it. A

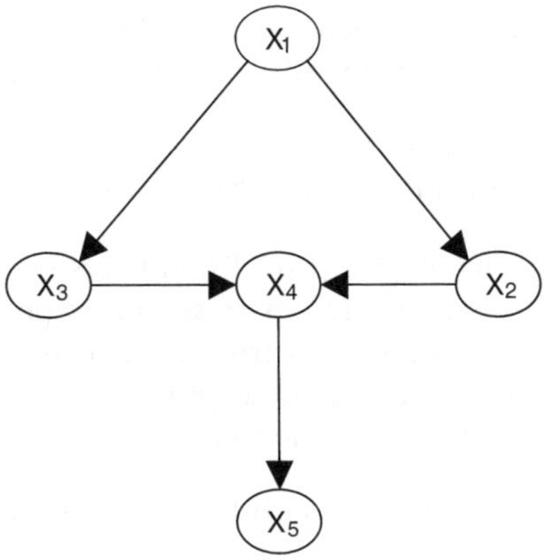

Figure 5.1 A graphical representation of Model I

sequence of consecutive edges in a directed graph G is called a *path*. A *directed* path P from X to Y is a sequence of vertices starting with X and ending with Y such that for every pair of variables A and B that are adjacent in the sequence in that order, the edge $A \rightarrow B$ occurs in G, and no vertex occurs more than once in P. Likewise, an *undirected* path U from X to Y is a sequence of variables starting with X and ending with Y such that for every pair of variables A and B that are adjacent in the sequence, A and B are adjacent in G, and no vertex occurs more than once in U. Y is a *collider* on an undirected path U if and only if there exist edges $X \rightarrow Y$ and $Z \rightarrow Y$ in U. And Y is an *unshielded collider* on U if and only if there exist edges $X \rightarrow Y$ and $Z \rightarrow Y$ in U and, in addition, Z and X are not adjacent in G. When there is a directed acyclic path from X to Y or $X = Y$, then X is said to be an *ancestor* of Y, and Y a *descendant* of X. A DAG is another way of representing a causally sufficient recursive structure. If the possibility of feedback is ruled out, the class of DAGs that can be built from a set of variables $\boldsymbol{V}$ constitutes the class of all causal models that can be true of $\boldsymbol{V}$. For now, we restrict our analysis to recursive structures and denote the class of DAGs that can be built from $\boldsymbol{V}$ by Ω.

5.2.4 Conditional independence data

The GT approach takes the independencies true in the joint distribution of $\boldsymbol{V}$, i.e. $P(\mathbf{V})$, as the evidence for making inference about the causal structure true of $\boldsymbol{V}$. Let X and Y be two variables in $\boldsymbol{V}$. X and Y are independent if their joint probability density $P(x, y)$ equals the product of the marginal densities $P(x)$ and $P(y)$, for all values x and y such that $P(y) > 0$. The independence of X and Y is usually shown by $X \perp Y$:

$$X \perp Y \quad \text{if and only if} \quad P(x/y) = P(x) \quad \text{whenever } P(y) > 0 \tag{5.1}$$

Similarly X and Y are independent conditional on Z if $P(x/y,z)$ equals the product of $P(x/z)$ and $P(y/z)$, for all values x, y, and z such that $P(y,z)$ is greater than zero:

$$X \perp Y/Z \quad \text{if and only if } P(x/y,z) = P(x/z) \quad \text{whenever} \quad P(y,z) > 0 \quad (5.2)$$

These definitions can be extended to disjoint sets of variables.[6] The conditional independence relation possesses several important properties that allow deriving new independencies from an existing set of independencies. Appendix 5.B lists some of these properties. We denote the set of independencies true in the distribution $P(\mathbf{V})$ over variables $\boldsymbol{V}$ by Ind_P.

5.2.5 Assumptions relating probability to causal relations

The GT approach introduces two principles to link independence data to a causal structure (DAG). The first is the causal Markov condition, which generalizes the two principles of path analysis. In its simplest form, the condition says that in a recursive causal structure every variable, conditional on its direct causes, is probabilistically independent of all other variables in the structure except its effects:

> **Markov condition**: A DAG G over a set of variables $\boldsymbol{V}$ and a probability distribution $P(\mathbf{V})$ satisfy the Markov condition if and only if for every X in $\boldsymbol{V}$ and every set $\boldsymbol{Z}$ of variables in $\boldsymbol{V}$ such that no member of $\boldsymbol{Z}$ is a descendant nor a parent of X, X and $\boldsymbol{Z}$ are independent conditional on the parents of X. (Spirtes *et al.*, 1993: 35)[7]

The Markov condition characterizes how a DAG represents independence relations. It says a variable X in DAG G, conditional on its parents, is independent of all its non-descendants in G. Applying the condition to Figure 5.1 yields the following independencies:

$X_2 \perp X_3/X_1$

$X_4 \perp X_1/(X_2, X_3)$

$X_5 \perp (X_1, X_2, X_3)/X_4$

These independencies entail additional independencies that are not immediately obtained by applying the Markov condition to the graph. An example is $X_5 \perp X_3/\{X_2, X_4\}$.[8] Pearl (1988) proposes a graph theoretic criterion, called *d-separation*, which allows reading from a DAG the entire list of independencies entailed by applying the Markov condition to the DAG. The criterion reads as follows:

> **Definition:** Let X and Y be two variables among the vertices in graph G, and $\boldsymbol{Z}$ a subset of the vertices in G. A path p is said to be d-separated

(or blocked) by $\mathbf{Z}$ if and only if (i) it contains a chain $X \rightarrow W \rightarrow Y$ or a fork $X \leftarrow W \rightarrow Y$ such that the middle variable W is in $\mathbf{Z}$, or (ii) it contains an unshielded collider $X \rightarrow W \leftarrow Y$ such that neither the middle variable W nor any of its descendants in G are in $\mathbf{Z}$. $\mathbf{Z}$ is then said to *d*-separate X from Y if and only if $\mathbf{Z}$ blocks every path from X to Y. (Pearl, 1998: 238)

Geiger *et al.* (1990) show that there is a one-to-one correspondence between the independence relations entailed by applying the Markov condition to a DAG G and the triples (X,Z,Y) that satisfy the *d*-separation criterion in G. In Figure 5.1, X_2 and X_3 are *d*-separated by X_1. But X_2 and X_3 are not *d*-separated by X_4, since X_4 is an unshielded collider on the path $X_2 \rightarrow X_4 \leftarrow X_3$. Nor are X_2 and X_3 *d*-separated by $\{X_1, X_5\}$, since X_5 is a descendant of the unshielded collider X_4. Applying the *d*-separation criterion to every DAG G in Ω yields all the independencies implied by G. We use Ind_G to denote the set of independencies implied by DAG G over $\boldsymbol{V}$ in order to distinguish it from Ind_P that denotes the set of independencies true in $P(\mathbf{V})$.

Using the *d*-separation criterion, Appendix 5.C shows that the Markov condition applied to a DAG over variables $\mathbf{V} = \{X_1, \ldots, X_n\}$ implies the following variant of the common cause principle: if X_i and X_j are correlated and neither X_i is a cause of X_j nor X_j is a cause of X_i, there are common causes of X_i and X_j in $\boldsymbol{V}$ conditional on which X_i and X_j are independent. The Markov condition therefore implies that every correlation among a causally sufficient recursive set of variables with independent errors has a causal explanation. The GT approach generalizes this implication to every correlation in the world by making the following metaphysical assumption:

The completeness hypothesis: For every set of recorded variables $\boldsymbol{O}$, either the set forms a causally sufficient set with uncorrelated errors or it can be embedded in a larger set of variables $\boldsymbol{V}$ that is causally sufficient with uncorrelated errors. (Scheines, 1997: 197; Spirtes *et al.*, 1993: 51)

Joined with this hypothesis, the Markov condition entails that every probabilistic dependency in the world reflects either a direct causal connection or the presence of latent common causes.[9]

The other assumption about the link between probability and causation is the *faithfulness* condition, which says that every independency true in the joint distribution of a set of observables represents the absence of a direct causal connection. Put differently, no two directly causally related variables are ever independent. Formally,

Faithfulness condition: Let G be a causal graph over variables $\boldsymbol{V}$ and $P(\mathbf{V})$ a probability distribution generated by G. $\langle G, P \rangle$ satisfies the faithfulness condition if and only if every conditional independence relation true in

P(V) is entailed by the Causal Markov condition applied to *G*. (Spirtes *et al.*, 1993: 56)

Faithfulness excludes independencies that are not implied by the topology of a DAG. For a possible case of such independency, consider the graph in Figure 5.2 below, which describes a conjecture about the relations among minimum wage, the economy and individual income.

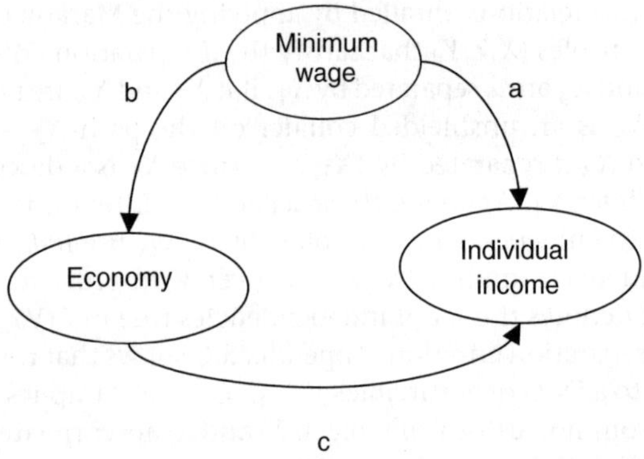

Figure 5.2 An unfaithful structure

Suppose the effect of minimum wage through the economy on individual income was such that it exactly offset its direct effect on individual income, i.e. $a = -(bc)$. In that case, the structure would generate an independency that did not follow from applying the Markov condition to it. If the world contained such structures, it would be wrong to infer the absence of causation from independence data. In the current example, one would wrongly conclude that minimum wage does not affect income, even though it does. Faithfulness excludes such structures from the world. It says all independencies are structural in the sense that they follow from the topology of the true graph, not from the particular parameter values attached to the links among the variables. Appendix 5.D shows how faithfulness underlies other methods of causal inference.

5.3 Causal inference

Causal inference in the GT approach proceeds by: (i) estimating the joint probability distribution of the variables of interest, *V*; (ii) deriving the independencies true in *P*(V); and (iii) constructing a graph (or graphs) that, given the Markov condition and faithfulness, is consistent with the independencies. The concern, here, is with the final stage, which has to do with the move from the independencies true in *P*(V) to a graph that could have generated the joint distribution. We describe this stage of inference in some detail to prepare the ground for a critical appraisal of the GT approach in section 3.5.

5.3.1 Inference with causal sufficiency

We begin our exposition by assuming that the variables under study are causally sufficient, and then describe graph-theoretic causal inference in general. Specifically, we work with variables $\mathbf{V} = \{X_1, \ldots, X_5\}$, assuming that $\boldsymbol{V}$ is causally sufficient. And, we hypothesize that

$$Ind_P = \{X_2 \perp X_3 / X_1$$
$$X_4 \perp X_1 / (X_2, X_3)$$
$$X_5 \perp (X_1, X_2, X_3) / X_4\}$$

Causal sufficiency implies that the set of DAGs, Ω, that can be true of variables $\boldsymbol{V}$ is finite. Thus, the solution to the causal inference problem involves finding a DAG G from Ω that is consistent with the independencies in Ind_P. To explain how such a DAG can be found, note that, given the Markov condition, if a DAG G generated the data, G would not imply any independency that is not in Ind_P. As a result, for any DAG G in Ω, if Ind_G contains an independency that is not in Ind_P, the DAG does not satisfy the Markov condition. The Markov condition excludes all those DAGs in Ω that entail at least one independency that is not in Ind_P. On the other hand, according to the faithfulness condition, the distribution $P(\mathbf{V})$ is faithful to a DAG G in Ω if every independency in Ind_P follows from the *d*-separation criterion applied to G. This means that if a DAG G in Ω fails to imply *all* the independencies in Ind_P, the DAG is not faithful to $P(\mathbf{V})$. Faithfulness excludes all those DAGs in Ω that fail to imply all the independencies in Ind_P. Altogether, these conditions imply that a DAG G in Ω with independencies Ind_G is consistent with the independencies in Ind_P if and only if there is a one-to-one correspondence between Ind_P and Ind_G. The inference problem can then be solved by deriving the set of independencies Ind_G implied by each DAG G in Ω and investigating whether they have a one-to-one correspondence with the independencies in Ind_P.

The above description gives all that there is in the *GT* approach under the causal sufficiency assumption. Nevertheless, the above implications of the Markov condition and faithfulness lead to a basic theorem that simplifies the procedure for constructing a DAG consistent with Ind_P. The theorem, proved by Verma and Pearl (1990), says:

> **Theorem**: Distribution $P(\mathbf{V})$ satisfies the Markov and faithfulness conditions for DAG G if and only if (i) any two vertices X and Y are adjacent in G if and only if they are statistically dependent conditional on every subset of vertices in G not containing them, and (ii) $X \rightarrow Y \leftarrow Z$ is an unshielded collider in G, then X, Z are not independent conditional on Y.

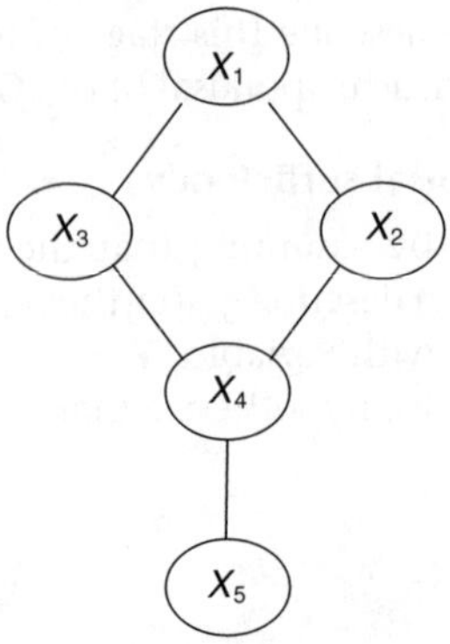

Figure 5.3 A partially connected skeleton

The procedure begins with a complete *skeleton*; that is, a graph in which every variable is connected by an undirected edge to every other variable. In the first phase, the procedure tests every pair of variables X and Y and removes the edge between them if $X \perp Y$ is in Ind_P. Next, for every pair X and Y, it tests whether there is a subset $\boldsymbol{Z}$ of variables that does not contain X and Y but renders them independent. If so, the edge between X and Y is removed. The process creates an undirected graph from which some of the edges are removed. In our example, the process results in a partially connected skeleton given in Figure 5.3.

In the second phase, the procedure considers every triple of vertices X, Y, and Z in $\boldsymbol{V}$. If there is an edge between X and Y, and an edge between Z and Y, but no edge between X and Z, and X and Z are not independent given Y, the edges are directed towards Y. In Figure 5.3, there is an edge between X_2 and X_4, an edge between X_3 and X_4, but no edge between X_2 and X_3. The edges are thus directed towards X_4. Or else, the resulting DAG will not entail $X_4 \perp X_1/(X_2, X_3)$, violating faithfulness. Similarly, the edge between X_4 and X_5 is directed towards X_5 to avoid violating faithfulness. The edges between X_1 and X_2, and X_1 and X_3 cannot *both* be directed towards X_1. Any such orientation makes X_2 and X_3 dependent conditional on X_1, which contradicts faithfulness. The independencies Ind_P impose no further restrictions on the edges. The graph in Figure 5.1 is consistent with the independencies in Ind_P.

5.3.2 Inference without causal sufficiency

Causal sufficiency is hardly true, and even if it were true it would not *a priori* be known. To claim any success, a data-driven method of causal inference should deal with the causal inference problem regardless of whether the recorded variables are causally sufficient or not. In the absence of causal sufficiency, a correlation between measured variables X and Y no longer implies that either X causes Y or Y causes X. The correlation might be due to latent common causes. Thus, the general problem of statistical causal inference is to determine when and how it is possible by analysis of a set of measured variables containing X and Y to conclude whether X causes Y, or Y causes X, or whether the correlation between X and Y is due to latent common causes.

In the GT approach, the burden of generalizing the solution to the inference problem under causal sufficiency to cases where the truth of the condition is not known is on the completeness hypothesis (Scheines, 1997: 197). According to this hypothesis, for every set of *measured* variables $\boldsymbol{O}$, which is not causally sufficient, there is in reality a DAG $G(\mathbf{O}, \mathbf{L})$ with independent errors that is responsible for the dependencies among the observed variables $\boldsymbol{O}$, with $\boldsymbol{L} = \boldsymbol{V}\backslash\boldsymbol{O}$ being the latent common causes of $\boldsymbol{O}$. Thus, the joint probability distribution of the recorded variables $P(\mathbf{O})$ is regarded as the marginal of an unknown distribution $P^*(\mathbf{V})$ that satisfies both the Markov and faithfulness conditions. From this perspective, statistical causal inference involves learning about the true DAG $G(\mathbf{O}, \mathbf{L})$ from the marginal distribution $P(\mathbf{O})$.

With causal sufficiency, the object of inference is a DAG in which every adjacency between X and Y is represented by an arrow, meaning that either X causes Y or Y causes X. As causal sufficiency is withdrawn, a different graphical object is needed to state that an adjacency is due to latent common causes. Several objects suitable for representing latent common causes are available. We use the so-called *hybrid graph*, which in addition to one-directional edges $\rightarrow$ contains bidirectional edges $\leftrightarrow$ to denote latent common causes.[10] To illustrate the simplest hybrid graph, let $X \leftarrow Z \rightarrow Y$ be the DAG true of X, Y and Z. When Z is unknown, the hybrid graph for this DAG is given by $X \leftrightarrow Y$; the bidirected link represents the latent common cause Z.

Learning about the true DAG $G(\mathbf{O}, \mathbf{L})$ from the independencies true in $P(\mathbf{O})$ requires knowing the independencies that would occur among the recorded variables $\boldsymbol{O}$ if $G(\mathbf{O}, \mathbf{L})$ were the DAG generating the data. An answer to this question is given in Pearl and Verma (1991). To explain the answer, we need to introduce a further graph-theoretic notion – an *inducing path*. An undirected path U between X and Y is an inducing path over $\boldsymbol{O}$ in $G(\mathbf{O}, \mathbf{L})$ if and only if (i) every member of $\boldsymbol{O}$ on U (except the endpoints) is a collider on U, and (ii) from every collider on U there is a directed path to X or Y. Figure 5.4 shows an inducing path between X and Y over $\mathbf{O} = \{X, Z, Y\}$.

Pearl and Verma (1991) have shown that there is an inducing path between recorded variables X and Y in $G(\mathbf{O}, \mathbf{L})$ over $\boldsymbol{O}$ if and only if X and Y are not independent conditional on any subset of $\mathbf{O}\backslash\{X, Y\}$. This means that if there is a directed path in the hybrid graph between X and Y that is into Y, then X is a (possibly indirect) cause of Y. If the path is into X, then Y is a (possibly indirect) cause of X. And, if the path is both into X and into Y, then there is a common cause (or causes) in $G(\mathbf{O}, \mathbf{L})$ affecting

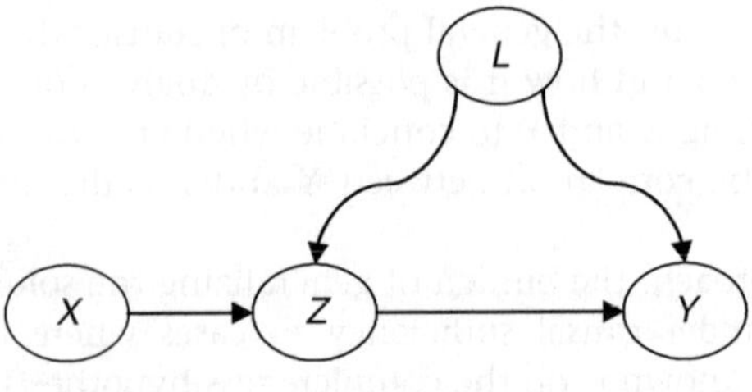

Figure 5.4 Inducing path graph

both X and Y. Accordingly, given the conditions, one can learn about the true structure $G(\mathbf{O}, \mathbf{L})$ by investigating the hybrid graph consistent with the independence data.

The intuitions behind these results can be explained by analysing some simple examples. As a first example, we withdraw the causal sufficiency assumption about the variables $\{X_1, \ldots, X_5\}$ studied earlier while retaining the same set of independence relations:

$$Ind_P = \{X_2 \perp X_3 / X_1, X_4 \perp X_1 / (X_2, X_3), X_5 \perp (X_1, X_2, X_3) / X_4\}$$

Starting from a skeleton over $\mathbf{O}$, these independencies lead to the same graph as in Figure 5.3. Faithfulness requires directing the edges between X_2 and X_4, and X_3 and X_4 towards X_4, and the edge between X_4 and X_5 towards X_5. No DAG $G(\mathbf{O}, \mathbf{L})$, containing variables that d-separate X_4 and X_5, can be true of the data. Any such DAG fails to entail $X_5 \perp X_2 / X_4$ and is unfaithful to $P(\mathbf{O})$. The true DAG $G(\mathbf{O}, \mathbf{L})$ thus contains an inducing path between X_4 and X_5 that is into X_5, meaning that X_4 causes X_5. Since cycles have been ruled out, X_5 is not a cause of X_4. Also, no DAG that renders both dependencies between X_1 and X_2 and X_1 and X_3 spurious can be faithful to $P(\mathbf{O})$. In any such DAG, X_1 is a collider incapable of d-separating X_2 from X_3. Finally, only one of the edges in $X_2 \rightarrow X_4 \leftarrow X_3$ can be due to latent common causes. A DAG that renders both edges spurious fails to entail $X_5 \perp X_1 / (X_2, X_3)$. Figure 5.5 shows two hybrid graphs consistent with the independencies:

This example shows how the Markov condition and faithfulness are used to conclude whether a variable causes another variable. To set the stage for our later discussion, let us also consider an example from Glymour (1997a: 218), intended to demonstrate a case where the conditions entail that an association is *definitely* due to latent common causes. Let $\mathbf{O} = \{X_1, \ldots, X_4\}$ and

$$Ind_P = \{X_1 \perp X_2, X_1 \perp X_3, X_2 \perp X_4\}$$

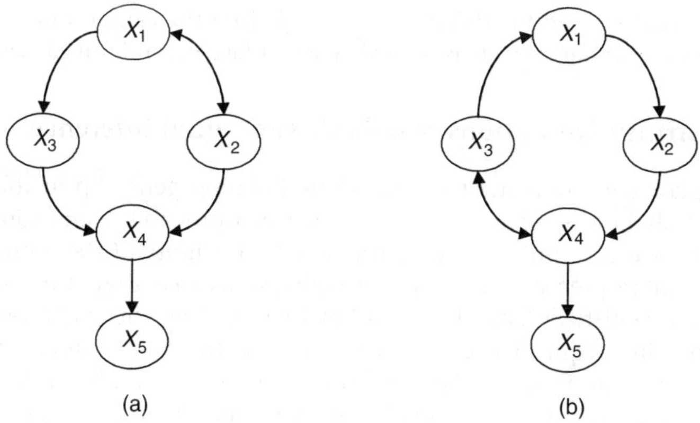

Figure 5.5 Equivalent hybrid graphs

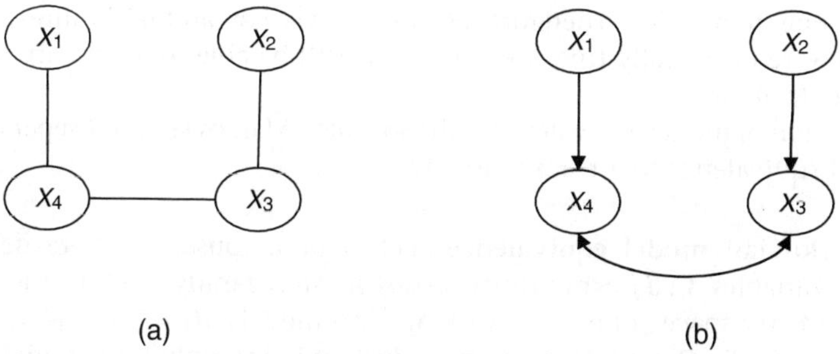

Figure 5.6 Latent common causes: the bidirected edge in (b) stands for unmeasured common causes

Starting from a skeleton over **O**, these independencies lead to undirected graph (a) in Figure 5.6. Faithfulness requires directing the edges between X_2 and X_3 and between X_4 and X_3 towards X_3, and the edges between X_1 and X_4 and between X_3 and X_4 towards X_4. These create a bidirected edge between X_3 and X_4, as shown in Figure 5.6(b) below. The bidirected edge reveals an inducing path in $G(\mathbf{O}, \mathbf{L})$ that is into both X_3 and X_4, revealing the existence of a common cause for the variables.

This conclusion is based on the consideration that any DAG $G(\mathbf{L}, \mathbf{O})$ not containing some variables responsible for the correlation between X_3 and X_4 violates either the Markov condition or faithfulness. Consider, for example, a DAG $G(\mathbf{L}, \mathbf{O})$ in which X_3 causes X_4. Such a DAG does not entail $X_2 \perp X_4$ which is in Ind_P, and hence violates faithfulness. Since there is by assumption no feedback among the variables, the correlation between X_3 and X_4 must be due to latent common causes. Given the completeness hypothesis, the

Markov condition and faithfulness allow inferring the causal influence of a variable on another, as well as the existence of latent common causes.

5.4 Intrinsic limitations of data-driven causal inference

The Markov condition and faithfulness are the most general principles that can possibly be true of the connection between probability and causation. As before, we continue to assume the universal validity of these principles to study more precisely the kinds of conclusions that they warrant us to draw from statistical data. This requires investigating the statistical indistinguishability (equivalence) of causal models, the key to understanding intrinsic limitations of any data-driven method of causal inference. We will show that, given any causal model fitting the data, there is always a simple rule that allows generating a class of statistically equivalent causal models. These models usually have very little or nothing in common, particularly because the sign and significance of the coefficient estimates can vary from one model to another. Therefore, even if the Markov and faithfulness principles were universally true, we would not still be able to learn very much from data alone.

A notion of model equivalence is the so-called Markovian (or *d*-separation) model equivalence that reads as follows:

> **Markovian model equivalence**: Let S_i be a causal structure defined on variables $\boldsymbol{V}$, F_i a multivariate distribution family over $\boldsymbol{V}$ and Θ_i a parameter space compatible with S_i. Two models $M_1 = \langle S_1, F_1, \Theta_1 \rangle$ and $M_2 = \langle S_2, F_2, \Theta_2 \rangle$ are Markovian-equivalent if and only if they imply the same Markovian independencies; i.e. if and only if $Ind_{P1} = Ind_{p2}$.

Another stronger concept of model equivalence is the so-called *distributional model equivalence*:

> **Distributional model equivalence:** Two models $M_1 = \langle S_1, F_1, \Theta_1 \rangle$ and $M_2 = \langle S_2, F_2, \Theta_2 \rangle$ are distributionally equivalent if and only if for every parameterization of M_1 generating distribution f_1 there is a parameterization of M_2 generating distribution f_2 such that f_1 and f_2 are the same.

These notions coincide in the case of causally sufficient recursive models (Pearl, 2000: 146). Outside this category, there are Markovian-equivalent models that are not distributionally equivalent (Sprites *et al.*, 1996; Raykov and Penev, 1999). Nevertheless, the generality of our argument is preserved even by focusing on the Markovian model equivalence. So we will not discuss distributional model equivalence.[11] We first consider recursive causal models and then turn to non-recursive models.

5.4.1 Recursive equivalent models

Recursive causal models can be divided into causally sufficient and causally insufficient models. An original contribution to the study of statistical indistinguishability of causally sufficient recursive models (DAGs) is due to Stelzl (1986), who studied the statistical equivalence of path models. Other early contributions are Frydenberg (1990), Lee and Hershberger (1990), and Verma and Pearl (1990).[12] In path analysis, data are characterized by sample covariance matrices and the implications of a model are defined, as seen, in terms of its zero partial correlations. A path model is compatible with the data if its vanishing partials are compatible with the sample covariance matrix of the variables being modelled. So, if path models M_1 and M_2 entail the same vanishing partials, and if M_1 is compatible with the data, M_2 is also compatible with the data and vice versa. On the other hand, if either M_1 or M_2 entails a zero partial correlation that is not implied by the other, the models are not equivalent. This suggests the following definition of path model equivalence:

> **Path model equivalence**: Two path models M_1 and M_2 are equivalent if and only if they constrain the same set of partial correlations to zero.

Stelzl (1986) noted that the zero partial correlations implied by a path model were invariant with respect to certain changes in the ordering of the variables in the model. He located several invariant properties of vanishing partials and used them to define four rules for transforming a path model into another statistically equivalent model. The invariant properties underpinning Stelzl's rules can be reduced to two very simple properties. Consider a path model over variables $\{X, Y, Z\}$, with path diagram (i) in Figure 5.7.

Graph (i) implies $\rho_{XY.Z} = 0$ but no other zero restriction. Inverting arrow $X \to Z$ or both arrows yields graph (ii) or (iii) that have the same zero restrictions as (i). Inverting arrow $Z \to Y$ in (i) or $X \to Z$ in (iii), however, creates unshielded collider (iv) that does not imply $\rho_{XY.Z} = 0$; the only zero restriction it implies is $\rho_{XY} = 0$. Alternatively, consider inverting one or both of the arrows in (iv). This yields one of the models (i) through (iii). These models fail to entail model (iv)'s zero restriction but entail a vanishing partial that is

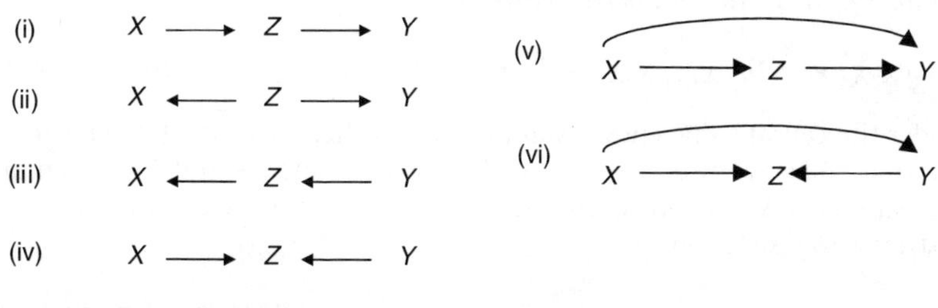

Figure 5.7 Equivalent path models

not implied by the model. This suggests that any arrow inversion in a path diagram that creates or destroys an unshielded collider destroys or creates a zero restriction, which yields a statistically different path model.

Now, consider graph (v), which is a complete graph in the sense that there is a link between every two variables in it. A complete graph implies no zero partial correlation (Wermuth, 1980). Therefore, any change in the graph that turns it into another (non-cyclic) complete graph yields an equivalent path model. Redirecting arrow $Z \rightarrow Y$, for instance, gives rise to graph (vi) which is equivalent to graph (v). On the other hand, removing an arrow from these two models yields a model with a new zero restriction.

This analysis points to two types of changes in a path diagram that alter its zero restrictions: (i) deletion or creation of a new link; and (ii) creation or destruction of an unshielded collider. In general, Verma and Pearl (1990) and Frydenberg (1990) show that:

> **Theorem 4.1**: Two DAGs G and G^* are Markovian- (covariance) equivalent if and only if they have (i) the same links and (ii) the same unshielded colliders.[13]

In light of this, an edge $X \rightarrow Y$ in a DAG G can be inverted to form an equivalent DAG $G*$ as long as the inversion neither destroys nor creates an unshielded collider. This happens only if every parent of X is a parent of Y and every parent of Y (except X) is a parent of X (Chickering, 1995; and Meek, 1995). The result leads to the following rule for converting a DAG G into another equivalent DAG G^* (Appendix 5.E outlines a proof):

> **The DAG inversion rule**: An arrow $X \rightarrow Y$ in a DAG G can be inverted to form an equivalent DAG G^* only if every parent of X is a parent of Y and every parent of Y (except X) is a parent of X.

Since equivalence relation is reflexive, symmetric and transitive, by repeatedly applying the rule one can generate all possible models equivalent to a DAG. Applying the rule to the path model described in Section 5.2 yields two more equivalent models. The original model corresponds to graph (a) in Figure 5.8, with the zero partial correlations:

$$\rho_{X_2X_3.X_1} = 0; \rho_{X_4X_1.X_2X_3} = 0; \rho_{X_5X_2.X_4} = 0; \rho_{X_5X_3.X_4} = 0; \rho_{X_5X_1.X_4} = 0$$

Under the causal sufficiency assumption, no other arrow in DAG (a) can be inverted. Take arrow $X_4 \rightarrow X_5$. X_4 has two parents X_2 and X_3 which are not parents of X_5. Inverting the arrow creates new unshielded colliders that destroy zero restrictions:

$$\rho_{X_5X_2.X_4} = 0; \ \rho_{X_5X_3.X_4} = 0; \ \rho_{X_5X_1.X_4} = 0$$

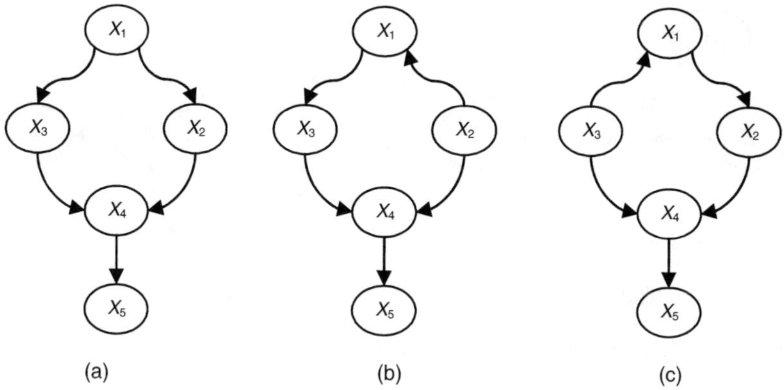

Figure 5.8 Markovian equivalent DAGs

This analysis shows that once a DAG is fitted to the data, there is a simple rule to transform it into another statistically equivalent DAG. Thus, even with the causal sufficiency assumption, the 'true' structure cannot be discovered from independence data alone. If causal sufficiency is not assumed, however, a graph (model) over measured variables $\boldsymbol{O}$ can be changed into another equivalent graph not only by inverting some of the directed edges but also by replacing them with bidirected edges $\leftrightarrow$, which represent latent common causes. In discussing Markovian equivalence of causally insufficient models, we continue to assume the completeness hypothesis. The equivalence of two DAGs over observed variables $\boldsymbol{O}$ can then be defined as follows:

Markovian equivalence over O: Two DAGs $G(\mathbf{O}, \mathbf{L})$ and $G^*(\mathbf{O}, \mathbf{L}^*)$ are Markovian-equivalent over $\boldsymbol{O}$ if they imply the same set of *d*-seperation triples over $\boldsymbol{O}$.[14]

Building on Stelzl's (1986), Lee and Hershberger (1990) establish a simple condition for replacing an arrow $X \to Y$ in the graph of a covariance structural model with a bidirected edge $X \leftrightarrow Y$ that suggests that the correlation between X and Y is due to correlation among errors. Based on the completeness hypothesis, a correlation among errors represents latent common causes. Lee and Hershberger's condition can, therefore, be viewed as a condition for converting a hybrid graph into another equivalent hybrid graph. We restate Lee and Hershberger's result in theorem 4.2 and outline a proof for it in Appendix 5.F:

Theorem 4.2: Let $G(\mathbf{O}, \mathbf{L})$ be a DAG, X and Y in $\boldsymbol{O}$, and $X \to Y$ hold in $G(\mathbf{O}, \mathbf{L})$. Let $G^*(\mathbf{O}, \mathbf{L}^*)$ be the same as $G(\mathbf{O}, \mathbf{L})$except that $X \to Y$ is replaced with $X \leftrightarrow Y$. $G(\mathbf{O}, \mathbf{L})$ and $G^*(\mathbf{O}, \mathbf{L}^*)$ are Markovian-equivalent over $\boldsymbol{O}$ if for

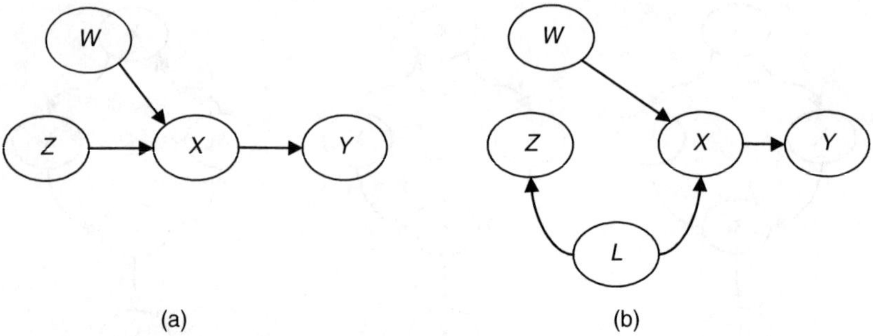

Figure 5.9 Graph (b) represents a legitimate edge replacement

every variable Z in $\boldsymbol{O}$ that is a parent of X in G, Z is also a parent of Y. Also, if $X \leftrightarrow Y$ is in $G(\mathbf{O}, \mathbf{L})$, the bidirected edge can be replaced with $X \rightarrow Y$ if every parent of X is a parent of Y.

Pearl (2000: 146) notes that, when the requirement of the DAG inversion rule holds of an arrow $X \rightarrow Y$ in a hybrid graph, replacing it with a bidirected edge neither generates nor destroys an unshielded collider, and yields an equivalent hybrid graph. The rule, he argues, can be used to transform a hybrid graph into another equivalent hybrid graph. However, unlike the condition in Theorem 4.2, the DAG inversion rule requires every parent of X or Y (except X) to be a parent of both, which is unnecessarily strong. Consider graph (a) in Figure 5.9. Here, X has a direct cause, W, which is not a cause of Z. But replacing the arrow $Z \rightarrow X$ with a bidirected edge neither destroys nor creates an independence relation among the recorded variables. Both graphs (a) and (b) imply the same independencies over $\mathbf{O} = \{X, Y, Z, W\}$.

As required by theorem 4.2, in order to replace an arrow $X \rightarrow Y$ with a bidirected arrow $X \leftrightarrow Y$ without destroying or creating an unshielded collider it is sufficient that every parent of X is a parent of Y. The theorem, however, does not exhaustively characterize the class of DAGs that are Markovian-equivalent to $G(\mathbf{O}, \mathbf{L})$ over $\boldsymbol{O}$. This is because creation of a new unshielded collider in certain situations leaves the independencies implied by $G(\mathbf{O}, \mathbf{L})$ over $\boldsymbol{O}$ unchanged. An example is given by graph (a) in Figure 5.10.[15] Theorem 4.2 permits replacing $Z \rightarrow Y$ with a bidirected edge to create equivalent graph (b) but does not allow replacing $X \rightarrow Y$ in (b) with a bidirected edge, since X has a parent that is no longer a parent of Y. Nevertheless, such a replacement neither destroys nor creates an independency. Even though graph (c) contains an extra unshielded collider, all three graphs are Markovian-equivalent over $\boldsymbol{O}$.

Due to such cases, establishing a rule that defines necessary and sufficient conditions for transforming a hybrid graph into another equivalent

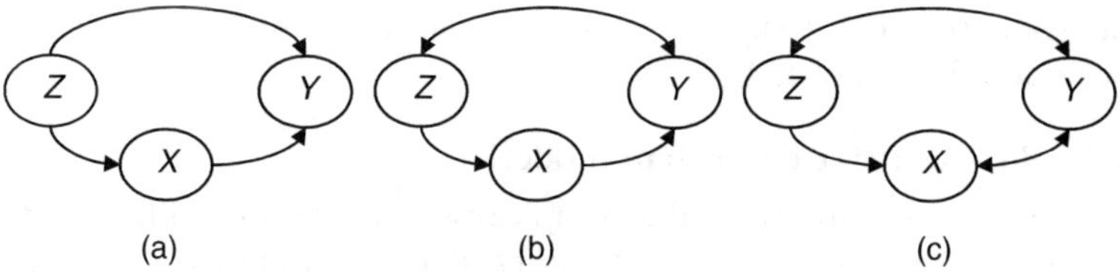

Figure 5.10 Equivalent graphs with different unshielded colliders

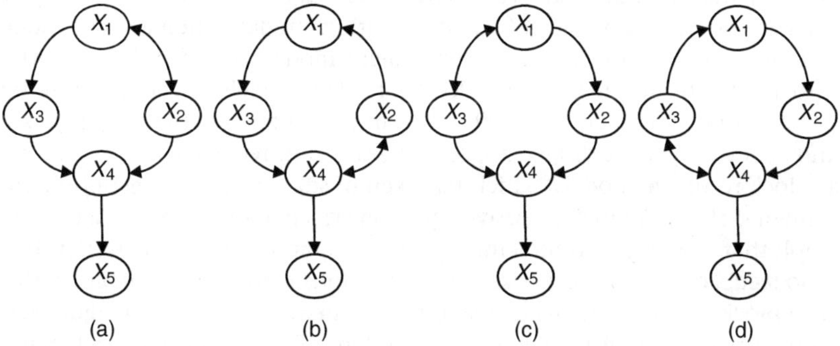

Figure 5.11 Semi-Markovian equivalent DAGs

hybrid graph demands specifying the conditions under which creating a new unshielded collider does not alter the independencies. Pearl (2000: 147) takes some steps towards this aim but acknowledges that his requirements are not sufficient. All the same, theorem 4.2 gives way to the following rule for the creation of a partial set of equivalent hybrid acyclic graphs:

> **The bi-directed edge replacement rule**: An arrow $X \to Y$ in a hybrid graph $G(\mathbf{O}, \mathbf{L})$ can be replaced with a bidirected edge $X \leftrightarrow Y$ to form an equivalent hybrid graph $G^*(\mathbf{O}, \mathbf{L}^*)$ if the parents of Y in $G(\mathbf{O}, \mathbf{L})$ include the parents of X. Conversely, under the same condition, a bidirected edge $X \leftrightarrow Y$ can be replaced with a directed edge $X \to Y$.

Applying this rule to the example used throughout the chapter adds four more models to the equivalent models listed in Figure 5.8. The new models are shown in Figure 5.11. Graph (b) is obtained by applying the DAG inversion rule to arrow $X_1 \to X_2$ and replacing it with a bidirected edge. Similarly, graph (d) is obtained by applying the DAG inversion rule to arrow $X_1 \to X_3$ and replacing it with a bidirected edge.

The rule does not permit replacing arrow $X_4 \to X_5$ with a bidirected edge, since X_4 has parents which are not parents of X_5. Given the Markov and faithfulness conditions, the only conclusion that can be inferred from the independence data is that X_4 is a (possibly indirect) cause of X_5, and X_5 has no causal influence over X_4.

5.4.2 Non-recursive equivalent models

Allowing feedback increases the complexity of causal modelling. Notably, the Markov condition, as defined earlier, does not hold for non-recursive (cyclic) models and must be replaced with a more general one.[16] Feedback also adds to the complexity of the conditions under which two cyclic models are *d*-separation-equivalent. This in turn makes it even more difficult to characterize the necessary and sufficient conditions under which a cyclic model can be transformed into another equivalent model. For the sake of brevity, instead of considering the equivalence of cyclic models in general, building on the works of Frydenberg (1990), Lee and Hershberger (1990) and Raykov and Penev (1999), we discuss a specific class of non-recursive models, known as block-recursive models, which has been of some interest in econometrics (Kmenta, 1986). A block-recursive equation system corresponds to a directed graph that can be partitioned into several subgraphs (blocks) such that there is no feedback across the blocks but the relations among the variables within each block can be either recursive or non-recursive. Graph (a) in Figure 5.12 represents a block-recursive equation system. There is no feedback across the blocks separated by the line. If, in addition, the graph (equation system) contains an acyclic subgraph (block), the graph is said to be a *limited block-recursive graph* (system) (Lee and Hershberger, 1990: 317). Following Lee and Hershberger (1990), we name an acyclic subgraph a *focal* subgraph.

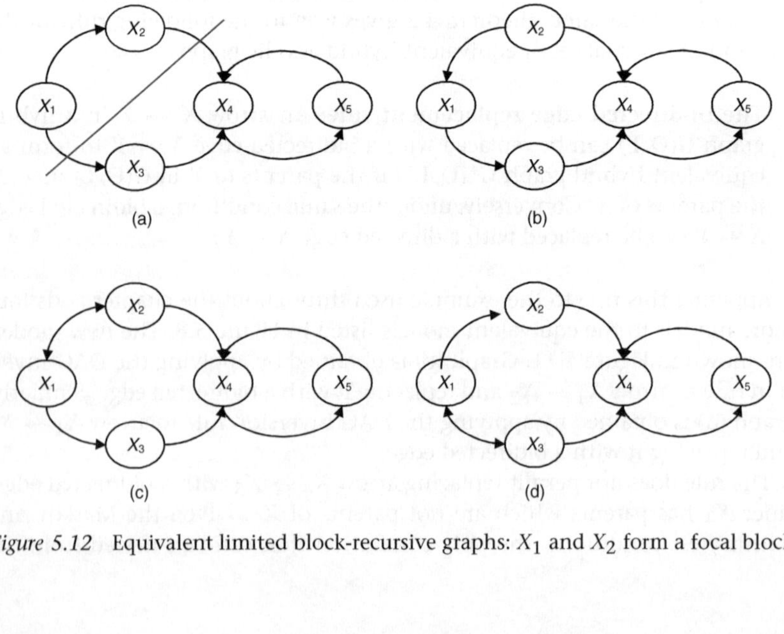

Figure 5.12 Equivalent limited block-recursive graphs: X_1 and X_2 form a focal block

Theorem 4.3 captures the result available about the *d*-separation equivalence of limited block-recursive models. Appendix 5.G outlines a proof, based on a theorem due to Raykov and Penev (1999):

> **Theorem 4.3**: Let $G^*(\mathbf{O}, \mathbf{L}^*)$ be the same limited block-recursive graph as $G(\mathbf{O}, \mathbf{L})$ over $\boldsymbol{O}$ except that $X \leftrightarrow Y$ is in $G^*(\mathbf{O}, \mathbf{L}^*)$ instead of $X \to Y$. Then, $G(\mathbf{O}, \mathbf{L})$ and $G^*(\mathbf{O}, \mathbf{L}^*)$ are *d*-separation-equivalent over $\boldsymbol{O}$ if for every variable Z in $\boldsymbol{O}$ that is a parent of X in $G(\mathbf{O}, \mathbf{L})$, Z is also a parent of Y. Furthermore, if $X \leftrightarrow Y$ is in $G(\mathbf{O}, \mathbf{L})$, the edge can be replaced with $X \to Y$ if every parent of X is a parent of Y.

This theorem makes it possible to establish a rule similar to the bidirected edge replacement rule that allows transforming a limited block-recursive graph into another equivalent limited block-recursive graph.[17] Figure 5.12 depicts four equivalent models. The set $\{X_1, X_2\}$ in graph (a) forms a focal block. Using the theorem, we can replace the arrow $X_1 \to X_2$ to obtain the equivalent graph (b) or replace it with a bidirected edge to obtain graph (c).[18] The set $\{X_1, X_3\}$ also forms a focal block. The arrow $X_1 \to X_3$ can be replaced with a bidirected edge to obtain graph (d).

Although the discussion of non-recursive models has been confined to limited block-recursive models, the scope of the result is not that limited. It is usually possible to locate a focal block in most non-recursive models. Theorem 4.3 applies to most cyclic models.

The above rules permit generating a class of equivalent models for a large class of structural models. The outcome of the GT algorithms, as stressed by the founders of the GT approach, is not therefore the true graph but a class of equivalent graphs that could have generated the data. More precisely, the outcome of the GT algorithms is a *pattern* – a graphical object that represents the directed edges common to all the members of the equivalent class but leaves the direction of other edges unspecified. These common edges define what can be learnt from the data using the GT techniques.

5.4.3 Causal inference in practice

A proposal to curb the multiplicity of equivalent models is to consider the temporal order of the variables. A cause is said to temporally precede the effect, which means if X precedes Y, Y cannot be a cause of X. This suggestion is of some help but falls short of narrowing the class of equivalent models to a single model. The suggestion does not apply to feedback models, and it is often difficult to ascertain whether a variable precedes another. Moreover, even if the temporal order of the variables were known and only recursive models were permitted, there would still be many models fitting the data. As a simple example, suppose that $\mathbf{O} = \{X, Y, Z\}$ is the set of recorded variables, X temporally precedes Y, Y temporally precedes Z and that $X \perp Z/Y$ is true in $P(\mathbf{O})$. The only conclusion that can be derived from this information is

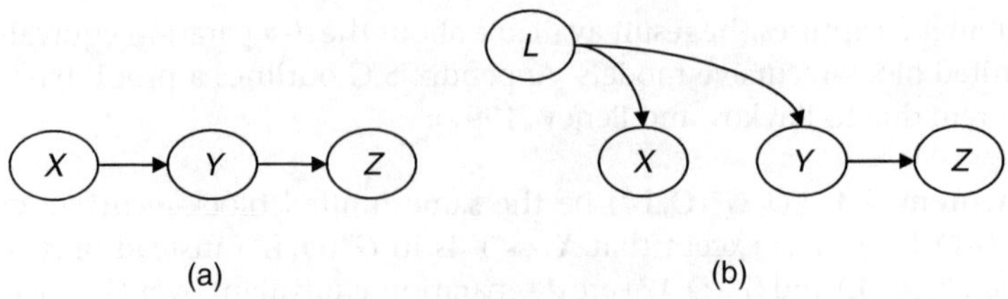

Figure 5.13 Time ordering and Markovian model equivalence

that *Y* causes *Z*. Both graphs (a) and (b) in Figure 5.13 are consistent with the data. In fact, *L* stands for all the temporally precedent variables that can affect both *X* and *Y*. This means infinitely many models could have generated the independence data. Even with the imposition of temporal order, the class of equivalent models may be large.

Table 5.1 Contrived covariance data

	X	*Y*	*Z*
X	1	0.26	0.30
Y	0.26	1	0.22
Y	0.30	0.22	1

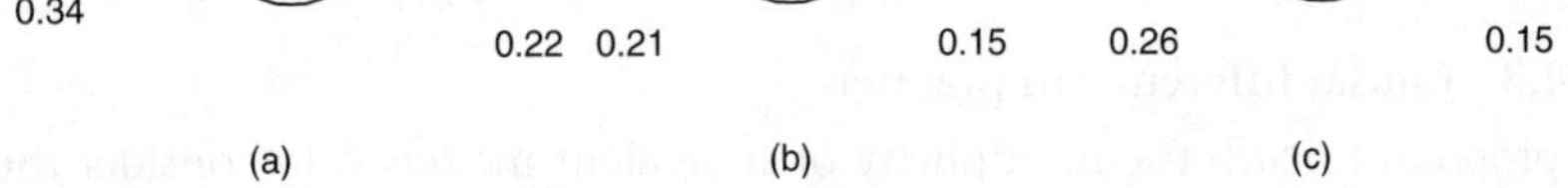

Figure 5.14 Markovian equivalent models with varying coefficient estimates

Now, a very important point, which often goes unnoticed, is that *in practice* the class of models (graphs) equivalent with a causal model fitting the data usually have little or even nothing in common. The reason is that coefficient estimates do not remain invariant across various members of an equivalence class; they vary as we move from one member of the class to another. Consider the covariance matrix shown in Table 5.1. Figure 5.14 depicts three equivalent graphs consistent with these data.

As these graphs illustrate, the parameter estimate for a link between two variables does not remain invariant across the members of the equivalent class. A coefficient estimate may be significant in some members of the class but not in others. Or it may be positive in some members of the class but negative in others. Moreover, the change in the sign and significance of coefficient estimates is by no means confined to the coefficients of the edges varying across the equivalent models. The sign and significance of the coefficients of common edges can also vary from one model to another (Williams *et al.*, 1996: 286). The coefficient estimate associated with a common edge may be significant in some members of the equivalent class but not in others. Or it may be positive in some equivalent models but in others negative. MacCallum *et al.* (1993) contains several real examples vividly illustrating this phenomenon.

Since probabilities are unknown and one has to rely on their estimates, and since coefficient estimates vary across equivalent models, in practice the members of an equivalent class usually have little in common. As a result, even by granting the Markov and faithfulness conditions, little can be learnt from data alone. The claim that one can infer substantive causal conclusions by inspecting the edges common among equivalent models is contingent on the invariance of coefficient estimates, which is not always the case. Substantive conclusions from data demand subject-matter information in order to narrow down the class of equivalent models fitting the data. One, in particular, needs information on the sign and significance of the coefficients.

5.5 Assumptions revisited

The claim that the GT approach can discover the class of statistically equivalent causal models that includes the true model hinges on the universal validity of the Markov and faithfulness conditions. That is, it hinges on the presumption that the conditions can be applied to any correlation or independency found in the data. In this section, we examine justifications usually set forth for the conditions. We also examine some of the objections raised against them, and put forward some new criticisms. It will be seen that the conditions are by no means generally valid. Reliable causal inference calls for reliable causal subject-matter information.

5.5.1 The causal Markov condition

The advocates of the GT approach have set forth several justifications for the Markov condition. Glymour argues that variants of the principle underlie other methods of causal inference, and in this respect the GT approach is the same as other causal inference methods (1997a: 203–5). This claim means that the conclusions obtained using the GT techniques are as valid as those obtained using other methods. This in itself offers no justification for the condition. Also, it has sometimes been argued that if one does not assume the universal validity of the Markov condition, some correlations remain unexplained. Implicit in this defence is that if a correlation does not have a causal explanation it has no explanation. But this is the very claim that one must defend for establishing the validity of the condition; one cannot simply take it for granted.

The central justification for the Markov condition is said to come from the fact that it is provably true of recursive, pseudo-indeterministic, causally sufficient structures, with independently distributed disturbance terms (Kiiveri and Speed, 1982).[19] Koster (1999) and Spirtes *et al.* (1998) have shown that a more general property, called the global Markov condition, is true of both recursive and non-recursive causally sufficient, homogeneous and pseudo-indeterministic linear structures, with independently distributed errors.[20] In what follows, the focus of analysis will be on the Markov condition defined in Section 5.2, even though the analysis is also relevant to the global Markov condition.

The proof of the Markov condition is a piece of mathematics. To relate it to the world, it is necessary to show that the underlying requirements are true of the world. Of these conditions, recursiveness is not a critical issue (at least in the case of linear models), as the global Markov condition is true of both recursive and non-recursive (linear) structures that satisfy the remaining conditions. The pseudo-indeterminism requirement has come under attack by critics concerned with the outcomes of quantum mechanical experiments that seem to point to indeterminism. At the quantum level, the world is said to be genuinely indeterministic, and the Markov condition does not apply. Since the universal validity of the condition can successfully be challenged without taking sides on indeterminism, we take pseudo-indeterminism for granted, and focus on the causal sufficiency and independence of the error requirements. These conditions are not usually true of variables under study. To apply the conditions in general, as we saw, the founders of the GT approach introduced:

> **The completeness assumption**: For every set of recorded variables ***O***, either the set forms a causally sufficient set with uncorrelated errors or it can be embedded in a larger set of variables ***V*** that is causally sufficient with uncorrelated errors. (Scheines, 1997: 197)

On this basis, the Markov condition is generalized to every set of variables, at least at the level of description with which social scientists, economists and biologists are concerned. As a consequence, the universal validity of the Markov condition depends on the validity of the completeness hypothesis. We concentrate our analysis on this hypothesis.

Before proceeding, we should again stress that exact independencies are not known. We have access to only an estimate of the joint probability distribution of the variables, obtained from a finite sample, and need to take approximately zero correlations as exact independencies. This means that to make any causal inference we need to replace the (population) Markov condition with the *sample* Markov condition:

> **The sample Markov condition**: Let $\hat{P}(\mathrm{V})$ be a joint probability distribution estimated from *a finite sample* of observations on variables $\boldsymbol{V}$. The pair $\langle G, \hat{P} \rangle$ satisfies the sample Markov condition if and only if every variable X in $\boldsymbol{V}$ conditional on its parents is *almost independent* of every variable Y in $\boldsymbol{V}$ that is not a descendant of X.

5.5.1.1 *Aggregation over heterogeneous units*

We consider several circumstances in which completeness can fail. An important case was pointed out by G. Udny Yule in his seminal paper (1903) on the theory of association of attributes in statistics where he noted that mixing heterogeneous units could lead to creation of spurious correlations at the population level that did not exist at the level of sub-populations. An illustration of such a phenomenon is presented in Table 5.2.

In both female and male sub-populations treatment and recovery as well as non-treatment and non-recovery are uncorrelated. When the two sub-populations are mixed together, however, recovery becomes statistically related to treatment and non-recovery to non-treatment. Such examples show that mixing populations, which either have different causal structures or have the same causal structure but different probability distributions, can create associations that do not exist at the sub-population level. Since such associations are by-products of mixing, the mixed population violates the Markov condition.

Spirtes *et al.* (1993: 57) describe in some detail Yule's example, which is similar to the above example, to explain why it presents no real problem for the Markov condition. The variables in Yule's example, they argue, exclude a variable that is the cause of membership in a sub-population. Once the omitted variable is included and the measured variables are conditioned on it, the

Table 5.2 Aggregation over heterogeneous units

	Male population		**Female population**		**Mixed population**	
	Treated	*Untreated*	*Treated*	*Untreated*	*Treated*	*Untreated*
Alive	4/99	16/99	20/99	10/99	24/99	26/99
Dead	8/99	32/99	6/99	3/99	14/99	35/99

spurious correlations disappear. In the above example, the measured variables exclude gender. Once we include gender and condition treatment and recovery and non-treatment and non-recovery on it, the spurious correlations will disappear and the population will satisfy the Markov condition.[21]

It may be possible in simple situations like the current case to locate classifying variables that can be considered as common causes. In more complex cases of aggregation over heterogeneous units, ubiquitous in the social sciences, there exists no small set of classifying variables capable of explaining away spurious correlations that can be considered as common causes of the recorded variables. In social contexts, what is required to explain away a spurious correlation at the aggregate level is a full description of the system at the micro-level, including the laws governing the behaviour of the individuals, their interactions with each other, and, more critically, the socio-economic processes determining variables that affect behaviour. A description of the system at the micro-level cannot be considered as a common cause of the variables at the aggregate level. To highlight this point, we borrow an example from the next chapter that studies the complexities arising from aggregating over heterogeneous units. The example revolves around a simple economy studied in Lippi (1988: 174). The economy has two consumers, each having a slightly different demand function. The demand function for each individual follows the static routine:

$$Y_{it} = \Pi_i X_{it} \qquad i = 1, 2 \tag{5.3}$$

which has no stochastic term. Y_{it} and X_{it} are respectively consumption and income of the ith individual in period t, and the parameter Π_i for each individual is *different*. Each consumer operates in a slightly different environment in the sense that the independent micro-variable X_{it} for each individual follows a different autoregressive routine:

$$X_{it} = a_i X_{it-1} + v_{it} \qquad 0 < a_i < 1 \tag{5.4}$$

where the parameter a_i for each individual is *different* and the v_{it} are orthogonal white-noise processes.[22] As shown in Appendix 5.E of the next chapter, the function relating aggregate consumption $Y_t = Y_{1t} + Y_{2t}$ to aggregate income $X_t = X_{1t} + X_{2t}$ is given by

$$Y_t = \alpha Y_{t-1} + \beta X_t + \gamma X_{t-1} + u_t \tag{5.5}$$

with u_t being a white-noise process. The function has among its arguments lagged aggregate consumption Y_{t-1} and income X_{t-1}. Furthermore, as the number of consumers increases, the function will contain an increasingly larger number of lagged predictors. Now, since the last period individual consumption Y_{it-1} does not appear in the individual demand function, setting Y_{t-1} by intervention at certain value would not affect Y_t. Therefore, the dependence of Y_t on Y_{t-1}in (5.5) cannot be causal; the function simply represents a statistical connection.

To explain the spurious correlation, one needs a description of the economy at the micro-level, including a description of the choice situation faced by each individual. In real-life situations, providing such a description is impossible. What is more, the description would involve a tremendously large number of classificatory variables (e.g. 'being a farmer', 'being a banker'), which cannot be considered as the common causes of the aggregate variables, say, Y_t and Y_{t-1}. As this example shows, in social contexts, where decision makers are different and operate in different choice situations, aggregation over heterogeneous units produces variables that neither stand in a causal relation with each other nor are part of a larger causally sufficient set of variables. In such situations, completeness and hence the Markov condition fail.

5.5.1.2 Selection bias

Aggregation over heterogeneous units is only one of the situations in which completeness fails. Another situation in which completeness fails is when there is 'selection bias'; that is, when a population is defined by conditioning on some variable Z that is a common effect of two or more of the variables under study (or their causes) that have no mutual influence on each other (Glymour, 1997a: 208). There has been a growing interest in studying the implications of selection bias for causal inference.[23] Here, we concentrate on a problem that selection bias creates for the completeness hypothesis, examine a proposal that some GT theorists have put forward to deal with it, and argue why, because of the possibility of selection bias, an important claim of the GT approach must be abandoned. We first consider an illustration discussed in Spirtes *et al.* (1996). Suppose a survey of college students is done to determine whether there is a link between *Intelligence* (I) and *Sex drive* (D). Let *Student status* (S) be a binary variable that takes value 1 when one is studying in a college and zero otherwise. Also, as in graph (a) in Figure 5.15, suppose *Age* (A) causes *sex drive,* and *age* and *intelligence* cause *student status* (here, *age* is taken to be a proxy for a combination of biological and mental states associated with age).

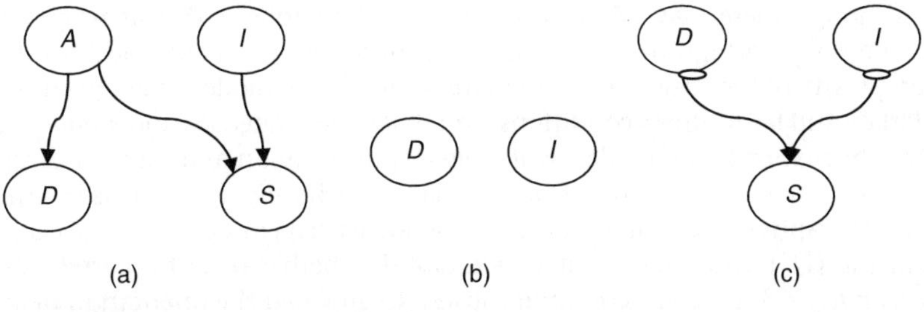

Figure 5.15 An example of selection bias

Since the sample is gathered from college students, the variables under study or their causes, i.e. I and A, influence whether one is in the sample, and this can create a correlation among the *recorded* variables, i.e. I and D. If the graph in Figure 5.15(a) is an accurate description of the causal relations among $\mathbf{V} = \{A, D, I, S\}$, the correlation between I and D is spurious, as there is no causal connection among them (see graph Figure 5.15(b)). Moreover, $\mathbf{V}$ contains no common cause of I and D that can screen off the correlation. The Markov condition is not true of the recorded variables I and D. Nor is there a larger DAG with the common causes of I and D satisfying the condition – hence a failure of completeness.

A number of proposals have been set forth to counter the danger of selection bias, calling for the use of domain-specific information and sensitivity analysis (Scharfstein *et al.*, 2003). Against these approaches, following Wermuth *et al.* (1994), Cooper (1995) argues that selecting a unit to include in the sample is a causal event. It can be represented by a variable and treated as a genuine part of the causal structure.[24] He thus proposes to incorporate the process of unit (case) selection into the structure, adding an extra assumption to the arsenal of the assumptions underlying the GT approach:

> **Selection bias assumption**: Case selection is a causal event that can be modelled within a causal directed graph that has a variable representing whether a case was selected or not. (Cooper, 2000)

A similar assumption underlies an attempt by Spirtes *et al.* (1996) to extend the GT techniques to data that might be affected by selection bias. On this proposal, the set $\{I, D\}$ does not exhaust all the recorded variables. The recorded variables are $\{I, D, S\}$, where S is a selection variable taking value 1 for the students and zero for non-students. Therefore, the dependence $\neg(D \perp I)$ appearing in the sample should be interpreted as $\neg(D \perp I/(S = 1))$, which means the graph in Figure 5.15(b) ought to be replaced with the graph in Figure 5.15(c) (the small ovals indicate that each arrow can be replaced with a bidirected edge $\leftrightarrow$). There are many ways to embed graph (c) into a DAG to make it consistent with the Markov condition. Figure 5.16 depicts two possibilities.

Although there may be nothing theoretically wrong with this proposal, it comes with a high price. The inclusion of selection variables adds to the complexity of the structure. This enlarges the class of models that, given the Markov and faithfulness conditions, could have generated the independence data. In that case, the models will have less in common and much less can be learnt about the structure from the data. Specifically, the increase in the class of graphs consistent with the independence data undermines the claim that the GT techniques are able to establish whether or not a correlation is *definitely* due to latent common causes. Recall when the orientation of an undirected graph leads to a bidirected edge, the edge is taken as evidence that

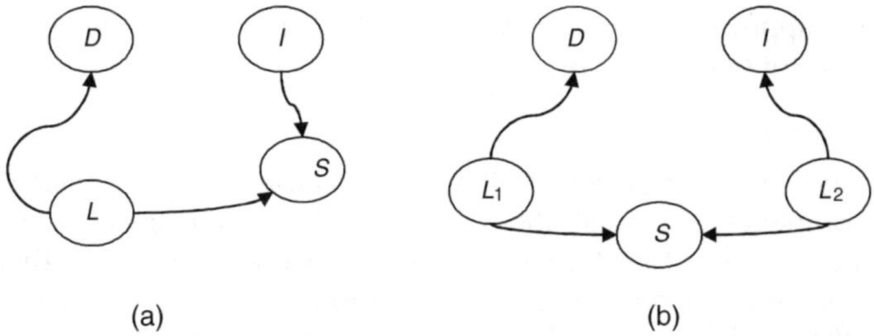

Figure 5.16 Equivalent DAGs with a case-selection variable

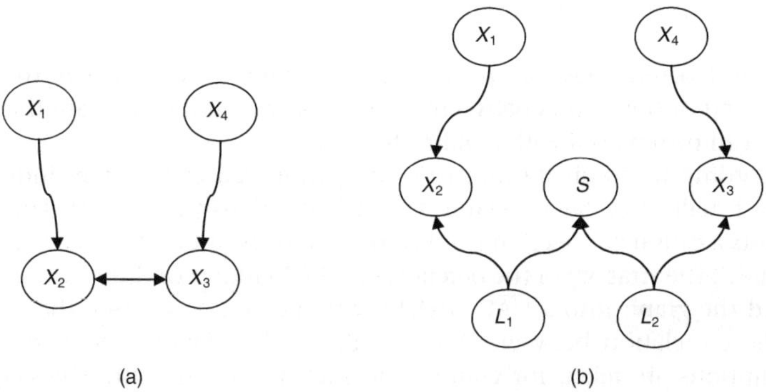

Figure 5.17 Causal inference in the presence of selection bias

the correlation is *definitely* due to a latent common cause. In the analysis of the second example in Section 5.3, faithfulness required placing a bidirected edge between X_2 and X_3 and we concluded that the correlation was due to latent common causes. When the possibility of selection bias is acknowledged, this inference is no longer warranted, because the bidirected edge can be due to selection bias. An example of such an explanation is given in the graph in Figure 5.17b above, which is also found in Spirtes *et al.* (1996).

Graph (b) implies all the independencies over the recorded variables in graph (a). Yet it contains no variable affecting both X_2 and X_3. If structures like graph (b) are permitted, a bidirected edge can no longer be taken as the evidence for a common cause. Such an interpretation demands ensuring that the bidirected edge is not the result of selection bias. The GT approach provides no formal guidance how to decide whether a data set is affected by selection bias or not. It too must rely on domain-specific information or sensitivity analysis to counter the threat of selection bias. Finally, allowing selection-variables in a causal structure demands revising the main theorem of the GT approach given in Glymour (1997a: 219). The theorem assumes the absence of selection bias.

5.5.1.3 *Concomitants*

Mistaking a cause with a concomitant of the cause creates another situation where completeness can fail (Sobel, 1995: 29). In such cases it is wrong to admit the outcome of the GT techniques that a variable causes another. As an illustration, suppose we are given data on four variables: *Mother's Genotype* (G), *Mother's childhood nutrition* (N), *Mother's occupation* (O) and *Children's intelligence* (I). It is plausible to assume that the following independencies are approximately true in the sample:

$$Ind_p = \{G \perp N, G \perp I/O, N \perp I/O\}$$

These independencies lead to the graph in Figure 5.18(a), where the ovals at the end of the arrows between G and O, and N and O indicate that each arrow can be replaced with a bidirected edge $\leftrightarrow$.

According to graph (a) mother's occupation causes (possibly indirectly) child's intelligence. Such a claim is not taken seriously at present. The graph suggests a causal connection from O to I that does not exist. Assuming completeness, the strategy of the defenders of the Markov condition would be to embed the graph into a DAG $G(\mathbf{O}, \mathbf{L})$ with a common cause L that screens off the correlation between O and I. But if the Markov and faithfulness assumptions are taken for granted, no such DAG can exist. The graph in Figure 5.18(b) shows a typical DAG capable of explaining away the correlation between O and I. Any such graph entails neither $G \perp I/O$ nor $N \perp I/O$, and is not faithful to the distribution of the recorded variables. In the present example, completeness can be restored only at the expense of faithfulness and faithfulness can be retained only at the expense of completeness. In either case, the immediate conclusion is that an irremovable arrow, such as

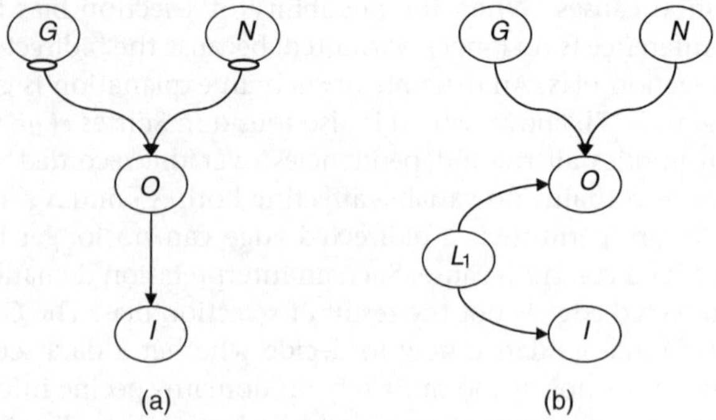

Figure 5.18 Concomitants and completeness

the one from O to I, cannot automatically be taken as evidence of a causal connection; the correlation may have arisen from mistaking a concomitant of a cause with the cause. Like other approaches to causal inference, the GT method cannot establish that a variable causes another variable.

The solution to the problem created by concomitants is not to search for a larger set of variables that includes the original ones but to search for the right variables. Spirtes *et al.* (1993: 63) come close to a similar conclusion when dealing with a counter-example to the common cause principle put forward by Wesley Salmon, termed *interactive forks*.[25] The apparent counter-example, they argue, arises because one has failed to pick up the right variables to describe the situation in hand. This simply means that the Markov condition generates sensible results only when applied to the right variables. Moreover, one cannot rely on formal principles to decide on the right set of variables to describe a situation. One needs domain-specific information.[26]

The analysis has so far dealt with the aspect of the completeness conjecture that says for every causally insufficient set of variables $\boldsymbol{O}$ there is a causally sufficient set $\boldsymbol{V}$ that embeds $\boldsymbol{O}$. It remains to investigate the claim that the disturbance terms associated with variables in a causally sufficient set are independently distributed. Pearl argues that this condition is not an extra assumption but follows from the causal sufficiency assumption and the common cause principle, which is basic for linking probability with causation (2000: 30). Other GT theorists have also taken a similar line (Richardson and Spirtes, 1999). These principles, however, do not entail the independence of the errors. A disturbance term u associated with an exogenous variable X in $\boldsymbol{V}$ represents the aggregate effect of all the variables outside $\boldsymbol{V}$ that influence X. Aggregation can make independently distributed micro-variables dependent. Therefore, even if all the variables affecting those in $\boldsymbol{V}$ are pairwise independent, when they are aggregated, they might become correlated (Cartwright, 2001). The independence requirement is an additional assumption that lacks a justification. Altogether, these analyses reveal why the completeness hypothesis cannot be taken for granted and why, as a result, the Markov condition cannot be applied universally.

5.5.2 The faithfulness condition

Faithfulness rules out any structure that fails to entail all independencies in the data. Several considerations are usually set forth to support an *a priori* exclusion of such structures. Glymour (1997a: 210) begins his defence of faithfulness by showing that it underlies other approaches to causal inference. This provides no justification for conclusions based on the GT techniques. Scheines defends faithfulness by arguing that it increases our inferential power and without it nothing can be learnt from data about causal directionality (1997: 194). Again, the increase in inferential power is no evidence for the soundness of the conclusions, and as such provides no support for faithfulness.

5.5.2.1 *The measure theoretic argument*

The main justification of faithfulness is of a Bayesian nature. Spirtes *et al.* have argued that, for any linear structural model, the set of parameterizations of the model that lead to violations of faithfulness is of Lebesgue measure zero. Therefore, any Bayesian whose prior over the model's parameters is absolutely continuous with the Lebesgue measure assigns a zero *prior* probability to the violations of faithfulness (Spirtes *et al.*, 1993: 68–9).[27] A quick challenge to this argument, also noted by Scheines *et al.* (1998: 82), is to ask why one has to have a prior that is absolutely continuous with respect to the Lebesgue measure. If one adopts a prior that lacks this feature, the measure theoretic argument has no force. This criticism is sufficient to challenge the argument. Nevertheless, more can be learnt by analysing what is involved in having a prior that assigns zero probability to violations of faithfulness. To explain this, we follow Robins and Wasserman (1999) and Robins (2003). Consider a normally distributed, causally sufficient set of variables $\mathbf{V} = \{X, Y, Z, U, V, W\}$, and let $\mathbf{O} = \{X, Y, Z\}$ be the recorded variables. Suppose X precedes Y, and Y precedes Z. Also assume we have an extremely large sample of data on X, Y and Z so that estimation problems can be left aside. Finally, suppose the following dependencies and independencies are true in the data:[28]

$$\rho_{XY} = 0.5; \quad \rho_{YZ} = 0.5; \quad \rho_{XZ} = 0.25; \quad \rho_{XZ.Y} = 0$$

Explanation (1): A possible explanation of these data is given by the graph in Figure 5.19(a). According to this graph, X causes Y, Y causes Z, and they have no common causes in $\mathbf{V}$.

Another representation of the same causal facts is given by the graph in Figure 5.19(b), where the lower-case letters denote path coefficients. Thus represented, the explanation implies that

$$u_1 u_2 = 0,\ v_1 v_2 = 0,\ w_1 w_2 = 0 \text{ but } a \neq 0 \text{ and } b \neq 0$$

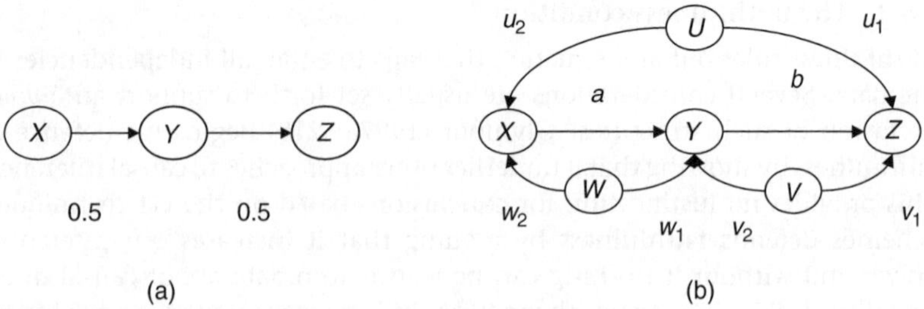

Figure 5.19 A faithful explanation
Note: Graphs (a) and (b) provide a faithful explanation of the independence data.

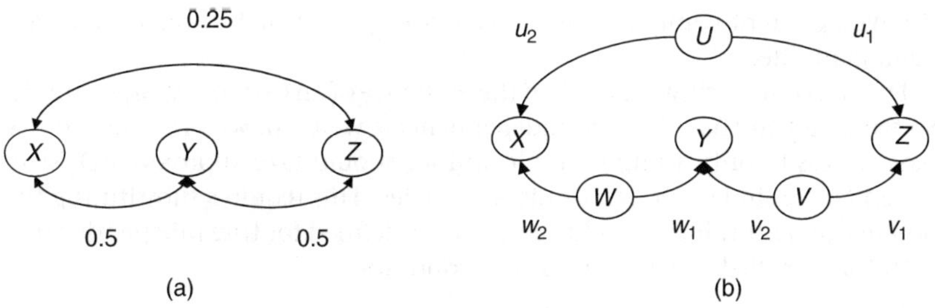

Figure 5.20 An unfaithful explanation
Note: Graphs (a) and (b) provide an unfaithful explanation of the independence data.

Explanation (2): A second possible explanation is offered by the graph in Figure 5.20(a) above. According to this graph, neither X causes Y nor Y causes Z. The dependencies and vanishing partial $\rho_{XZ.Y} = 0$ are due to particular residual correlations between X and Z, X and Y, and Y and Z – as shown by the numbers on the bidirected edges linking the variables.

If we explain residual correlation in terms of latent common causes, the graph in Figure 5.20(b) above provides an alternative representation of the causal facts in Figure 5.20(a). On this graph, U, V, and W are confounders. This means

$$u_1 u_2 \neq 0, \; v_1 v_2 \neq 0, \; w_1 w_2 \neq 0 \quad \text{but } a = 0 \text{ and } b = 0$$

Both explanations are possible. The measure theoretic argument draws on the fact that the subset of values for the coefficients $\{u_1, u_2, v_1, v_2, w_1, w_2\}$ that yields the vanishing partial $\rho_{XZ.Y} = 0$, when $u_1 u_2 \neq 0$, $v_1 v_2 \neq 0$, and $w_1 w_2 \neq 0$, has Lebesgue measure zero in R^6. If one has a prior over the parameter space that is absolutely continuous with the Lebesgue measure of the space, one has to regard explanation (2) as *a prior* unlikely, and accept explanation (1), which is faithful to the data. The difficulty with this argument is that the move from the claim that explanation (2) is *a priori* unlikely to the acceptance of explanation (1) is not warranted. Explanation (1) implies that $u_1 u_2 = 0$, $v_1 v_2 = 0$, and $w_1 w_2 = 0$. Now, the Lebesgue measure of each of these events is also zero in two-dimensional parameter space R^2. If one has a prior over the parameter space that is absolutely continuous with the Lebesgue measure, one also has to consider these events as *a priori* unlikely. Therefore, as far as the measure theoretic considerations are concerned, both explanations are equally unlikely. The only way the balance can be tilted in favour of explanation (1) is to rule out *a priori* any latent common cause for the recorded variables.[29] If the existence of common causes is not *a priori* ruled out, both explanations are *a priori* equally likely, and no causal conclusion can be inferred from the data. This means, to believe that violations of faithfulness are *a priori* unlikely, one must believe that X and Y, and Y and

Z have no latent common causes. Such an *a priori* belief, though, does not seem plausible.

The above analysis was based on the existence of an extremely large sample. So we assumed that the true independencies were known. In practice, we have access to only a finite sample and we should take approximately zero dependencies in lieu of exact independencies. This requires substituting the population faithfulness condition, which is defined for true independencies, with the so-called *sample* faithfulness condition:

> **The sample faithfulness assumption**: In a large sample if X and Y are *almost* independent conditional on Z, that is evidence that X and Y are not directly causally connected except through Z. (Glymour *et al.*, 1999: 345)

In light of this, what is needed to be excluded *a priori* is the set of parameter values that *nearly* cancel each other out. Such a set always has a non-zero Lebesgue measure and cannot be excluded on measure theoretic grounds. The Bayesian argument applies, if at all, only when the true independencies are known. It has no force in practice where almost-zero partial correlations should be taken in place of exact independencies.

5.5.2.2 *Stable unfaithfulness*

Another line of defence of faithfulness has been pursued in Pearl's writings. Pearl's concept of a causal model is influenced by the views of early econometricians, who define a structural model as a system of equations each representing an *autonomous* causal mechanism that can be manipulated without affecting other equations in the model. Autonomy, the early econometricians argued, is an essential feature that a model must have to be useful for evaluating actions and policies. Influenced by this tradition, Pearl argues that the reason we search for causal models is the need for evaluating actions and policies, and a key feature that a model ought to have to be useful for analysis of actions and policies is the autonomy of the model equations. Since the equations of unfaithful models break down with a slight change in the conditions sustaining one of the equations, the models lack autonomy, and are not useful for evaluating actions and policies. They should not therefore be taken seriously (Pearl, 2000: 63).[30]

A number of authors have rightly challenged this claim. Cartwright (1999: 118) and Hoover (2001: 170) point out that one of the ways that we minimize damages in our social and medical regimes is by arranging the system so that conflicting causal forces counterbalance the effect of each other. Unfaithful structures can be of significant interest in designing efficient social and medical regimes. Moreover, what is really at issue here is whether faithfulness is a reliable guide to discovery of autonomous relations. A definition of autonomy and a recommendation to avoid using unstable relations in policy analysis cannot serve as a guide in searching for structural relations.

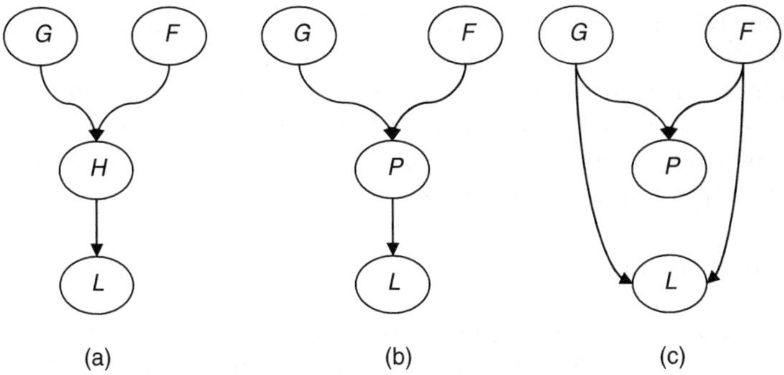

Figure 5.21 Stable spurious independence data (graph (b))

Pearl may also be taken as arguing that because unfaithful structures are unstable they do not last long enough to generate data for a reliable estimate of the distribution. Any independencies embedded in a distribution estimated from an adequately large homogeneous sample arise from a faithful structure. It is therefore a sound practice to rely on faithfulness to infer causation from reliably estimated independencies. This reasoning assumes that there can be no 'stable' unfaithful independencies. This is wrong, however. Mistaking concomitants for causes can easily produce *stable* independencies that do not represent absence of causation. Consider the structure depicted in the graph in Figure 5.21(a), which represents a possible causal structure between Genotype (*G*), Family background (*F*), Heavy smoking (*H*), and Lung cancer (*L*).

According to this structure, conditional on H, L is independent of G and F, which means there is no direct causal link from genotype and family background to lung cancer; they cause lung cancer through causing heavy smoking. Now suppose H is replaced with one of the concomitants of heavy smoking such as 'Having yellowed teeth' (*P*). Assuming that the conditional independence relation $L \perp \{G, F\}/H$ is true in the data, the conditional independency $L \perp \{G, F\}/P$ is also most likely true, and if one picks up variables $\{G, F, P, L\}$ instead of $\{G, F, H, L\}$, one ends up with the graph in Figure 5.21(b). The graph entails that, conditional on having yellowed teeth, lung cancer is independent of genotype and family background. Based on our current state of knowledge, independence relations $L \perp G/P$ and $L \perp F/P$ do not genuinely represent absence of causal connections. Assuming Figure 5.21(a) is true, when 'heavy smoking' is dropped from the graph, there will be causal links from G and F to L, as shown in Figure 5.21(c). Moreover, the spurious independencies $L \perp G/P$ and $L \perp F/P$ are stable; they are true as long as the structure (a) is true. Such examples, which are by no means rare, illustrate cases of stable unfaithfulness that are neither generated by exact cancellation of parameter values nor by mixing of heterogeneous units, the Simpson Paradox.[31] Pearl's stability argument may be useful for excluding violations of faithfulness arising from exact cancellation of parameter values. But it has no force in ruling out stable unfaithful independencies arising from mistaking concomitants with genuine causes. Like the Markov condition, faithfulness cannot be applied universally either.

5.6 Conclusion

The strongest possible assumptions about the link between causation and probability are the Markov condition, i.e. every probabilistic dependency has a causal explanation, and faithfulness, i.e. every probabilistic independency reflects the lack of a causal connection. These hypotheses are false. A correlation or independency can arise for reasons other than causal reasons. Hence, the class of explanations possible for a correlation or independency is larger than the class of possible causal explanations. As a result, there can never be an entirely data-driven causal inference method. Causal inference first and foremost involves eliminating non-causal explanations that could possibly be responsible for a dependency or independency. This requires some subject-matter information about the system. In the simple economy described in the text, it is essential to know the rules governing the behaviour of the individuals as well as the character of the environment in which they operate to determine whether the correlation between the aggregates reflect a causal connection or is an artefact of aggregation. The Markov and faithfulness conditions become relevant only after non-causal candidate explanations are eliminated.

Even after excluding non-causal explanations, the Markov and faithfulness conditions are not sufficient to pin down a single causal model, due to the ubiquitous existence of statistically equivalent causal models. There is always a simple rule to generate a class of equivalent causal models for every model fitting the data. Because the coefficient estimates of the common edges vary across the models, and their sign and significance usually differ from one model to another, very little can be learnt from data alone. Extra subject-matter information is particularly necessary to reduce the class of statistically equivalent models by excluding unlikely but possible causal models.

The reliability of the GT algorithms and indeed any data-driven method of causal inference depends on the sample size and the joint probability distribution of the variables under study. The GT algorithms proceed by assuming that the data comes from a multivariate normal distribution. When the sample is large, this assumption may be justified, and one can reliably test independence hypotheses. In practice, where the samples are small, the normality assumption can lead to wrong conclusions. As a general rule, since the number of known multivariate distribution families is very limited and they make the restrictive assumption that the marginal distributions of the variables belong to the same distribution family, testing independence hypotheses needs great care in practice.

Also, for analysis of actions and policies, one needs to know not only whether an equation represents a causal relation but also the circumstances under which it remains invariant. Recall Haavelmo's famous remark about the relation between pressure on the throttle and acceleration of the car (1944). To predict the effect of taking a car to an unexplored territory, we need to know not only whether putting pressure on the throttle makes the car accelerate but also the circumstances under which the relation remains invariant. The GT methods are at best suited for discovering a causal structure, defined as a complex of type-level causal connections. They are not suitable for understanding the circumstances under which the structure continues to operate. This needs knowledge of the chance set-up, to use Cartwright's phrase (1997: 357), which has given rise to and sustains the causal relations.

These analyses have major implications for modelling bounded rationality. Most notably, understanding how people are able to make causal inferences from usually small samples necessitates an approach that emphasizes the interaction between domain-specific causal knowledge and statistical learning (Griffiths *et al.*, 2004). The causal information is to restrict plausible causal relations, their functional form, and strength. This limits the space of plausible models, making it possible to infer causal conclusions from small samples. We again encounter the basic question of where the domain-specific information comes from. One thing is certainly clear about this question. The information does not come from a purely statistical analysis of data. The IS hypothesis does not provide a full account of human causal learning.

6
The Economy as an Interactive System: An Appraisal of the Microfoundations Project

6.1 Introduction

> In order to have a useful theory of relations among aggregate, it is necessary that they be defined in a manner derived from the theory of individual behaviour. In other words, even the definition of such magnitudes as national income cannot be undertaken without a previous theoretical understanding of the underlying individual phenomena. (Arrow, 1968)

Several difficulties stand in the way of establishing a structural model of the economy. Notably, for social and practical reasons, the economy cannot be subjected to controlled experiments to establish causal relations true at the economy level. And, because of the theoretical difference between a causal and statistical relation, atheoretical analysis of aggregate data is inadequate for establishing causation. What is more, aggregate data are inherently imprecise, a fact that further aggravates the difficulties in making causal inferences from economic data. The key to the success of macroeconomics is to overcome these difficulties, which make the establishment of causal relations at the economy level problematic.

According to mainstream economists, these difficulties can be evaded by starting with a model of individual behaviour. It is argued that we often know intuitively how human beings make decisions, and even if intuition fails to lead us to the laws of behaviour, we can experimentally study human behaviour to establish an accurate theory of economic behaviour. Having established a theory of behaviour, we can transform it into a theory of the economy using aggregation procedures. Aggregate data can then be used to estimate the model and obtain a quantitative model of the economy. Since the structure is determined by the laws of behaviour and the model is based on behavioural laws, it correctly describes the economy. Specifically, it describes how aggregate variables relate to each other, classifies them into exogenous and endogenous categories, defines the conditions under which the aggregate equations remain invariant, and fixes the interpretation of the aggregate model parameters. So, the model provides all the information necessary for policy analysis.

The enterprise of deriving the theory of the economy as a whole from microeconomic theory – the *microfoundations project* – is the hallmark of modern theoretical macroeconomics. Two assumptions underlie the project. The first is that it is possible to establish an empirically adequate theory of economic behaviour. The second is that the theory of behaviour can be turned into a theory of the economy using aggregation procedures, without having to introduce any substantive assumption about the economy. The previous four chapters studied some of the commonly accepted tenets in economics about individual behaviour. This chapter takes up the second hypothesis which has to do with the move from the micro- to the macro-level.

The search for microfoundations is the concern of all those who view macroeconomics as something more than the art of summarizing data and who aim at establishing models suitable for policy analysis. Both new classical and Keynesian economists have searched for microfoundations. Nevertheless, most systematic attempts to derive models of macroeconomic phenomena from assumptions about individual behaviour have taken place in new classical economics. For this reason, this chapter confines itself to an analysis of the efforts made in new classical economics. Even so, since the analysis deals with the general issue of moving from individualistic assumptions to a theory of the economy, it equally applies to any attempt at deriving a theory of the economy from a microeconomic theory.

New classical economics sometimes takes microeconomic theory to be the analysis of a single decision maker, either a consumer or a firm; the consumer is modelled as an expected utility maximizer, the firm as an expected profit optimizer. On this account, a call for microfoundations is a call for a model in which the starting-point is an expected utility or profit maximization problem. To model some aspect of the economy, a utility or profit maximization problem is set up for an individual and solved subject to his or her budget constraint to derive a model of the micro-variables of interest. The model is then elevated to the economy level. We termed this approach to macroeconomics the 'representative agent' modelling approach.

An alternative view of microeconomic theory is presented by the Walrasian general equilibrium theory in which the decision problems of various sectors of the economy, each represented by a representative agent, are simultaneously solved. To account for uncertainty about the future, the theory is supplemented by the rational expectations hypothesis. From this perspective, the microfoundations project is an attempt to derive the laws of the economy from the Walrasian theory and the rational expectations hypothesis. Since the Walrasian theory makes minimal assumptions about the structure of the economy, this account of the microfoundations project is known as the strict microfoundations thesis (Rizvi, 1994: 357).

This chapter criticizes both interpretations of the microfoundations thesis. In a nutshell, the representative agent modelling approach conceives of the economy as a society of identical isolated individuals. The strict microfoundations thesis, on the other hand, conceives of the economy as a collection of few sectors, each being populated by identical decision makers, who only interact with each other through equilibrium prices. Most macroeconomic phenomena, however, arise from informational differences, behavioural heterogeneities, coordination failures and interactions among market participants. A satisfactory explanation of macroeconomic phenomena therefore calls for thinking of the economy as a society of heterogeneous interactive individuals. In such a society, the relations true of the aggregates are fundamentally different from those true of the micro-variables, and there is no way that the former can be derived from the latter alone. Besides the microeconomic relations, one also needs to know a great deal about the structure of the society in order to derive the correct form of the aggregate relations.

6.2 The representative agent modelling approach

Modern economies consist of millions of decision makers, either as individuals or organized groups, each pursuing their own disparate interest in a limited part of the economy. These individual and group activities are somehow coordinated, leading to certain regularities at the economy level, which form the subject-matter of macroeconomics. If we were in a position to simultaneously study the behaviour of every decision-making unit in the economy and model its interaction with other decision-making units, we would be able to predict the emergence of macroeconomic regularities by simulating the evolution of the economy. However, we are not omniscient and this avenue is closed to us. All the same, many individuals or groups often encounter similar choice situations, have similar tastes and demographic characteristics, and behave similarly. Moreover, individual idiosyncratic differences sometimes neutralize each other in real life. A satisfactory understanding of the economy does not necessarily require simulating the whole system including the details of each decision-making unit. It is sufficient to work with an idealized, smaller, model economy in which the behaviour of each group of 'similar' decision-making units is represented by an average unit (agent). Some economists, like Jevons, have taken this consideration to an extreme. According to Jevons, 'accidental and disturbing causes will operate, in the long run, as often in one direction as the other, so as to neutralize each other.' Thus, 'the general forms of the laws of economics are the same in the case of individuals and the nations' (Jevons, 1965 [1871]: 16–17).[1] Hicks has even gone further to suggest that microeconomic theory has greater relevance for aggregate data, arguing that the variations in circumstances of individual households are averaged out to negligible proportions in the aggregate, leaving only systematic effects of variation in prices and budgets (Hicks, 1956).[2] Such thoughts have led to the emergence of a modelling approach that views the economy as a single average individual, implying that whatever is true of the individual is also true of the economy, hence the nomenclature of representative agent modelling.

6.2.1 The structure of the representative agent approach

New classical economics makes two assumptions about individual behaviour: the expected utility optimization principle and the rational expectations hypothesis. The point of departure in building a representative agent model, then, is to specify the optimization problem of an agent (a household or a firm) and solve it subject to his or her budget constraint and rational expectations. The solution yields the relationships among the individual variables. The well-defined *individual* model is taken to be exactly true at the aggregate level. And aggregate variables are substituted for the individual variables to obtain a model of the economy. If the model fits aggregate data, the conformity is taken as evidence for the truth of the microeconomic model. If it does not fit the data, the blame is placed on the individual assumptions built into the model. The representative-agent methodology seeks to meet all the challenges of macroeconomic modelling. It aims to specify the form of the relations among aggregate variables, the conditions under which the model equations remain invariant, and the proper interpretation of the macromodel parameters. On this interpretation of the microfoundations thesis, only those macro-models that are grounded on utility optimization subject to rational expectations are regarded as acceptable for policy evaluation.

6.2.2 A historical example

Before examining the requirements of the representative-agent methodology, we study a typical representative-agent model that has been the subject of many debates in macroeconomics. The study helps bring to the fore various assumptions underpinning such a model.[3] An issue in economics concerns the relation between aggregate consumption and aggregate income. Several empirical studies during the third quarter of the last century implied that aggregate income was a good predictor of aggregate consumption (Blanchard and Fisher, 1989). This seemed to contradict the belief that people form expectations rationally, and make their consumption decisions according to the permanent income hypothesis. In a classic paper, Robert Hall (1978) set out to shed light on this issue by testing the hypothesis. He did this by following the representative-agent modelling method.[4]

The permanent income hypothesis suggests that a household decides on his or her expenditure at time t as part of a plan that takes into account future uncertainty in income by optimizing over time with regard to available wealth. To be precise, let r be the real rate, T the length of economic life and $u_i(.)$ a strictly concave one-period utility function. Also, let C_{it} be consumption by consumer i in period t, Y_{it} income in period t, A_{it} assets apart from human capital, and δ the consumer's rate of subjective time preference so that £1 now and £$(1 + \delta)1$ next period are equally valued. The permanent income hypothesis says that, in each period t, family i decides on its consumption plan by maximizing the expected lifetime utility:

$$E_t \sum_{\tau=0}^{T-t} (1+\delta)^{-\tau} u_i(C_{it+\tau}) \tag{6.1}$$

subject to the amount of available wealth:

$$\sum_{\tau=0}^{T-\tau} (1+r)^{-\tau} (C_{it+\tau} - Y_{it+\tau}) = A_{it} \tag{6.2}$$

E_t in (6.1) denotes mathematical expectation conditional on all information available at t including $C_{it-\tau}$, $Y_{it-\tau}$ and $A_{it-\tau}$, for $\tau = 0, 1, 2, \ldots$. Hall also assumes that the real rate of interest r is constant, the subjective rate of time preference δ is equal or less than r, incomes Y_{it} are stochastic and are the only source of uncertainty, and lets T go to infinity. The first-order necessary condition for maximization of equation (6.1) subject to constraint (6.2) is the well-known Euler equation:

$$E_t u_i'(C_{it+1}) = [(1+\delta)/(1+r)] u_i'(C_{it}) \tag{6.3}$$

where $u'(C) = du(C)/dC$. Equation (6.3) says that the expected marginal utility next period is the same as the marginal utility this period, except for a trend associated with the rate of time preference δ and the real rate of interest r. Another way to express the same idea is

$$u_i'(C_{it+1}) = \gamma u_i'(C_{it}) + \varepsilon_{it+1} \tag{6.4}$$

where $\gamma = (1+\delta)/(1+r)$ and ε_{it+1} is the difference between the marginal utility next period and its current expected value. Assuming that expectations are rational, ε_{t+1} is a random variable with expected value zero at time t, when consumption C_{it} is decided. So, no information available at time t apart from C_{it} helps predict C_{it+1}. Once C_{it} is taken into account, individual income and assets at time t or earlier, and past consumptions, C_{it-j}, for $j > 0$, are irrelevant for predicting the next period marginal utility.

Hall further simplifies matters by taking the utility function to be quadratic; that is, $u_i(C_{it}) = -(\overline{C}_i - C_{it})^2/2$, where $\overline{C}$ is the bliss level of consumption.[5] This leads to the individual consumption function:

$$C_{it+1} = \lambda C_{it} + \varepsilon_{it+1} \tag{6.5}$$

Thus, the change in individual consumption is the amount warranted by innovations in expectations about future labour income. Formally, this means that individual consumption obeys a random walk.[6] As a consequence, no other variable observed in period t or earlier has a non-zero coefficient when included in equation (6.5).

Hall next assumes that if individual consumption exhibits random walk behaviour, aggregate consumption also by and large mimics random walk behaviour. Therefore, if the above assumptions are approximately true of a typical household, the equation

$$C_{t+1} = \lambda C_t + \varepsilon_{t+1} \tag{6.6}$$

provides a good approximation of the behaviour of aggregate consumption C_t. Accordingly, the permanent income hypothesis, in Hall's view, rules out the systematic influence of any variable on future aggregate consumption other than current aggregate consumption. Hall tested equation (6.6) by regressing aggregate consumption changes on lags of aggregate consumption, income, and stock prices. In the data, aggregate income did not help predict aggregate consumption but stock prices were highly correlated with aggregate consumption changes.[7] Hall concluded that while the data on income confirmed the hypothesis, the data on stock prices disconfirmed it (1989: 157). Flavin (1981) also studied the relation between aggregate income and consumption in a similar setting, but found enough predictive power for aggregate income to reject the permanent income hypothesis.

6.2.3 The requirements of the representative-agent approach

Hall's analysis is a typical example of the representative-agent methodology. An analysis of this approach requires examining: (i) the conditions under which a collection of individuals can be modelled as a single individual; (ii) the plausibility of the conditions; and (iii) the usefulness of representative-agent models for understanding macroeconomic phenomena. We begin with the first issue.

Consider an economy of n consumers and m goods. Each individual i has utility function $u_i(.)$, income (expenditure) X_{it} at time t, and demands $\mathbf{Y}_{it} = (Y_{it1}, \ldots, Y_{itm})$ for m goods at time t. Further, suppose everyone in the economy faces the common price vector $\mathbf{P}_t = (P_{t1}, \ldots, P_{tm})$.[8] Each agent i maximizes his or her utility subject to budget constraint, arriving at the individual consumption function:

$$\mathbf{Y}_{it} = f_i(X_{it}, \mathbf{P}_t) \tag{6.7}$$

The aggregate demand of m goods will be

$$\mathbf{Y}_t = \sum_i f_i(X_{it}, \mathbf{P}_t) = G(X_{1t}, \ldots, X_{nt}, \mathbf{P}_t) \tag{6.8}$$

where $\mathbf{Y}_t = \sum_i Y_{it}$. Finally, let $\mathbf{X}_t = \sum_i X_{it}$ denote aggregate expenditure. The question about the conditions under which a representative agent exists has two parts. The first concerns the conditions under which there exists an aggregate function $F(\mathbf{X}_t, \mathbf{P}_t)$ such that

$$\mathbf{Y}_t = G(X_{1t}, \ldots, X_{nt}, \mathbf{P}_t) = F(\mathbf{X}_t, \mathbf{P}_t) \tag{6.9}$$

The second relates to the conditions under which $F(\mathbf{X}_t, \mathbf{P}_t)$ can be derived from maximization of a utility function subject to total income $\mathbf{X}_t$ and price vector $\mathbf{P}_t$. Note that this setting is general in the sense that individual function f_i can take any form and X_{it} and Y_{it} can be interpreted in different ways. For instance, as in Hall's model, Y_{it} can be current consumption and X_{it} lagged consumption. To preserve consistency, for the time being, we take Y_{it} to be consumption and X_{it} income.

Gorman (1953) establishes the necessary and sufficient conditions for the existence of macro-function $F(\mathbf{X}_t, \mathbf{P}_t)$ in a static setting. Theorem 2.1 states these conditions:

> **Theorem 2.1:** Aggregate consumption function (6.9) exists if and only if the individual demand functions (6.7) take the form:
>
> $$\mathbf{Y}_{it} = a_i(\mathbf{P}_t) + b(\mathbf{P}_t)X_{it} \tag{6.10}$$
>
> that is, if and only if the individual demand functions are (i) linear in income and (ii) are identical up to the addition of a term that depends only on the common price vector. (Gorman, 1953)[9]

Individual demand function (6.10), known as the *Gorman polar form*, restricts individual differences to the intercept term $a_i(\mathbf{P})$, requiring the slope term to be common to all the consumers.[10] If the *adding up* condition, $\mathbf{Y}_{it}.\mathbf{P}_t = X_{it}$, is imposed, it follows that $a_i(\mathbf{P}_t).\mathbf{P}_t = 0$ and $b(\mathbf{P}_t).\mathbf{P}_t = 1$. When individual demand equations take the Gorman polar form (6.10), the aggregate demand function can be derived as

$$\mathbf{Y}_t = \sum_i a_i(\mathbf{P}_t) + b(\mathbf{P}_t) \sum_i X_{it} \tag{6.11}$$

Gorman's theorem requires individual demand functions to be linear in income. This means the proportion of income spent by a person on consumption is independent of the size of his or her income; he or she spends the same portion of income on goods regardless of how large that income grows. Also, the theorem demands identical marginal propensities to consume. That is, the income proportion spent by Bill Gates on a good should be same as the income proportion spent by a poor person. These requirements entail that aggregate consumption equation (6.9) exists if and only if total consumption is independent of the income distribution. If there were two groups of households with different marginal reactions to income changes, a transfer of income from one group to the other would alter total consumption. In that case, there would be distributional effects that are not accounted for by total income.

As an illustration, consider an economy consisting of one rich family and three poor families. The rich household receives £50 per month and spends 5 per cent of its income on food. Each poor family receives £10 per month and spends 25 per cent of its income on food. Aggregate monthly expenditure on food in the economy is £10. A transfer of £5 from each poor household to the rich reduces total food expenditure to £7. However, if the same amount, i.e. £15, is taken from the rich and evenly distributed among the poor households, aggregate expenditure rises to £13, even though aggregate income in either case is the same. What effect does an increase of £10 in total income have on total expenditure? Again, it all depends on who gets the income. If the rich household receives the extra income, total expenditure changes by 50 pence. If any of the poor families receives the extra income, aggregate expenditure rises by £2.5. The point is that, with different marginal responses, knowledge of total income is not sufficient to determine total consumption.

Gorman (1953; 1961) also established the conditions under which aggregate equation $F(\mathbf{X}_t, \mathbf{P}_t)$ is integrable or, in other words, can be derived from maximization of a utility function subject to a budget constraint. The result draws on the notion of homotheticity. A monotone preference relation $\geq$ on a choice set $\mathbf{X} \subseteq \mathbf{R}_+^L$ is called *homothetic* just in case $\mathbf{x} \geq \mathbf{y} \Leftrightarrow \alpha\mathbf{x} \geq \alpha\mathbf{y}$ for all $\alpha > 0$.[11] Homothetic preferences can be represented by a monotonic transformation of a homogeneous of degree 1 function. Having said this, Gorman's conditions can be stated as follows:

> **Theorem 2.2:** (Gorman 1953; Nataf, 1948): Suppose the individual demand function (6.10) is integrable; that is, it can be derived from maximization of a utility function $u(.)$. Then, aggregate demand function $F(\mathbf{X}_t, \mathbf{P}_t)$ exists and is integrable if and only if $u(.)$ is a homothetic utility function. (See Shafer and Sonnenschein, 1982, for a proof)[12]

The market demand function can be interpreted as a consumer demand function if and only if each individual demand function f_i is derived from a homothetic utility function $u(.)$ common to all consumers. In that case, for all i, $F = f_i$.[13] Non-homotheticity makes the marginal propensity to consume dependent on the income level, which renders total consumption dependent on the income distribution in the society. As an illustration, following Shafer and Sonnenschein (1982), consider an economy with two goods and two consumers who have identical but non-homothetic preferences represented by $u(x, y) = xy + y$. Let the price vector be (1,1). An income distribution of $m_1 = £1$ and $m_2 = £1$ leads to a different demand than an income distribution of $m_1 = 2$ and $m_2 = 0$ does. In the first case, total demand for y is £2 and for x is zero, whereas in the second case total demand for y is £3/2 and for x is £0.5. With strictly non-negative incomes, the homotheticity condition can be replaced with quasi-homotheticity, which is a weaker condition.[14]

6.2.3.1 *Identical marginal propensity throughout time*

Theorems 2.1 and 2.2 give the conditions for the existence of a representative agent in a static setting. As one moves to a dynamic setting, the existence of a representative agent calls for further conditions. To explore these conditions, note that theorem 2.1 requires the slope function $b(p)$ to be independent of the level of individual income. This requirement necessitates identical marginal propensity to consume over time regardless of whether one is young, employed, or retired. Hall implicitly introduces this condition into his model economy by assuming that people live an infinite life. They do not then need to worry about their future income.

Clarida (1991) replaced the infinite lifespan assumption of Hall's model with the assumption that people live for a finite period and, as a result, their propensity to consume declines monotonically with age. In this setting, aggregation can generate an aggregate consumption function quite different from the individual function, and the assumption of a finite lifespan, as noted by Clarida, can shed light on several stylized facts discernible in aggregate economic data. Specifically, Clarida considered a simple economy in which each consumer lives for n periods, earns income Y_t during m $(m < n)$ working periods, and receives nothing during the retirement periods $(n-m)$. Consumption during retirement is financed by saving a portion of labour income. Individual income Y_t follows a random walk with drift g:

$$Y_t = g + Y_{t-1} + \varepsilon_t \tag{6.12}$$

Further, the interest rate is zero and, as in Hall's economy, everyone acts according to the life-cycle permanent income hypothesis. In this economy, even though individual consumption is a random walk, aggregate consumption is not a random walk. In fact, if n is taken to be three and m two, average consumption change follows:

$$\Delta\overline{C}_t = \overline{g} + \alpha\overline{\varepsilon}_t + \beta\overline{\varepsilon}_{t-1} + \gamma\overline{\varepsilon}_{t-2}, \tag{6.13}$$

where the sign '$^{-}$' denotes average (Deaton, 1992: 169). Appendix 6.A explains the steps from (6.12) to (6.13).

Therefore, when people have a finite lifespan, and face different levels of income during their life, average (aggregate) consumption is not orthogonal to lagged innovations; both parameters β and γ are non-zero. Nor does average consumption respond one-for-one to innovations in current income. The economy exhibits a correlation between consumption change and past income (known as 'excess sensitivity'), and the variance of consumption changes is much less than the variance of income changes (known as 'excess smoothness').[15] In a dynamic setting, the representative-agent methodology not only requires the households to have identical marginal propensity to consume at any time but also requires them to have identical marginal propensity to consume *over* time. Otherwise, aggregation can produce relations that are not representative of relations at the individual level.

6.2.3.2 *Identical aggregate and individual income processes*

Another requirement for a representative consumer in a dynamic setting is that individual income and aggregate income follow the same stochastic process. If different processes generate the individual and aggregate income, and consumers lack full knowledge of the aggregate income process, aggregation over individual consumption functions can easily create a macro-consumption function that is entirely different from the individual functions. Pischke (1995) was the first to note this requirement. He considers an economy similar to Hall's economy but supposes that individual and aggregate income follow different processes.[16] Specifically, he assumes that the average income in the economy follows a random walk with drift, i.e.

$$\overline{Y}_t = g + \overline{Y}_{t-1} + \varepsilon_t \tag{6.14}$$

He, however, takes individual income to be the average income plus an idiosyncratic component that is purely transitory, represented by a white noise:

$$Y_{it} = \overline{Y}_t + u_{it} \tag{6.15}$$

with innovations ε_t and u_{it} being uncorrelated. The first difference of individual income is the first difference of the random walk, including the drift term, plus the first difference of the white noise term:

$$\Delta Y_{it} = g + \varepsilon_t + u_{it} - u_{it-1} \tag{6.16}$$

The households, Pischke notes, are not in a position to infer the contemporaneous aggregate shock ε_t. As a consequence, they cannot separate the macro-shock from the idiosyncratic component (private shock), u_{it}. Each individual can at best estimate the sum of these terms, which amounts to estimating the moving average process:

$$\Delta Y_{it} = g + \eta_{it} - \lambda\eta_{it-1} \tag{6.17}$$

With this result and Hall's conditions, the change in individual consumption follows $\Delta C_{it} = (1 - \lambda/1 + r)\eta_{it}$, and individual consumption obeys a random walk:

$$C_{it} = C_{it-1} + (1 - \lambda/1 + r)\eta_{it} \tag{6.18}$$

Aggregate consumption is not a random walk. It follows a second-order autoregressive process (see Appendix 6.B):

$$C_t = (\lambda + 1)C_{t-1} - \lambda C_{t-2} + \varsigma_t, \tag{6.19}$$

where $\varsigma_t = (1 - \lambda/1 + r)\varepsilon_t$. The difference would disappear if households knew the history of aggregate income including Y_t *and* were able to infer the aggregate income process correctly. This would enable the households to separate the common contemporaneous shock ε_t from the private shock u_{it}. In that case, the aggregate and individual consumption function would coincide (Pischke, 1995: 809).

In a dynamic setting, for a representative consumer to exist, the processes generating individual and aggregate income should be the same. Or individuals should have complete knowledge of the aggregate income history to infer the aggregate income process. In fact, full knowledge of the aggregate income history is not enough. It must also be assumed that individuals with the same information always make the same inferences (Grossman and Shiller, 1982). Otherwise, they may infer different processes from the full history of aggregate income, which could result in a difference between the individual and aggregate functions. Thus, in a dynamic setting, the representative-agent methodology necessitates a variant of the Harsanyi doctrine that people with the same information always form the same probabilistic beliefs. Critical analysis of objective Bayesianism has shown critical flows in the Harsanyi doctrine, partly because there is no unique prior representing the state of ignorance.[17] Also, information on the current values of aggregate variables is hardly available. Even the interested econometricians receive such information with a delay of a quarter or more. What is more, there seems to be no rationale for people to obtain such information. Gathering such information is often costly.

6.2.3.3 *Absence of interaction among economic agents*

Gorman's result requires the parameters in the individual consumption functions to be independent of the explanatory variables that vary across the individuals. Since the aggregate consumption function is derived by summing over the individual functions, the same condition must hold for the aggregate parameters. This requirement necessitates the absence of any interaction among decision makers in the economy. Whenever there are interdependencies among decision makers, the parameters of the aggregate function depend on the explanatory variables that vary across the individuals. In that case, the aggregate function will no longer be the same as the individual functions. To see this, consider Hall's model again. In setting up his model, Hall regards the real rate of interest r as constant, thus assuming that it is independent of the (current) consumption level. The assumption is reflected in the individual consumption function (6.5), restated here as

$$C_{it+1} = \left[\frac{(1+\delta)}{(1+r)}\right] C_{it} + \varepsilon_{it+1} \tag{6.20}$$

In this setting, the agent takes the interest rate as given in deciding how to allocate his income between consumption and saving. This is reasonable. If he saves a little bit more or less, his action won't affect the real interest rate. But if everyone makes a similar decision, the real interest rate moves. If everybody saves less, the real interest rate rises, pushing asset prices down. Alternatively, if everybody saves more, the real interest rate falls, pushing asset prices up.[18] Contrary to Hall's assumption, aggregate consumption and the real interest rate do not move independently. The real interest rate depends on the consumption level and vice versa; one cannot hold one of these as constant and let the other vary. So, although in modelling individual consumption the real interest rate r can be considered as independent of the individual consumption level C_{it}, in modelling aggregate consumption the real interest rate r cannot be considered as independent of the aggregate consumption level C_t. It would be conceptually wrong to write the aggregate function as

$$C_{t+1} = \left[\frac{(1+\delta)}{(1+r)}\right] C_t + \varepsilon_{t+1} \tag{6.21}$$

Since the interest rate depends on aggregate consumption, the relation between the current and future aggregate consumption is non-linear (Hartley, 1997: 156).

In fact, with interaction, the differences between the micro- and macro-functions do not end here. If everyone decides to save less, the decision increases the real interest rate, lowering the asset prices. This increases the opportunity cost of current consumption, moderating the increase in the current consumption actually achieved. Alternatively, if everyone decides to save more, the decision lowers the real interest rate, pushing the asset prices up. This lowers the opportunity cost of current consumption, moderating the reduction in the current consumption actually achieved. Such endogenous fluctuations in the interest rate and asset prices restrain intertemporal arrangement of consumption. The inhibition can create a tighter link between future consumption and current income than is predicted by Hall's model, which abstracts from fluctuations in the interest rate and asset prices. So, even if (6.20) were true of the individual, the aggregate consumption function might still include variables other than current aggregate consumption.

As a consequence, in an interactive system the behaviour of an aggregate variable cannot be modelled in isolation from the mechanisms generating the (independent) variables affecting the variable. In the above setting, this means that one cannot establish an adequate theoretical model of consumption without simultaneously modelling the mechanisms generating income, asset prices, and interest rate. Since aggregate consumption also influences these variables, the interdependencies necessitate a non-recursive model to account for the feedback. In an interactive system, even though a recursive model may accurately describe individual consumption behaviour, to describe the aggregate consumption behaviour, one may have to adopt a non-recursive model.[19]

To sum up, the existence of a representative individual requires that the dependent variable in the micro-functions be linear in the explanatory variables, the coefficient in the micro-functions (except the intercept) be the same across the individuals, the coefficients be constant over time, the mechanisms generating the individual and aggregate explanatory variables be the same or the agents have full knowledge of the mechanisms generating the aggregate explanatory variables, and there be no interaction among the individuals. These assumptions are incredibly strong, and, even as gross approximation, are hardly true of modern economies.

6.2.4 Problems with the representative-agent approach

The requirements of the representative-agent methodology are extremely stringent, and cannot be true of real economies, even as remote approximations. This is not, however, the most critical difficulty with the methodology. For many reasons, the approach is, in principle, unsuitable for studying the economy, and can lead to fallacious results.

To begin with, the approach views the economy as a society of identical individuals, operating in isolated homogeneous choice situations. In such a society, there is no room for money, which is a means of exchange among agents with different needs, preferences, beliefs, and attitudes towards risk (Friedman and Hahn, 1990: xii). Nor does such a society provide a room for monetary institutions. These institutions are for coordinating among differently situated agents with different needs and beliefs, who do not exist in a society of identical individuals (Colander, 1996: 62). Also, if people had identical preferences, had access to identical information, held the same beliefs, and faced identical choice situations, there would be no trade in securities. There is no room for security markets in a society of identical agents. These markets arise because people have access to different information, make different inferences from the same data, and have different attitudes towards risk. Any attempt at explaining security markets, their effects on the economy, and the role of related institutions, demands taking individual heterogeneities seriously (Arrow, 1986: 212). The difficulty with the representative-agent approach, as these considerations reveal, is not that it abstracts away certain aspects of the economy; any modelling methodology proceeds with abstraction and idealization. The fundamental difficulty is that it abstracts away the very same features that are necessary for understanding basic economic phenomena.[20]

Also, the representative-agent methodology implies that every proposition true of the individual is true of the economy, and every proposition true of the economy is true of the individual. This is wrong. In general, when one moves from the individual level to the economy level, the causal status of the variables affected by individual decisions changes. Coffee scarcity is exogenous to one's decision but it is the people who altogether cause coffee scarcity (Schelling, 1978: 78); economic growth is exogenous to one's decision but it is the external effects of individuals' capital accumulation that causes growth (Romer, 1994); asset prices are exogenous to one's decision but it is the individuals' saving, consumption and investment decisions that determine the prices (Lucas, 1978); and the interest rate is exogenous to one's decision but it is the individuals' saving decisions that determine it. Coffee scarcity, the interest rate, asset prices, unemployment level, economic growth, and population density should be regarded as exogenous in modelling behaviour. But, it is the individual decisions that should be considered as exogenous in modelling the economy. It is wrong to think that if a variable is exogenous to the agent it is also exogenous to the economy, or if a variable is endogenous to the economy it is also endogenous to the individual. Failure to recognize this point results in fallacious conclusions about the economy.

Theoretical differences between the individual and the economy do not end here. There is also a multitude of other types of propositions that apply to the individual but not the economy or apply to the economy but not the individual. Consider an example from Schelling (1998) that concerns the pattern of sales of best-seller novels, fictions and biographies by new unknown authors. Sales data show that the sales of such works in a society follow a logistic path, growing exponentially at first, then passing an inflection point, and finally declining exponentially until the left-over copies are remaindered. A possible explanation for this pattern, Schelling says, is the following. 'People who read the book, if they like it, *they* talk about it, some people more than others; the more people who read the book, the more people there are to talk about it. Some of the people they talk to buy the book; if they like it, they talk about it. Talk is proportionate to the number of people who have read the book; if all talk is equally effective, the number talking about it grows exponentially. But there is a limit to the number of people likely to be recruited; eventually most of those who would be interested have already heard of the book, maybe bought it, and when they want to talk about it find that there's hardly anybody left who hasn't already heard about it. If there were initially L potentially interested readers, and N have now read it and want to talk about it, and everybody who has read it meets and talks about it with n out of the L per week, there will be $N \times n \times L$ contacts per week, with $N \times n \times (L - N)$ of them potentially productive, and N will grow logistically' (Schelling, 1998: 34). The logistic curve found in the data on the sale of best-sellers by unknown authors cannot be attributed to a single individual. The curve emerges as a consequence of the finiteness of the number of readers in a society, and does not depend on the specific decision-making process driving one to buy the book.[21] Similar patterns are likely to emerge in sales data for newly invented durable goods.

Finally, a further problem relates to the suitability of the representative-agent models for policy analysis. Policies are usually designed to work by changing certain distributional aspects of the economy. Monetary policies, for instance, operate by reducing or increasing the consumption of those who are facing liquidity constraints, and their effects depend on the distribution of assets in the economy (Stiglitz, 1991: 26). But this goes against the assumption of the representative-agent models that the value of an aggregate dependent variable (here, aggregate consumption) is independent of the distribution of the explanatory micro-variables (here, income and assets). On these models, as long as the effect of a policy shift is limited to a change in the distribution of independent micro-variables, the policy has no impact on the dependent variable. If the possibility of influencing the economy through distributional channels is granted, then one has to search for models that are sensitive to the distributional features of the economy (Martel, 1996: 140). In general, an analysis of economic policies calls for some information about the joint distribution of the micro-variables that affect decisions. In addition, it requires predicting how a policy changes the distribution, and how the distributional change affects the economy's structure. None of these issues can be settled within the representative-agent modelling framework.

6.3 Modelling heterogeneous behaviour

It is essential for understanding large-scale economic phenomena to think of the economy as a system of interactive heterogeneous individuals. Individual heterogeneity and interaction generate difficult aggregation issues, making the relation between micro- and macro-models extremely complicated. The interest in aggregation over interactive heterogeneous agents is relatively recent (Hansen, 1998: 240–1). The remainder of this chapter studies some of the issues directly relevant to the question of whether, in the presence of heterogeneity and interaction, the correct form of the aggregate model can be derived from the micro-models alone, or whether inferring the correct form of the macro-model necessitates a substantial amount of information concerning the economy.

This section concentrates on aggregation problems arising from individual heterogeneity. It discusses the fundamental theorem of *exact aggregation*, due to Lau (1982). The theorem specifies the conditions that are necessary in the presence of heterogeneity for the micro-models alone to determine the aggregate model. An analysis of these conditions enables us to understand precisely the circumstances under which the microfoundations programme may succeed.

6.3.1 The fundamental theorem of exact aggregation

Individuals differ in many respects that are relevant to economic decisions. They differ in their tastes, opinions, information, incomes, demographic attributes, and environment. Such differences usually give rise to differences in preferences, making people with identical income exhibit different patterns of consumption behaviour, and thus affect aggregate consumption. Of all possible individual heterogeneities, Lau (1982) considers demographic attributes, such as age and number of children. To explain Lau's result, we need to extend the framework used earlier to state Gorman's theorems. In particular, we need to extend the micro-functions to include arguments referring to individual demographic attributes.[22] That is

$$\mathbf{Y}_{it} = f_i(X_{it}, \mathbf{A}_{it}, \mathbf{P}_t) \qquad i = 1, \ldots, N \tag{6.22}$$

where $\mathbf{Y}_{it}$ is the individual consumption vector at time t, X_{it} is individual income, $\mathbf{A}_{it}$ is the vector of individual attributes, $\mathbf{P}_t$ is the vector of prices at time t, and N is the number of households. Aggregate demand $\mathbf{Y}_t$ is given by the sum of the individual demands:

$$\mathbf{Y}_t = \sum_i^N f_i(X_{it}, \mathbf{A}_{it}, \mathbf{P}_t) \tag{6.23}$$

Evidently, calculating total consumption using equation (6.23) requires knowing, besides the individual demand functions, the distribution of income and attributes in the economy. The search for an aggregate function involves finding a function that reduces the information needed for calculating total consumption. To achieve this, the function should dispense with the need for full knowledge of the distribution, and make it possible to compute total consumption using a small number of statistics (indices) summarizing it. The macro-function should take the form:

$$\begin{aligned} \mathbf{Y}_t &= \sum_i f_i(X_{it}, \mathbf{A}_{it}, \mathbf{P}_t) \\ &= F(g_1(X_{1t}, \ldots, X_{Nt}, \mathbf{A}_{1t}, \ldots, \mathbf{A}_{Nt}), \ldots, \\ &\quad g_L(X_{1t}, \ldots, X_{Nt}, \mathbf{A}_{1t}, \ldots, \mathbf{A}_{Nt}), \mathbf{P}_t) \end{aligned} \tag{6.24}$$

where each function g_l, $l = 1, \ldots, L$, is an index of the joint distribution of income and attributes, such as $\sum_i^N X_{it}$ and $\sum_i^N X_{it}\mathbf{A}_{it}$.

Equation (6.24) must satisfy several conditions to reduce the information necessary for computing total consumption:

1. The number of statistics g_l must be smaller than the number of the micro-functions (i.e. $L < N$) for any reduction to occur in the information needed for calculating aggregate consumption.

2. The value of a statistic is invariant with respect to the ordering of the units in the population. This means each function $g_l(X_{it}, \ldots, X_{nt}, \mathbf{A}_{1t} \ldots, \mathbf{A}_{nt})$ must be invariant with respect to whether individual i possesses attributes $\mathbf{A}^*$ and income x or individual j possesses attributes $\mathbf{A}^*$ and income x. Swapping the income and attributes of two individuals should not affect the value of the statistic. In consequence, each index function g_l must be *symmetric* with respect to subscript i through N. As shown in Appendix 6.C, this requires the individual demand functions to be identical up to the addition of a term that is independent of the individual attributes and expenditure (Jorgenson *et al.*, 1982: 113). Formally

$$f_i(X_{it}, \mathbf{A}_{it}, \mathbf{P}_t) = f(X_{it}, \mathbf{A}_{it}, \mathbf{P}_t) + k_i(\mathbf{P}_t). \tag{6.25}$$

   Consequently, in order for aggregate function (6.24) to exist, all individual demand functions for the same commodity must be identical up to the addition of a function that is independent of variables that vary across individuals (Lau, 1982: 122).
3. Index functions g_l, $l = 1, \ldots, L$, must be functionally independent. Or else, some of the indices play no genuine role in reducing the distributional information necessary for calculating aggregate consumption, and can be omitted without harm.
4. Aggregate function $F(g_1, g_2, \ldots, g_L, \mathbf{P}_t)$ must also be *invertible* in the indices $g_1, \ldots, g_L$. Specifically, there must be a price vector $\mathbf{P}_t$ such that $F(g_1, g_2, \ldots, g_L, \mathbf{P}_t)$ is invertible in $g_1, \ldots, g_L$. To see the necessity of this condition, consider function $F(G(g_1, g_2), g_3, \ldots, g_L, \mathbf{P}_t)$. There is no price vector $\mathbf{P}_t$ such that $F(G(g_1, g_2), g_3, \ldots, g_L, \mathbf{P}_t)$ is invertible in $g_1, \ldots, g_L$. The difficulty is with g_1 and g_2, which are effectively a single function, namely G (Lau, 1982: 126). Taken together, functional independence and invertibility ensure that the aggregate function is represented by a minimal number of index functions g_l's.
   Individual demand functions that can be aggregated into an aggregate function of the form (6.24) are said to be exactly aggregable. The reason for this nomenclature is that, when there is an aggregate function like (6.24), masking some aspects of the income-attribute distribution through aggregation does not jeopardize the ability to correctly compute aggregate consumption (Heineke and Shefrin, 1988). Lau (1982) establishes a theorem that defines the conditions under which individual functions (6.22) can be exactly aggregated:

The fundamental theorem of exact aggregation: Aggregate function (6.24) exists, is continuously differentiable, and satisfies conditions (1) through (4) if and only if the individual functions (6.22) can be written as

$$f_i(X_{it}, \mathbf{A}_{it}, \mathbf{P}_t) = b_1(\mathbf{P}_t) g_1^*(X_{it}, \mathbf{A}_{it}) + \ldots + b_q(\mathbf{P}_t) g_L^*(X_{it}, \mathbf{A}_{it}) + a_i(\mathbf{P}_t),$$
$$i = 1, \ldots, N, \tag{6.26}$$

> that is, if and only if the individual demand functions can be represented as sums of products of separate functions of prices and individual income and attributes. (Jorgenson *et al.*, 1982: 104)

Equation (6.26) imposes several restrictions on individual demand functions. It requires the functions to be identical up to an additive term that is independent of the variables varying across individuals. In this respect, Lau's theorem does not depart from Gorman's result. Secondly, equation (6.26) excludes heterogeneity in marginal responses only when income *and* attributes are identical. The theorem is, therefore, a significant generalization of Gorman's result, which excludes heterogeneity in marginal responses with identical incomes. Thirdly, equation (6.26) requires individual functions to be linear in a number of functions of individual income and attributes. Unlike in Gorman's polar form, these functions are permitted to depend non-linearly on the individual income and attributes.

When individual functions can be stated as (6.26), each index g_l in aggregate equation (6.24) corresponds to the sum of individual functions $g_l^*(X_{it}, \mathbf{A}_{it})$, i.e. $g_l = \sum_i g_l^*(X_{it}, \mathbf{A}_{it})$, $(l = 1, \ldots, L)$. Therefore, a corollary of the exact aggregation theorem is that the indices in the aggregate function are expressible as sums of some functions, each depending only on x_{it} or $\mathbf{A}_{it}$ (Jorgenson *et al.*, 1982: 106). The aggregate function can then be derived from the individual equations by substituting the sum of $g_l^*(X_{it}, \mathbf{A}_{it})$ for index function g_l.

Exactly aggregable functions defined by equation (6.26) are the only class of functions where individual functions alone determine the aggregate function, and the meaning of the individual parameters fixes the meaning of the aggregate parameters. But this does not imply that if individual functions are integrable, the aggregate function is also integrable. It is only when individual functions can be stated in terms of two terms $g_l^*(X_{it}, \mathbf{A}_{it})$, $l = 1, 2$, that the integrability of the functions guarantees the integrability of the aggregate function, and hence the existence of a representative agent (Muellbauer, 1975; 1976).

While Lau's theorem takes a major step in making room for individual heterogeneity, it does not yield much support for the microfoundations project. In fact, by reflecting on Lau's requirements, one begins to see enormous complications that individual heterogeneity creates even when individual functions are exactly aggregable. Recall when Gorman's conditions are in place, computing total consumption requires no information about the income distribution. As soon as one moves away from this unrealistic situation to a situation where the conditions for exact aggregation hold, one requires quite a good deal of information about the income distribution to calculate aggregate consumption. As an illustration, consider a simple example adapted from Stoker (1993). Suppose there are two small and two large families, with different marginal propensities to consume. Let the demand function for the small families be $Y_{it} = b_0(\mathbf{P}_t)X_{it}$ and for the large families be

$Y_{it} = b_1(\mathbf{P}_t)X_{it}$. Let attribute vector $\mathbf{A}_{it}$ be a qualitative variable, with A_{it}=1 denoting a small family and $A_{it} = 0$ a large family. The demand function for each household can be written as

$$Y_{it} = b_0(\mathbf{P}_t)A_{it}X_{it} + b_1(\mathbf{P}_t)(1 - A_{it})X_{it} \tag{6.27}$$

which is of the form (6.26). The aggregate demand model can be written as

$$Y_t = b_1(\mathbf{P}_t)\sum_i X_{it} + [b_0(\mathbf{P}_t) - b_1(\mathbf{P}_t)]\sum_i A_{it}X_{it} \tag{6.28}$$

Now, suppose each small family currently receives £40 as income and spends a fourth of its income on goods and each large family receives £60 as income and spends half of its income on food. The aggregate equation (6.28) predicts total food consumption to be £80. If total income is doubled, depending on who receives the additional income the aggregate model yields different results. If all the income goes to the small families, the model forecasts total consumption to be £130. If all the income goes to the large families, the model forecasts total consumption to be less then £180. Other income distributions lead to different predictions of total consumption. Predicting total consumption using equation (6.28) demands information on the amount of total income going to the small or large families. In real economies, the micro-parameters $b_l(\mathbf{P}_t)$ are not known, and econometricians turn to aggregate data to estimate them. This practice yields useful results if the relevant aspects of the distribution of the individual explanatory variables are not masked in the data. In the present case, the data should not be so aggregated that the total income going into the small families cannot be distinguished from the total income going into the large families; the income of these family groups should be kept separate (Stoker, 1993: 1836). As we consider real economies, the diversity of market participants turns out to be much richer and more complex and more disaggregated information is needed for estimating the correct aggregate model. The problem is that such information is difficult to obtain.

There is also no guarantee that exactly aggregable functions can always be stated as equation (6.26) using a small number of terms $g_l^*(X_{it}, \mathbf{A}_{it})$. The effort to state individual functions in the form necessary for exact aggregation may require a large number of terms $g_l^*(X_{it}, \mathbf{A}_{it})$, which results in an aggregate function with a large number of indices $g_l(.)$, again making it difficult to estimate the function reliably from normally available samples. In practice, to counter this complexity, the analyst may need to work with a simplified aggregate function that is substantially different from the exact aggregate equation. The existence of a true aggregate function is one thing and the practicality or usefulness of the function is another. The microfoundations thesis wrongly implies that not only does a true aggregate function exist but it is also simple enough to be estimated and used in practice.

6.3.2 The effect of non-linearity

The requirements of exact aggregation are not appropriate in modelling many economic phenomena. In reality, a household's income must reach a certain level to be able to afford a car, purchase a house, save, go on a holiday, send its children to private schools, move house, buy a luxury car, and so forth. The demand for such commodities is not linearly dependent on income. And this necessitates working with a non-linear individual consumption model. When behaviours follow a non-linear pattern, the aggregate function cannot be inferred from the individual functions alone. To derive the function, it is also necessary to know the joint distribution of the explanatory variables (income and attributes) in the economy (Cameron, 1990: 207). This necessity would in fact remain even if there were no heterogeneity in individual functions. A simple example best illustrates the point.

Following Stoker (1993), suppose that the concern is to study the purchase of a single unit of a product such as a car, and that we only observe whether it is bought ($Y_{it} = 1$) or not ($Y_{it} = 0$). Suppose the value to family i of buying the product depends on the product's price P_t and family's income X_{it}. Specifically, suppose the utility of the product for family i is given by $1 + \beta_1 \ln P_t + \beta_2 X_{it}$. A model of family i's decision to purchase the product could, then, be the discrete model:

$$\begin{aligned} Y_{it} &= f(X_{it}, P_t) \\ &= 1 \text{ if } 1 + \beta_1 \ln P_t + \beta_2 X_{it} \geq 0 \qquad (6.29) \\ &= 0 \text{ otherwise.} \end{aligned}$$

The objective is to model the average demand $\overline{Y}_t = N_t^{-1} \sum Y_{it}$, i.e. the proportion of families buying the product. This requires estimating the probability that family i buys the product, $p(1+\beta_1 \ln P_t + \beta_2 X_{it} \geq 0)$, which depends on the distribution of income X_t in the economy. When the income distribution is known, the probability that a purchase is made can be calculated, and the derivation of the aggregate model will be straightforward. If the distribution of X_t is, say, lognormal with $\ln X_t$ having mean μ_t and variance υ_t^2, the model will be

$$E_t(y) = \Phi\left[\frac{1}{\beta_2 \upsilon_t}(1 + \beta_1 \ln P_t + \beta_2 E_t(x) - \beta_2 \frac{\upsilon_t^2}{2})\right] \qquad (6.30)$$

where $E_t(y)$ denotes the expected number of families purchasing the product, and $\Phi(.)$ is the univariate normal *cumulative* distribution function. If there were behavioural heterogeneity, that is, if the parameters β_1 and β_2 varied across the families, further information about the probability distribution of households would be needed to compute aggregate demand correctly, and the aggregate consumption model would depart even further from the individual consumption models.[23]

This example points to some significant differences between aggregating over linear and non-linear models. In the former case, when the exact aggregation requirements hold, the individual models alone determine the correct macro-model. In the case of non-linear models, even when the same model is precisely true of every individual, the correct form of the aggregate model depends on the distribution of the explanatory micro-variables, and cannot be inferred from the micro-models alone. An assumption about the distribution of the micro-explanatory variables is an assumption about the configuration of the society. In the case of non-linear models therefore the microfoundations thesis, which only permits macro-models that can be derived solely from purely individualistic assumptions, falters. Moreover, and quite importantly, it is difficult to see how the distribution of the explanatory variables can be estimated in a large economy. Economic data are hardly disaggregated enough to permit estimation of the distributions required for aggregating over non-linear choice models (Cameron, 1990: 212).

6.3.3 The effect of dynamics

Lau laid down the requirements for exact aggregation in a static setting. But the agent lives in an uncertain environment and, to make decisions, needs to rely on his or her expectations of future values of variables affecting his or her decisions. Ideally, he or she estimates the required expectations on the basis of some observable variables, whose values are already known. In that case, as in Hall's (1978) study, the appropriate model of individual behaviour is a dynamic model, which, in the presence of heterogeneity, further complicates aggregation issues. In fact, aggregation over extremely simple heterogeneous dynamic models can produce a complex macro-model that is different from the individual models, and cannot be given the behavioural interpretation available for the micro-models. The simplest instance of this phenomenon occurs in the case of aggregating over heterogeneous first-order autoregressive processes, $AR(1)$. Consider the aggregation of the two $AR(1)$ processes:

$$X_{it} = \alpha_i X_{it-1} + \varepsilon_{it} \qquad i = 1, 2 \tag{6.31}$$

where ε_{1t} and ε_{2t} are a pair of independent, zero-mean, white-noise series.[24] A simple calculation shows that aggregate variable $X_t = X_{1t} + X_{2t}$ follows the autoregressive moving average (2,1) process:

$$X_t = \alpha X_{t-1} + \beta X_{t-2} + \eta_{t-1} + \eta_t \tag{6.32}$$

In general, Box and Jenkins (1976) and Granger and Morris (1976) have shown that if N time series each following an $AR(1)$ model with different parameter values are added, their sum follows an $ARMA(N, N-1)$

(Appendix 6.D).[25] As a result, if the number of heterogeneous decision makers is large as in real economies, the true aggregate function contains an extremely large number of parameters, making it impossible to estimate the function from ordinarily available samples. Also, due to the high number of parameters, the model is not practically useful (Granger, 1980a: 230–1). The relation between the micro- and macro-parameters is also so complicated that it makes it problematic to ascribe much behavioural interpretation to the aggregate model's parameters (Stoker, 1993: 1861).

6.3.4 The effect of heterogeneous environments

Lau's theory is solely concerned with the conditions where individual functions alone determine the aggregate equation. The theory pays no attention to environmental heterogeneities that ubiquitously exist in the economy. To give an example, the processes generating incomes in various sectors of the economy are by no means the same. A banker and a farmer, for instance, may not only have different preferences and demographic attributes but may also face quite different income-generating mechanisms. When there is no behavioural heterogeneity, such differences are immaterial. But when people behave differently, environmental differences affect the shape of the regularities that emerge at the economy level, and enormously aggravate the disparities between the micro- and macro-levels. We return to Lippi's example (1988) discussed in the last chapter to bring to the fore some of the complications that environmental heterogeneities create for modelling the economy.

The example concerns an economy consisting of two consumers with demands following static routines:

$$Y_{it} = \Pi_i X_{it} \qquad i = 1, 2 \tag{6.33}$$

Y_{it} and X_{it} are respectively the consumption and income of the ith agent at time t, and Π_i are different, i.e. $\Pi_1 \neq \Pi_2$. Moreover, X_{it} follow the autoregressive process:

$$X_{it} = a_i X_{it-1} + v_{it} \qquad 0 < a_i < 1 \tag{6.34}$$

with a_i being different for each individual, and v_{it} being orthogonal white-noise processes. The variables representing the state of the economy are aggregate demand $Y_t = Y_{1t} + Y_{2t}$ and aggregate income $X_t = X_{1t} + X_{2t}$. The consumption function for this economy, as established in Lippi (1988), follows (see Appendix 6.E):

$$Y_t = \alpha Y_{t-1} + \beta X_t + \gamma X_{t-1} + u_t \tag{6.35}$$

The error term u_t is a white-noise process, and the parameters are defined as

$$\alpha = \frac{(\Pi_1 - k)a_1 + (k - \Pi_2)a_2}{(\Pi_1 - \Pi_2)} \tag{6.36a}$$

$$\beta = k = \frac{Cov(\Pi_{1t}v_{1t} + \Pi_2 v_{2t}, v_{1t} + v_{2t})}{Var(v_{1t} + v_{2t})} \tag{6.36b}$$

$$\gamma = \frac{(\Pi_1 - k)\Pi_2 a_1 + (k - \Pi_2)\Pi_1 a_2}{(\Pi_1 - \Pi_2)} \tag{6.36c}$$

Aggregate demand equation (6.35) markedly differs from micro-demand functions (6.33); it contains variables that are absent in the micro-consumption functions. Moreover, the equation's parameters depend in a highly complex manner on both the parameters of micro-consumption functions (6.33) and those of the environmental functions (6.34), which represent the processes that generate individual incomes.

This example is simple but teaches us several key lessons about the connection between the micro- and macro-levels in a real economy. To begin with, when agents encounter heterogeneous choice situations and behave differently, the correct aggregate model is partly defined by the mechanisms that generate explanatory micro-variables. To derive the model, then, some knowledge of the structure of the economy, such as the causal process generating income in the banking sector, is needed. Secondly, as the number of heterogeneous decision makers in the economy increases, the complexity of the aggregate function also increases beyond control. In fact, even when the number of decision makers does not exceed a single digit, the aggregate equation is more complex than most aggregate equations used in practice. Consequently, the true aggregate model, even if it were known, would not be of any practical use. Thirdly, in the presence of behavioural and environmental heterogeneity, the parameters of the aggregate model depend in a highly complex manner on both the parameters of the behavioural equations and those of the environmental functions, which describe the mechanisms generating explanatory micro-variables. This makes it impossible to ascribe any behavioural meaning to the aggregate model. Indeed, inspecting equalities (6.36a) through (6.36c), one wonders what interpretation can be given to the parameters in (6.35) except that they are by-products of aggregation. Even in this simple case, the very existence of an aggregate (demand) function, which meaningfully relates to the behavioural functions, is in doubt. Economists have rarely come to grip with the issues arising from aggregation over heterogeneous individuals operating in different situations. But those who have come to realize the severity of the complications have felt bound to abandon the nomenclature of a true aggregate function. Referring to Theil (1954)'s seminal work on aggregation, Zellner (1969) writes:

> His [Theil] main result that the mathematical expectation of macro-coefficient estimators will in general depend on a complicated combination of corresponding and noncorresponding micro-coefficients was so disturbing to him that he seriously considered the following question in his concluding chapter (1954: 180) 'Should not we abolish these [macro] models altogether?' (Zellner, 1969: 365)

6.3.5 Heterogeneity and policy evaluation

The dependence of aggregate models on processes generating micro-independent variables also suggests the sensitivity of the models to changes in policy regimes. Economic policies are often designed to work by modifying the mechanisms that determine micro-independent variables such as income. In the presence of heterogeneity, policies that lead to different income-generating mechanisms, for instance, could give rise to different aggregate models. In that case, it would not be appropriate to use an aggregate model valid under one policy regime to predict the effects of an alternative policy regime. This could potentially lead to very wrong predictions about the effects of the new policy. Several authors have noted the sensitivity of aggregate models to changes in policy regimes, and have emphasized its implications for the microfoundations project. To highlight the matter, we discuss a simple example from Geweke (1985), who uses it for a slightly different purpose.

Geweke considers an industry in a small country that produces a single output, Y_t, ultimately sold competitively in a world market. The production technology is the same for all the firms in the industry. To be specific, for the ith firm at time t:

$$Y_{it} = aX_{it} + dX_{it}^2 \qquad a > 0, d < 0 \tag{6.37}$$

where X_{it} is an input factor used to produce Y_t. Firms are distributed throughout the country and, as a consequence, the price for the output of each firm P_{it} varys, say, with access to deep-water ports. Output price varies through time but relative output prices across firms never vary.[26] The output price for the ith firm may be stated as

$$P_{it} = P_t P_i \tag{6.38}$$

Input price r_t is the same across the country. Equation (6.37) is exactly aggregable, and can be estimated using time-series data on aggregate (average) input factor X_t and aggregate (average) output Y_t. Equations (6.37) and (6.38) lead to average supply function:

$$Y_t = \frac{-a^2}{4d} + \frac{r_t^2}{4dP_t^2 E(P_i^2)} \tag{6.39}$$

where $E(.)$ stands for average. Suppose the aim is to predict the effect on production of an *ad rem* subsidy that amounts to substituting (6.38) with a new price regime:

$$P_{it} = P_t P_i + u \qquad u > 0. \tag{6.40}$$

Supply function (6.39) predicts the effect of the subsidy on average supply to be

$$(r_t^2/4dP_t^2 E(P_i^2))\{(1 + (u/P_t)]^{-2} - 1\} \tag{6.41}$$

However, when new price regime (6.40) is in place, the actual average supply function is

$$Y_t = \frac{-a^2}{4d} + \frac{r_t^2}{4dP_t^2} E\left(P_i + \frac{u}{P_t}\right)^{-2} \tag{6.42}$$

and the actual effect of the subsidy on average supply is

$$(r_t^2/4dP_t^2)E\{[P_i + (u/P_t)]^{-2} - P_i^{-2}\} \tag{6.43}$$

which is different from the predicted change. The change in the individual price functions invalidates the aggregate production function. The function can no longer be used to predict the policy outcome.[27] New classical economists argue for establishing economic models on features of human behaviour such as tastes that, unlike expectations, are invariant to policy shifts. Geweke's example reveals that the perils of ignoring aggregation may not be less than those of ignoring expectations.

The analysis of aggregation over heterogeneous individuals shows how individual heterogeneity limits the circumstances where the microfoundations project can succeed. It is only when micro-functions are identical and (intrinsically) linear, and identical processes generate micro-explanatory variables, that the individual functions alone determine the macro-model.[28] If any of these conditions fails, substantial information regarding the structural features of the economy, including the processes generating the micro-explanatory variables, is needed to derive the aggregate model. This necessity of relying on macroeconomic phenomena (i.e. the processes generating micro-explanatory variables) to model other macroeconomic phenomena undermines the central thesis of the microfoundations project that 'the economist should start at the level of isolated individual' (Kirman, 1989: 138; Rizvi, 1994: 372). Modelling the economy always requires making substantive assumptions about the economy's structure.

6.4 Modelling interaction

The analysis of the representative-agent modelling approach showed that in studying the economy one could not take a single individual as the unit of analysis. Explaining macroeconomic phenomena requires viewing the economy as an interactive system of heterogeneous decision making units. This means one has to take 'a collection of interactive heterogeneous individuals' as the unit of analysis. We have studied some of the implications of individual heterogeneity for the microfoundations project. It is now time to investigate some of the issues that arise from the presence of interactions (or, interdependencies) in the economy.

6.4.1 Market interactions

The earliest model of economic interaction is the theory of Walrasian general equilibrium, which is still a basic model of the market in economics (Ackerman, 1999). New classical economists often interpret the call for microfoundations as a call for deducing the laws of aggregates from the theory of general equilibrium joined with the rational expectations hypothesis (Lucas and Sargent, 1979). The basic idea of the general equilibrium theory is that one cannot model a sector of the economy such as the consumption sector while treating the influences impinging on the sector by the rest of the economy as constant. Various sectors of the economy are interdependent and must be modelled simultaneously. The nuts and bolts of the Walrasian theory can be explained by considering an economy that, in addition to the consumption sector, has a single production sector. Specifically, consider an economy consisting of n consumers who own non-negative initial endowments of capital goods and labour and consume q goods, and m firms producing the q goods using as input labour and capital services provided by the consumers. The Walrasian theory introduces several basic assumptions about the consumers and firms of the economy. I rely on Leigh Tesfatsion's notes on macroeconomics (2003: 2) to state these assumptions, while adding to her list the assumption of rational expectations:[29]

A1: Consumers are (subjective) expected utility maximizers.

A2: Firms are (subjective) expected profit optimizers.

A3: 'The preferences of each consumer are exogenously given.'

A4: 'The income of consumers comes from dividends and from the sale of capital services and labour services.'

A5: 'Market for services and consumption goods are *complete*. That is, for each valued service and consumption good, there is a market price at which it can be bought or sold.'

A6: 'Consumers, taking expected good prices, wages, rental rates and dividends as given, choose demand for consumption goods and supplies of capital and labour services to maximize their utility subject to a budget constraint and physical feasibility conditions (non-negativity and endowment constraints).'

A7: 'Firms, taking expected good prices, wages and rental rates as given, choose supplies of goods and demands for capital and labour services to maximize expected profits subject to technological feasibility conditions.'

A8: 'All purchase and sale agreements are costlessly enforced.'

A9: Expectations are rational.

In addition to these assumptions, the theory introduces certain technical restrictions regarding the utility functions as well as production functions including continuity, convexity, and monotonicity of preferences. These are to ensure the existence of a Walrasian equilibrium, which is a set of relative prices and corresponding demand and supply quantities at which all consumers are maximizing their utility conditional on their expected prices and dividends, all producers are optimizing their profits conditional on their expected prices, and markets for all goods clear. Altogether, these assumptions entail that the economy is in equilibrium, prices fully reflect all the relevant information and there is no conflict across business plans. In a Walrasian world, a decision maker has no need to communicate with others or adjust his or her decisions to those of others in the market. He or she only needs to consider prices to decide on the optimal course of action. Since in such a world all interactions take place through prices, the Walrasian economic model is referred to as a model of *market* or *indirect* interaction.

The call to establish the laws of the aggregates on the general equilibrium theory is an attempt to derive the laws of the economy from the assumptions about individual behaviour, firm behaviour, tastes, technologies, and endowments as well as the postulates necessary for the existence of an equilibrium (Rizvi, 1994). A question taken up by Sonnenschein (1972), Mantel (1976) and Debreu (1974) (henceforth, SMD) is whether the Walrasian assumptions impose any restrictions on the regularities emerging at the economy level. To be precise, these theorists have enquired if the conditions imply any restrictions for the excess demand curve of the economy. The authors have found that, given the Walrasian assumptions, *only* three properties carry over from the individual's excess demand curves to the aggregate excess demand curve. They are: '(i) continuity; (ii) that the value of total excess demand must equal zero at all positive prices, i.e. that the budget constraint for the economy as a whole be satisfied (Walras' law); and (iii) the excess demand is homogeneous of degree zero (only relative prices count)' (Kirman, 1992: 122).[30] A Walrasian economy can exhibit any aggregate excess demand curve that satisfies these three requirements (Appendix 6.F states the SMD theorem).

The SMD theorem can be traced to the analysis of the subjective expected utility theory in Chapter 2. The theory, as seen, is a method for solving a decision problem. Almost any observed behaviour can be rationalized by re-specifying the problem the agent is trying to solve. Substantive implications attributed to the theory originate from the exogenous assumptions introduced to specify the agent's model of his or her choice situation and definition of the decision problem. The assumption that consumers (or firms) are subjective expected utility maximizers imposes little restriction on behaviour. The other assumption in the Walrasian theory, possibly restricting behaviour, is the market-clearing condition. Yet, as explained in Chapter 2, when expectations of endogenous variables are involved, which is almost always the case in economics, the condition falls short of pinning down any particular behaviour. Infinitely many price vectors usually clear the market.

Also, in the presence of behavioural heterogeneity, aggregate functions can take unlimited forms, regardless of the form of the individual functions. It is therefore never possible to derive the relations emerging in an economy from the assumptions of the Walrasian theory, which entirely overlooks heterogeneities, and pays no attention to how people model their choice situations, define their decision problems, and interact with each other (Kirman, 1989: 128). The issue, again, is not whether the Walrasian assumptions are true. The problem is that, even if they were true, they would not be adequate to fix aggregate regularities. It is wrong to think that 'significant results could be obtained by starting from very general hypotheses about the behaviour of economic agents' (Ingrao and Israel, 1990: 316).

The Walrasian theory also provides no explanation of who sets the equilibrium prices. It simply assumes that the economy is in equilibrium, suggesting that prices are exogenous to the economy. Moreover, by supposing that all business plans are costlessly enforced, the theory rules out the existence of transaction costs, and, hence, money, which is a means for facilitating the coordination of the entire economy, finds no room in the theory (Debreu, 1959). Finally, by supposing that prices convey all information relevant for making decisions, and thus ruling out any direct interaction among market participants, the theory excludes the possibility of coordination failures. As a result, it fails to make room for central macroeconomic phenomena that arise from the inability of market participants in a decentralized economy to coordinate their actions. An understanding of the process of price formation, market crashes, depressions, convergence to equilibrium, the role of money and economic institutions calls for questioning the Walrasian view and allowing direct interaction into economic models.

6.4.2 Non-market interactions

Attempts at modelling economic phenomena not explainable within the Walrasian setting have given rise to a view of the economy as a society of *directly* interacting heterogeneous individuals. This change of view has in turn led to the development of formal models of the economy that allow for the state of each person (i.e. strategies, preferences, and expectations) to depend on the states (i.e. strategies, preferences, and expectations) of other participants in the economy (Glaeser and Scheinkman, 2001). These models are still simple, and based on competing assumptions. They can nevertheless serve us to explain some basic lessons about the relation between the individual and aggregate levels in an economy of interactive heterogeneous individuals. For simplicity, we use the modelling approach provided by game theory, which views the economy as a many-person game or as a collection of interdependent teams. Specifically, we consider the stag hunt production (or coordination) game, studied in Bryant (1994), Cooper (1999) and Tesfatsion (2003).[31]

Consider an economy of N agents indexed $i = 1, 2, \ldots, N$, who live on N separate locations. Each agent is endowed with L units of leisure and likes to consume two goods, leisure C_1 and bread C_2. Each agent has a strictly increasing and concave differentiable utility function $u(C_1, C_2)$. The agents work to produce grains, and grains are carried out to a location to produce bread. N different types of grains are needed to produce bread, each produced by a different individual. Also, one unit of leisure produces one unit of grain, and one unit of bread is produced by N units of grain – one unit for each type of grain. Bread production follows the relation:

$$Q(g_1, \ldots, g_N) = N.\min\{g_1, \ldots, g_N\} \tag{6.44}$$

where g_i is the amount of grain produced by the ith agent, and a surplus of any of the grains is discarded as waste. The bread is *equally* distributed among all individuals:

$$\frac{Q(g_1, \ldots, g_N)}{N} = \min\{g_1, \ldots, g_N\} \tag{6.45}$$

Each agent knows the common leisure endowment L, the common utility function $u(C_1, C_2)$, the production function (6.44), and the distribution rule (6.45). He also knows that everyone is rational, that everyone knows that everyone is rational, and that everyone knows that everyone knows the structure of the game, and so forth.

Each individual decides how many hours of leisure to sacrifice for producing grain. A player's optimal decision depends on other players' strategies or, more precisely, on what she thinks of other players' strategies. Let e_i be the effort made by agent i to produce grain g_i, and $\bar{e}$ be the vector of all other agents' efforts. Output g_i, then, depends on $\bar{e}$, i.e., $g_i = f(e_i, \bar{e})$. Let $\Pi(e_i, e)$ denote the pay-off of agent i from action e_i when other agents take action e and $\hat{e}_i(\bar{e})$ denote the optimal response of agent i when other agents take action e. Since any effort made by agent i above the minimum effort made by some other agent j is wasted, if other agents are choosing action e, it is in the interest of agent i to select e. That is, $\hat{e}_i(e) = e$. Also, suppose the more leisure is sacrificed the less pleasant it is but if all individuals equally sacrifice leisure to produce grain, the additional output produced by the increased effort more than compensates for the added pain of the sacrifice. This means all individuals are better off if all exert the maximum effort possible. The game, then, has a continuum of (symmetric) Nash equilibria defined by

$$\mathbf{S} = \{e \in [0, L] | \Pi_1(e, e) = 0\} \tag{6.46}$$

where the subscript in Π_1 denotes a partial derivative. $\boldsymbol{S}$ includes an optimal equilibrium corresponding to the case when everyone devotes maximal effort level to production. Let s^* denote the optimal equilibrium. The continuum of Nash equilibria in $\boldsymbol{S}$ is Pareto ranked as

$$0 \leq s \leq s^* \tag{6.47}$$

Any Nash equilibrium s below s^* is a *coordination failure*, representing a situation where 'mutual gains, potentially attainable from a feasible all-around change in agent behaviour (strategies) are not realised because no *individual* agent has an incentive to deviate from his [*sic*] current behaviour.'[32] This is in sharp contrast to general equilibrium models where all possible equilibria are efficient.[33]

While this model abstracts away complexities of the real world, it successfully captures the important notion of strategic uncertainty (i.e. uncertainty about expectations and strategies of others), which can lead to coordination failures. The model thereby offers a general framework for thinking about many subjects central to economics. To see how, for example, a recession may occur, suppose there is a fall in the money supply. In that case, firms need to cut their prices to maximize their profit. But each firm's profit depends not only on its pricing decision but also on the decisions made by other firms. If no firm cuts its price, the amount of real money is low, a recession ensues, and the firm makes a low profit. If all firms cut their prices, real money balances are high, a recession is avoided, and each firm makes a high profit. Although all firms prefer to avoid a recession, none can do by its own action. Whether a firm cuts its price or not may depend on its expectations of other firms' decisions. If every firm expects other firms to cut their price, it cuts its price. If every firm expects other firms to keep their price, it may not cut its price, and a recession may follow – a typical coordination failure (Mankiw, 1993). Similar considerations play a vital part in explaining business cycles, involuntary unemployment, stock market crashes, and even financial institutions. Any theory aiming to deal with these phenomena should view the economy as an interactive system, place strategic uncertainty at the centre of its analysis, and exploit the notion of coordination failure (Bryant, 1996).

The production game allows investigating two general aggregation issues arising in any interactive economy. The first relates to the existence of a production function $Q = G(\mathrm{L})$ that maps aggregate leisure $\boldsymbol{L}$ to aggregate production Q such that $G(\mathrm{L}) = N.\min\{g_i, \ldots, g_N\}$. The second relates to the connection between the aggregate production function and the micro-production functions $g_i = f(e_i, \bar{e})$.

As for the first query, an important thing to note is that the game has many solutions. Even when the players' beliefs are consistent with each other, and the structure of the game is common knowledge, there is a continuum of Nash equilibria, each giving rise to a different output. This means aggregate output is not *solely* a function of aggregate inputs in the economy – here, total leisure. Depending on what everyone thinks of everyone else's strategy, almost any aggregate output is possible. There is therefore no function $G(\mathbf{L})$ that correctly predicts aggregate output Q from aggregate input $\boldsymbol{L}$. If there is an aggregate production function, the function should contain variables referring to equilibrium conditions, or more generally, the interdependencies among the players in the game. Now if we agree that strategic uncertainty is a central feature of modern societies, a similar conclusion also applies to the economy. The prevalence of strategic uncertainty, and hence multiple equilibria, call into question the existence of aggregate production functions that correctly predict aggregate output from physical and human factors of production in the economy (Bryant, 1996: 168). An aggregate production function describing an economy, if one exists at all, certainly contains variables representing the level of coordination in the economy.

The point just raised about the aggregate production function first appeared in a criticism of Klein's treatment of the aggregation problem. Klein argued that

> there are certain equations in microeconomics that are independent of the equilibrium conditions and we should expect the corresponding equations of macroeconomics will also be independent of the equilibrium conditions. The principal equations that have this independence property... are the technological production functions. The aggregate production function should not depend upon profit maximisation, but purely on technological factors. (1946b: 303)

He therefore rejected using the entire micro-model with the profit maximization assumption to derive the production function of the economy. May (1947) rightly criticized Klein's position by arguing that even the production function of a firm results from a decision-making process, and is not solely a technical relationship. Nor is there any global decision maker who allocates resources optimally in the economy. For these reasons, aggregate production functions are also entirely fictitious:

> The aggregate production function is dependent on all the functions of the micromodel, including the behaviour equations such as profit-maximisation conditions, as well as upon all exogenous variables and

> parameters. This is the mathematical expression of the fact that the productive possibilities of an economy are dependent not only upon the productive possibilities of the individual firms (reflected in production functions) but on the manner in which these technological possibilities are utilized, as determined by the socio-economic framework (reflected in behaviour equations and institutional parameters). Thus the fact that our aggregate production function is not purely technological corresponds to the social character of aggregate production. (May, 1947: 63)

Led by similar thoughts, Colander (1986) also rejected the conventional aggregate function $Q = f(K, L)$, which takes aggregate output Q to be a function of total labour supply L and total capital K.[34] Instead, he proposed an aggregate function that takes the form $Q = f(K, L, C)$, where C refers to the degree of coordination in the economy. The level of coordination in the economy depends to a large extent on the institutional character of the society. This means aggregate output depends not only on capital, labour, land and other factors of production but also on the society's institutional structure. Two economies may be identical with respect to the production factors but due to their institutional structures generate different levels of outputs. A similar consideration applies to the consumption sector, as what one consumes can depend on what other people consume.

Now, let us return to the question concerning the relation between the aggregate and individual functions in an interactive economy. A necessary condition for deriving an aggregate function from individual functions is that every variable in the function can somehow be defined by aggregating over the individual variables. Variable C, which refers to the level of coordination or perceived interdependencies in the economy, cannot be derived by aggregating over individual variables. The variable is not, in fact, an aggregate. This means the functions describing an interactive system cannot be derived by aggregating over the individual functions. Indeed, to describe individual behaviour in an interactive system, the individual models, as in the stag hunt production game, should contain variables referring to the state of the economy. Thus, to be precise, the individual models are not individualistic; they are of a social character.

As a final point, it may make sense to introduce in the aggregate production function variables such as C that refer to the coordination level of the economy. But it is difficult to envision how such variables can be operationalized. The difficulties in accepting the existence of an aggregate production function and those in operationalizing variables such as C yield strong support for a view of macroeconomics akin to the position set forth in Basmann (1972) and Sims (1980) (Colander, 1996: 66). Sims, as we learnt earlier, regards models of economic aggregates as efficient summaries of data with no clear link to the processes at the individual level.

6.5 Conclusion

Although the representative-agent approach is prevalent in theoretical economic modelling, particularly in economic dynamics, the requirements for the existence of a representative agent are extremely stringent. In fact, they cannot be true of the economy even as remote approximations. More important, representative-agent models lead to fallacious conclusions. Variables such as prices, economic growth, the interest rate, unemployment level and inflation, which should be taken as exogenous in individual models, are determined within the economy. It is thus wrong to apply causal statements implied by individual models to the economy. What is more, representative-agent models consider individual differences as entirely irrelevant. They are not therefore suitable for evaluating economic policies, which usually work by affecting some distributional features of the economy.

An understanding of most large-scale economic phenomena demands thinking of the economy as a society of interactive, heterogeneous individuals. This necessity leads to complications that fundamentally blur the connection between the micro- and macro-levels in the economy. In a society of heterogeneous individuals, aggregate models depend on not only individual models but also the distribution of micro-explanatory variables, such as income and the mechanisms generating them. As a consequence, assumptions about the structure of the economy become an integral part of the aggregate models, and there remains no resemblance between the laws of the individual and the economy. Also, the parameters of the aggregate models depend on the parameters of the processes generating micro-explanatory variables. This makes it inappropriate to ascribe a behavioural interpretation to the models.

Moreover, in the presence of individual heterogeneity, the aggregate model is sensitive to changes in the distributional configuration of the economy, and the mechanisms generating micro-explanatory variables. This means a policy shift, which affects the distributional feature of the economy, can invalidate the true aggregate model. As a result, correctly specified aggregate models are not adequate for policy analysis. Policy analysis requires knowing how a policy will affect the distributional configuration of the economy, and how the distributional change affects the fitted model. Information on the distribution of micro-explanatory variables or the mechanisms generating them is normally hard to obtain. This makes the task of establishing models useful for policy analysis enormously difficult.

The difficulties arising from individual and environmental heterogeneities undermine the aim of deriving a macroeconomic model from individual models alone. Yet, complications arising from direct interaction among market participants are even more detrimental to the microfoundations project. Modelling the behaviour of an individual in an interactive environment requires introducing variables referring to preferences, expectations, and strategies of other decision makers. Such variables cannot be aggregated. More important, the ubiquitous existence of multiple equilibria in models of interactive markets excludes the very existence of a true aggregate 'function' linking explanatory aggregate variables (e.g. capital and labour) to the aggregate dependent variable (e.g. output). If there is a true model of the aggregates, it must involve a variable or variables referring to the interdependencies in the economy. It is, though, difficult to see how such variables could be operationalized. Nor are they aggregate of any micro-variables.

These reflections on the connection between the micro- and macro-levels do not rule out the emergence of regular patterns at the economy level that can be modelled statistically. What they reject is that the emerging patterns are in any simple manner related to the processes at the individual level. The analysis of aggregation issues, particularly those relating to the effects of interaction, supports the view of macroeconomics put forward by econometricians, such as Sims (1980), who regard large-scale economic models as efficient summaries of data, not as representations of a structure.

Finally, the existence of multiple equilibria in models of interactive markets casts doubts on the existence of causal relations among economic aggregates. And so there seems to be no point in applying structural modelling tools to aggregate economic data. There are no causal relations among the aggregates to be discovered.

Finale

'The moral … is this: if you put very little in, you get very little out.' (Sonnenschein, 1973: 405)

This book has studied some general issues at the heart of the theoretical approach to macroeconomics. The issues relate to the possibility of establishing an explanatory and predictive microeconomic theory *and* transforming it into a theory of the economy as a whole using aggregation methods. It is now time to bring together the results of the analysis.

Early in the book, we showed that the proposal that 'homo economicus' behaves like a decision scientist, understood in terms of one or another expected utility theory, contributes very little to the understanding of behavioural matters and hence economic phenomena. The expected utility theories take as given how the agent specifies his choice situation and defines his decision problem. They only state how the agent solves an already well-structured decision problem. But accurate prediction and explanation of behaviour depend critically on how the agent models his choice situation and defines his decision problem than on the *specific* method by which he solves the problem. To predict how an agent models his choice situation, and defines the decision problem, we need a theory which tells us how the agent processes information, models the causal structure of his choice situation, adapts goals, forms preferences, and modifies them as a result of subsequent experiences or information. Without such a theory, there is no prospect for accurately predicting or explaining behaviour in a dynamic and changing environment; we can only rationalize actions *ex post*.

The proposal to model 'homo economicus' as an intuitive econometrician is an intriguing and substantive step towards understanding how the agent models his or her choice situation and modifies it in response to new information. The trouble is that there is no 'tight enough' theory of statistical learning capable of fully, and accurately, explaining the central phases of learning from data – in particular model formulation and re-specification. Reflection on non-parametric inference reveals that there can be no algorithm that receives an ordinarily sized sample and yields the model that, given the data, best approximates the underlying data-generating mechanism. The choice of a model at a deep level requires various subjective judgements. With ordinarily sized samples, even non-parametric learning of an interpretable model of few variables, representing a simple choice situation, is theoretically impossible. In real-life inference situations, learning of an interpretable model of several variables calls for starting with a parametric model.

However, any statistical theory of parametric learning necessarily presupposes a reservoir of models or, more precisely, a reservoir of basic probabilistic assumptions that can be used for creating models. It also requires information on the pre-estimation implications of the models, and methods for exploring their post-estimation consequences. None of these can be explained within a statistical theory of parametric inference. Therefore, within the framework of the intuitive statistician hypothesis, any explanation of how the agent comes to model his or her choice situation is necessarily bound to be incomplete.

Statistical theories of causal inference are also of limited power. Because of the possibility of selection bias, mistaking concomitants for genuine causes, taking barren proxies for real causes, aggregation over heterogeneous units, and so on, the class of explanations possible in general for a statistical dependency or independency is larger than the class of causal explanations. As a result, an essential step in drawing causal inferences from observational data is to first exclude non-causal explanations. Only then do statistical tools become relevant for inferring causal conclusions. Even at this stage, statistical analysis can at best infer a class of statistically indistinguishable models, which in practice usually have little or nothing in common. Selecting a causal model calls for substantive causal background information at every level. However, for the reasons mentioned above, this information cannot come from a theory of statistical learning.

One outcome of this analysis is that the description level at which the econometrician (statistician) works is inappropriate for establishing a predictive model of human learning. To specify how a person processes data, conceptualizes the environment, models the choice situation, defines the decision problem, and learns from experience, it is necessary to work at a far deeper, and more refined, level of description. One, in particular, needs to establish a theory of cognition, object representation, pattern recognition, and even preference formation, as well as a detailed history of the person's experiences (Arthur, 1994). A precise theory of human cognition and decision making may eventually arise. However, because of the level of description the theory is defined for, the theory may not be of much use for economic analysis. The basic problem in establishing a predictive theory of economic behaviour is of mismatched levels – an empirically rich theory of behaviour may require working at a description level useless to economics.

The connection between the individual and aggregate levels is also highly complex. To explain large-scale economic phenomena it is necessary to view the economy as a society of interactive, and heterogeneous, agents. However, the regularities that emerge at the aggregate level in an interactive and heterogeneous economy are not directly related to the laws operating at the micro-level. The regularities are the joint outcome of individual interactions *and* the processes characterizing the physical and institutional environment. In light of this, modelling the emergent regularities requires starting with a great deal of information about the structure of the economy. It is therefore wrong to attribute any purely behavioural interpretation to the regularities. Moreover, due to the ubiquitous existence of multiple equilibria in models of interactions, the relations that emerge among economic aggregates are simply statistical. They are not causal.

These considerations yield strong support to atheoretical macroeconomics. The position views aggregate models as efficient summaries of data with no direct link to behavioural mechanisms driving individual decision makers. The models are useful for short-run *ex post* and *ex ante* predictions. Beyond this, any claim of macroeconomics is fraught with a multitude of uncertain personal decisions concerning the structural model of the economy. In fact, because of the inherent imprecision of aggregate economic data one even has to be cautious about *ex ante* and *ex post* predictions of large-scale economic models.

Appendices

2 Rational behaviour and economic theory

Appendix A: homothetic utility function

A monotone preference relation $\geq$ on a choice set $\mathbf{X} \subseteq \mathbf{R}^L_+$ is called *homothetic* just in case $\mathbf{x} \geq \mathbf{y} \Leftrightarrow \alpha\mathbf{x} \geq \alpha\mathbf{y}$ for all $\alpha > 0$. Homothetic preferences can be represented by a monotonic transformation of a homogeneous of degree 1 utility function. Informally, homothetic preferences mean that the agent always spends a fixed proportion of his or her income on each good.

Appendix B: satisficing

Satisficing is a choice procedure. Following Rubinstein (1998:12), let $\boldsymbol{A}$ be some 'grand' set of options (or the set of all possible options), O an ordering of the set $\boldsymbol{A}$, and $\mathbf{S} \subseteq \mathbf{A}$ the set of satisfactory alternatives. For any choice problem C, satisficing involves sequentially examining the alternatives in $\boldsymbol{A}$ according to the ordering O, until an alternative s is found such that $s \in \mathbf{S}$.

Appendix C: Fair's voting equation

As in the text, let V_{it} be a variable that is equal to one if voter i votes for the Democratic candidate in period t and zero if he votes for the Republican candidate. Also, let

$$\psi_i = \xi_i^r - \xi_i^d \tag{A2.1}$$

$$q_t = \beta_1 \frac{M_{td1}}{(1+\rho)^{t-td1}} + \beta_2 \frac{M_{td2}}{(1+\rho)^{t-td2}} - \beta_3 \frac{M_{td1}}{(1+\rho)^{t-tr1}} - \beta_4 \frac{M_{tr1}}{(1+\rho)^{t-tr2}} \tag{A2.2}$$

The expected utility theory implies that:

$$V_{it} = \begin{cases} 1 & \text{if} \quad q_t > \psi_i \\ 0 & \text{if} \quad q_t < \psi_i \end{cases}$$

which means the voter votes for the Democratic candidate if $\psi_i < q_t$. Now, recall the aggregation assumptions (A5) and (A6), restated here as:

A_5: ψ_i is evenly distributed across voters in each election between some numbers $a + \delta_t$ and $b + \delta_t$, where $a < 0$ and $b > 0$. a and b are constant but δ_t can vary across elections.

A_6: There are an infinite number of voters in each election.

These assumptions imply that ψ is uniformly distributed between $a+\delta_t$ and $b+\delta_t$, where the subscription is now dropped from ψ_i. The probability-density function for ψ , denoted by $f_t(\psi)$ is

$$f_t(\psi) = \begin{cases} \frac{1}{b-a} & \text{for } a+\delta_t < \psi < b+\delta_t \\ 0 & \text{otherwise} \end{cases} \tag{A2.3}$$

and the cumulative distribution function for ψ, denoted as $F_t(\psi)$, is

$$F_t(\psi) = \begin{cases} 0 & \psi < a+\delta_t \\ \frac{\psi-a-\delta_t}{b-a} & a+\delta_t < \psi < b+\delta_t \\ 1 & \psi > b+\delta_t \end{cases} \tag{A2.4}$$

Because of δ_t, the probability density and distribution functions are different for each election. Let V_t denote the percentage of the vote that goes to the Democratic candidate in election t. Since a person votes for the Democrat candidate if $\psi_i < q_t$, the probability that he votes for the Democrat candidate is $p(\psi < q_t)$. The proportion of voters voting for the Democrat candidate in election t is $np(\psi < q_t)/n = p(\psi < q_t)$, which means V_t is equal to the probability that ψ is less than or equal to q_t. Since the probability density function of ψ is given by (A2.3), V_t is equal to $F_t(q_t)$. Using (A2.4), V_t can be stated as

$$V_t = \frac{-a}{b-a} + \frac{q_t}{b-a} - \frac{\delta_t}{b-a} \tag{A2.5}$$

Substituting q_t in (A2.5) yields:

$$\begin{aligned} V_t = \alpha_0 + \beta_1^* \frac{M_{td1}}{(1+\rho)^{t-td1}} + \beta_2^* \frac{M_{td2}}{(1+\rho)^{t-td2}} \\ - \beta_3^* \frac{M_{td1}}{(1+\rho)^{t-tr1}} - \beta_4^* \frac{M_{tr1}}{(1+\rho)^{t-tr2}} + v_t \end{aligned} \tag{A2.6}$$

where

$\alpha_0 = -a/(b-a)$ $\qquad\beta_3^* = \beta_3/(b-a)$

$\beta_1^* = \beta_1/(b-a)$ $\qquad\beta_4^* = \beta_4/(b-a)$

$\beta_2^* = \beta_2/(b-a)$ $\qquad v_t = -\delta_t/(b-a)$

3 'Homo economicus' as an intuitive statisfician (1)

Appendix A: product kernel independence

Notice that although the estimator

$$\hat{f}(x,y) = \frac{1}{Nh^2} \sum_{i=1}^{N} K\left(\frac{x-x_i}{h}\right) K\left(\frac{y-y_i}{h}\right) \tag{A3.1}$$

uses kernel independence, this does not imply that the variables X and Y are independently distributed. If the variables were independent, the kernel estimator would have the form:

$$\hat{f}(x,y) = \left(\frac{1}{Nh_x}\sum_{i=1}^{N} K\left(\frac{x-x_i}{h_x}\right)\right) \times \left(\frac{1}{Nh_y}\sum_{i=1}^{N} K\left(\frac{y-y_i}{h_y}\right)\right) \tag{A3.2}$$

Appendix B: decomposition (Eubank, 1988)

This result is based on a lemma established in Searle (1971, ch. 2) and mentioned in Eubank (1988: 402). Let $\boldsymbol{Z}$ be an $n \times 1$ vector with mean $\mathbf{m}$ and variance-covariance matrix Σ. Suppose W is a symmetric $n \times n$ matrix. Then

$$E(\mathbf{Z}'W\mathbf{Z}) = \mathbf{m}'W\mathbf{m} + tr(W\Sigma) \tag{A3.3}$$

where $tr(W\Sigma)$ is the trace of $W\Sigma$.

Now let $\{(y_i, x_i), \ldots, (y_n, x_n)\}$ be a vector of observations from

$$\mathbf{y} = f(\mathbf{x}) + \varepsilon$$

where $\mathbf{y}$ is the vector of responses, $f(\mathbf{x})$ the vector of unknown means, and ε the vector of zero mean, uncorrelated random errors with common variance σ^2. Further let $\hat{f}_h(\mathbf{x})$ be a linear estimator of $f(\mathbf{x})$. The mean average squared residuals for $\hat{f}_h(\mathbf{x})$ is given by

$$E(ASR(h)) = n^{-1}\sum_{i=1}^{n} E\{y_i - \hat{f}_h(\mathbf{x}_i)\}^2 \tag{A3.4}$$

which can be rewritten as

$$\begin{aligned} E(ASR(h)) &= n^{-1}E(\mathbf{y} - W(h)\mathbf{y})^2 \\ &= n^{-1}E[(\mathbf{y} - W(h)\mathbf{y})(\mathbf{y} - W(h)\mathbf{y})] \\ &= n^{-1}E[\mathbf{y}'(\mathbf{I} - W(h))(\mathbf{I} - W(h))\mathbf{y}] \\ &= n^{-1}E[\mathbf{y}'(\mathbf{I} - W(h))^2\mathbf{y}] \end{aligned} \tag{A3.5}$$

where $W(h)$ is the smoother matrix and $\mathbf{y}$ the vector of responses. Let $\Sigma = \sigma^2\mathbf{I}$, and note that $W(h)$ is symmetric. Applying (A3.3) to (A3.5) yields the result:

$$\begin{aligned} E(ASR(h)) &= n^{-1}f(\mathbf{x})'(\mathbf{I} - W(h))^2 f(\mathbf{x}) + n^{-1}\sigma^2 tr[(\mathbf{I} - W(h))^2] \\ &= n^{-1}f(\mathbf{x})'(\mathbf{I} - W(h))^2 f(\mathbf{x}) + \sigma^2 + n^{-1}\sigma^2 tr[(W(h))^2] \\ &\quad - 2n^{-1}\sigma^2 tr[W(h)] \end{aligned} \tag{A3.6}$$

Now consider applying the technique to average mean prediction error:

$$APE(h) = n^{-1} \sum_{i=1}^{n} E(y_i^* - \hat{f}_h(x_i))^2 \tag{A3.7}$$

which can be restated as

$$\begin{aligned}
&= \sigma^2 + n^{-1} \textstyle\sum_{i=1}^{n} E(f(x_i) - \hat{f}_h(x_i))^2 \\
&= \sigma^2 + n^{-1} E[f(x) - \hat{f}_h(x))'(f(x) - \hat{f}_h(x))] \\
&= \sigma^2 + n^{-1} E[f(x) - W(h)\mathbf{y})'(f(x) - W(h)\mathbf{y})] \\
&= \sigma^2 + n^{-1} E[f(x) - W(h)(f(x) + \varepsilon))'(f(x) - W(h)(f(x) + \varepsilon)] \\
&= \sigma^2 + n^{-1} f(x)(\mathbf{I} - W(h))^2 (f(x) + n^{-1} \sigma^2 tr[(\mathbf{I} - W(h))^2]
\end{aligned} \tag{A3.8}$$

which is the same as equation (3.28) in the text.

Appendix C: bootstrap estimates of prediction error

Without any loss of generality, let $D = \{(x_i, y_i)\}_{i=1}^{N}$ be an IID sample from bivariate distribution π, $\hat{f}$ be an estimate of the regression function f, and $\hat{f}(x_i)$, the predicted value of Y at point x_i.

Let $\Delta = [y_i, \hat{f}(x_i)]$ denote a measure of the distance (error) between the response y_i and prediction $\hat{f}(x_i)$. In regression, $\Delta = [y_i, \hat{f}(x_i)]$ is often chosen to be $[y_i - \hat{f}(x_i)]^2$.

Let denote the prediction error for $\hat{f}$ by

$$Perr(D, f) = E_{\pi}^{*}\{\Delta[y^*, \hat{f}(x^*)]\} \tag{A3.9}$$

where the expectation is taken over a new observation (x^*, y^*) from distribution π. The apparent error rate is

$$Aerr(D, \hat{f}) = \frac{1}{N} \sum_{i=1}^{N} \Delta[y_i, \hat{f}(x_i)] \tag{A3.10}$$

Let $D^b = \{(x_j^b, y_j^b)\}_{j=1}^{N}$ be a bootstrap sample. The simplest bootstrap error estimator generates B bootstrap samples, estimates the model on each, and then applies it to the *original sample* to give B estimates of prediction error:

$$err(D^b, \hat{f}) = \frac{1}{N} \sum_{i=1}^{N} \Delta[y_i, \hat{f}_b(x_i)] \tag{A3.11}$$

In this expression, $\hat{f}_b(x_i)$ is the predicted outcome at x_i based on model $\hat{f}_b$ estimated from bootstrap data set D^b. The overall prediction error estimate is the average of these B estimates:

$$\overline{Perr}_{boot} = \frac{1}{B}\sum_{b=1}^{B}\sum_{i=1}^{N}\Delta[y_i, \hat{f}_b(x_i)]/N \tag{A3.12}$$

$\overline{Perr}_{boot}$ is not a good estimate, since the training and test samples overlap, causing an underestimation of prediction error $Perr(D, \hat{f})$.

A second way to employ the bootstrap technique is to estimate the bias (or optimism) of the apparent error rate $Aerr(D, \hat{f})$ as an estimate of prediction error $Perr(D, \hat{f})$, and obtain an estimate of the error by adding the bias term to $Aerr(D, \hat{f})$. Let us denote the bias by

$$\omega(\hat{f}) = Perr(D, \hat{f}) - Aerr(D, \hat{f}) \tag{A3.13}$$

The bootstrap estimate of $\omega(\hat{f})$ is given by

$$\hat{\omega}(\hat{f}) = \frac{1}{B.N}\left\{\sum_{b=1}^{B}\sum_{i=1}^{N}\Delta\left[y_i, \hat{f}_b(x_i)\right] - \sum_{b=1}^{B}\sum_{i=1}^{N}\Delta\left[y_{bi}, \hat{f}_b(x_{bi})\right]\right\} \tag{A3.14}$$

An alternative bootstrap estimate of the prediction error is then given by

$$\overline{Perr}_{boot2}(D, \hat{f}) = Aerr(D, \hat{f}) + \hat{\omega}(\hat{f}) \tag{A3.15}$$

For each data point (x_i, y_i) the bootstrap samples can be divided into those that contain (x_i, y_i) and those that do not. The prediction error for (x_i, y_i) will likely be smaller for a bootstrap sample containing it. It can be shown that the percentage of points belonging to both the original sample and the bootstrap sample is approximately 63.2%. A possible way to construct a better error estimator is to take as test samples only those data points that are not in D^b. That is

$$\overline{Perr}_{boot3}(D, \hat{f}) = \frac{1}{N}\sum_{i=1}^{N}\frac{1}{B_i}\sum_{i\in I_i}\Delta[y_i - \hat{f}(x_i)] \tag{A3.16}$$

where I_i is the set of indices of the bootstrap sample D^b that do not contain (x_i, y_i), and B_i is the number of such bootstrap samples. Since the samples used to obtain $\overline{Perr}_{boot3}$ have no common elements with the test samples, they are likely to give rise to a pessimistic estimate of the error. In contrast, 63.2% of the bootstrap samples contain (x_i, y_i). These samples are likely to lead to an optimistic estimate of the error. The 0.632 bootstrap estimator is defined by the weighted average of the apparent error estimate $Aerr(D, \hat{f})$ and the error estimate $\overline{Perr}_{boot3}$:

$$\overline{Perr}_{.632} = 0.368 \times Aerr(D, \hat{f}) + 0.632 \times \overline{Perr}_{boot3} \tag{A3.17}$$

4 'Homo economicus' as an intuitive statistician (2)

Appendix A: Lindley's paradox

Lindley's paradox shows a disagreement between sampling theory and Bayesian methods, first noted by Jeffreys (1961 [1939]). The paradox illustrates that a 'sharp null hypothesis may be strongly rejected by a standard sampling ... theory test of significance and yet be awarded a high odds by a Bayesian analysis based on a small prior probability for the null hypothesis and a diffuse distribution of one's remaining probability over the alternatives' (Shafer, 1998: 2257). As an illustration, following Bernardo and Smith (1994: 394), suppose for data $D = \{x_1, \ldots, x_n\}$ the set of candidate models are M_1 and M_2. The models correspond to the simple and composite hypotheses about θ in $N(x_i \mid \theta, \phi)$:

$$M_1: \quad p_1(D) = \prod_{i=1}^{n} N(x_i \mid \theta_0, \phi), \quad \theta_0, \phi \text{ known;}$$

$$M_2: \quad p_2(D) = \int \prod_{i=1}^{n} N(x_i \mid \theta, \phi) N(\theta | \varphi, \eta) d\theta, \quad \phi, \varphi, \eta \text{ known.}$$

Here, ϕ is taken to be precision, defined as $1/\sigma^2$. Since $\bar{x} = N^{-1} \sum_{i=1}^{N} x_i$ under both models is a sufficient statistic, the Bayes factor in favour of M_1 against M_2 is given by

$$B_{12} = \frac{N(\bar{x} \mid \theta_0, n\phi)}{\int N(\bar{x} \mid \theta, n\phi) N(\theta \mid \varphi, \eta) d\theta}$$

$$= \left(\frac{\eta + n\phi}{\eta}\right)^{1/2} \frac{\exp\left\{2^{-1}(\eta^{-1} + (n\phi)^{-1})^{-1}(\bar{x} - \varphi)^2\right\}}{\exp\left\{2^{-1} n\phi(\bar{x} - \theta_0)^2\right\}}$$

For any fixed sample D, $B_{12} \to \infty$ as the prior precision η in M_2 approaches zero. This drives the posterior probability $p(M_1 \mid D)$ towards unity, regardless of the data. In many cases, however, the null hypothesis is rejected by the sampling significance tests. See Lee (1997: 128) for an example.

The general lesson learnt from the paradox is that, in any Bayesian model comparison, the Bayes factor can depend on the prior distributions specified for the parameters of each model (Bernardo and Smith, 1994: 394), and the effect of the priors on the Bayes factor remains even when the sample size grows (Kass, 1993: 555).

Appendix B: Bayesian normal/chi-squared model

Following Lee (1997: 65–71), consider the case where we have a set of observations $D = \{x_1, \ldots, x_n\}$ thought to come from distribution $N(\theta, \phi)$, with θ

and ϕ both unknown. So,

$$p(x/\theta,\phi) = (2\pi\phi)^{-1/2} \exp\left\{-\frac{(x-\theta)^2}{2\phi}\right\} \tag{A4.1}$$

The likelihood function is given by

$$\ell(\theta,\phi/x) \propto p(x/\theta,\phi) \propto \phi^{-n/2} \exp\left\{-\frac{\sum(x_i-\theta)^2}{2\phi}\right\}$$

$$= \phi^{-n/2} \exp\left[-\frac{\left\{\sum(x_i-\bar{x})^2 + n(\bar{x}-\theta)^2\right\}}{2\phi}\right]$$

$$= \phi^{-n/2} \exp\left[-\frac{\{S + n(\bar{x}-\theta)^2\}}{2\phi}\right] \tag{A4.2}$$

where

$$S = \sum(x_i - \bar{x})^2 \tag{A4.3}$$

The conjugate prior distribution of ϕ is (a multiple of) an inverse chi-squared on ν_0 degrees of freedom. That is

$$p(\phi) \propto \phi^{-\nu_0/2-1} \exp(-S_0/2\phi) \tag{A4.4}$$

The conjugate prior distribution of θ conditional on ϕ is normal with mean θ_0 and variance ϕ/n_0. Then

$$p(\theta/\phi) = (2\pi\phi/n_0)^{-1/2} \exp\left\{-\frac{(\theta-\theta_0)^2}{2(\phi/n_0)}\right\} \tag{A4.5}$$

The joint prior distribution is thus a normal /chi-squared distribution with density function:

$$p(\theta,\phi) = p(\phi)p(\theta/\phi) \propto \phi^{-(\nu_0+1)/2-1} \exp\left[-\frac{1}{2}\{S_0 + n_0(\theta-\theta_0)^2\}/\phi\right]$$

$$= \phi^{-(\nu_0+1)/2-1} \exp\left\{-\frac{1}{2}\{Q_0(\theta)/\phi\right\} \tag{A4.6}$$

where

$$Q_0(\theta) = n_0\theta^2 - 2(n_0\theta_0)\theta + (n_0\theta_0^2 + S_0) \tag{A4.7}$$

The posterior is

$$p(\theta,\phi/D) \propto p(\theta,\phi)\ell(\theta,\phi/D)$$
$$\propto \phi^{-(\nu_0+n+1)/2-1} \times \exp\left[-\frac{1}{2}\{(S_0+S)+n_0(\theta-\theta_0)^2+n(\theta-\bar{x})^2\}/\phi\right]$$
$$= \phi^{-(\nu_1+1)/2-1} \times \exp\left\{-\frac{1}{2}\{Q_1(\theta)/\phi\}\right\} \quad \text{(A4.8)}$$

where

$$\nu_1 = \nu_0 + n \quad \text{(A4.9)}$$

and

$$Q_1(\theta) = (S_0+S)+n_0(\theta-\theta_0)^2+n(\theta-\bar{x})^2$$
$$= (n_0+n)\theta^2 - 2(n_0\theta_0+n\bar{x})\theta + (n_0\theta_0^2+n\bar{x}^2+S_0+S)$$
$$= S_1 + n_1(\theta-\theta_1)^2$$
$$= n_1\theta^2 - 2(n_1\theta_1)\theta + (n_1\theta_1^2+S_1) \quad \text{(A4.10)}$$

where

$$n_1 = n_0 + n;$$
$$\theta_1 = (n_0\theta_0+n\bar{x})/n_1; \text{ and}$$
$$S_1 = S_0+S+n_0\theta_0^2+n\bar{x}^2-n_1\theta_1^2$$
$$= S_0+S+(n_0^{-1}+n^{-1})^{-1}(\theta_0-\bar{x})^2 \quad \text{(A4.11)}$$

The posterior for ϕ is

$$\phi \sim S_1\chi_{\nu_1}^{-2} \quad \text{(A4.12)}$$

and that for θ given ϕ is

$$\theta/\phi \sim N(\theta_1, \phi/n) \quad \text{(A4.13)}$$

5 'Homo economicus' as an intuitive statistician (3)

Appendix A: path analysis principles

We state the proofs of the two principles for the case where there are only three variables X, Y and Z under study. Extension to more general cases is straightforward. Since for the current purpose there is no interest in the first moments, each variable is expressed as a deviation from its mean.

Proof of the first principle:
Let

$$X = u_x$$
$$Z = \alpha_{xz}X + u_z \tag{A5.1}$$
$$Y = \alpha_{yz}Z + u_y$$

Assumption (i): u_x, u_z, and u_y are uncorrelated.
Assumption (ii): u_z and X, and u_y and Y are uncorrelated.

Given these assumptions, the objective is to establish that $\rho_{xy.z} = 0$. Multiply both sides of the equation for Z with X. Taking expectations of both sides of the equation gives

$$E(XZ)/E(X^2) = \rho_{xz} = \alpha_{xz} \tag{A5.2}$$

Also multiply both sides of the equation for Y with Z. Taking expectations of both sides of the equation yields

$$E(YZ)/E(Z^2) = \rho_{yz} = \alpha_{yz} \tag{A5.3}$$

Multiplying both sides of the equation for Y with X and taking expectations of both sides of the equation leads to

$$E(YZ)/E(X^2) = \rho_{xy} = \alpha_{xz}\alpha_{yz} \tag{A5.4}$$

Therefore

$$\rho_{xy} = \rho_{xz}\rho_{yz}$$

Finally, recall the expression for partial correlation:

$$\rho_{xy.z} = (\rho_{xy} - \rho_{xz}\rho_{yz})/(1 - \rho_{xz}^2)^{1/2}(1 - \sigma_{yz}^2)^{1/2} \tag{A5.5}$$

Since the numerator is zero (because $\rho_{xy} = \rho_{xz}\rho_{yz}$), $\rho_{xy.z} = 0$.

The proof for the second principle is similar. We replace (A5.1) with

$$Z = u_z$$
$$X = \alpha_{xz}Z + u_x \tag{A5.6}$$
$$Y = \alpha_{yz}Z + u_y$$

and compute ρ_{xz}, ρ_{yz}, and ρ_{xy}.

Appendix B: the conditional independence properties

Some of the properties of conditional independence, studied by Dawid (1979), include:

(1) *Symmetry*: $(X \perp Y/Z) \Rightarrow (Y \perp X/Z)$;
(2) *Decomposition*: $(X \perp YW/Z) \Rightarrow (X \perp Y/Z)$;
(3) *Weak union*: $(X \perp YW/Z) \Rightarrow (X \perp Y/ZW)$;
(4) *Contraction*: $(X \perp Y/Z) \& (X \perp W/ZY) \Rightarrow (X \perp YW/Z)$;
(5) Intersection: $(X \perp W/ZY) \& (X \perp WY/ZW) \Rightarrow (X \perp YW/Z)$.

For a detailed discussion of these properties see Pearl (1988: 82–3).

Appendix C: The common cause principle

Consider a DAG G true of variables $\mathbf{V} = \{X_1, \ldots, X_n\}$. Define X_c as a common cause of X_a and X_b in $\boldsymbol{V}$ just in case there is a directed path from X_c to X_a and a directed path from X_c to X_b. Let $\mathbf{C}$ denote the set of common causes of X_a and X_b in the $\boldsymbol{V}$ (the proof to follow is based on Arntzenius, 1999).

> **Claim**: Suppose X_a and X_b are conditionalized on $\mathbf{C}$. If X_a is not a cause of X_b and X_b is not a cause of X_a, then every path between X_a and X_b in G is d-separated (inactive or blocked).

For any path P between X_a and X_b, either (i) P departs from X_a (i.e. is out of X_a) or (ii) it arrives at X_a (i.e. is into X_a).

Case (i): Suppose P is a path out of X_a. Since X_a is not a cause of X_b, the path cannot be a directed path, and therefore along the way to X_b it must reach a collider X_d. Since neither X_d nor any of its descendent is in $\boldsymbol{C}$, X_d blocks (d-separates) the path between X_a and X_b.

Case (ii): Suppose P is a path into X_a. Since X_b is not a cause of X_a, the path cannot be a directed path, and therefore somewhere along the way it must change direction. Starting from X_a and moving along the path towards X_b, there are two general possibilities:

(a): P changes direction at a variable X_c from which there is a directed path into X_b. In that case, X_c is a common cause of X_a and X_b and in $\boldsymbol{C}$, d-separating the path between X_a and X_b.

(b): Suppose the path from X_c to X_b is not a directed path. In that case, it must contain a collider X_d, as in Figure A5.1

Figure A5.1

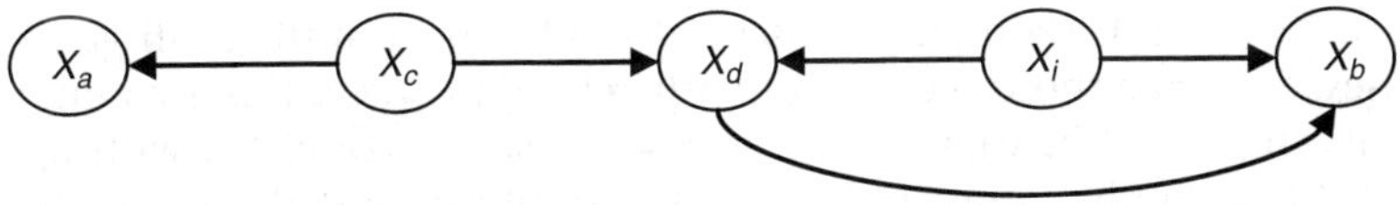

Figure A5.2

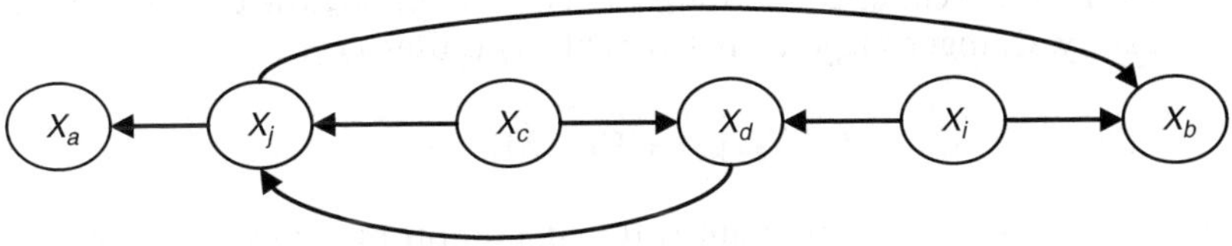

Figure A5.3

To take up this possibility, it is enough to concentrate on path P* between X_d and X_b. As before, these paths can be of two types. Either they are into X_d or they are out of X_d.

For any path P* that is into X_d, the whole path between X_a and X_b, created by joining the sub-paths between X_a and X_d, and X_d and X_b, is inactive, as neither X_d is in $\mathbf{C}$ nor a descendant of it.

For any path P* between X_d and X_b which is out of X_d there are also two possibilities. Either it changes direction at some points between X_d and X_b or it forms a directed path towards X_b. If it forms a directed path and intersects with no node between X_c and X_a as shown in Figure A5.2, node X_c will be a common cause and is included in $\mathbf{C}$. The whole path between X_a and X_b will be *d*-separated.

On the other hand, if the directed path has a common node X_j with the path between X_a and X_c, there will then be a directed path from X_j to X_d. In that case, X_j will be a common cause of X_a and X_b, as shown in Figure A5.3.

Since X_j is in $\mathbf{C}$, the whole path between X_a and X_b, formed by joining the (sub) path from X_a to X_j with the path from X_j to X_b, is *d*-separated. This exhausts all the possibilities that matter, and therefore the desired conclusion.

Appendix D: the use of faithfulness in traditional methods

Variants of the faithfulness condition underlie traditional approaches to causal inference. Suppes (1970) defines an event C^*_t to be a *prima facie* cause of event E_t if and only if (i) t^* refers to a time point prior to t, (ii) C^*_t has positive probability, and (iii) and C^*_t is positively relevant to E_t, that is,

$P(E_t/C_t^*) > P(E_t)$. He then gives several conditions to distinguish genuine causes of E_t from those events spuriously related to E_t. On this account, the events that could be causes of E_t are those that are correlated with it; an event C_t^* cannot be a cause of E_t if it is statistically unrelated with E_t. This is nothing but the faithfulness condition.

As another example, consider Granger's theory of causation (Granger, 1980b). Let Ω_t denote the complete history of the world up to and including discrete time t, excluding deterministic relations among the components of this history. Granger suggests that variable X_t causes Y_{t+1} if

$$P(Y_{t+1} \in A/\Omega_t) \neq P(Y_{t+1} \in A/\Omega_t - X_t)$$

for some set A. He operationalizes this definition by replacing Ω_t with a limited information set I_t that includes information on the history of the variables considered, i.e. $I_t = (X_t, Y_t, Z_t, \ldots)$, and relativizes the definition of causation with respect to I_t. Thus, he takes a confirmation of the hypothesis

$$P(Y_{t+1} \in A/I_t) = P(Y_{t+1} \in A/I_t - X_t)$$

by the data as the evidence that X_t does not causes Y_{t+1}. The inference from the independence of Y_{t+1} and X_t conditional on the information set $I_t - X_t$ to the denial of a causal link from X_t to Y_{t+1} is a special case of faithfulness (Robins, 2003: 89).

Appendix E: the DAG inversion rule

Let G be any DAG containing edge $X \rightarrow Y$, and G^* be a graph the same as G except that edge $X \rightarrow Y$ is replaced with $X \leftarrow Y$. Then, G^* is a DAG equivalent to G if and only if every parent of X is a parent of Y, and every parent of Y, except X, is a parent of Y (Chickering, 1995).

Part I (if part): Suppose G^* is not a DAG (i.e. contains a cycle). Since the only difference between G and G^* is that $X \rightarrow Y$ is replaced with $X \leftarrow Y$, and since G is a DAG, there has to be a directed path from X to a variable Z which is a parent of Y. This means Y has a parent in G which is not a parent of X, contrary to the assumption. So, G^* is a DAG.

Now suppose G and G^* are not equivalent. By theorem 4.1 in the text, either G or G^*contains an unshielded collider that is not present in the other. Since the only difference between G and G^* is that $X \rightarrow Y$ in G^* is replaced with $X \leftarrow Y$, the unshielded collider ought to be formed from $X \leftarrow Y$ and $X \leftarrow Z$, while Z is not a parent of Y. This implies that X in G has a parent that is not a parent of Y, contradicting the assumption. The same argument applies if G contains an unshielded collider that is not in G^*.

Part II (only if): Suppose X has a parent in G that is not a parent of Y. Substituting $X \rightarrow Y$ with $X \leftarrow Y$ creates an unshielded collider in G^*. Alternatively, suppose Y has a parent that is not a parent of X. Substituting $X \rightarrow Y$

with $X \leftarrow Y$ destroys an unshielded collider which is in G. In either case, G and G^* are not equivalent.

Appendix F: the semi-Markovian model equivalence theorem

> **Theorem 4.2**: Let $G(\mathbf{O}, \mathbf{L})$ be a DAG, X and Y in $\boldsymbol{O}$, and edge $X \rightarrow Y$ hold in $G(\mathbf{O}, \mathbf{L})$. Let $G^*(\mathbf{O}, \mathbf{L}^*)$ be the same as $G(\mathbf{O}, \mathbf{L})$ except that $X \rightarrow Y$ is replaced in $G^*(\mathbf{O}, \mathbf{L}^*)$ with bidirected edge $X \leftrightarrow Y$. (i) $G(\mathbf{O}, \mathbf{L})$ and $G^*(\mathbf{O}, \mathbf{L}^*)$ are Markovian-equivalent over $\boldsymbol{O}$ if for every variable Z in $\boldsymbol{O}$ that is a parent of X in G, Z is also a parent of Y. (ii) If $X \leftrightarrow Y$ is in $G(\mathbf{O}, \mathbf{L})$, the bidirected edge can be replaced with $X \rightarrow Y$ when every parent of X in $G^*(\mathbf{O}, \mathbf{L}^*)$ is also a parent of Y.

The proof of this theorem follows from a theorem established in Spirtes and Verma (1992). Several graph-theoretic notions are needed to introduce the theorem:

Inducing path relative to $\boldsymbol{O}$: If $G(\mathbf{O}, \mathbf{L})$ is a DAG over variables $\boldsymbol{V}$, $\boldsymbol{O}$ is a recorded subset of $\boldsymbol{V}$ containing X and Y, where $X \neq Y$, then an undirected path U between X and Y is an inducing path relative to $\boldsymbol{O}$ if and only if every member of $\boldsymbol{O}$ on U except the end points (i.e. X and Y) is a collider on U, and every collider on U is an ancestor of either X or Y.
Inducing path graph over $\boldsymbol{O}$: G^* is an inducing path graph over $\boldsymbol{O}$ for DAG $G(\mathbf{O}, \mathbf{L})$ if and only if there is an edge between variables X and Y with an arrow directed at Y if and only if X and Y are in $\boldsymbol{O}$ and there is an inducing path in $G(\mathbf{O}, \mathbf{L})$ between X and Y relative to $\boldsymbol{O}$ that is into Y.
Partially oriented inducing path graph over $\boldsymbol{O}$: Recall when causal sufficiency is not assumed, the process of inference starts by constructing a skeleton over $\mathbf{O}$. For every pair X and Y in $\mathbf{O}$, it is checked whether X and Y are independent. If so, the edge between them is removed. It is then searched if there is any subset $\boldsymbol{Z}$ of $\mathbf{O}\backslash\{X, Y\}$ such that conditional on $\boldsymbol{Z}$, X and Y are independent. If so, the edge between X and Y is removed. The process is repeated for every pair of variables in $\boldsymbol{O}$. The outcome is an undirected graph. Every endpoint between $X - Y$ admits two possibilities, i.e. '-' and '>'. To make these possibilities explicit, let us represent the undirected edge $X - Y$ between every connected pair X and Y by $Xo - oY$.

Next, we check every triple (X, Y, Z). If there is an edge between X and Y, an edge between Y and Z, and no edge between X and Z, we replace $Xo - oYo - oZ$ with $Xo \rightarrow Y \leftarrow oZ$.

Then, for every $-oYo-$, it is checked if there can be a graph consistent with the data such that both 'o' are replaced with arrows, i.e. $\rightarrow Y \leftarrow$. If no such graph is consistent with the data, $-oYo-$, is replaced with $-o\underline{Y}o-$. The resulting graphical object represents all that can be learnt from the independence data about the underlying causal structure. The graph is referred to as a partially oriented inducing path graph over $\boldsymbol{O}$.

Using these preliminaries, Spirtes and Verma establish the following:

> **Theorem** (Spirtes and Verma, 1992): If G is a DAG over $\boldsymbol{V}$, G^* is a DAG over $\boldsymbol{V}^*$, $\boldsymbol{O}$ is a subset of $\boldsymbol{V}$ and of $\boldsymbol{V}^*$, then G and G^* have the same d-separation relations among the variables in $\boldsymbol{O}$ if and only if they have the same partially oriented inducing path graph over $\boldsymbol{O}$.

Given this theorem, the proof of theorem 4.2 is straightforward:

(i) Suppose $G(\mathbf{O}, \mathbf{L})$ and $G^*(\mathbf{O}, \mathbf{L}^*)$ are defined as in the first part of theorem 4.2 but are not Markovian-equivalent over $\boldsymbol{O}$. By the above theorem, $G^*(\mathbf{O}, \mathbf{L}^*)$ has a partially oriented inducing path graph over $\boldsymbol{O}$ different from that of $G(\mathbf{O}, \mathbf{L})$. This can only happen if in $G(\mathbf{O}, \mathbf{L})$ X has a parent Z in $\boldsymbol{O}$ that is not a parent of Y, and Z and Y are d-separated conditional on X. In that case, $G^*(\mathbf{O}, \mathbf{L}^*)$ includes subgraph $Z \to X \leftarrow L \to Y$ that makes Z and Y dependent conditional on X. But, every parent of X in $\boldsymbol{O}$ is by assumption a parent of Y in $G(\mathbf{O}, \mathbf{L})$. Therefore, both DAGs have the same partially oriented inducing path graph over $\boldsymbol{O}$, and are Markovian-equivalent over $\boldsymbol{O}$.

(ii) Suppose $G(\mathbf{O}, \mathbf{L})$ and $G^*(\mathbf{O}, \mathbf{L}^*)$ are as defined in the second part of the theorem. That is, they just differ in that $X \leftrightarrow Y$ is in $G(\mathbf{O}, \mathbf{L})$ but $X \to Y$ in $G^*(\mathbf{O}, \mathbf{L}^*)$. If $G(\mathbf{O}, \mathbf{L})$ and $G^*(\mathbf{O}, \mathbf{L}^*)$ are not Markovian-equivalent, it follows that $G(\mathbf{O}, \mathbf{L})$ and $G^*(\mathbf{O}, \mathbf{L}^*)$ produce different partially oriented inducing path graphs over $\boldsymbol{O}$. Again, this can only happen if X in $G^*(\mathbf{O}, \mathbf{L}^*)$ has a parent Z in $\boldsymbol{O}$ that is not a parent of Y, and Z and Y conditional on X are independent (d-separated). By assumption, every parent of X in $\boldsymbol{O}$ is also a parent of Y in $G^*(\mathbf{O}, \mathbf{L}^*)$. Both DAGs therefore generate the same partially oriented inducing path graph over $\boldsymbol{O}$ and are Markovian-equivalent over $\boldsymbol{O}$.

In either case, the condition given in the lemma is sufficient for the equivalence of $G(\mathbf{O}, \mathbf{L})$ and $G^*(\mathbf{O}, \mathbf{L}^*)$.

Appendix G: the limited block-recursive theorem

A proof of theorem 4.3 follows from a proposition established in Raykov and Penev (1999: 238–43). We outline the proof to explain how it can be checked whether two models are equivalent. Several technical notions are needed to state the proposition:

Let M_1 and M_2 stand for two models, with parameter spaces Θ and Θ^* respectively. Call $\mathbf{g} : \Theta \to \Theta^*$ a parameter transformation (mapping) if for each $\theta \in \Theta$ there is an $\theta^* \in \Theta^*$ such that θ is mapped into θ^* by g; that is, $\theta^* = \mathbf{g}(\theta)$.

The mapping $\mathbf{g} : \Theta \to \Theta^*$ is called surjective if for each $\theta^* \in \Theta^*$ there exists an $\theta \in \Theta$ such that θ^* is mapped into θ by g. A surjective transformation is an 'onto' mapping. And, M_1 and M_2 are said to satisfy $\sum$-condition if, for all $\theta \in \Theta$, there is a g such that

$$\sum\nolimits_1 (\theta) = \sum\nolimits_2 [\mathbf{g}(\theta)] \tag{A5.7}$$

where $\sum_1 (\theta)$ is the covariance matrix implied by the parameter vector θ for model M_1 and $\sum_2 [\mathbf{g}(\theta)]$ is the derived covariance matrix for model M_2.

Raykov and Penev's proposition (1999: 206) can now be stated as follows:

> **General Model Equivalence Proposition**: Two models M_1 and M_2 are equivalent if and only if they fulfil the $\sum$-condition with a surjective transformation $\mathbf{g} : \Theta \to \Theta^*$ relating their parameters. (Raykov and Penev, 1999: 206)

Informally, two models are equivalent if a transformation of the parameters of one of the models can be found that preserves the model's covariance matrix, and covers the whole parameter space of the other.

The proof of theorem 4.3 involves establishing that there is a transformation g such that: (i) the model before applying the theorem, denoted by M_1, and the model obtained by applying the theorem, denoted by M_2, satisfy the $\sum$-condition; and (ii) g is surjective. To state the proof, some further notations and preliminaries are needed:

1. Notations:

M_1: the model before the replacement of $X \to Y$ with bidirected edge $X \leftrightarrow Y$;
M_2: the model after the replacement of $X \leftrightarrow Y$ for $X \to Y$;
$\mathbf{P} = (P_1, \ldots, P_m)'$: the vector of common explanatory variables (parents) of X and Y;
$\mathbf{Q} = (Q_1, \ldots, Q_n)'$: the vector of additional explanatory variables (parents) of Y $(m, n \geq 0)$.

Every limited block-recursive model can in principle be decomposed into three blocks. They are the *preceding* block, *focal* block, and *succeeding* block. So, M_1 can be decomposed into a preceding block (PB) with variables $\mathbf{V}_p$, a focal block (FB) with $\mathbf{V}_f (\equiv (X, Y))$, and a succeeding block (SB) with $\mathbf{V}_s$. Several assumptions are made about M_1:

(i) The relations across $\mathbf{V}_p$, $\mathbf{V}_f$ and $\mathbf{V}_s$ are recursive.
(ii) The relations within the focal block $\mathbf{V}_f$ are only recursive.
(iii) M_1 is identified.

Thus, M_1 can be stated as

$$\begin{aligned}
\mathbf{V}_p &= \mathbf{A}_{pp}\mathbf{V}_p + \mathbf{E}_p \\
X &= \mathbf{a}'\mathbf{P} + u, \\
Y &= \mathbf{b}'\mathbf{P} + \mathbf{c}'\mathbf{Q} + \lambda X + v \\
&= (\mathbf{b}' + \lambda.\mathbf{a}')\mathbf{P} + \mathbf{c}'\mathbf{Q} + (\lambda u + v), \quad \lambda \neq 0 \\
\mathbf{V}_s &= \mathbf{A}_{ps}\mathbf{V}_p + \mathbf{K}\mathbf{V}_f + \mathbf{L}\mathbf{V}_s + \mathbf{E}_s
\end{aligned} \tag{A5.8}$$

where

- $\mathbf{A}_{pp}$ is a $p \times p$ matrix containing all regression coefficients in the PB;
- $\boldsymbol{a}$ and $\boldsymbol{b}$ are $m \times 1$ vectors containing the partial regression coefficients of X and Y upon the common explanatory variables of X and Y;
- c is an $n \times 1$ vector containing the partial regression coefficients of Y on its additional explanatory variables;
- $\mathbf{A}_{ps}$ is the coefficient matrix relating the SB-variables to the PB variables;
- $\boldsymbol{K}$ contains two columns, representing the coefficients of X and Y, relating the variables in the succeeding block to X and Y;
- $\boldsymbol{L}$ is a coefficient matrix relating the SB-variables to each other; and
- u and v are uncorrelated.

Model M_2, obtained by replacing $X \leftrightarrow Y$ for $X \rightarrow Y$, is defined as

$$\begin{aligned}
\mathbf{V}_p &= \mathbf{A}_{pp}\mathbf{V}_p + \mathbf{E}_p, \\
X &= \mathbf{a}'\mathbf{P} + u, \\
Y &= \mathbf{B}'\mathbf{P} + \mathbf{c}'\mathbf{Q} + w \\
\mathbf{V}_s &= \mathbf{A}_{ps}\mathbf{V}_p + \mathbf{K}\mathbf{V}_f + \mathbf{L}\mathbf{V}_s + \mathbf{E}_s
\end{aligned} \tag{A5.9}$$

u and w are no longer assumed to be uncorrelated. Note that the replacement leaves all the equations except the one for Y unchanged, and in this equation nothing has changed regarding the variables in $\mathbf{Q}$, which do not enter into the equation for X. Before showing that M_1 and M_2 are equivalent, it is useful to state some rules for calculating the required covariance matrices.

2. Simple rules of covariance algebra (Bollen, 1989):

(I) For any random variable X with finite second-order moment,

$$Cov(X, X) = Var(X)$$

(II) For any random variables X, Y, Z and U with finite second-order moments, and any real numbers a, b, c, and d:

$$Cov(aX + bY, cZ + dU) = acCov(X, Z) + adCov(X, U) + bcCov(Y, Z) + bdCov(Y, U)$$

To establish that M_1 and M_2 are equivalent it must be shown that there is a surjective transformation vector function g, mapping every element of Θ onto Θ^*, and it satisfies the $\sum$-condition. The replacement of $X \to Y$ with $X \leftrightarrow Y$ leaves all the elements of the parameter vector θ for M_1 unchanged, except $(b_1, \ldots, b_m)$, λ, and σ_{vv}, where σ_{vv} is the variance of v. One then only needs to find a surjective mapping g for these parameters. For the rest of the elements in θ, the required mappings g are simply identity functions. To define the transformation g for the parameters changed by the replacement, the parameters of M_1 are held as fixed to define the corresponding parameters of M_2 as

$$\begin{aligned} B_1 &= b_1 + \lambda a_1 \\ B_2 &= b_2 + \lambda a_2 \\ &\ldots \\ B_m &= b_m + \lambda a_m \\ \sigma_{uw} &= \lambda \sigma_{uu} \\ \sigma_{ww} &= \lambda^2 \sigma_{uu} + \sigma_{vv} \end{aligned} \tag{A5.10}$$

With g thus defined, it remains to show that M_1 and M_2 satisfy the $\sum$-condition and that g is surjective. For model M_1, let

$\sum_{pp}^1$ the covariance matrix of the preceding block;
$\sum_{ff}^1$ the covariance matrix of the focal block;
$\sum_{ss}^1$ the covariance matrix of the succeeding block;
$\sum_{pf}^1$ the covariance matrix of the variables in preceding and focal block;
$\sum_{ps}^1$ the covariance matrix of the variables in preceding and succeeding block;
$\sum_{fs}^1$ the covariance matrix of the variables in the focal and succeeding block.

Table A5.1 Model 1

	$\mathbf{V}_p$	$\mathbf{V}_f$	$\mathbf{V}_s$
$\mathbf{V}_p$	$\sum_{pp}^{1}(\theta)$		
$\mathbf{V}_f$	$\sum_{fp}^{1}(\theta)$	$\sum_{ff}^{1}(\theta)$	
$\mathbf{V}_s$	$\sum_{sp}^{1}(\theta)$	$\sum_{sf}^{1}(\theta)$	$\sum_{ss}^{1}(\theta)$

The covariance matrix implied by model M_1 for parameter vector θ can be partitioned as in Table A5.1:

Similarly, the covariance matrix implied by model M_2 for $\theta^* = \mathbf{g}(\theta)$ can be partitioned as in Table A5.2:

Table A5.2 Model 2

	$\mathbf{V}_p$	$\mathbf{V}_f$	$\mathbf{V}_s$
$\mathbf{V}_p$	$\sum_{pp}^{2}[\mathbf{g}(\theta)]$		
$\mathbf{V}_f$	$\sum_{fp}^{2}[\mathbf{g}(\theta)]$	$\sum_{ff}^{1}[\mathbf{g}(\theta)]$	
$\mathbf{V}_s$	$\sum_{sp}^{2}[\mathbf{g}(\theta)]$	$\sum_{sf}^{2}[\mathbf{g}(\theta)]$	$\sum_{ss}^{2}[\mathbf{g}(\theta)]$

To establish the $\sum$-condition, it must be shown that

$$\sum\nolimits_{ij}^{1}(\theta) = \sum\nolimits_{ij}^{2}[\mathbf{g}(\theta)], \quad (i, j = s, f, p) \tag{A5.11}$$

The transformation $\mathbf{g} : \Theta \to \Theta^*$, defined by equation (A5.10) leaves $\sum_{pp}^{1}$, $\sum_{ss}^{1}$, $\sum_{fs}^{1}$, and $\sum_{ps}^{1}$ unchanged. For these matrices, equation (A5.11) is trivially true. It remains to show that

(i) $\sum_{ff}^{1}(\theta) = \sum_{ff}^{2}[\mathbf{g}(\theta)]$

(ii) $\sum_{fp}^{1}(\theta) = \sum_{fp}^{2}[\mathbf{g}(\theta)]$

The process of establishing (i) and (ii) is similar. So, we describe the steps in establishing (ii). Let V_{pi} be any variable from the preceding block $\mathbf{V}_p$. Since the equation for X in both models is the same, the covariance of X with V_{pi} remains unchanged by g. To establish (ii), it is therefore enough to show that the covariance of Y with each V_{pi} in $\mathbf{V}_p$ satisfies the $\sum$-condition.

Let $\mathbf{A}_{pp}(i)$ be the row of coefficients in the coefficient matrix $\mathbf{A}_{pp}$ relating V_{pi} to its predictors. Using the covariance rules (I) and (II), for any V_{pi} in $\mathbf{V}_P$

in model M_1 we have

$$Cov(Y, V_{pi}) = \mathbf{A}_{pp}(i)Cov(\mathbf{V}_p, \mathbf{P})(\mathbf{b}' + \lambda.\mathbf{a}') + \mathbf{A}_{pp}(i)Cov(\mathbf{V}_p, \mathbf{Q})\mathbf{c} \qquad \text{(A5.12)}$$

Applying transformation g, defined by (A5.10), to the right-hand side of this equation yields:

$$\mathbf{A}_{pp}(i)Cov(\mathbf{V}_p, \mathbf{P})\mathbf{B} + \mathbf{A}_{pp}(i)Cov(\mathbf{V}_p, \mathbf{Q})\mathbf{c} \qquad \text{(A5.13)}$$

Applying the covariance rules (I) and (II) to model M_2 to compute the covariance of Y with any variable V_{pi} in $\mathbf{V}_P$ yields:

$$\mathbf{A}_{pp}(i)Cov(\mathbf{V}_p, \mathbf{P})\mathbf{B} + \mathbf{A}_{pp}(i)Cov(\mathbf{V}_p, \mathbf{Q})\mathbf{c} \qquad \text{(A5.14)}$$

which is identical with (A5.13). So, condition (ii) holds. A similar reasoning can be used to establish (i). The two models satisfy the $\sum$-condition. It remains to show that g is surjective.

Recall in equation (A5.10), we hold the parameters of M_1 fixed to define the parameters of M_2. To establish the surjectivity of g, the parameters of M_2 are held fixed in order to define the parameters of M_1, which yields:

$$\begin{aligned}
b_1 &= B_1 - (\sigma_{uw}/\sigma_{uu})a_1 \\
b_2 &= B_2 - (\sigma_{uw}/\sigma_{uu})a_2 \\
&\ldots \\
b_m &= B_m - (\sigma_{uw}/\sigma_{uu})a_m \\
\sigma_{vv} &= \sigma_{ww} - (\sigma_{uw}/\sigma_{uu})^2\sigma_{uu} \\
\lambda &= \sigma_{uw}/\sigma_{uu}
\end{aligned} \qquad \text{(A5.15)}$$

The surjectivity of g is established by deriving the covariance $Cov(Y, V_{pi})$ of each variable V_{pi} in $\mathbf{V}_P$ of M_2 using rules (I) and (II), restating the result using equation (A5.15), and checking that the result is the same as the one obtained by applying the rules to M_1 to compute $Cov(Y, V_{pi})$ for each V_{pi} in $\mathbf{V}_P$. This will show that the two models are equivalent.

The proof of the second part of the theorem follows a similar path, with the difference that we start with M_2. To define g, the parameters of M_2 are held fixed and the parameters of M_1 are accordingly derived (as done in (A5.15)). It is then shown that the implied covariance matrices are the same. Raykov and Penev's method is quite general. It can be used for checking the Markovian equivalence of any two structural models.

6 The economy as an interactive system

Appendix A: Clarida's life-cycle model

As in the text, we state the simplest possible case of Clarida's model, which is also discussed in Deaton (1992). The case is built around an economy with

the following features:
Assumption 1: Each worker lives for three periods, working in the first two periods of his or her life and retiring in the third. It is assumed that only one person is born in each period.
Assumption 2: In period t, each person receives an identical amount of labour income Y_t while working, but zero during retirement. Consumption during retirement is financed from assets accumulated during the working periods.
Assumptions 3: Y_t follows a random walk with drift

$$Y_t = g + Y_{t-1} + \varepsilon_t \tag{A6.1}$$

The per capita labour income also follows a random walk:

$$\frac{2Y_t}{3} = \frac{2g}{3} + \frac{2Y_{t-1}}{3} + \frac{2\varepsilon_t}{3}$$

Assumption 4: Interest rate is zero, and each person decides to leave no asset behind.
Assumption 5: Everyone is a pure permanent income life-cycler.

Note that labour income received by each individual does not follow a random walk; by assumption labour income is zero with probability one during retirement. Assuming rational expectations, each individual best forecast of labour income during the next working period is the current labour income plus the cumulative drift, i.e. $g + Y_1$.

Thus, a person who is born in period t consumes $2Y_t + g/3$ during his first working period and $2Y_t + g/3 + \varepsilon_{t+1}/2$ during the second working period and retirement period.

Table A6.1 below shows the individual consumptions during the first five periods of the life of the economy.

Now consider total consumption change between periods 4 and 3:

$$\Delta C_4 = C_4 - C_3 = \frac{2Y_4 + g}{3} + \frac{\varepsilon_4}{2} - \frac{2Y_1 + g}{3} - \frac{\varepsilon_2}{2} \tag{A6.2}$$

Table A6.1

Period 1	Period 2	Period 3	Period 4	Period 5	Period 6
$\frac{2Y_1+g}{3}$	$\frac{2Y_1+g}{3} + \frac{\varepsilon_2}{2}$	$\frac{2Y_1+g}{3} + \frac{\varepsilon_2}{2}$	Dead		
	$\frac{2Y_2+g}{3}$	$\frac{2Y_2+g}{3} + \frac{\varepsilon_3}{2}$	$\frac{2Y_2+g}{3} + \frac{\varepsilon_3}{2}$	Dead	
		$\frac{2Y_3+g}{3}$	$\frac{2Y_3+g}{3} + \frac{\varepsilon_4}{2}$	$\frac{2Y_3+g}{3} + \frac{\varepsilon_4}{2}$	Dead
			$\frac{2Y_4+g}{3}$	$\frac{2Y_4+g}{3} + \frac{\varepsilon_5}{2}$	...

Writing Y_4 in terms of Y_1 yields:

$$Y_4 = 3g + Y_1 + \varepsilon_2 + \varepsilon_3 + \varepsilon_4 \tag{A6.3}$$

Substituting (A6.3) for Y_4 in (A6.2) yields:

$$\Delta C_4 = 2g + \frac{7\varepsilon_4}{6} + \frac{2\varepsilon_3}{3} + \frac{\varepsilon_2}{6} \tag{A6.4}$$

If we consider total consumption change at time t in general, rather than at period 4, total consumption change for the economy is given by

$$\Delta C_t = 2g + \frac{7\varepsilon_t}{6} + \frac{2\varepsilon_{t-1}}{3} + \frac{\varepsilon_{t-2}}{6} \tag{A6.5}$$

which is of the same form as the result stated in the text. Average consumption change follows:

$$\Delta\overline{C}_t = \frac{2}{3}g + \frac{7}{18}\overline{\varepsilon}_t + \frac{2}{9}\overline{\varepsilon}_{t-1} + \frac{\overline{\varepsilon}_{t-2}}{18} \tag{A6.6}$$

Appendix B: Pischke's incomplete information model

The following assumptions define Pischke's economy.

Assumption I: Average income follows a random walk with drift.

Let Y_t stand for average income and g for the drift term. Then, average income is given by

$$Y_t = g + Y_{t-1} + \varepsilon_t \tag{A6.7}$$

Assumption II: Each consumer income is the average income plus an idiosyncratic component that is purely transitory, represented by a white noise:

$$Y_{it} = Y_t + u_{it} \tag{A6.8}$$

The first difference of individual income is given by

$$\begin{aligned}
\Delta Y_{it} &= Y_t + u_{it} - Y_{t-1} - u_{it-1} \\
\Delta Y_{it} &= g + Y_{t-1} + \varepsilon_t + u_{it} - Y_{t-1} - u_{it-1} \\
\Delta Y_{it} &= g + \varepsilon_t + u_{it} - u_{it-1}
\end{aligned} \tag{A6.9}$$

Assumption III: Each person only observes the sum of the contemporaneous macro- and private shocks and cannot separate them. He only estimates the moving average process:

$$\Delta Y_{it} = g + \eta_{it} - \lambda\eta_{it-1} \tag{A6.10}$$

Assumption IV: Every household satisfies the infinite-life permanent income model (Hall's model).

Individual consumption, therefore, follows a random walk:

$$\Delta C_{it} = \left(1 - \frac{\lambda}{1+r}\right)\eta_{it} \tag{A6.11}$$

The change in average consumption C_t is obtained by averaging over (A6.11):

$$\Delta C_t = \left(1 - \frac{\lambda}{1+r}\right)\eta_t \tag{A6.12}$$

Now, since the real first difference of individual income is

$$\Delta Y_{it} = g + \varepsilon_t + u_{it} + u_{it-1}$$

and

$$\Delta Y_t = \sum \Delta Y_{it} + g + \varepsilon_t + \sum u_{it}/N + \sum u_{it-1}/N$$

we have

$$\Delta Y_t = g + \varepsilon_t \tag{A6.13}$$

(because u_{it} is a white noise, $\sum u_{it}/N$ and $\sum u_{it-1}/N$ are equal to zero; in other words, the idiosyncratic components by assumption have zero means over the population).

On the other hand, since the derived first difference of individual income is

$$\Delta Y_{it} = g + \eta_{it} + \lambda\eta_{it-1}$$

and

$$\Delta Y_t = \sum \Delta Y_{it} + g + \sum \eta_{it} + \sum \lambda\eta_{it-1}/N$$

we have

$$\Delta Y_t = g + \eta_t - \lambda\eta_{t-1} \tag{A6.14}$$

From (A6.13) and (A6.14) we have

$$\varepsilon_t = \eta_t - \lambda\eta_{t-1}$$

and

$$\eta_t = \varepsilon_t + \lambda\eta_{t-1} \tag{A6.15}$$

Combining (A6.12) and (A6.15) yields:

$$\Delta C_t = \left(1 - \frac{\lambda}{1+r}\right)(\varepsilon_t + \lambda \eta_{t-1})$$

$$\Delta C_t = \left(1 - \frac{\lambda}{1+r}\right)\varepsilon_t + \left(1 - \frac{\lambda}{1+r}\right)\lambda \eta_{t-1}$$

$$\Delta C_t = \left(1 - \frac{\lambda}{1+r}\right)\lambda \eta_{t-1} + \left(1 - \frac{\lambda}{1+r}\right)\varepsilon_t$$

From (A6.12) we have

$$\Delta C_t = \lambda \Delta C_{t-1} + \left(1 - \frac{\lambda}{1+r}\right)\varepsilon_t$$

which yields the average consumption function as

$$C_t = (\lambda + 1)C_{t-1} - \lambda C_{t-2} + \left(1 + \frac{\lambda}{1+r}\right)\varepsilon_t \tag{A6.16}$$

Appendix C: Lau's theorem (1982)

The individual functions $f_i(X_{it}, \mathbf{A}_{it}, \mathbf{P}_t)$ are of the form:

$$f_i(X_{it}, \mathbf{A}_{it}, \mathbf{P}_t) = f(X_{it}, \mathbf{A}_{it}, \mathbf{P}_t) + k_i(\mathbf{P}_t) \tag{A6.17}$$

only if the index functions $g_l(.)$ are symmetric.

Suppose $g_l(.)$ are not symmetric. In that case, exchanging the income X_{rt} and attributes $\mathbf{A}_{rt}$ of agent r with those of agent s changes the value of $g_l(.)$. Hence

$$\sum f_i(X_{it}, \mathbf{A}_{it}, \mathbf{P}_t) \neq \sum_{i \neq s, i \neq r} f_i(X_{it}, \mathbf{A}_{it}, \mathbf{P}_t) + f_s(X_{rt}, \mathbf{A}_{rt}, \mathbf{P}_t) + f_r(X_{st}, \mathbf{A}_{st}, \mathbf{P}_t) \tag{A6.18}$$

After eliminating the identical terms and reordering, we obtain:

$$f_s(X_{rt}, \mathbf{A}_{rt}, \mathbf{P}_t) - f_r(X_{rt}, \mathbf{A}_{rt}, \mathbf{P}_t) \neq f_r(X_{st}, \mathbf{A}_{st}, \mathbf{P}_t) - f_s(X_{st}, \mathbf{A}_{st}, \mathbf{P}_t) \tag{A6.19}$$

which only holds if the individual functions cannot be stated as (A6.17). Therefore, the index functions $g_l(.)$ must be symmetric for (A6.17) to hold.

Appendix D: aggregation over heterogeneous time series

Suppose that X_{1t} and X_{2t} are a pair of series generated by

$$X_{1t} = \alpha_1 X_{1t-1} + \varepsilon_{1t} \tag{A6.20a}$$

$$X_{2t} = \alpha_2 X_{2t-1} + \varepsilon_{2t} \tag{A6.20b}$$

where ε_{1t} and ε_{2t} are a pair of independent, zero-mean white-noise series. Equation system (A6.20) can be written as

$$(1-\alpha_1 L)X_{1t} = \varepsilon_{1t} \tag{A6.21a}$$

$$(1-\alpha_2 L)X_{2t} = \varepsilon_{2t} \tag{A6.21b}$$

Or

$$X_{1t} = \varepsilon_{1t}/(1-\alpha_1 L) \tag{A6.22a}$$

$$X_{2t} = \varepsilon_{2t}/(1-\alpha_2 L) \tag{A6.22b}$$

The polynomials are usually written as $\alpha_i(L)$ but for the sake of simplicity is written here as $\alpha_i L$. Let $X_t = X_{1t} + X_{2t}$. It follows that

$$(1-\alpha_1 L)X_t = (1-\alpha_1 L)X_{1t} + (1-\alpha_1 L)X_{2t}$$

$$(1-\alpha_2 L)(1-\alpha_1 L)X_t = (1-\alpha_2 L)(1-\alpha_1 L)X_{1t} + (1-\alpha_2 L)(1-\alpha_1 L)X_{2t} \tag{A6.23}$$

Using (A6.22a) and (A6.22b), aggregate equation (A6.23) can be restated as

$$(1-\alpha_2 L)(1-\alpha_1 L)X_t = (1-\alpha_2 L)\varepsilon_{1t} + (1-\alpha_1 L)\varepsilon_{2t} \tag{A6.24}$$

Based on the definition of ε_{1t} and ε_{2t}, the right-hand side of (A6.24) is equivalent to

$$(1-\alpha L)\varepsilon_t = (1-\alpha_2 L)\varepsilon_{1t} + (1-\alpha_1 L)\varepsilon_{2t} \tag{A6.25}$$

Combining (A6.24) and (A6.25) gives the desired result:

$$(1-\alpha_2 L)(1-\alpha_1 L)X_t = (1-\alpha L)\varepsilon_t \tag{A6.26}$$

which is an ARMA (2,1). This exercise is an example of a general theorem proved by Granger and Morris (1976) and Box and Jenkins (1976).

Appendix E: Lippi's simple economy

As in Lippi (1988), we work with the two-consumer economy. Let Y_{it} denote the consumption of the ith agent and X_{it} the income of the ith agent, where $i = 1, 2$. Suppose individual consumptions follow the static rules:

$$\begin{cases} Y_{1t} = \Pi_1 X_{1t} \\ Y_{2t} = \Pi_2 X_{2t} \end{cases} \qquad \Pi_1 \neq \Pi_2 \tag{A6.27}$$

while the process-generating individual incomes are given by

$$\begin{cases} X_{1t} = \alpha_1 X_{1t-1} + v_{1t} \\ X_{2t} = \alpha_2 X_{2t-1} + v_{2t} \end{cases} \qquad \alpha_1 \neq \alpha_2 \tag{A6.28}$$

v_{it} s are white-noise process. Also, for the sake of simplicity, assume that v_{1t} and v_{2t} are independent. Aggregate consumption Y_t and aggregate income X_t are defined as

$$\begin{cases} Y_t = Y_{1t} + Y_{2t} \\ X_t = X_{1t} + X_{2t} \end{cases} \tag{A6.29}$$

The concern is to infer aggregate consumption function $Y_t = f(X_t)$. Equation (A6.28) can be restated as

$$\begin{cases} (1 - \alpha_1 L)X_{1t} = v_{1t} \\ (1 - \alpha_2 L)X_{2t} = v_{2t} \end{cases} \tag{A6.30}$$

where $\alpha_i L$ s are polynomials in the lag operator L and $\alpha_i(0) = 1$. Then

$$\begin{pmatrix} X_{1t} \\ X_{2t} \end{pmatrix} = \begin{pmatrix} \frac{1}{1-\alpha_1 L} & 0 \\ 0 & \frac{1}{1-\alpha_2 L} \end{pmatrix} \begin{pmatrix} v_{1t} \\ v_{2t} \end{pmatrix} \tag{A6.31}$$

From (A6.27) and (A6.29), for vector (Y_t, X_t) we have

$$\begin{pmatrix} Y_t \\ X_t \end{pmatrix} = \begin{pmatrix} \Pi_1 & \Pi_2 \\ 1 & 1 \end{pmatrix} \begin{pmatrix} X_{1t} \\ X_{2t} \end{pmatrix} \tag{A6.32}$$

Combining (A6.31) and (A6.32) yields

$$\begin{pmatrix} Y_t \\ X_t \end{pmatrix} = \begin{pmatrix} \Pi_1 & \Pi_2 \\ 1 & 1 \end{pmatrix} \begin{pmatrix} \frac{1}{1-\alpha_1 L} & 0 \\ 0 & \frac{1}{1-\alpha_2 L} \end{pmatrix} \begin{pmatrix} v_{1t} \\ v_{2t} \end{pmatrix} \tag{A6.33}$$

Represent (A6.33) as

$$\begin{aligned} \begin{pmatrix} Y_t \\ X_t \end{pmatrix} &= \begin{pmatrix} \Pi_1 & \Pi_2 \\ 1 & 1 \end{pmatrix} \begin{pmatrix} \frac{1}{1-\alpha_1 L} & 0 \\ 0 & \frac{1}{1-\alpha_2 L} \end{pmatrix} \\ &\quad \times \begin{pmatrix} \Pi_1 & \Pi_2 \\ 1 & 1 \end{pmatrix}^{-1} \begin{pmatrix} \Pi_1 & \Pi_2 \\ 1 & 1 \end{pmatrix} \begin{pmatrix} v_{1t} \\ v_{2t} \end{pmatrix} \end{aligned} \tag{A6.34}$$

And let

$$\begin{pmatrix} W_{1t} \\ W_{2t} \end{pmatrix} = \begin{pmatrix} \Pi_1 & \Pi_2 \\ 1 & 1 \end{pmatrix} \begin{pmatrix} v_{1t} \\ v_{2t} \end{pmatrix}$$

Like v_{it}, W_{it} are also white-noise processes. Then, we have

$$\begin{pmatrix} Y_t \\ X_t \end{pmatrix} = \begin{pmatrix} \frac{\Pi_1}{1-\alpha_1 L} & \frac{\Pi_2}{1-\alpha_2 L} \\ \frac{1}{1-\alpha_1 L} & \frac{1}{1-\alpha_2 L} \end{pmatrix} \begin{pmatrix} \frac{1}{\Pi_1-\Pi_2} & \frac{-\Pi_2}{\Pi_1-\Pi_2} \\ \frac{-1}{\Pi_1-\Pi_2} & \frac{1}{\Pi_1-\Pi_2} \end{pmatrix} \begin{pmatrix} W_{1t} \\ W_{2t} \end{pmatrix} \tag{A6.35}$$

To simplify matters, let

$$\begin{aligned} A &= (1-\alpha_1 L) \\ B &= (1-\alpha_2 L) \\ C &= \Pi_1 - \Pi_2 \\ E &= ABC. \end{aligned} \tag{A6.36}$$

Equation system (A6.35) can be written as

$$\begin{pmatrix} Y_t \\ X_t \end{pmatrix} = \begin{pmatrix} \frac{\Pi_1 B - \Pi_2 A}{E} & \frac{(A-B)\Pi_1\Pi_2}{E} \\ \frac{B-A}{E} & \frac{A\Pi_1 - B\Pi_2}{E} \end{pmatrix} \begin{pmatrix} W_{1t} \\ W_{2t} \end{pmatrix} \tag{A6.37}$$

Still to simplify further the necessary calculations, let the first matrix on the right-hand side of (A6.37) be rewritten as

$$\begin{pmatrix} F & G \\ H & I \end{pmatrix}$$

and call it M. Multiplying both sides of (A6.37) by the adjoint of M yields:

$$\begin{pmatrix} I & -G \\ -H & F \end{pmatrix} \begin{pmatrix} Y_t \\ X_t \end{pmatrix} = \begin{pmatrix} FI - GH & 0 \\ 0 & FI - GH \end{pmatrix} \begin{pmatrix} W_{1t} \\ W_{2t} \end{pmatrix} \tag{A6.38}$$

From (A6.38) we have

$$\begin{cases} -IY_t - GX_t = (FI - GH)W_{1t} \\ -HY_t + FX_t = (FI - GH)W_{2t} \end{cases} \tag{A6.39}$$

Multiply the second equation in (A6.39) by a scalar k and subtract it from the first one. This yields:

$$(I + kH)Y_t = (G + kF)X_t + (FI - GH)(W_{1t} - kW_{2t}) \tag{A6.40}$$

After substituting the definitions of F, G, H, and I into (A6.40), we need only some elementary algebra to derive the equation:

$$\left(1 - \frac{\Gamma_1\alpha_1 L + \Gamma_2\alpha_2 L}{\Pi_1 - \Pi_2}\right) Y_t = \left(k - \frac{\Gamma_1\Pi_2\alpha_1 L + \Gamma_2\Pi_1\alpha_2 L}{\Pi_1 - \Pi_2}\right) X_t + u_t \tag{A6.41}$$

where

$$\Gamma_1 = \Pi_1 - k$$

$$\Gamma_2 = k - \Pi_2$$

$$u_t = W_{1t} - kW_{2t}$$

$$k = \frac{Cov(W_{1t}, W_{2t})}{Var(W_{2t})} = \frac{Cov(\Pi_{1t}v_{1t} + \Pi_2 v_{2t}, v_{1t} + v_{2t})}{Var(v_{1t} + v_{2t})}$$

The aggregate consumption function of the economy is given by

$$Y_t = \left(\frac{\Gamma_1\alpha_1 L + \Gamma_2\alpha_2 L}{\Pi_1 - \Pi_2}\right) Y_{t-1} + kX_t - \left(\frac{\Gamma_1\Pi_2\alpha_1 L + \Gamma_2\Pi_1\alpha_2 L}{\Pi_1 - \Pi_2}\right) X_{t-1} + u_t \tag{A6.42}$$

Appendix F: the SMD theorem

There are several variants of the SMD theorem available. For a simple statement, consider an exchange economy with a finite number l of goods and N consumers. Define the following notations:

$e(a)$: a positive bundle of initial endowment of all goods for individual a;
$\phi(a, \mathbf{p})$: a demand function for individual a derived from a strictly convex monotone utility function, with $\boldsymbol{P}$ being the price vector;
$Z(a, \mathbf{p}) = \phi(a, \mathbf{p}) - e(a)$: the excess demand for individual a;
$Z(\mathbf{p}) = \sum Z(a, \mathbf{p})$: the aggregate excess demand function of the economy obtained by summing over the excess demands of the N individuals.

For this economy, the SMD theorem reads as follows (Kirman, 1989: 129):

Theorem: Given a continuous function $f : \mathbf{p} \rightarrow R^l$ satisfying Walras' Law, i.e. $\mathbf{p}f(\mathbf{p}) = 0$ for all $\boldsymbol{p}$ in $\boldsymbol{P}$, then for any positive ε there is an economy ε with consumers with strictly convex monotone preferences such that

$$f(\mathbf{p}) = Z_\varepsilon(\mathbf{p}), \quad \text{for all } \boldsymbol{p} \text{ in } \Delta_\varepsilon$$

Here $Z_\varepsilon(.)$ is the excess demand of the economy ε and Δ_ε is the price simplex with prices above ε, i.e.

$$\left\{\mathbf{p} | \textstyle\sum_i p_i = 1 \text{ and } p_i \leq 0 \text{ for all } i\right\}$$

In other words, for any arbitrary function $f : \Delta_\varepsilon \rightarrow R^l$ satisfying the Walras Law, there is an economy with N consumers with strictly convex monotone preferences whose excess demand function for prices in Δ_ε coincides with the arbitrary function. Thus the aggregate excess demand function of an economy of N consumers with strictly convex monotone preferences can be any arbitrary continuous function satisfying the Walras Law. The standard restrictions on preferences do not restrict the class of functions to which the excess demand function belongs.

Notes

1 Theoretical versus Atheoretical Macroeconomics

1. The following view of the economy is borrowed from Granger (1990b).
2. See Janssen (1993: ch. 1) for various notions of macroeconomics.
3. For the history of the Cowles Commission Foundation see Darnell and Evans (1990), and Epstein (1987).
4. We adopt the usual convention of denoting random variables by upper-case letters, and their values by the corresponding lower-case letters. Likewise, we denote random vectors by bold upper-case letters and their values by the corresponding bold lower-case letters.
5. See Hurwicz (1962) for the connection between causal and structural relations.
6. A necessary requirement for this exercise is that ε_1 be independent of P, ε_2 independent of Q, and ε_1 independent of ε_2.
7. For further discussion see Goldberger (1992), Pearl (2000), and Woodward (2003).
8. The description to follow draws on Lucas (1976) and Cooley and LeRoy (1984).
9. Z_t may be the same as Y_t.
10. Fair (1987: 271) defines various notions of predictions.
11. This is true if no other sufficient set of causes is present.
12. See Cartwright (1989) for a full discussion.
13. Woodward (2003) and Pearl (2000) argue that the orthogonality condition is neither necessary nor sufficient for the causal interpretation of a regression equation.
14. The ordinary least squares regression coefficient of X is given by $E(YX)/E(XX)$. If we define β as equal to $E(YX)/E(XX)$, we have

$$\varepsilon = Y - \beta X$$

$$X\varepsilon = XY - \beta(XX)$$

$$E(X\varepsilon) = E(YX) - \beta E(XX) = 0$$

15. This example is borrowed with some changes from Spirtes *et al.* (1998).
16. The phrase inside the bracket is added.
17. See Koopmans (1971 [1949]: 169) for an example.
18. A thorough analysis of the identification problem is given in Manski (1995).
19. A similar view regarding the obviousness of the laws of economic behaviour is explicit in Mill's *Principles of Political Economy*, where he writes, 'Happily, there is nothing in the laws of Value which remains for the present writer or any future writer to clear up; the theory of the subject is complete' (1990 [1848]:420).
20. Italics are added. See also the same article, footnote 11.
21. For a history of atheoretical macroeconomics see Simkins (1999).
22. Cartwright (1989), Epstein (1987) and Leamer (1985) suggest a similar interpretation.
23. Similar remarks are found in Sims (1996: 113).
24. Before Sims, Liu (1960) had argued that no variable could be regarded as exogenous in macroeconomics.

25. This follows from the assumption that the present does not influence the past, and the fact that all the variables on the right-hand side of (1.15) are lagged except for u_t.
26. A Wold causal chain is a system of equations in which the shock to Y_1 contemporaneously affects $Y_2, Y_3, \ldots, Y_n$ while the shock to Y_2 contemporaneously affects $Y_3, Y_4, \ldots, Y_n$ but influences Y_1 with a lag, and so on.
27. Swanson and Granger's approach has been extended by Demiralp and Hoover (2003).
28. In (1.17), each error, except for m_t, is a linear function of the innovation terms appearing earlier in the model and a stochastic component.
29. See Hoover (2001: ch. 5) for a discussion of Hayek's position.

2 Rational Behaviour and Economic Theory

1. See Sen (1987) for different notions of behavioural rationality, and historical references.
2. For a discussion of Savage's theory see Fishburn (1970: ch. 14) and (1981).
3. 'iff' stands for 'if and only if'.
4. Savage favours the normative interpretation (1972 [1954]: 20).
5. A similar classification is found in Lane *et al.* (1996).
6. Kreps (1988) offers a thorough review of rational choice theories.
7. A principle of economic thinking is that opportunity costs and out-of-pocket costs should be treated alike. This implies that preferences should depend on only relevant differences between options, not on how they are represented.
8. This is not to deny conditional restrictions that Savage's postulates impose on observed behaviour, such as those tested in Allais' paradox (Allais, 1953).
9. Simon (1986) and Conslik (1996) also mention this example. Another example, relating to Becker's work on the marriage market, is given in Lam (1988).
10. Our account of Becker's work is based on Goldberger (1989).
11. For a definition of homotheticity see Appendix 2.A.
12. See Appendix 2.B for a definition of satisficing.
13. For simplicity, the case when the voter is indifferent is not considered here.
14. t is a time trend that takes, for instance, a value 8 in 1916, 9 in 1920, and so on.
15. ψ_i is voter's 'expected utility bias' in favour of the Republican candidate; it is voter i's expected utility difference between the Republican and Democratic parties before any consideration is given to their past performances.
16. The key assumption is that this difference differs across voters in a uniform way (Fair, 1987: 162).
17. The RE hypothesis and subjective expected utility can be reconciled through de Finetti's (1937) exchangeability result. Suppose there are repeated trials of some random process; and that individuals are indifferent between receiving a dollar conditional on some sequence of outcomes and receiving a dollar conditional on any other sequence of outcomes of each type; if there exist limiting frequencies of different types of outcomes, and individuals put strictly positive probability on the truth, then each individual's conditional beliefs converge to these limiting relative frequencies (Morris, 1995: 232–3).
18. Agents in a multi-agent economy is said to have *perfect foresight* if the following two conditions hold: (a) people's beliefs are correct; and (b) there are no exogenous shock terms impinging on the economy, so that all expectations are correct without error, i.e. $(E_t(V_{t+k}) = V_{t+k})$.

19. This method is known as the method of undetermined coefficients. See Pesaran (1987: 80–81) for alternative methods.
20. The equilibrium price is now $p_t = (e_1 - \alpha e_2)^{-1} M_t + (e_1/e_2)^t c$.
21. Economists have introduced extra principles to select a unique equilibrium. A proposal is due to MacCallum (1983: 144) that blocks introduction of 'extraneous' terms such as c. Such suggestions are inadequate. They also lack a behavioural justification (Lucas, 1986).
22. New classical economists have often realized the tension between the RE hypothesis and policy intervention. Sargent writes: 'In formal work, this contradiction is evaded by regarding analyses of policy interventions as descriptions of different economies, defined on different probability spaces. The mental comparison is among economies identical with respect to private agents' preferences and technologies, but differing in government policy regime' (1984: 413). This move raises more questions than it solves. It is not clear how the agents in the economy governed by the existing policy regime come to know the joint distribution of the variables of the economy governed by the new regime.

3 'Homo Economicus' as an Intuitive Statistician (1)

1. The IS hypothesis has a long history in cognitive psychology. An interesting discussion of the proposal is found in Cheng and Holyoak (1995), who focus on how people, like statisticians, learn about the causal structure of their environment. The hypothesis also occupies a central place in Shanks (1995)'s monograph on the psychology of learning.
2. In Bray (1982), agents know the supply curve and must only form price expectations to plug into it.
3. Sargent (1993) raises this question, assuming that it has a positive answer.
4. This section builds on the works of Granger (1990b; 1999), Lindley (1982), Spanos (1986; 1999) and Spanos and McGuirk (2001).
5. Granger (1999: ch. 1) touches on some of the difficulties at this stage of specification analysis.
6. See Spanos (1999: 263–7) for a concrete example.
7. This is because even estimating a univariate distribution from a random sample involves estimating infinitely many parameters, which is impossible with a finite sample.
8. Although the intuitive notion of smoothness is adequate for our purpose, there is not yet a complete understanding of the abstract idea of 'smoothness', usually defined in terms of 'the number of derivatives'. For a critical discussion see Marron (1996).
9. Yatchew (1998) offers a readable review of non-parametric inference, aimed at economists.
10. Our exposition draws on Härdle (1990; 1993), Silverman (1986), and Scott (1992).
11. See Silverman (1986: 100–10) for the adaptive kernel estimator.
12. Although the expression (3.6) uses kernel independence, this does not imply the independence of the variables (See Appendix 3.A).
13. N stands for the sample size at time t.
14. A sizeable number of studies of learning in economics utilize neural network inference procedures (e.g. Salmon, 1995). Neural Networks were initially viewed as an independent field aiming to tackle complex learning tasks that were not usually considered in statistics. It soon emerged that the procedures were nothing but

variants of non-parametric methods and are subject to similar strengths and limits (Friedman, 1994; Cheng and Titterington, 1994; Ripley, 1993). The methods cannot solve any learning problem that theoretically falls beyond the reach of non-parametric inference.

15. This example is from Härdle (1990: 258). For further discussion of the curse of dimensionality see Bellman (1961: 94); Friedman (1991; 1994), Friedman and Stuelzle (1981: 817), Scott (1992), Bishop (1995), Härdle (1990), and Silverman (1986: 129).
16. Friedman (1994) and Hastie and Tibshirani (1994) review some of the non-parametric multivariate approximation methods.
17. See Ripley (1996) for the proof.
18. The prime in $f(x)'$ stands for transpose.
19. These selectors are discussed in Härdle (1990: ch. 5).
20. See Breiman (1992), Breiman and Spector (1992), Efron (1983; 1986), and Efron and Tibshirani (1993; 1997).
21. For a definition of this error estimator see Appendix 3.C.
22. A K-nearest neighbour classifier considers K-nearest neighbours and assigns the class by majority vote.
23. Fisher's iris dataset contains three classes of fifty instances each, where each class refers to a type of iris plant (Fisher, 1936).
24. This is another way of stating Goodman's riddle of induction (Goodman, 1955). See Howson (2000) for an exposition.
25. This model has been constructed based on a similar example in Forster (2000).
26. This point is evident from the reformulation of the leave-one-out cross-validation given in (6.9).

4 'Homo Economicus' as an Intuitive Statistician (2)

1. Classic sources for the DB theorem are F.P. Ramsey (1926 [1980]) and B. de Finetti, (1980 [1937]).
2. This assumption can be weakened. All that is needed is that if you have a degree of belief in H, it is reflected in the price you are ready to pay for a bet on or against H.
3. The dollar sign is omitted in what follows.
4. '[B]etting quotients are ... just odds normalized so that they lie within the half-open interval [0,1); this is extended to the closed-unit interval [0,1] by allowing the odds to take the "value" ∞' (Howson, 2000: 125).
5. For a further discussion of this point see Howson (1995: 4–5).
6. In a new manuscript, Howson (2004) substantially reformulates the argument for the probability axioms as consistency constraints on partial beliefs, effectively rejecting the traditional formulation embodied in the DB theorem. In this new setting the value additivity assumption is introduced 'as a constraint on the solution assignment of fair betting quotients' (2004: 18). The formulation more vividly supports the conclusions drawn in the text about the scope of the Bayesian theory.
7. Here it is assumed that the sum of the bets is equivalent to an additional bet, which is not generally the case.
8. As Howson points out, Ramsey set forth this view of the laws of probability within the theoretical framework of axiomatic utility, not the theory of logic. Recent defenders of epistemic probability have made every effort to disentangle entirely the proof of the probability axioms from formal utility considerations (Howson, 2004: 5–6).

9. Classic statements of the DB theorem only establish finite additivity. Williamson (1999) has extended the theorem to countable additivity.
10. This argument for the quotient rule is adapted from Howson and Urbach (1993).
11. Williams (1980) derives the BCR from the minimum information principle.
12. This can be seen by applying the rule to E itself.
13. $Q(H) = Q(E)Q(H/E) + Q(\neg E)Q(H/\neg E)$.
14. A lucid discussion of these issues is found in Diaconis and Zabell (1985).
15. Hierarchical models have further distributional assumptions relating to the distribution of hyperparameters.
16. A review of Bayesian model selection is found in Kass and Raftery (1995).
17. See Spanos (1999) for definitions of the notions used in the graph.
18. Another interesting use of the theorems in modelling the duration of unemployment is found in Kiefer (1988).
19. For how to deal with identical observations see Bradley (1968: 48–56).
20. Kendall (1955) and Mann (1945) provide similar distribution-free tests of randomness. See Bradley (1968: 287–8) for an exposition.
21. Kadane and Wolfson (1998) review the literature on prior elicitation.
22. An 'a-fractile of a continuous distribution is a point z(a) such that a random variable with this distribution has probability a of being less than or equal to z(a)' (Berger, 1985: 79).
23. When Z is a standard normal variable $p(Z < -1/\sqrt{2.16}) = 1/4$.
24. The median is zero, and it can be checked that $\int_{-\infty}^{-1} 1/\pi([1 + \theta^2])d\theta = 1/4$.
25. De Finetti's representation theorem implies that coherent like-minded individuals who share symmetries (like exchangeability) in their beliefs are led to common likelihoods. These data models are simplified in terms of mental constructs called *parameters* (Poirier, 1988: 131). A proof of the theorem is given in Bernardo and Smith (1994: 172–80).
26. Let F denote the class of data-density functions $f(x/\theta)$, defined by θ. A class P of prior distributions is said to be a conjugate family for F if $\pi(\theta/x)$ is also in the class P for all $f \in F$ and $\pi \in P$ (Berger, 1980: 96).
27. The priors must be related according to $\pi(\theta)d\theta = \pi^*(\phi)d\phi$.
28. Seidenfeld (1979) offers an appraisal of the invariance approach.
29. The Beta function can be stated in terms of the Gamma function as $B[\alpha, \beta] = \Gamma[\alpha]\Gamma[B]/\Gamma[\alpha + \beta]$.
30. If $X_1, X_2, \ldots X_n$ are NIID (standard normal) $Y = \sum X_i^2 \sim \chi^2(n)$.
31. See Bayarri and Berger (1999) for other objections to the prior predictive approach.
32. Gilks *et al.* (1996) contains a collection of articles on Markov Chain Monte Carlo techniques.
33. A well-fitted model will produce residuals that are approximately independent random variables with zero mean, constant variance, and, possibly, a normal distribution (Gilchrist, 1984: 138).
34. See Rubin (1984: 1168) on how a statistic may be defined to tell whether the data come from a normal or a Cauchy distribution. Geweke and McCausland (2001: 5-6) contains a discussion on the choice of diagnostic statistics for assessing models of financial returns.
35. The simulations discussed in this section were performed using Bugs software, available on [http://www.mrc-bsu.cam.ac.uk/bugs].
36. An ARMA model can be interpreted as an approximation to an autoregression model of some order p (Spanos, 1999: 452).

37. A sufficient statistic for θ is a function of the data which summarizes all available sample information concerning θ. For example, if an independent sample $X_1, \ldots, X_N$ for $N(\mu, \sigma^2)$ distribution is to be taken, it is known that $T(\overline{X}, S^2)$ is a sufficient statistic for $\theta = (\mu, \sigma^2)$, where $\overline{X}$ stands for the sample mean and $S^2 = \sum (X_i - \overline{X})^2 / N - 1$ (Berger,1985: 35). This definition, which underlies the sufficiency principle, assumes that the model is true. Otherwise, a different definition of sufficiency is needed, and the sufficiency principle will no longer be valid (Hill, 1986: 217).
38. See Barnett (1999: 181-3).
39. When the issue is the structural specification of how known and unknown quantities are related, one cannot count on 'the data to swamp the priors' (Draper, 1995).

5 'Homo Economicus' as an Intuitive Statistician (3)

1. Quoted from Whittaker (1990).
2. Similar remarks are found in Pearl and Verma (1991).
3. We may intuitively think of event x as a value of (random) variable X.
4. The definitions to follow are adapted from Spirtes (1994).
5. Path analysis was developed by Sewell Wright (1934) and advanced by others including Simon (1954) and Blalock (1972). Blalock (1964) gives an introduction to the field. Irzik and Meyer (1987) contains a philosophically oriented discussion of path analysis.
6. See Pearl (1988: 82–3).
7. Glymour (1997a: 203–6) explains how traditional approaches to causal inference rely on variants of the Markov condition. Hans Reichenbach (1956) was the first philosopher to discuss the Markov properties of causal systems. Variants of the principle have also been discussed by Cartwright (1989), Salmon (1984), Skyrms (1980) and Suppes (1970).
8. This follows by first applying the weak union and then decomposition properties of independence relations to $X_5 \perp (X_1, X_2, X_3)/X_4$. See Appendix 5.B.
9. To deal with feedback systems, the GT theorists have introduced the so-called Global Markov Condition, which reads as follows: for a directed (cyclic or acyclic) graph G over vertices $\mathbf{V}$ and a probability distribution P over $\mathbf{V}$, the distribution satisfies the global Markov condition if and only if for any three disjoint sets of $\mathbf{X}$, $\mathbf{Y}$, and $\mathbf{Z}$ in V if $\mathbf{X}$ is d-separated from $\mathbf{Y}$ given $\mathbf{Z}$ in G, then, $\mathbf{X}$ is independent of $\mathbf{Y}$ given $\mathbf{Z}$ in P (Koster, 1999). Joined with the completeness hypothesis, this implies that every correlation has a causal explanation.
10. The term 'hybrid graph' is from Pearl and Verma (1991). They define a hybrid graph slightly differently as a graph in which links may be undirected, unidirected, or bidirected.
11. Appendix 5.G shows how it is in general possible to check whether two models are distributionally equivalent.
12. Further contributions include: Bollen (1989), Breckler (1990), Hershberger, (1994), Jöreskog and Sörborm (1993), Luijben (1991), MacCallum *et al.* (1993), and Raykov and Penev (1999).
13. This theorem also follows from proposition I in Raykov and Penev (1999: 206).
14. A necessary and sufficient criterion for testing the d-separation equivalence of two semi-Markovian models is given in Spirtes and Verma (1992).
15. A different example is found in Pearl (2000: 147).
16. Glymour (1997a: 208) describes a feedback model that does not satisfy the Markov condition.

17. Richardson (1996) defines the necessary and sufficient conditions under which two non-recursive models, limited block-recursive or not, are *d*-separation equivalent.
18. Graph (b) is obtained by first replacing $X_1 \rightarrow X_2$ with $X_1 \leftrightarrow X_2$ and then replacing it with $X_1 \leftarrow X_2$.
19. Kiiveri and Speed (1982) provided the first proof of the result. A simple proof also appears in Cartwright (2002: 451-42).
20. For a definition of the global Markov condition see note 9. The proofs by Koster (1999) and Spirtes *et al.* (1998) assume linearity of the structural model.
21. For further discussion of how correlations due to mixing heterogeneous units are dealt with, see Glymour (1997a: 207) and Meek and Glymour (1994: 1012).
22. The stochastic process $\{Z_t, t = 1, 2, \ldots\}$ is a white-noise process if $E(Z_t) = 0$ and $Cov(Z_t, Z_s) = \delta^2$ if $t = s$ and $Cov(Z_t, Z_s) = 0$ if $t \neq s$.
23. See Cooper (1995, 2000) and Spirtes *et al.* (1996).
24. In other words, it can be treated as a variable in a higher-dimensional probability space.
25. Consider variables X, Y, and Z. Suppose Z causes X and Y but there is no causal link between X and Y. Salmon calls such a case an interactive fork if P(X/Z)<P(X/Z&Y). For some examples see Salmon (1984: 168–74).
26. Another case where completeness may fail is raised in Sober (1987), discussed under the nomenclature of 'Co-evolving Processes'. Hoover (2003) offers an interesting analysis of Sober's counter-examples.
27. Lebesgue measure is the uniform distribution in Euclidean space, e.g. length, area, volume.
28. This example, originally from Sewell Wright (1934), is described in Irzik and Meyer (1987: 508–9).
29. In other words, one has to assign *a priori* non-zero probabilities to events $u_1 u_2 = 0$, $v_1 v_2 = 0$ and $w_1 w_2 = 0$.
30. Autonomy or invariance is defined with respect to a specific set of changes. See Woodward (2003).
31. Simpson's Paradox (Simpson, 1951) has been taken up by many authors in detail including Cartwright (1997) and Hausman (1998).

6 The Economy as an Interactive System

1. See also Marshall (1890 [1961]:174).
2. See Deaton and Muellbauer (1980: 149).
3. Hartley (1997) gives a thorough analysis of the representative-agent modelling approach.
4. Granger (1999: 42–8) provides a brief discussion of Hall's methodology.
5. A bliss utility level is a level beyond which the marginal utility of consumption is negative (Deaton, 1992: 179). Note that equation (6.5) is based on the assumption that δ equals r; otherwise, the equation includes an intercept.
6. A random walk sequence is an example of a martingale sequence. A sequence Z_t is a martingale if $E[Z_t / Z_{t-1}, Z_{t-2}, \ldots] = Z_{t-1}$. Z_t is then a random walk if $Z_t = Z_{t-1} + u_t$ where $Cov(u_t, u_s) = 0$ for all $t \neq s$.
7. Hall's exercise is an example of testing for non-Granger causality (Sargent, 1987: 94).
8. A weighted sum of the individual demand functions with each function multiplied by the price of the corresponding commodity is equal to expenditure $\sum p_m f_{mi} = x_i$.
9. For a simple statement of Gorman's proof see Brighi and Forni (1989: 5).

10. There is a vast literature on the requirements of a representative agent. It includes Antonelli (1886), Deaton and Muellbauer (1980), Gorman (1953), Green (1964); Heineke and Schefrin (1990), Jorgenson, *et al.* (1982); Lau (1977; 1982), Lewbel (1989), Muellbauer (1975; 1976), Nataf (1948), and Stoker (1984; 1993).
11. Here, homothetic preferences mean that the agent always spends a fixed proportion of his or her income on each good (Kirman, 1989: 132).
12. Also see Brighi and Forni (1989: app. 1).
13. An assumption underlying Gorman's result is the restriction of zero expenditure at zero income.
14. Quasi-homothetic preferences generalize homothetic preferences. Homothetic preferences imply Engle curves that are linear and pass through the origin. Quasi-homothetic preferences allow vertical non-zero intercepts, leading to Engle curves that do not necessarily pass through the origin. A utility function creating such Engle curves is called quasi-homothetic. Engle curves describe demand as a function of income.
15. Since α is less than 1. See Appendix 6.A.
16. The statement here draws on Deaton's (1992) discussion of Pischke's paper.
17. Goodfriend (1992) assumes that agents observe aggregate income with one lag period and use this information to guess about contemporaneous income shock. Consumption change is then shown to follow an AR(1) process.
18. A similar discussion is found in Dow (1988: 8), Leijonhufvud (1968: 210–11) and Snowdon *et al.* (1994: 370).
19. Aware of the interdependencies between consumption, income, and the interest rate, Michener (1984) adopted a general equilibrium approach to study aggregate consumption. In a general equilibrium setting, the permanent income hypothesis did not imply that aggregate consumption follows a random walk process. Quite the opposite, aggregate consumption change turned out to be a constant function of aggregate current income.
20. For a list of other phenomena that cannot occur in a society of identical, entirely isolated, individuals, see Stiglitz (1991).
21. See Schelling (1978: 49) for other propositions that are true of a closed interactive system but not true of the behaviour of each person, nor even of any groups smaller than the whole system. Also see Hartley (1997: 148-9) for an example from monetary economics, due to Laidler (1982).
22. For the theory of exact aggregation see Jorgenson *et al.* (1982), Lau (1977, 1982), and Heineke and Shefrin (1988).
23. Stoker (1984; 1986; 1993) and Cameron (1990) study aggregation of non-linear models.
24. The stochastic process $\{Z_t, t = 1, 2, 3, \ldots\}$ is said to be a white-noise process provided that (i) $E(Z_t) = 0$ and (ii) $Cov(Z_t, Z_s) = \sigma^2$ for $t = s$ and 0 for $t \neq s$.
25. See Granger (1999: 42–48) for a brief discussion.
26. This would be the case if price differentials were due to different transportation costs and the relative prices of output and transportation were unchanging.
27. Kupiec and Sharpe (1991) provide another example.
28. A relation that can be made linear by taking the logarithm of each side of the equation is called intrinsically linear.
29. Exact quotations are placed inside commas.
30. Rizvi (1994), Kirman (1989; 1992) offer accessible discussions of the SMD result.
31. Non-market interactions 'are interactions between individuals, which are not regulated by the price mechanism' (Glaeser and Schinkman 2001: 1). For a survey of the topic see Glaeser and Schinkman (2001), sec. 2.

32. Tesfatsion (1994), quoted in Bryant (1996: 157).
33. The game theoretic assumption that the state of every individual depends on the state of every other individual is not necessary for multiple solutions. For multiple solutions, it is enough that the states of some of the decision makers depend on the states of some others (Glaeser and Schinkman, 2001).
34. This function is quoted in Bryant (1996), where he refers to Colander (1986) but does not mention the reference. The underlying idea, though, is explicit in Colander (1996).

Bibliography

Abrevaya, J. and W. Jiang (2005). A Nonparametric Approach to Measuring and Testing Curvature. *Journal of Business and Economic Statistics* 23: 1–19.

Ackerman, F. (2002). Still Dead After All These Years: Interpreting the Failure of General Equilibrium Theory. *Journal of Economic Methodology* 9: 119–39.

Akaike, H. (1970). Statistical Predictor Information. *Annals of the Institute of Statistical Mathematics* 22: 203–17.

Akaike, H. (1974). A New Look at the Statistical Model Identification. *IEEE Transactions on Automatic Control* AC-19: 716–23.

Allais, M. (1953). Le Comportement de l'homme rationnel devant le risque: Critique des postulates et axioms de l'Ecole Americaine. *Econometrica* 21: 503–46.

Altaman, N. S. (1992). An Introduction to Kernel and Nearest-Neighbour Nonparametric Regression. *American Statistician* 46: 175–85.

Amemiya, T. (1980). Selection of Regressors. *International Economic Review* 21: 331–54.

Anscombe, F. J. (1963). Tests of Goodness of Fit. *Journal of the Royal Statistical Society, Series B* 25: 81–94.

Anscombe, F. J. and R. J. Aumann (1963). A Definition of Subjective Probability. *Annals of Mathematical Statistics* 34: 199–205.

Antonelli, G. B. (1986 [1971]). Sulla teoria matematica dell'economia politica, Pisa (English trans.), in J. S. Chipman, L. Hurwicz, M. K. Richter and H. F. Sonnenschein (eds), *Preferences, Utility and Demand: A Minnesota Symposium*. New York: Harcourt Brace Jovanovich, 333–60.

Arntzenius, F. (1999). Reichenbach's Common Cause Principle. *Stanford Encyclo paedia of Philosophy (on the World Wide Web).*

Arrow, K. (1968). Economic Equilibrium. *International Encyclopaedia of the Social Sciences*. London: Macmillan, vol. 4, 376–89.

Arrow, K. (1982). Risk Perception in Psychology and Economics. *Economic Inquiry* 20: 1–9.

Arrow, K. (1986). Rationality of Self and Others in an Economic System. *The Journal of Business* 59: S385-S399.

Arrow, K. (1994). Methodological Individualism and Social Knowledge. *American Economic Review* 84: 1–9.

Arthur, B. (2000). Cognition: The Black Box of Economics. D. Colander (ed.), *The Complexity Vision and the Teaching of Economics*. Northampton, MA: Edward Elgar Publishing, ch. 3.

Arthur, W. B. (1993). On Designing Economic Agents that Behave like Human Agents. *Journal of Evolutionary Economics* 3: 1–22.

Arthur, W. B. (1994). Inductive Reasoning and Bounded Rationality. *American Economic Review* 84: 406–11.

Arthur, W. B., J. H. Holland *et al.* (1997). Asset Pricing under Endogenous Expectations in an Artificial Stock Market. *Economic Notes* 26: 297–330.

Aumann, R. J. (1987). Correlated Equilibrium as an Expression of Bayesian Rationality. *Econometrica* 55: 1–18.

Barker, T. S. and M. H. Pesaran (eds) (1990). *Disaggregation in Econometric Modelling*. London: Routledge.

Barnard, G. A. (1962). Prepared Contribution and Discussion. L. J. Savage (ed.), *Foundations of Statistical Inference*. London: Methuen, 39–49.

Barnett, V. (1999). *Comparative Statistical Inference*. New York: Wiley.

Barron, A. R. and X. Xiangyu (1991). Discussion of 'Multivariate Adaptive Regression Splines' by J. H. Friedman. *Annals of Statistics* 19: 67–81.

Basmann, R. L. (1972). The Brookings Quarterly Econometric Model: Science or Number Mysticism? K. Brunner (ed.), *Problems and Issues in Current Econometric Practice*. Columbus, OH: College of Administrative Science, Ohio State University, ch. 1.

Bayarri, M. J. and J. O. Berger (1999). Quantifying Surprise in the Data and Model Verification (with discussion). J. M. Bernardo, J. O. Berger, A. P. Dawid and A. Smith (eds), *Bayesian Statistics 6: Proceedings of the Sixth Valencia International Meeting*. Oxford: Oxford University Press, vol. 6, 53–82.

Bayes, T. (1763). An Essay towards Solving a Problem in the Doctrine of Chances. *Philosophical Transactions of the Royal Society* 53: 370–418.

Becker, G. S. (1976). *The Economic Approach to Human Behaviour*. Chicago; London: University of Chicago Press.

Becker, G. S. (1981). *A Treatise on the Family*. Cambridge, MA: Harvard University Press.

Bellman, R. (1961). *Adaptive Control Processes: A Guided Tour*. Princeton, NJ: Princeton University Press.

Berger, J. (1980). *Statistical Decision Theory: Foundations, Concepts, and Methods*. New York: Springer.

Berger, J. O. (1985). *Statistical Decision Theory and Bayesian Analysis*. New York: Springer.

Bernardo, J. M. and A. F. M. Smith (1994). *Bayesian Theory*. New York; Chichester: John Wiley.

Bewley, T. F. (ed.) (1987). *Advances in Econometrics: Fifth World Congress*. Cambridge: Cambridge University Press.

Bicchieri, C. (1987). Rationality and Predictability in Economics. *The British Journal for the Philosophy of Science* 38: 501–13.

Bicchieri, C., R. Jeffrey *et al.* (eds) (1997). *The Dynamics of Norms*. Cambridge; New York: Cambridge University Press.

Bierens, H. J. (1987). *Kernel Estimators of Regression Functions*. Cambridge: Cambridge University Press.

Bishop, C. M. (1995). *Neural Networks for Pattern Recognition*. Oxford: Oxford University Press.

Black, F. (1982). The Trouble with Econometric Models. *Financial Analysis Journal* 38(March–April): 29–37.

Blalock, H. M. (1964). *Causal Inferences in Nonexperimental Research*. Chapel Hill: University of North Carolina Press.

Blalock, H. M. (1972). *Causal Models in the Social Sciences*. London: Macmillan.

Blalock, H. M. (1972). Four-variable Causal Models and Partial Correlations. H. M. Blalock (ed.), *Causal Models in the Social Sciences*. London: Macmillan.

Blanchard, O. and S. Fisher (1989). *Lectures on Macroeconomics*. Cambridge, MA: MIT Press.

Blanchard, O. J. and M. Watson (1982). Bubbles, Rational Expectations, and Financial Markets. P. Wachtel (ed.), *Crises in the Economic and Financial Structure: Bubbles, Bursts, and Shocks*. Lexington, MA: Lexington Books, 295–315.

Blume, L. E. and D. Easley (1995). What Has the Rational Learning Literature Taught Us? A. Kirman and M. Salmon (eds), *Learning and Rationality in Economics*. Oxford: Blackwell, 13–39.

Bollen, K. A. (1989). *Structural Equations with Latent Variables*. New York: John Wiley and Sons.

Boudon, R. (1968). A New Look at Correlation Analysis. H. M. J. Blalock and A. B. Blalock (eds), *Methodology in Social Research*. London: McGraw-Hill, 199–235.

Bowles, S. (1998). Endogenous Preferences: The Cultural Consequences of Markets and other Economic Institutions. *Journal of Economic Literature* 36: 75–111.

Box, G. E. P. (1980). Sampling and Bayes' Inference in Scientific Modelling and Robustness (with discussion). *Journal of the Royal Statistical Society, Series A* 143: 383–430.

Box, G. E. P. (1983). An Apology for the Ecumenism in Statistics. G. E. P. Box, T. Leonard and C.-F. Wu (eds), *Scientific Inference, Data Analysis, and Robustness*. New York: Academic Press, 51–84.

Box, G. E. P. (1994). Statistics and Quality Improvement. *Journal of the Royal Statistical Society, Series A* 157: 209–29.

Box, G. E. P. and G. M. Jenkins (1976). *Time Series Analysis: Forecasting and Control*. London: Holden Day.

Box, G. E. P., T. Leonard *et al.* (eds) (1983). *Scientific Inference, Data Analysis, and Robustness*. New York: Academic Press.

Bradley, J. V. (1968). *Distribution-Free Statistical Tests*. Englewood Cliffs, NJ: Prentice-Hall.

Bray, M. (1982). Learning, Estimation, and Stability of Rational Expectations. *Journal of Economic Theory* 26: 318–39.

Bray, M. (1983). Convergence to Rational Expectations Equilibrium. R. Frydman and E. S. Phelps (eds), *Individual Forecasts and Aggregate Outcomes*. Cambridge: Cambridge University Press.

Bray, M. (1989). Rational Expectations, Information, and Asset Markets. F. Hahn (ed.), *The Economics of Missing Markets, Information, and Games*. Oxford: Clarendon Press, 243–78.

Bray, M. and D. Kreps (1987). Rational Learing and Rational Expectations. G. R. Feiwel (ed.), *Arrow and the Ascent of Modern Economic Theory*. New York, NYU Press, 597–625.

Bray, M. and N. Savin (1986). Rational Expectations Equilibria, Learning, and Model Specification. *Econometrica* 54: 1129–60.

Breckler, S. (1990). Applications of Covariance Structure Modelling in Psychology: Cause for Concern? *Psychological Bulletin* 107: 260–73.

Breiman, L. (1992). The Little Bootstrap and other Methods for Dimensionality Selection in Regression: *x*-fixed Prediction Error. *Journal of the American Statistical Association* 87, 738–54.

Breiman, L., J. H. Friedman *et al.* (1984). *Classification and Regression Trees*. New York: Chapman and Hall.

Breiman, L. and P. Spector (1992). Sub-model Selection and Evaluation in Regression: The *x*-Random Case. *International Statistical Review* 60: 291–319.

Brighi, L. and M. Forni (1989). Aggregation across Agents in Demand Systems. Working Paper, Badia Fiesolana, San Domenico, European University Institute, 38.

Brinbaum, A. (1962). On the Foundations of Statistical Inference (with discussion). *Journal of the American Statistical Association* 57: 269–306.

Browne, M. W. (2000). Cross-Validation Methods. *Journal of Mathematical Psychology* 44: 108–32.

Bryant, J. (1994). Coordination Theory, the Stag Hunt and Macroeconomics. J. W. Friedman (ed.), *Problems of Coordination in Economic Activity*. Norwell, MA: Kluwer Academic Publisher, 207–27.

Bryant, J. (1996). Team Coordination Problems and Macroeconomic Models. D. Colander (ed.), *Beyond Microfoundations: Post Walrasian Macroeconomics*. Cambridge: Cambridge University Press, 157–71.

Bullard, J. (1994). Learning Equilibria. *Journal of Economic Theory* 64, 468–85.

Cagan, P. (1956). The Monetary Dynamics of Hyperinflation. M. Friedman (ed.), *Studies in Quantity Theory of Money*. Chicago: University of Chicago Press, 25–120.

Cameron, A. C. (1990). Aggregation in Discrete Choice Models: An Illustration of Nonlinear Aggregation. T. S. Barker and M. H. Pesaran (eds), *Disaggregation in Economic Modelling*. London: Routledge, 206–34.

Cartwright, N. (1989). *Nature's Capacities and Their Measurement*. Oxford: Oxford University Press.

Cartwright, N. (1995). Probabilities and Experiments. *Journal of Econometrics* 67: 47–59.

Cartwright, N. (1997). What is the Causal Structure. McKim and Turner (eds), *Causality in Crisis? Statistical Methods and the Search for Causal Knowledge in the Social Sciences*, 343–57.

Cartwright, N. (1999). *The Dappled World: Essays on the Perimeter of Science*. New York: Cambridge University Press.

Cartwright, N. (2001). What Is Wrong with Bayes Nets? *The Monist* 84: 242–64.

Cartwright, N. (2002). Against Modularity, the Causal Markov Condition and Any Link between the Two: Comments on Hausman and Woodward. *British Journal for the Philosophy of Science* 53: 411–53.

Chari, V. V. (1999). Nobel Laureate Robert E. Lucas, Jr.: Architect of Modern Macroeconomics. *Federal Reserve Bank of Minneapolis Quarterly Review* 23: 2–12.

Chatfield, C. (1995). Model Uncertainty, Data Mining and Statistical Inference. *Journal of the Royal Statistical Society, Series A* 158: 419–66.

Chen, X. and H. White (1998). Nonparametric Adaptive Learning with Feedback. *Journal of Economic Theory* 82: 190–222.

Cheng, B. and D. M. Titterington (1994). Neural Networks: A Review from a Statistical Perspective. *Statistical Science* 9: 2–54.

Cheng, P. W. and K. J. Holyoak (1995). Complex Adaptive Systems as Intuitive Statisticians: Causality, Contingency, and Prediction. J. A. Meyer and H. Roitblat (eds), *Comparative Approaches to Cognition*. Cambridge, MA: MIT Press, 271–302.

Cherkassky, V., J. H. Friedman *et al.* (eds) (1994). *From Statistics to Neural Networks, Theory and Pattern Recognition Applications*. Nato ASI Series, New York: Springer-Verlag 1.

Chickering, D. (1995). A Transformational Characterization of Bayesian Network Structures. P. Besnard and S. Hanks (eds), *Uncertainty in Artificial Intelligence*. San Francisco: Morgan Kaufmann, vol. 2, 87–98.

Christensen, D. (1991). Clever Bookies and Coherent Beliefs. *Philosophical Review* 100: 229–47.

Christensen, D. (1996). Dutch Books Depragmatized: Epistemic Consistency for Partial Believers. *The Journal of Philosophy* 93: 450–79.

Clarida, R. H. (1991). Aggregate Stochastic Implications of the Life Cycle Hypothesis. *The Quarterly Journal of Economics* 106: 851–69.

Clogg, C. C. and A. Haritou (1997). The Regression Method of Causal Inference and a Dilemma Confronting This Method. McKim and Turner (eds), *Causality in Crisis*, 83–112.

Colander, D. (1996). *Beyond Microfoundations: Post Walrasian Macroeconomics*. Cambridge; New York: Cambridge University Press.

Collingwood, R. G. (1948). *An Essay on Metaphysics*. Oxford: Clarendon Press.

Congdon, P. (2001). *Bayesian Statistical Modelling*. Chichester; New York: John Wiley.

Conslik, J. (1996). Why Bounded Rationality? *Journal of Economic Literature* 34: 669–700.
Cooley, T. F. and S. F. LeRoy (1984). Econometric Policy Evaluation: Comments. *American Economic Review* 74: 467–70.
Cooley, T. F. and S. LeRoy (1985). Atheoretical Macroeconomics: A Critique. *Journal of Monetary Economics* 16: 283–308.
Cooper, G. (1995). Causal Discovery from Data in the Presence of Selection Bias. *Proceedings of the Workshop on Artificial Intelligence and Statistics*, 140–50.
Cooper, G. (2000). A Bayesian Method for Causal Modelling and Discovery Under Selection. *Proceedings of the Conference on Uncertainty in Artificial Intelligence (2000)*. San Francisco: Morgan Kaufmann, 98–106.
Cooper, R. W. (1999). *Coordination Games: Complementarities and Macroeconomics*. Cambridge: Cambridge University Press.
Cox, D. R. (1958). Some Problems Connected with Statistical Inference. *The Annals of Mathematical Statistics* 29: 357–72.
Cox, D. R. (1992). Causality: Some Statistical Aspects. *Journal of the Royal Statistical Society, Series A* 155: 291–301.
Cox, D. R. and N. J. H. Small (1978). Testing Multivariate Normality. *Biometrika* 65: 263–72.
Cox, D. R. and E. J. Snell (1981). *Applied Statistics*. London: Chapman & Hall.
Cox, D. R. and A. Stuart (1955). Some Quick Sign Tests for Trend in Location and Dispersion. *Biometrika* 42: 80–95.
Craven, P. and G. Whaba (1979). Smoothing Noisy Data with Spline Functions. *Numerische Mathematik* 31: 377–403.
Cyert, R. and M. H. DeGroot (1974). Rational Expectations and Bayesian Analysis. *Journal of Political Economy* 82: 521–36.
D'Agostino, R. B. (1986). Graphical Analysis. R. B. D'Agostino and M. A. Stephenes (eds), *Goodness-of-Fit Techniques*. New York: Marcel Dekker, 7–62.
D'Agostino, R. B. and M. A. Stephenes (eds) (1986). *Goodness-of-Fit Techniques*. New York; Basel: Marcel Dekker.
Darnell, A. C. and J. L. Evans (1990). *The Limits of Econometrics*. Aldershot: Elgar.
Dawid, A. P. (1979). Conditional Independence in Statistical Theory. *Journal of the Royal Statistical Society, Series A* 41: 1–31.
Dawid, A. P. (1982). Intersubjective Statistical Models. G. Koch and F. Spizzichino (eds), *Exchangeability in Probability and Statistics*. Amsterdam: North-Holland, 217–32.
Dawid, A. P. (1983). Invariant Prior Distributions. *Encyclopaedia of Statistical Sciences*, ed. S. Kotz and N. L. Johnson. New York: John Wiley, 228–36.
Dawid, A. P. (2002). Probability, Causality and Empirical World: A Bayes–de Finetti–Popper–Borel Synthesis. Unpublished technical report, University College London.
Deaton, A. (1992). *Understanding Consumption*. Oxford and New York: Oxford University Press.
Deaton, A. and J. Muellbauer (1980). *Economics and Consumer Behaviour*. Cambridge: Cambridge University Press.
Debreu, G. (1959). *The Theory of Value*. New York: Wiley.
Debreu, G. (1974). Excess Demand Functions. *Journal of Mathematical Economics* 1: 15–23.
De Finetti, B. (1972). *Probability, Induction, and Statistics*. New York: Wiley.
De Finetti, B. (1980 [1937]). Foresight: Its Logical Laws, Its Subjective Sources. H. E. Kyburg, Jr. and H. E. Smokler (eds), *Studies in Subjective Probability*. New York: Krieger, 51–131.

Demiralp, S. and K. D. Hoover (2003). Searching for the Causal Structure of a Vector Autoregression. *Oxford Bulletin of Economics and Statistics* 65, Supplement: 745–67.

Dempster, A. P. (1971). Model Searching and Estimation in the Logic of Inference (with discussion). *Foundations of Statistical Inference (Proc. Sympos., Univ. Waterloo, Waterloo, Ont., 1970)*. Toronto, Ont.: Holt, Rinehart and Winston of Canada, 56–81.

Dempster, A. P. (1983). Purposes and Limitations of Data Analysis. *Scientific Inference, Data Analysis, and Robustness*. G. E. P. Box, T. Leonard and C.-F. Wu (eds), New York: Academic, 117–33.

Diaconis, P. and M. Shahshahani (1984). On Nonlinear Functions of Linear Combinations. *SIAM Journal of Scientific and Statistical Computing* 5: 175–91.

Diaconis, P. and S. L. Zabell (1985). Some alternatives to Bayes' rule. B. Grofman, G. Owen (eds), *Information and Group Decision Making, Proc. Second Univ. of Calif. Irvine Conf. Political Economy*. Greenwich, CT: Jai Press, 25–38.

Dow, S. (1988). Post Keynesian Economics: Conceptual Underpinnings. *British Review of Economic Issues* 10: 1–18.

Draper, D. (1995). Assessment and Propagation of Model Uncertainty (with Discussion). *Journal of the Royal Statistical Society, Series B* 57: 45–97.

Draper, D. (1996). Utility, Sensitivity Analysis, and Cross-Validation in Bayesian Model-Checking. Discussion of 'Posterior Predictive Assessment of Model Fitness via Realized Discrepancies', by A. Gleman *et al. Statistica Sinica* 6: 28–35.

Draper, D., J. S. Hodges *et al.* (1993). Exchangeability and Data Analysis (with discussion). *Journal of the Royal Statistical Society, Series A* 156: 9–37.

Dreze, J., H. (1987). *Essays on Economic Decisions under Uncertainty*. Cambridge: Cambridge University Press.

du Toit S. H. C., A. G. W. Steyn *et al.* (1986). *Graphical Exploratory Data Analysis*. New York: Springer Verlag.

Earman, J. (1992). *Bayes or Bust? A Critical Examination of Bayesian Confirmation Theory*. Cambridge, MA: MIT Press.

Efron, B. (1983). Estimating the Error Rate of a Prediction Rule: Some Improvement on Cross Validation. *Journal of the American Statistical Association* 78: 316–33.

Efron, B. (1986). How Biased is the Apparent Error Rate of a Prediction Rule? *Journal of the American Statistical Association* 81: 461–70.

Efron, B. and G. Gong (1983). A Leisurely Look at the Bootstrap, the Jacknife, and Cross-Validation. *American Statistician* 37: 36–48.

Efron, B. and R. J. Tibshirani (1993). *An Introduction to the Bootstrap*. New York; London: Chapman & Hall.

Efron, B. and R. J. Tibshirani (1997). Improvements on Cross-Validation: The 0.632 + Bootstrap Method. *Journal of the American Statistical Association* 92: 548–60.

Engle, R., D. Hendry and J. F. Richard (1983). Exogeneity. *Econometrica* 51: 277–304.

Epstein, R. J. (1987). *A History of Econometrics*. Amsterdam: Elsevier Science Publishers.

Eubank, R. L. (1988). *Spline Smoothing and Nonparametric Regression*. New York; Basel: Marcel Dekker.

Evans, G. W. and S. Honkapohja (2001). *Learning and Expectations in Macroeconomics*. Princeton, NJ: Princeton University Press.

Fair, R. C. (1978). The Effect of Economic Events on Votes for President. *The Review of Economics and Statistics* 60: 159–73.

Fair, R. C. (1987). Macroeconomic Models. *The New Palgrave: A Dictionary of Economics*, ed. J. Eatwell, M. Milgate and P. Newman. London: Macmillan, vol. 3, 269–73.

Faraway, J. (1998). Data Splitting Strategies for Reducing the Effect of Model Selection on Inference. *Computing Science and Statistics* 30: 332–41.

Felipe, J. and F. M. Fisher (2003). Aggregation in Production Functions: What Applied Economists Should Know. *Macroeconomica* 54: 208–62.

Feller, W. (1971). *An Introduction to Probability Theory and its Applications*. New York; Chichester: Wiley.

Fischer, G., Z. Carmon *et al.* (1999). Goal-based Construction of Preference: Task Goals and Prominence Effect. *Management Science* 45: 1057–75.

Fishburn, P. C. (1970). *Utility Theory for Decision Making*. New York: Wiley.

Fishburn, P. C. (1981). Subjective Expected Utility: A Review of Normative Theories. *Theory and Decision* 13: 139–99.

Fisher, F. M. (1989). Games Economists Play: A Noncooperative View. *RAND Journal of Economics* 20: 113–23.

Fisher, R. A. (1922). On the Mathematical Foundations of Theoretical Statistics. *Philosophical Transactions of the Royal Society of London, Series A* 222: 309–68.

Fisher, R. A. (1936). The Use of Multiple Measurements in Taxonomic Problems. *Annals of Eugenics* 7: 179–88.

Flavin, M. A. (1981). The Adjustment of Consumption to Changing Expectations about Future Income. *Journal of Political Economy* 89: 1020–37.

Forster, M. (2000). Key Concepts in Model Selection: Performance and Generalizability. *Mathematical Psychology* 44: 205–31.

Freedman, D. A. (1981). Some Pitfalls in Large Econometric Models: A Case Study. *Journal of Business* 54: 497–500.

Freedman, D. A. (1987). As Others See Us: A Case Study in Path Analysis (with Discussion). *Journal of Educational Statistics* 12: 101–223.

Freedman, D. A. (1997). From Association to Causation via Regression. McKim and Turner (eds), *Causality in Crisis? Statistical Methods and Search for Causal Knowledge in the Social Sciences*, 113–82.

Friedman, B. M. and F. H. Hahn (1990). Preface to the Handbook. B. M. Friedman and F. H. Hand (eds), *Handbook of Monetary Economics*. Amsterdam: Elsevier Science Publishers, vol. 1.

Friedman, J. H. (1991). Multivariate Adaptive Regression Splines (with Discussion). *Annals of Statistics* 19: 1–141.

Friedman, J. H. (1994). An Overview of Predictive Learning and Function Approximation. V. Cherkassky, J. H. Friedman and H. Wechsler (eds), *From Statistics to Neural Networks, Theory and Pattern Recognition Applications*. Berlin: Springer, 1–61.

Friedman, J. H. and W. Stuelzle (1981). Projection Pursuit Regression. *Journal of the American Statistical Association* 76: 817–23.

Friedman, J. W. (1994). *Problems of Coordination in Economic Activity*. Boston, MA; Dordrecht; London: Kluwer Academic Publishers.

Friedman, M. and J. Savage (1952). The Expected Utility Hypothesis and the Measurability of Utility. *Journal of Political Economy* 60: 464–74.

Friedman, M. and A. J. Schwartz (1963). *A Monetary History of the United States 1867–1960*. Princeton, NJ: Princeton University Press, for the National Bureau of Economic Research.

Frydenberg, M. (1990). The Chain Graph Markov Property. *Scandinavian Journal of Statistics* 17: 333–53.

Frydman, R. and E. S. Phelps (1984). *Individual Forecasting and Aggregate Outcomes: 'Rational Expectations' Examined*. Cambridge; New York: Cambridge University Press.

Fuller, W. (1976). *Introduction to Stochastic Time Series*. New York: Wiley.

Galambos, J. (1982). Characterizations of Distributions. *Encyclopaedia of Statistical Sciences*. New York: Wiley, vol. 1, 422–28.

Gasking, D. (1955). Causation and Recipes. *Mind* 64: 479–87.

Geiger, D., T. S. Verma *et al.* (1990). Identifying Independence in Bayesian Networks. *Networks* 20: 507–34.

Geisser, S. and W. Eddy (1979). A Predictive Approach to Model Selection. *Journal of the American Statistical Association* 74: 153–60.

Gelfand, A. E., D. K. Dey *et al.* (1992). Model Determination Using Predictive Distributions, with Implementation via Sampling-Based Methods (with discussion). J. M. Bernardo J. O. Berger, A. P Dawid and A. F. M. Smith (eds), *Bayesian Statistics*. Oxford: Oxford University Press. **4**: 147–67.

Gelman, A. (2002). Exploratory Data Analysis for Complex Models. New York: Columbia University, 1–26.

Gelman, A., J. B. Carlin *et al.* (1995). *Bayesian Data Analysis*. London; New York: Chapman & Hall.

Gelman, A., X. L. Meng *et al.* (1996). Posterior Predictive Assessment of Model Fitness via Realized Discrepancies. *Statistica Sinica* 6: 733–807.

Geman, S., Bienenstock, E. and Doursat, R. (1992). Neural Networks and the Bias/Variance Dilemma. *Neural Computation* 4: 1–58.

Geweke, J. (1985). Microeconomic Modelling and the Theory of Representative Agent. *American Economic Review* 75: 206–10.

Geweke, J. (1999). Simulation Methods for Model Criticism and Robustness Analysis. J. M. Bernardo, J. O. Berger, A. P. Dawid, and A. F. M Smith (eds), *Bayesian Statistics*. Oxford: Oxford University Press, vol. 6, 53–82.

Geweke, J. and W. McCausland (2001). Bayesian Specification Analysis in Econometrics. *American Journal of Agricultural Economics* 83: 1181–86.

Gilchrist, W. (1984). *Statistical Modelling*. New York: John Wiley & Sons.

Gilks, W. R., S. Richardson *et al.* (1996). *Markov Chain Monte Carlo in Practice*. London; New York: Chapman & Hall.

Glaeser, E. L. and J. A. Scheinkman (2001). Non-market Interaction. Unpublished Technical Report, Economics Department, Harvard University.

Glymour, C. (1997a). A Review of Recent Work on the Foundations of Causal Inference. Mckim and Turner (eds), *Causality in Crisis? Statistical Methods and the Search for Causal Knowledge in the Social Sciences*, 210–48.

Glymour, C. (1997b). Representations and Misrepresentations, Reply to Humphreys and Woodward. Mckim and Turner (eds), *Causality in Crisis?*, 317–22.

Glymour, C., D. Madigan *et al.* (1996). Statistical Inference and Data Mining. *Communications of ACM* 39: 35–41.

Glymour, C., P. Spirtes *et al.* (1999). Response to Rejoinder. C. Glymour and G. Cooper (eds), *Computation, Causation, and Discovery*. Cambridge, MA: AAAI Press, 343–5.

Gnanadesikan, R. (1977). *Methods for Statistical Data Analysis of Multivariate Observations*. New York: John Wiley.

Goldberger, A. S. (1971). Discerning a Causal Pattern among Data on Voting Behaviour. H. M. Blalock (ed.), *Causal Models in the Social Sciences*, 33–49.

Goldberger, A. S. (1989). Economic and Mechanical Models of Intergenerational Transmission. *American Economic Review* 79: 504–13.

Goldberger, A. S. (1992). Models of Substance; Comments on N. Wermuth, 'On Block-Recursive Linear Regression Equations'. *Brazilian Journal of Probability and Statistics* 6: 1–56.

Goodfriend, M. (1992). Information-Aggregation Bias. *American Economic Review* 82: 508–19.

Goodman, N. (1955). *Fact, Fiction, and Forecast.* Cambridge, MA: Harvard University Press.

Gorman, W. M. (1953). Community Preference Fields. *Econometrica* 21: 63–80.

Gorman, W. M. (1961). On a Class of Preference Fields. *Macroeconomica* 13: 53–6.

Granger, C. W. J. (1980a). Long Memory Relationships and the Aggregation of Dynamic Models. *Journal of Econometrics* 14: 227–38.

Granger, C. W. J. (1980b). Testing Causality: A Personal Viewpoint. *Journal of Economic Dynamics and Control* 2: 329–52.

Granger, C. W. J. (ed.) (1990a). *Modelling Economic Series: Reading in Economic Methodology.* Oxford: Oxford University Press.

Granger, C. W. J. (1990b). Aggregation of Time Series Variables. I. T. Barker and M. H. Pesaran (eds), *Disaggregation in Econometric Modelling.* London: Routledge: 17–34.

Granger, C. W. J. (1999). *Empirical Modelling in Economics: Specification and Evaluation.* Cambridge: Cambridge University Press.

Granger, C. W. J. and M. Morris (1976). Time Series Modelling and Interpretation. *Journal of the Royal Statistical Society, Series A* 38: 246–57.

Green, H. A. J. (1964). *Aggregation in Economic Analysis, an Introductory Survey.* Princeton, NJ: Princeton University Press.

Green, P. and B. Silverman (1994). *Nonparametric Regression and Generalised Linear Models: A Roughness Penalty Approach, Monographs on Statistics and Applied Probability.* New York: Chapman & Hall.

Greene, W. H. (1990). *Econometric Analysis.* New York: Macmillan.

Griffiths, T. L., E. R. Baraff *et al.* (2004). Using Physical Theories to Infer Hidden Causal Structure. To appear in *Proceedings of the 26th Annual Conference of the Cognitive Science Society* [http://cog.brown.edu/~gruffydd/papers/hidden.pdf].

Griliches, Z. and M. D. Intriligator (1984). *Handbook of Econometrics.* Amsterdam; Oxford: North-Holland.

Grossman, S. and R. J. Shiller (1982). Consumption Correlatedness and Risk Measurement in Economics with Non-traded Assets and Heterogeneous Information. *Journal of Financial Economics* 10: 195–210.

Guttman, I. (1967). The Use of the Concept of a Future Observation in Goodness-of-Fit Problems. *Journal of the Royal Statistical Society, Series B* 29: 83–100.

Haavelmo, T. (1943). The Statistical Implications of a System of Simultaneous Equations. *Econometrica* 11: 1–12.

Haavelmo, T. (1944). The Probability Approach in Econometrics. *Econometrica* 12 (Supplement).

Hacking, I. (1967). Slightly More Realistic Personal Probability. *Philosophy of Science* 34: 311–25.

Hall, P. (1983). Large Sample Optimality of Least Squares Cross-Validation in Density Estimation. *The Annals of Statistics* 11: 1156–74.

Hall, P. (1989). On Convergence Rates of Nonparametric Problems. *International Statistical Review* 57: 45–58.

Hall, R. E. (1978). Stochastic Implications of the Life Cycle–Permanent Income Hypothesis: Theory and Evidence. *Journal of Political Economy* 86: 971–87.

Hall, R. E. (1989). Consumption. R. Barro (ed.), *Modern Business Cycle Theory.* Oxford: Basil Blackwell and Harvard University Press.

Hansen, L. P. (1998). New Approaches to Macroeconomic Modeling: Evolutionary Stochastic Dynamics, Multiple Equilibria, and Externalities as Field Effects (book review). *Journal of Economic Literature* 36: 239–41.

Härdle, W. (1990). *Applied Nonparametric Regression.* Cambridge: Cambridge University Press.

Härdle, W. (1993). Applied Nonparametric Methods. R. Engle and D. McFadden (eds), *Handbook of Econometrics*. Amsterdam: North-Holland, ch. 38.

Harsanyi, J. C. (1965). Bargaining and Conflict Situations in the Light of a New Approach to Game Theory. *The American Economic Review* 55: 447–57.

Hartley, J. (1997). *The Representative Agent in Macroeconomics*. London: Routledge.

Hastie, T. J. and R. J. Tibshirani (1990). *Generalized Additive Models.* London: Chapman & Hall.

Hastie, T. J. and R. J. Tibshirani (1994). Nonparametric Regression and Classification. V. Cherkassky (ed.), *From Statistics to Neural Networks, Theory and Pattern Recognition Applications*. New York: Springer-Verlag 1.

Hausman, D. M. (1998). *Causal Asymmetries*. Cambridge; New York: Cambridge University Press.

Hausman, J., B. H. Hall, *et al.* (1984). Econometric Models for Count Data with an Application to the Patents–R&D Relationship. *Econometrica* 52: 909–38.

Hayek, F. A. (1979). *The Counter-Revolution in Science: Studies in the Abuse of Reason.* Indianapolis, Liberty Press.

Hedströöm, P. and R. Swedberg (1998). *Social Mechanisms: An Analytical Approach to Social Theory*. Cambridge: Cambridge University Press.

Heineke, J. M. and H. Shefrin (1988). Exact Aggregation and the Finite Basis Property. *International Economic Review* 29: 525–38.

Heineke, J. M. and H. Schefrin (1990). Aggregation and Identification in Consumer Demand Systems. *Journal of Econometrics* 44: 377–90.

Hempel, C. (1965). *Aspects of Scientific Explanation and other Essays in the Philosophy of Science*. New York: Free Press.

Hempel, C. and P. Oppenheim (1965 [1948]). Studies in the Logic of Explanation. C. Hempel (ed.), *Aspects of Scientific Explanation and Other Essays in the Philosophy of Science*. New York: The Free Press, 245–90.

Hendry, D. F. (1993). *Econometrics: Alchemy or Science? Essays in Econometric Methodology.* Cambridge and Oxford: Blackwell.

Hendry, D. F. and N. R. Ericsson (1991). An Econometric Analysis of U.K. Money Demand in 'Monetary Trends in the United States and the United Kingdom' by Milton Friedman and Anna J. Schwartz. *American Economic Review* 81: 8–38.

Hershberger, S. L. (1994). The Specification of Equivalent Models before Collection of Data. A. Von Eye and C. C. Clogg (eds), *Latent Variables Analysis*. Thousand Oaks, CA: Sage, 68–108.

Hicks, J. R. (1939). *Value and Capital: An Inquiry into some Fundamental Principles of Economic Theory*. Oxford: Oxford University Press.

Hicks, J. R. (1956). *A Revision of Demand Theory*. Oxford: Oxford University Press.

Hicks, J. R. (1979). *Causality in Economics*. Oxford: Basil Blackwell.

Hill, B. M. (1986). Some Subjective Considerations in the Selection of Models (with discussion). *Econometric Review* 1: 191–288.

Hill, B. M. (1990). A Theory of Bayesian Data Analysis. S. Geisser, J. S. Hodges, S. J. Press and A. Zellner (eds), *Bayesian and Likelihood Methods in Statistics and Econometrics.* Amsterdam: North-Holland, 40–73.

Hodges, J. S. (1987). Uncertainty, Policy Analysis and Statistics (with discussion). *Statistical Science* 2: 259–91.

Hodges, J. S. (1990). Can/May Bayesians Do Pure Tests of Significance? S. Geisser, J. S. Hodges and A. Zellner (eds), *Bayesian and Likelihood Methods in Statistics and Econometrics*. Amsterdam: North-Holland, 75–90.

Honkapohja, S. (1995). Bounded Rationality in Macroeconomics: A Review Essay. *Journal of Monetary Economics* 35: 509–18.

Hoover, K. (2003). Nonstationary Time Series, Cointegration, and the Principle of the Common Cause. *British Journal for the Philosophy of Science* 54: 527–51.

Hoover, K. D. (2001). *Causality in Macroeconomics*. Cambridge; New York: Cambridge University Press.

Howitt, P. (1987), Macroeconomics: Relations with Microeconomics. J. Eatwell, M. Milgate and P. Newman (eds), *The New Palgrave: A Dictionary of Economics*. London: The Macmillan Press Limited, 3: 273–6.

Howson, C. (1993). Dutch Books and Consistency. *PSA*. M. F. D. Hull and K. Okruhlik (eds). East Lansing, MI: Philosophy of Science Association, 161–8.

Howson, C. (1995). Theories of Probability. *British Journal for the Philosophy of Science* 46: 1–32.

Howson, C. (1997). Bayesian Rules of Updating. *Erkenntnis* 45: 195–208.

Howson, C. (2000). *Induction: Hume's Problem*. Oxford: Clarendon.

Howson, C. (2004). Chapter 3: The Laws of Probability (part of an unpublished manuscript). London: London School of Economics and Political Sciences: 31 pps.

Howson, C. and P. Urbach (1993). *Scientific Reasoning: The Bayesian Approach*. Chicago: Open Court.

Huber, P. (1985). Projection Pursuit (with discussion). *Annals and Statistics* 13: 135–75.

Hurwicz, L. (1962). On the Structural Form of Interdependent Systems. E. Nagel, P. Suppes and A. Tarski (eds), *Logic, Methodology, and the Philosophy of Science*. Stanford, CA: Stanford University Press, 232–9.

Ingrao, B. and G. Israel (1990). *The Invisible Hand: Economic Equilibrium in the History of Science*. Cambridge, MA: MIT Press.

Irzik, G. (1996). Can Causes Be Reduced to Correlations? *British Journal for the Philosophy of Science* 47: 249–70.

Irzik, G. and E. Meyer (1987). Causal Modelling: New Directions for Statistical Explanation. *Philosophy of Science* 54: 495–514.

Jacobs, D. P., E. Kalai *et al.* (eds) (1998). *Frontiers of Research in Economic Theory*. Econometric Society Monographs. Cambridge: Cambridge University Press.

Janssen, M. C. W. (1993). *Microfoundations: A Critical Inquiry*. London: Routledge.

Jeffrey, R. (1968). Probable Knowledge. I. Lakatos (ed.), *The Problem of Inductive Inference*. Amsterdam: North-Holland: 166–80.

Jeffreys, H. (1946). An Invariant Form for the Prior Probability in Estimation Problems. *Proceedings of the Royal Society, Series A* 186: 453–61.

Jeffreys, H. (1955). The Present Position of Probability Theory. *The British Journal for the Philosophy of Science* 5: 275–89.

Jeffreys, H. (1961 [1939]). *Theory of Probability*. Oxford: Clarendon Press.

Jeffreys, H. (1973 [1931]). *Scientific Inference*. London: Cambridge University Press.

Jevons, W. S. (1965 [1871]). *The Theory of Political Economy*. New York: A. M. Kelley.

Johnson, N. L., S. Kotz *et al.* (1994). *Continuous Univariate Distributions*. New York: John Wiley.

Johnson, N. L., S. Kotz *et al.* (1997). *Discrete Multivariate Distributions*. New York; Chichester: John Wiley.

Jöreskog, K. and D. Sörborm (1990). Model Search with Tetrad and LISREL. *Sociological Methods and Research* 19: 93–106.

Jorgenson, D. W., L. J. Lau *et al.* (1982). The Transcendental Logarithmic Model of Aggregate Consumer Behaviour. R. L. Basmann and G. Rhodes (eds), *Advances in Econometrics*. Greenwich, CN: JAI Press, 97–238.

Judge, G. G., W. E. Griffiths *et al.* (1985). *The Theory and Practice of Econometrics*. New York: John Wiley.

Kadane, B. J., J. M. Dickey *et al.* (1980). Interactive Elicitation of Opinion for a Normal Linear Model. *Journal of the American Statistical Association* 75: 845–54.

Kadane, J. B. (1980). Predictive and Structural Methods for Eliciting Prior Distributions. A. Zellner (ed.), *Bayesian Analysis in Econometrics and Statistics*. Amsterdam: North-Holland Publishing Company: 89–93.

Kadane, J. B. and L. J. Wolfson (1998). Experiences in Elicitation. *Journal of the Royal Statistical Society, Series D* 47: 3–19.

Kahneman, D. (1996). New Challenges to the Rationality Assumption. K. Arrow, Mark Perlman and Christian Schmidt (eds), *The Rational Foundations of Economic Behaviour*. London: Macmillan Press, 203–19.

Kahneman, D. (2003). Maps of Bounded Rationality: Psychology for Behavioral Economics. *American Economic Review* 93: 1449–75.

Kahneman, D. and A. Tversky (1973). On the Psychology of Prediction. *Psychological Review* 80: 237–51.

Kalai, E. and E. Lehrer (1993). Rational Learning Leads to Nash Equilibrium. *Econometrica* 61: 1019–45.

Kass, R.E. (1993). Bayes Factors in Practice. *The Statistician* 42:551–60.

Kass, R. E. and A. E. Raftery (1995). Bayes Factors. *Journal of the American Statistical Association* 90, 773–95.

Kass, R. E. and L. Wasserman (1996). The Selection of Prior Distribution by Formal Rules. *Journal of the American Statistical Association* 91: 1343–70.

Kendall, M. G. (1955). *Rank Correlation Methods*. New York: Hafner Publishing Co.

Kenny, D. A. (1979). *Correlation and Causality*. New York: John Wiley.

Keynes, J. M. (1936). *The General Theory of Employment, Interest and Money*. London: Macmillan.

Kiefer, M. N. and Y. Nyarko (1995). Savage Bayesian Models of Economics. A. Kirman and M. Salmon (eds), *Essays in Learning and Rationality in Economics and Games*. Oxford: Basil Blackwell Press, 42–62.

Kiefer, N. M. (1988). Economic Duration Data and Hazard Functions. *Journal of Economic Literature* 26: 646–79.

Kiiveri, H. T. and T. P. Speed (1982). Structural Analysis of Multivariate Data: A Review. S. Leinhardt (ed.), *Sociological Methodology*. San Francisco: Jossey Bass: 209–89.

Kirman, A. (1989). The Intrinsic Limits of Modern Economic Theory: The Emperor Has No Clothes. *Economic Journal* 99: Conference:126–39.

Kirman, A. (1992). Whom or What Does the Representative Individual Represent? *Journal of Economic Perspectives* 6: 117–36.

Kirman, A. P. and M. Salmon (1995). *Learning and Rationality in Economics*. Oxford; Cambridge, MA: Blackwell.

Klein, L. R. (1946a). Macroeconomics and the Theory of Rational Behaviour. *Econometrica* 14: 93–108.

Klein, L. R. (1946b). Remarks on the Theory of Aggregation. *Econometrica* 14: 303–12.

Kmenta, J. (1986). *Elements of Econometrics*. New York: Macmillan Publishing Company.

Knight, F. H. (1964 [1921]). *Risk, Uncertainty, Profit*. New York: Augustus M. Kelley.

Kohavi, R. (1995). A Study of Cross-Validation and Bootstrap for Accuracy Assessment and Model Selection. International Joint Conference on Artificial Intelligence *(IJCAI)*: 1137–45.

Koopmans, I. C. (1947a). Identification Problems in Economic Model Construction. *Econometrica* 17: 125–44.

Koopmans, I. C. (1947b). Measurement without Theory. *The Review of Economic Statistics* 29(3): 161–72.

Koopmans, T. C. (1971 [1949]). The Econometric Approach to Business Fluctuations. *American Economic Review* 39: 64–73.

Koster, J. (1999). On the Validity of the Markov Interpretation of Path Diagrams of Gaussian Structural Equation Systems of Simultaneous Equations. *Scandinavian Journal of Statistics* 26: 413–31.

Kramer, G. H. (1971). Short Term Fluctuations in U.S. Voting Behavior 1896–1964. *The American Political Science Review* 65: 131–43.

Kreps, D. (1988). *Notes on the Theory of Choice*. Boulder, CO and London: Westview Press.

Kupiec, P. H. and S. A. Sharpe (1991). Animal Spirits, Margin Requirements, and Stock Price Volatility. *Journal of Finance* 46: 717–31.

Kyburg, H. E., Jr. and H.E. Smokler (eds) (1980). *Studies in Subjective Probability*. New York: Krieger.

Laidler, D. E. W. (1982). *Monetarist Perspectives*. Oxford: Philip Allan.

Lam, D. (1988). Marriage Markets and Assortive Mating with Household Public Goods: Theoretical Results and Empirical Implications. *Journal of Human Resources* 23: 462–87.

Lane, D. (1986). Comments. *Econometric Review* 4: 253–58.

Lane, D., F. Marlerba *et al.* (1996). Choice and Action. *Journal of Evolutionary Economics* 6: 43–76.

Lau, L. J. (1977). Existence Conditions for Aggregate Demand Functions: The Case of Multiple Indexes, Unpublished technical report No.249, Institute for Mathematical Studies in the Social Sciences, Stanford University.

Lau, L. J. (1982). A Note on the Fundamental Theorem of Exact Aggregation. *Economic Letters* 9: 119–26.

Leamer, E. E. (1978). *Specification Searches: Ad Hoc Inference with Nonexperimental Data*. New York: Wiley.

Leamer, E. E. (1983). Model Choice and Specification Analysis. Z. Griliches and M. D. Intriligator (eds), *Handbook of Econometrics*. Amsterdam: North-Holland, I: ch.5.

Leamer, E. E. (1985). Vector Autoregressions for Causal Inference. K. Brunner and A. H. Meltzer (eds), *Understanding Monetary Regimes*. Amsterdam: North-Holland: 255–304.

Leamer, E. (1990). A Conversation on Econometric Methodology with Date Poirier and David Hendry. *Journal of Econometric Theory* 6(2), 171–261.

Lee, P. M. (1997). *Bayesian Statistics: An Introduction*. London: Arnold.

Lee, S. and S. L. Hershberger (1990). A Simple Rule for Generating Equivalent Models in Covariance Structure Modeling. *Multivariate Behavioral Research* 25: 313–34.

Lehmann, E. L. (1990). Model Specification: The Views of Fisher and Neyman, and Later Developments. *Statistical Science* 5: 160–8.

Lehmann, E. L. and H. J. M. D'Abrera (1975). *Nonparametrics: Statistical Methods Based on Ranks*. San Francisco: Holden-Day.

Leijonufvud, A. (1968). *On Keynesian Economics and the Economics of Keynes*. New York: Oxford University Press.

Levene, H. (1952). On the Power Function of Tests of Randomness Based on Runs Up and Down. *Annals of Mathematical Statistics* 23: 34–56.

Lewbel, A. (1989). Exact Aggregation and a Representative Consumer. *Econometrica* 57: 701–6.

Lewis, D. (1986). Causal Explanation. *Philosophical Papers*. New York: Oxford: Oxford University Press, vol. 2, 214–41.

Lichtenstein, S. and P. Slovic (1971). Reversals of Preferences between Bids and Choices in Gambling Decisions. *Journal of Experimental Psychology* 89: 46–55.

Lindley, D. V. (1968). The Choice of Variables in Multiple Regression (with discussion). *Journal of the Royal Statistical Society, Series B* 30: 31–66.

Lindley, D. V. (1980). Discussion of Professor Box's Paper. *Journal of the Royal Statistical Society*, series A: 143: 423.

Lindley, D. V. (1982). The Bayesian Approach to Statistics. J. Taago de Oliveria, and Benjamin Epstein (eds), *Some Recent Advances in Statistics*. New York: Academic Press, 65–87.

Lindley, D. V. (1983). Theory and Practice of Bayesian Statistics. *The Statistician* 32: 1–11.

Lindley, D. V. (1990). The 1988 Wald Memorial Lectures: The Present Position in Bayesian Statistics. *Statistical Science* 5: 44–89.

Lindley, D. V. and L. D. Phillips (1976). Inference for a Bernoulli Process (a Bayesian View). *American Statistician* 30: 112–19.

Linhart, H. and W. Zucchini (1986). *Model Selection*. New York: John Wiley & Sons.

Lippi, M. (1988). On the Dynamics of Aggregate Macroequations: from Simple Microbehaviours to Complex Macrorelations. G. Dosi, C. R. Freeman, G. Silvergerg and L. Soete (eds), *Technical Change and Economic Theory*. London: Pinter, 170–96.

Lippi, M. (1992). Microfoundations of Dynamic Macroequations. *Themes in Modern Macroeconomics*. H. Brink. Basingstoke and London: The Macmillan Press, 35–49.

Lippi, M. and M. Forni (1990). On the Dynamic Specification of Aggregate Models. T. S. Barker and M. H. Pesaran (eds), *Disaggregation in Econometric, Modelling*. London: Routledge.

Liu, T. C. (1960). Underidentification, Structural Estimation, and Forecasting. *Econometrica* 28: 855–65.

Lucas, R. E. (1978). Asset Prices in an Exchange Economy. *Econometrica* 46: 1429–45.

Lucas, R. E. (1976). Econometric Policy Evaluation: A Critique. K. Brunner and A. H. Meltzer (eds), *The Phillips Curve and Labour Market*. Amsterdam: North-Holland, vol. 1: 19–46.

Lucas, R. E. (1981). *Studies in Business-Cycle Theory*. Oxford: Basil Blackwell.

Lucas, R. E. (1987). *Models of Business Cycles*. Oxford: Basil Blackwell.

Lucas, R. E. (1986). Adaptive Behaviour and Economic Theory. *Journal of Business* 59: 5401–26.

Lucas, R. E. and T. Sargent (1979 [1981]). After Keynesian Macroeconomics. R. E. Lucas and T. Sargent (eds), *Rational Expectations and Econometric Practice*. Minneapolis, MN: University of Minnesota Press, 295–319.

Luijben, T. C. W. (1991). Equivalent Models in Covariance Structure Analysis. *Psychometrika* 56: 653–66.

MacCallum, B. T. (1983). On Non-Uniqueness in Rational Expectations Models. *Journal of Monetary Economics* 11: 139–68.

MacCallum, R., D. Wegener *et al.* (1993). The Problem of Equivalent Models in Applications of Covariance Structure Analysis. *Psychological Bulletin* 114: 185–99.

Machina, M. J. (1987). Choice under Uncertainty: Problems Solved and Unsolved. *Economic Perspectives* 1: 121–54.

MacNeill and G. J. Umphrey (eds) (1987). *Foundations of Statistical Inference.* Boston: Reidel.

Mallow, C. L. (1970). Some Comments on Bayesian Methods. D. L. Meyer and R. O. J. Collier (eds), *Bayesian Statistics.* Itasca, IL: Peacock, 71–84.

Mankiw, G. N. (1993). New Keynesian Economics. *Entry in the On-line Concise Encyclopedia of Economics.*

Mann, H. B. (1945). Nonparametric Tests against Trend. *Econometrica* 13: 245–59.

Manski, C. F. (1991). Regression. *Journal of Economic Literature* 29: 34–50.

Manski, C. F. (1995). *Identification Problems in the Social Sciences.* Cambridge, MA: Harvard University Press.

Mantel, R. (1976). Homothetic Preferences and Community Excess Demand Functions. *Journal of Economic Theory* 12: 197–201.

Marcoulides, A. G. and R. E. Schumacker (eds) (1996). *Advanced Structural Equation Modeling.* Mahwah, NJ: Lawrence Erlbaum Associates.

Mardia, K. V. (1970). *Families of Bivariate Distributions.* London: Griffin and Co.

Marrimon, R. (1997). Learning from Learning in Economics. D. Kreps and K. F. Wallis (eds), *Advances in Economics and Econometrics: Theory and Applications.* Cambridge: Cambridge University Press, 278–315.

Marron, J. (1996). A Personal View of Smoothing and Statistics. W. Härdle and M. Schimek (eds), *Statistical Theory and Computational Aspects of Smoothing.* Heidelberg: Physika Verlag, 1–9.

Marschack, J. (1953). Econometric Measurements for Policy and Prediction. J. Marschak (ed.), *Economic Information, Decision, and Prediction.* Dordrecht: Reidel, 1(1974).

Marshall, A. (1890 [1961]). *Principles of Economics,* (9th edn). New York: Macmillan.

Martel, R. (1996). Heterogeneity, Aggregation, and a Meaningful Macroeconomics. D. Colander (ed.), *Beyond Microfoundations.* Cambridge: Cambridge University Press, 127–44.

May, K. (1947). Technological Change and Aggregation. *Econometrica* 15: 51–63.

McCann, C. R. (1994). *Probability Foundations of Economic Theory.* London; New York: Routledge.

McCullagh, P. (1995). Discussion of Papers by Reid and Zeger and Liang. *Statistical Science* 10: 177–9.

McFadden, D. (1999). Rationality for Economics. *Journal of Risk and Uncertainty* 19: 73–105.

McKim, V. and S. Turner (eds) (1997). *Causality in Crisis?: Statistical Methods and the Search for Causal Knowledge in the Social Sciences.* Notre Dame, IN: University of Notre Dame Press.

Meek, C. (1995). Causal Inference and Causal Explanation with Background Knowledge. P. Besnard and S. Hanks (eds), *Uncertainty in Artificial Intelligence.* San Francisco: Morgan Kaufmann, vol. 2: 403–10.

Meek, C. and C. Glymour (1994). Conditioning and Intervening. *British Journal for the Philosophy of Science* 45, 1001–21.

Meng, X. L. (1994). Posterior Predictive *p*-values. *The Annals of Statistics* 22: 1142–60.

Michener, R. (1984). Permanent Income in General Equilibrium. *Journal of Monetary Economics* 13: 297–305.

Milgrom, P. and N. Stokey (1982). Inflation, Trade, and Common Knowledge. *Journal of Economic Theory* 26: 17–27.

Mill, J. S. (1974 [1874]). *A System of Logic*: Toronto: University of Toronto Press.

Mill, J. S. (1990). *Principles of Political Economy*. New York: The Colonial Press (first published 1848).

Moody, J. (1994). Prediction Risk and Architecture Selection for Neural Networks. V. Cherkassky, J. H. Friedman and H. Wechsler (eds), *From Statistics to Neural Networks: Theory and Pattern Recognition Applications*. New York: Springer.

Morris, S. (1995). The Common Prior Assumption in Economic Theory. *Economic and Philosophy* 11: 227–53.

Mosteller, F. and P. Nogee (1951). An Experimental Measurement of Utility. *Journal of Political Economy* 59: 371–404.

Muellbauer, J. (1975). Aggregation, Income Distribution and Consumer Demand. *Review of Economic Studies* 42: 525–43.

Muellbauer, J. (1976). Community Preferences and the Representative Consumer. *Econometrica* 44: 979–99.

Muth, J. F. (1961). Rational Expectations and the Theory of Price Movements. *Econometrica* 29: 315–35.

Nataf, A. (1948). Sur la possibilité de construction de certains macromodèles. *Econometrica* 16: 232–44.

Nyarko, Y. (1991). Learning in Mis-Specified Models and the Possibility of Cycles. *Journal of Economic Theory* 55: 416–27.

Nyarko, Y. (1997). Savage-Bayesians Play a Repeated Game. R. J. C. Bicchieri, and B. Skyrms (eds), *The Dynamics of Norms*. Cambridge: Cambridge University Press.

Nyarko, Y. (1998). Bayesian Learning and Convergence to Nash Equilibrium without Common Priors. *Economic Theory* 11(3), 643–56.

Nyarko, Y., N. Yannelis *et al.* (1994). Bounded Rationality and Learning. *Economic Theory* 4: 811–20.

Oakes, M. (1980). *Statistical Inference: A Commentary for the Social and Behavioural Sciences*. New York: John Wiley and Sons.

O'Hagan, A. (1994). *Kendall's Advanced Theory of Statistics. Vol. 2B, Bayesian Inference*. London: Edward Arnold.

O'Hagan, A. (2003). HSSS Model Criticism (with Discussion). P. J. Green, N. L. Hjort and S. Richardson (eds), *Highly Structured Stochastic Systems*. Oxford: Oxford University Press.

Pagan, A. (1987). Three Econometric Methodologies: A Critical Appraisal. *Journal of Economic Surveys* 1: 3–24.

Pearl, J. (1988). *Probabilistic Reasoning in Intelligent Systems: Networks of Plausible Inference*. San Nateo, CA: Morgan Kaufmann.

Pearl, J. (1998). Graphs, Causality, and Structural Equation Models. *Sociological Methods and Research* 27: 226–84.

Pearl, J. (1998). Tetrad and SEM. *Multivariate Behavioral Research* 33: 119–28.

Pearl, J. (2000). *Causality: Models, Reasoning, and Inference*. Cambridge: Cambridge University Press.

Pearl, J. and T. Verma (1991). A Theory of Inferred Causation. J. A. Allen, R. Filkes and E. Sandewall (eds), *Principles of Knowledge, Representation and Reasoning: Proceedings of the Second International Conference*. San Mateo, CA, Morgan Kaufmann: 441–52.

Peltzman, S. (1991). The Handbook of Industrial Organization: A Review Article. *Journal of Political Economy* 99: 201–17.

Pesaran, M. H. (1987). *The Limits to Rational Expectations*. Oxford: Basil Blackwell.

Pesaran, M. H. and R. P. Smith (1985). Evaluation of Macroeconomic Models. *Economic Modeling* 2: 125–34.

Pischke, J. S. (1995). Individual Income, Incomplete Information, and Aggregate Consumption. *Econometrica* 63: 805–40.

Poirier, D. J. (1988). Frequentist and Subjectivist Perspectives on the Problems of Model Building In Economics (with discussion). *Journal of Economic Perspectives* 2: 121–44.

Pollak, R. A. (2002). Gary Becker's Contributions to Family and Household Economics. *NBER Working Paper*.

Pratt, J. W. (1965). Bayesian Interpretation of Standard Inference Statements (with discussion). *Journal of the Royal Statistical Society, Series B* 27: 169–203.

Pratt, J. W. and R. Schlaifer (1988). On the Interpretation and Observation of Laws. *Journal of Econometrics* 39: 23–52.

Ramsey, F. P. (1926 [1980]). Truth and Probability. H. E. J. Kyburg and H. E. Smokler (eds), *Studies in Subjective Probability*. New York: Krieger, 25–52.

Ramsey, J. B. (1983). Perspective and Comment. *Econometric Reviews* 2: 241–8.

Raykov, T. and S. Penev (1999). On Structural Equation Model Equivalence. *Multivariate Behavioral Research* 34: 199–244.

Reichenbach, H. (1956). *The Direction of Time*. Berkeley, CA: University of Los Angeles Press.

Rice, J. (1984). Bandwidth Choice for Nonparametric Regression. *Annals of Statistics* 12: 1215–30.

Richardson, T. (1996). A Polynomial-Time Algorithm for Deciding Markov Equivalence of Directed Cyclic Graphical Models. E. Horvitz and F. Jensen (eds), *Proceedings of the 12th Conference on Uncertainty in Artificial Intelligence, Portland, Oregon*. San Francisco, CA: Morgan Kaufmann.

Richardson, T. and P. Spirtes (1999). Automated Discovery of Linear Feedback Models. G. Cooper and C. Glymour (eds), *Computation, Causation, and Discovery*. Cambridge, MA: MIT Press, 253–304.

Ripley, B. D. (1993). Statistical Aspects of Neural Networks. O. E. Barndorff-Nielsen, F. L. Jensen and W. S. Kendall (eds), *Networks and Chaos – Statistical and Probabilistic Aspects*. London: Chapman & Hall: 40–123.

Ripley, B. D. (1996). *Pattern Recognition and Neural Networks*. Cambridge; New York: Cambridge University Press.

Rizvi, S. A. T. (1994). The Microfoundations Project in General Equilibrium Theory. *Cambridge Journal of Economics* 18: 357–77.

Robins, J. M. (2003). General Methodological Considerations. *Journal of Econometrics* 112: 89–106.

Robins, J. M. and L. Wasserman (1999). On the Impossibility of Inferring Causation from Association without Background Knowledge. C. Glymour and G. Cooper (eds), *Computation, Causation, and Discovery*. Menlo Park, CA: Cambridge, MA: AAAI Press/The MIT Press: 305–21.

Romer, P. M. (1994). The Origins of Endogenous Growth. *Journal of Economic Perspectives* 8: 3–22.

Rubin, D. B. (1984). Bayesianly Justifiable and Relevant Frequency Calculations for the Applied Statistician. *The Annals of Statistics* 12: 1151–72.

Rubinstein, A. (1998). *Modeling Bounded Rationality*. Cambridge, MA: MIT Press.

Salmon, M. (1995). Bounded Rationality and Learning: Procedural Learning. A. Kirman and M. Salmon (eds), *Learning and Rationality in Economics*. Oxford: Blackwell.

Salmon, W. C. (1984). *Scientific Explanation and the Causal Structure of the World*. Princeton, NJ: Princeton University Press.

Sargent, T. J. (1984). Autoregressions, Expectations, and Advice. *American Economic Review,* 74: 408–15.

Sargent, T. J. (1987). *Dynamic Macroeconomic Theory*. Cambridge, MA: Harvard University Press.

Sargent, T. J. (1993). *Bounded Rationality in Macroeconomics: The Arne Ryde Memorial Lectures*. Oxford: Clarendon Press.

Savage, L. J. (1972 [1954]). *The Foundations of Statistics*. New York: Wiley.

Savage, L. J. (1967). Implications of Personal Probability for Induction. *Journal of Philosophy* 64: 593–607.

Savage, L. J. (1971). Letter from Leonard Savage to Robert Aumann. J. H. Dreze, *Essays on Economic Decisions under Uncertainty*: 78–81.

Savage, L. J. (1977). The Shifting Foundations of Statistics. R. Colodny (ed.), *Logic, Laws, and Life*. Pittsburgh: University of Pittsburgh Press, 3–18.

Scharfstein, D. O., M. J. Daniels *et al.* (2003). Incorporating Prior Beliefs about Selection Bias into the Analysis of Randomized Trials with Missing Outcomes. *Biostatistics* 4: 495–512.

Scheines, R. (1994). Inferring Causal Structure among Unmeasured Variables. P. Chessman and R. W. Oldford (eds), *Selecting Models from Data: AI and Statistics IV*. Berlin and New York: Springer-Verlag, 197–204.

Scheines, R. (1997). An Introduction to Causal Inference. McKim and Turner (eds), *Causality in Crisis?*, 185–200.

Scheines, R., P. Spirtes *et al.* (1998). The TETRAD Project: Constraint Based Aids to Causal Model Specification. *Multivariate Behavioral Research* 33: 65–118.

Schelling, T. C. (1978). *Micromotives and Macrobehavior*. New York: Norton.

Schelling, T. C. (1998). Social Mechanisms and Social Dynamics. P. Hedstrm (ed.), *Social Mechanisms: an Analytical Approach to Social Theory*. Cambridge: Cambridge University Press: 32–34.

Schick, F. (1986). Dutch Bookies and Money Pumps. *Journal of Philosophy* 83: 112–19.

Schumpeter, J. A. (1954). *History of Economic Analysis*. Oxford: Oxford University Press.

Scott, D. (1992). *Multivariate Density Estimation, Theory, Practice, and Visualization*. New York: John Wiley and Sons.

Searle, S.R. (1971). *Linear Models*. New York: John Wiley & Sons.

Seber, G. A. F. (1984). *Multivariate Observations*. New York: Wiley.

Seidenfeld, T. (1979). Why I am Not an Objective Bayesian: Some Reflections Promoted by Rosenkrantz. *Theory and Decision* 11: 413–40.

Sen, A. (1987). Rational Behaviour. *The New Palgrave: A Dictionary of Economics*, ed. J. Eatwell, M. Milgate, P. Newman, vol. 4: 68–74.

Sen, A. (1993). Internal Consistency of Choice. *Econometrica* 61: 495–521.

Shafer, G. (1986). Savage Revisited. *Statistical Science* 1: 463–501.

Shafer, G. (1998). Lindley's Paradox. *Encyclopaedia of Biostatistics*, ed. P. Armitage and T. Colton, Chichester, England: Wiley, vol. 3: 2257–8.

Shafer, W. and H. Sonnenschein (1982). Market Demand and Excess Demand Functions. K. J. Arrow and M. D. Intriligator (eds), *Handbook of Mathematical Economics*. Amsterdam: North-Holland, vol. 2: 670–93.

Shanks, D. R. (1995). *The Psychology of Associative Learning*. Cambridge: Cambridge University Press.

Shibata, R. (1981). An Optimal Selection of Regression Variables. *Biometrica* 68: 45–54.

Silverman, B. W. (1986). *Density Estimation for Statistics and Data Analysis*. London: Chapman & Hall.

Simkins, S. (1999). Measurement and Theory in Macroeconomics, Department of Economics, Merrick Hall, North Carolina A&T State University. 2005.

Simon, H. A. (1954). Spurious Correlation: A Causal Interpretation. *Journal of the American Statistical Association* 49: 467–79.

Simon, H. A. (1955). A Behavioral Model of Rational Choice. *Quarterly Journal of Economics* 69: 99–118.

Simon, H. A. (1956). Rational Choice and the Structure of the Environment. *Psychological Review* 63: 129–38.

Simon, H. A. (1960). *The New Science of Management Decision*, New York: Harper.

Simon, H. A. (1984). On the Behavioral and Rational Foundations of Economic Dynamics. *Journal of Economic Behaviour and Organization* 5: 35–55.

Simon, H. A. (1986). Rationality in Psychology and Economics. *Journal of Business* 59: S209–24.

Simon, H. (1990). Invariants of Human Behavior. *Annual Review of Psychology* 41: 1–20.

Simonson, I. and A. Tversky (1992). Choice in Context: Tradeoff Contrast and Extremeness Aversion. *Journal of Marketing Research* 29: 281–15.

Simpson, E. H. (1951). The Interpretation of Interaction in Contingency Tables. *Journal of the Royal Statistical Society, Series B,* 13: 238–41.

Sims, C. A. (1977). Exogeneity and Causal Ordering in Macroeconomic Models. Sims, *New Methods in Business Cycle Research*. Minneapolis, MN: Federal Reserve Bank of Minneapolis, 23–43.

Sims, C. A. (1980). Macroeconomics and Reality. *Econometrica* 48: 1–48.

Sims, C. A. (1981). What Kind of Science is Economics? *Journal of Political Economy* 89: 578–83.

Sims, C. A. (1982a). Policy Analysis with Econometric Models. *Brooking Papers on Economics Activity* 1: 107–64.

Sims, C. A. (1982b). Scientific Standards in Econometric Modelling. *Current Developments in the Interface: Economics, Econometrics, Mathematics*. Dordrecht; Boston; London: D. Reidel, 317–37.

Sims, C. A. (1986). Are Forecasting Models Usable for Policy Analysis? *Federal Reserve Bank of Minneapolis Quarterly Review* 10(Winter): 2–15.

Sims, C. A. (1987). Making Economics Credible. T. Bewley (ed.), *Advances in Econometrics: Fifth World Congress*. Cambridge: Cambridge University Press, 49–61.

Sims, C. A. (1991). Empirical Analysis of Macroeconomic Time Series: VAR and Structural Models: Comments. *European Economic Review* 34: 922–32.

Sims, C. A. (1996). Macroeconomics and Methodology. *Journal of Economic Perspectives*, 10: 105–20.

Sims, C. A. (2004). An Interview with Christopher A. Sims. *Macroeconomic Dynamics* 8: 273–94.

Skyrms, B. (1980). *Causal Necessity: A Pragmatic Investigation of the Necessity of Laws*. New Haven; London: Yale University Press.

Skyrms, B. (1986). *Choice and Chance: An Introduction to Inductive Logic*. Belmont, CA: Wadsworth.

Slovic, P. (1995). The Construction of Preference. *American Psychologist* 50: 364–71.

Slovic, P., D. Griffin *et al.* (1990). Compatibility Effects in Judgment and Choice. R. Hogarth (ed.), *Insights in Decision Making: A Tribute to Hillel J. Einhhorn*. Chicago: University of Chicago Press, 5–27.

Slovic, P. and S. Lichtenstein (1968). The Relative Importance of Probabilities and Payoffs in Risk-Taking. *Journal of Experimental Psychology, Monograph Supplement* 78: 1–18.

Slovic, P. and A. Tversky (1974). Who Accepts Savage's Axioms? *Behavioral Science* 19: 368–73.

Smith, A. F. M. (1984). Bayesian Statistics, Present Position and Potential Developments: Some Personal Views. *Journal of the Royal Statistical Society, Series A* 147: 245–59.

Smith, A. F. M. (1986). Some Bayesian Thoughts on Modelling and Model Choice. *The Statistician* 35: 97–102.

Snowdon, B., Vane, H., and Wynarczyk, P. (1994). *A Modern Guide to Macroeconomics*. Aldershot: Edward Elgar.

Sobel, J. (2000). Economists' Models of Learning. *Journal of Economic Theory* 94: 241–61.

Sobel, M. E. (1995). Causal Inference in the Social and Behavioral Sciences. G. Arminger, C. Clogg, and M.E. Sobel (eds), *Handbook of Statistical Modeling for the Social and Behavioral Sciences*. New York: Plenum Press, 1–38.

Sober, E. (1987). The Principle of the Common Cause. J. Fetzer (ed.), *Probability and Causation: Essays in Honor of Wesley Salmon*. Dordrecht: Reidel, 211–28.

Sonnenschein, H. (1972). Market Excess Demand Functions. *Econometrica* 40: 549–63.

Sonnenschein, H. (1973). The Utility Hypothesis and Market Demand Theory. *Western Economic Journal* 11: 404–10.

Spanos, A. (1986). *Statistical Foundations of Econometric Modelling*. Cambridge: Cambridge University Press.

Spanos, A. (1999). *Probability Theory and Statistical Inference: Econometric Modeling with Observational Data*. Cambridge; New York: Cambridge University Press.

Spanos, A. (2000). Where Do Statistical Models Come From? Revisiting the Problem of Specification. Blacksburg, Department of Economics, Virginia Tech, Unpublished.

Spanos, A. and A. McGuirk (2001). Econometric Methodologies for the Model Specification Problem: Addressing Old Problems in the New Century: The Model Specification Problem from a Probabilistic Reduction Perspective. *American Journal of Agricultural Economics* 83: 1168–76.

Spiegelhalter, D. J. (1995). Discussion of 'Assessment and Propagation of Model Uncertainty' by D. Draper. *Journal of the Royal Statistical Society, Series B* 57: 45–97.

Spirtes, P. (1994). Building Causal Graphs from Statistical Data in the Presence of Latent Variables. B. Prawitz, B. Skyrms and D. Westerstahl (eds), *Logic, Methodology, and the Philosophy of Science LX*. Amsterdam: Elsevier Science, 813–29.

Spirtes, P. (1997). Limits on Causal Inference from Statistical Data. Presented at American Economics Association Meeting [http://www.hss.cmu.edu/philosophy/people/directory/Peter_Spirtes.html], 1999.

Spirtes, P., C. Glymour and R. Scheines (1993). *Causation, Prediction, and Search*. New York: Springer-Verlag.

Spirtes, P., Meek, C., and Richardson, T. (1996). *Causal Inference in the Presence of Latent Variables and Selection Bias*. Technical Report CMU-77-Phil.

Spirtes, P., R. Richardson *et al.* (1998). Using Path Diagrams as a Structural Equation Modeling Tool. *Sociological Methods and Research* 27: 148–81.

Spirtes, P. and T. Richardson (1996). A Polynomial Time Algorithm for Determining DAG Equivalence in the Presence of Latent. *Proceedings of the 6th International Workshop on Artificial Intelligence and Statistics (January 4–7, Fort Lauderdale, FL).*

Spirtes, P. and R. Scheines (1997). Reply to Freedman. Turner and McKim (eds), *Causality in Crisis?*

Spirtes, P. and T. S. Verma (1992). Equivalence of Causal Models with Latent Variables, Unpublished technical report CMU-PHIL-33. Pittsburgh, PA: Department of Philosophy, Carnegie Mellon University.

Stelzl, I. (1986). Changing a Causal Hypothesis without Changing the Fit: Some Rules for Generating Equivalent Path Models. *Multivariate Behavioral Research* 21: 309–31.

Stigler, G. (1973). General Economic Conditions and National Elections. *The American Economic Review* 63: 160–7.

Stigler, G. and G. Becker (1977). De Gustibus Non Est Disputandum. *American Economic Review* 67: 76–90.

Stiglitz, J. E. (1991). Alternative Approaches to Macroeconomics: Methodological Issues and the New Keynesian Economics. Cambridge, MA: NBER Working Papers Series, Unpublished.

Stoker, T. M. (1984). Completeness, Distribution Restrictions, and the Form of Aggregate Functions. *Econometrica* 52: 887–907.

Stoker, T. M. (1986). Simple Tests of Distributional Effects on Macroeconomic Equations. *Journal of Political Economy* 94: 763–95.

Stoker, T. M. (1993). Empirical Approaches to the Problem of Aggregation over Individuals. *Journal of Economic Literature* 31: 1827–74.

Stone, M. (1974). Cross-Validatory Choice of and Assessment of Statistical Predictions. *Journal of the Royal Statistical Society, Series B* 36: 111–33.

Suppes, P. (1961). The Philosophical Relevance of Decision Theory. *The Journal of Philosophy* 58: 605–14.

Suppes, P. (1969). *Studies in the Methodology and Foundations of Science: Selected Papers from 1951 to 1969.* Dordrecht: D. Reidel.

Suppes, P. (1970). *A Probabilistic Theory of Causality.* Amsterdam: North-Holland Publishing.

Suppes, P. (1984). *Probabilistic Metaphysics.* Oxford: Blackwell.

Swanson, N. R. and C. W. J. Granger (1997). Impulse Response Functions Based on a Causal Approach to Residual Orthogonalisation in Vector Autoregressions. *Journal of American Statistical Association* 92: 357–67.

Teller, P. (1973). Conditionalization and Observation. *Syntheses* 26: 218–58.

Tesfatsion, L. (2003). Non-Walrasian Equilibrium: Illustrative Examples [http://www.econ.iastate.edu/classes/econ606/tesfatsion/syl606t.htm#Intro].

Theil, H. (1954). *Linear Aggregation of Economic Relations.* Amsterdam: North-Holland.

Thrall, R. M. (1954). Applications of Multidimensional Utility Theory. R. M. Thrall, C.H. Coombs and R. L. Davis (eds), *Decision Processes.* John Wiley, 181–6.

Tinbergen, J. (1939). *Statistical Testing of Business Cycle Theories*, 2 vols. Geneva: League of Nations.

Tversky, A. (1996) Rational theory and constructive choice. In K. J. Arrow, E. Colombatto, M. Perlman and C. Schmidt (eds), *The Rational Foundations of Economic Behavior.* London and New York: Macmillan and St Martin's Press: 185–202.

Tversky, A. and D. Kahneman (1981). The Framing of Decisions and the Psychology of Choice. *Science* 211: 453–8.

Tversky, A. and D. Kahneman (1986). Rational Choice and the Framing of Decisions. *Journal of Business* 59: 251–78.

Tversky, A. and E. Shafir (1992). Choice under Conflict: The Dynamics of Deferred Decision. *Psychological Science* 3: 358–61.

Tversky, A., P. Slovic *et al.* (1990). The Causes of Preference Reversal. *American Economic Review* 80: 204–17.

Tversky, A. and Thaler, R. H. (1990). Anomalies: Preference Reversals. *Journal of Economic Perspectives* 4: 201–11.

Vercelli, A. (1991). *Methodological Foundations of Macroeconomics: Keynes and Lucas*. Cambridge: Cambridge University Press.

Verma, T. S. and J. Pearl (1990). Equivalence and Synthesis of Causal Models. *Proceedings of the 6th Conference on Uncertainty in AI*, New York: Elsevier, 220–7.

Von Wright, G. H. (1971). On the Logic and Epistemology of the Causal Relation. E. Sosa and M. Tooley (eds), *Causation and Conditionals (1987)*. Oxford: Oxford University Press, 105–24.

Vriend, N. J. (1996). Rational Behaviour and Economic Theory. *Journal of Economic Behaviour and Organization* 29: 263–85.

Wahba, G. and S. Wold (1975). A Completely Automatic French Curve: Fitting Spline Functions by Cross Validation. *Communications in Statistics* 4: 125–42.

Wallace, N. (1980). The Overlapping Generations Model of Fiat Money. J. H. Kareken and N. Wallace (eds), *Models of Monetary Economics*. Minneapolis, MN: Federal Reserve Bank of Minneapolis.

Warner, B. and M. Manavendra (1996). Understanding Neural Networks as Statistical Tools. *The American Statistician* 50: 284–93.

Wasserman, L. (2000). Bayesian Model Selection and Model Averaging. *Journal of Mathematical Psychology* 44: 92–107.

Wermuth, N. (1980). Linear Recursive Equations, Covariance Selection, and Path Analysis. *Journal of the American Statistical Association* 75: 963–72.

Wermuth, N., D. R. Cox *et al.* (1994). Explanations for Multivariate Structures Derived from Univariate Recursive Regressions, University of Mainz.

White, H., (ed.) (1992). *Artificial Neural Networks: Approximation and Learning Theory*. Oxford: Blackwell.

Whittaker, J. (1990). *Graphical Models in Applied Multivariate Statistics*. Chichester: John Wiley & Sons.

Williams, L. J., H. Bozdogan *et al.* (1996). Inference Problems with Equivalent Models. A. G. Marcoulides and R. E. Schumacker (eds), *Advanced Structural Equation Modelling*. Mahwah, NJ: Lawrence Erlbaum Associates, 279–314.

Williams, P. M. (1980). Bayesian Conditionalisation and the Principle of Minimum Information. *British Journal for the Philosophy of Science* 31: 131–44.

Williamson, J. (1999). Countable Additivity and Subjective Probability. *British Journal for the Philosophy of Science* 50: 401–16.

Williamson, P. (1997). Learning and Bounded Rationality. *Journal of Economic Surveys* 11: 221–30.

Winkler, R. L. (1980). Prior Information, Predictive Distribution, and Bayesian Model-Building. A. Zellner (ed.), *Bayesian Analysis in Econometrics and Statistics*. Amsterdam: North-Holland.

Winkler, R. L. (1994). Model Uncertainty: Probabilities for Models? A. Mosleh, N. Siu, C. Smidts and C. Lui (eds), *Model Uncertainty: Its Characterization and Quantification*. Washington, DC: US Nuclear Regulatory Commission: 107–16.

Woodward, J. (1999). Causal Interpretation in Systems of Equations. *Synthese* 121: 199–257.

Woodward, J. (2003). *Making Things Happen: A Theory of Causal Explanation*. New York: Oxford University Press.

Wright, S. (1934). The Method of Path Coefficient. *Annals of Mathematical Statistics* 5: 161–215.

Yatchew, A. J. (1998). Nonparametric Regression Techniques in Economics. *Journal of Economic Literature* 36: 669–721.

Yule, G. U. (1903). Notes on the Theory of Association of Attributes in Statistics. *Biometrica* 2: 121–34.

Zellner, A. (1969). On the Aggregation Problem, a New Approach to a Troublesome Problem. *Estimation and Risk Programming: Essays in honor of Gehard Tintner*, ed. K. Fox, B. V. L. Narashimham and K. Sengupta. Berlin: Springer.

Zucchini, W. (2000). An Introduction to Model Selection. *Journal of Mathematical Psychology* 44: 41–61.

Index